ROUTLEDGE LIBRARY EDITIONS:
AGING

Volume 33

I0028292

DEPENDENCY
AND
INTERDEPENDENCY
IN OLD AGE

DEPENDENCY
AND
INTERDEPENDENCY
IN OLD AGE

Theoretical Perspectives and Policy Alternatives

Edited by
CHRIS PHILLIPSON,
MIRIAM BERNARD
AND
PATRICIA STRANG

Routledge
Taylor & Francis Group

LONDON AND NEW YORK

First published in 1986 by Croom Helm Ltd

This edition first published in 2024
by Routledge
4 Park Square, Milton Park, Abingdon, Oxon OX14 4RN

and by Routledge
605 Third Avenue, New York, NY 10158

Routledge is an imprint of the Taylor & Francis Group, an informa business

British Library Cataloguing in Publication Data
A catalogue record for this book is available from the British Library

ISBN: 978-1-032-67433-9 (Set)
ISBN: 978-1-032-71585-8 (Volume 33) (hbk)
ISBN: 978-1-032-71597-1 (Volume 33) (pbk)
ISBN: 978-1-032-71594-0 (Volume 33) (ebk)

DOI: 10.4324/9781032715940

Publisher's Note
The publisher has gone to great lengths to ensure the quality of this reprint but points out that some imperfections in the original copies may be apparent.

Disclaimer
The publisher has made every effort to trace copyright holders and would welcome correspondence from those they have been unable to trace.

DEPENDENCY AND INTERDEPENDENCY IN OLD AGE

Theoretical Perspectives and Policy Alternatives

Edited by CHRIS PHILLIPSON, MIRIAM BERNARD and PATRICIA STRANG

CROOM HELM
London • Sydney • Wolfeboro, New Hampshire
In association with the British Society of
Gerontology

©1986 British Society of Gerontology
Croom Helm Ltd, Provident House, Burrell Row,
Beckenham, Kent, BR3 1AT
Croom Helm Australia Pty Ltd, Suite 4, 6th Floor,
64-76 Kippax Street, Surry Hills, NSW 2010, Australia

British Library Cataloguing in Publication Data
Dependency and interdependency in old age.
  1. Aged — Care and hygiene
  I. Phillipson, Chris II. Bernard, Miriam
  III. Strang, Patricia IV. British Society
  of Gerontology
  362.6 HV1451

ISBN 0-7099-3987-6

Croom Helm, 27 South Main Street,
Wolfeboro, New Hampshire 03894-2069, USA
Library of Congress Cataloging-in-Publication Data
Dependency and interdependency in old age.

  Based on the British Society of Gerontology
conference proceedings at the University of Keele,
Sept. 1985.
  Includes index.
  1. Aged — Care and treatment — Congresses. 2. Aged —
Services for — Congresses. 3. Aged — Family relationships
— Congresses. 4. Aged — Social conditions — Congresses.
5. Dependency (Psychology) — Congresses. I. Phillipson,
Chris. II. Bernard, Miriam. III. Strang, Patricia.
IV. British Society of Gerontology.
HV1451.D46 1986   362.6'042   86-16752
ISBN 0-7099-3987-6

CONTENTS

Editors' Introduction

PART TWO : RESPONSES TO DEPENDENCY

PART THREE : EXPERIENCES OF GROWING OLD

Editors' Introduction

The theme of the 1985 Annual Conference of the British Society of Gerontology was: 'Understanding Dependency in Later Life: Theoretical Perspectives and Policy Alternatives'. The aim of the conference, as envisaged by the organisers, was that the plenaries, seminars and workshops should explore the various dimensions to dependency in old age, as well as review policy responses and implications for practitioners. It seemed an opportune time to mount a theoretical and policy evaluation of the idea of dependency, given the debate which had followed Peter Townsend's major article in Ageing and Society, outlining the causes and consequences of the structured dependency of the elderly. This article, along with equally important contributions from Carroll Estes, Anne-Marie Guillmard, Alan Walker and others, has had a significant influence on researchers and policy-makers. It seemed appropriate, therefore, that the British Society of Gerontology should debate the issues and perspectives arising from the critical, political economy-orientated gerontology of the late 1970s and 1980s.

The organisers were particularly fortunate in that so many of those who have made seminal contributions to the debate on the social construction of old age, also spoke at the conference and provided papers for this volume. However, along with established researchers, we have also included chapters from younger researchers, postgraduate students and workers in the social and health services. Taken together, we believe that the chapters demonstrate, despite the difficulties of funding, the strength and vitality of current gerontological research. They also illustrate, we believe, the diversity of themes currently being pursued by researchers. The areas covered include: the sociology of ageing, methodological issues, evaluations of service provision, ethnographies of growing old, historical studies and political perspectives on ageing. We urgently need a creative dialogue between the proponents of these themes and we hope that this book will help stimulate such a discussion.

Although the focus of the BSG conference started with the construction of dependency in old age, in the title of this book we also raise the issue of interdependence. This reflects the contribution of Maggie Kuhn who, in her plenary address to the conference, reminded us of the need for reciprocal, rather than one-sided (and dependent) relationships in old age. In this context, she attacked the way health and social services often seemed to diminish elderly recipients. She argued instead for non-ageist services which fostered interdependence rather than independence and dependence. This theme was subsequently taken up by many conference contributors and became an important theme in the discussions at Keele.

Finally, the editors would like to thank the many people involved in the organisation of the conference. In particular, we would pay tribute to Frank Glendenning and Arthur Creber, members of the conference steering committee, who worked hard to make the meeting a successful event. The committee was given excellent secretarial support by Sue Allingham and Ann Seaton.

Sue Allingham, along with Kim Pickerill, provided valuable assistance in the production of the volume. Finally we are grateful to Tim Hardwick at Croom Helm for his editorial support.

Chris Phillipson
Miriam Bernard
Patricia Strang

Prologue

SOCIAL AND POLITICAL GOALS

FOR AN AGEING SOCIETY

Maggie Kuhn

May I say that it is a privilege and an honour for my colleagues and myself to be with you today. We have come to encourage you, to learn from you, and conspire with you, to make the changes which are needed in our society. The Gray Panthers are a mix of people of different ages and different backgrounds who have come together for social justice and peace. Our movement emphasises old and young working together, striving to create a new society for a new age. All of us are getting old and all of us are subject to the finite quality of life. We believe, however, that life should be shared with people of all age groups, and that a coalition of young and old will be an effective means of dealing with the social and economic upheavals going on around us.

We are, at this moment in history, in the midst of two revolutions; one demographic, the other technological. People are living longer than at any time in recorded history, whilst, at the same time, technology is bringing enormous changes to all aspects of our lives. We in the Gray Panthers have tried to address some of the issues arising from these changes.

What are the priorities of the Gray Panthers? The first is for an enduring peace. We believe mankind to be an endangered species: the whole world, according to our Gray Panther analysis, is arming to destroy itself. We campaign, therefore, for an end to nuclear power and nuclear weaponry.

Another priority of the Gray Panthers is health. We yearn for what you in Britain have achieved with your National Health Service. We are working very hard for such a system and it angers us that your own health service should be in jeopardy: I hope it outrages you as well.

The third priority for the Gray Panthers is housing. We have in the streets of Philadelphia around five thousand people who are homeless. The bag ladies who carry all their possessions in paper shopping bags; and the vent men who sleep on the steam vents at night. These are tragic, lost people; people with no shelter. So we need housing, decent affordable housing for everyone.

How do we achieve these goals? Just let me run through some of our tactics. We have chosen, as you can see from that list of priorities, not old folk's issues, but societal issues because we believe that old people and any other marginalised group in Western society are not going to get a fair share of resources without facing societal change. And we, the wise ones who have made social changes, who have lived and coped with social changes, are the ones who ought to be probing the depths.

The Gray Panthers also raise issues about the organisation of health and welfare services. Many important services have been developed - in the United States and in Britain. Unfortunately, these often do no more than dull the pain: they do not change the human situation. Services can be paternalistic, demeaning and diminishing to older people. This must be changed and the Gray Panthers are striving with others to achieve this.

Gray Panthers are also building new models. For example, we have developed the concept of shared housing, with younger and older people living under the same roof and supporting each other. We have also been looking at the way in which health care can be delivered by the people themselves, through schemes of self-care and self-help care.

We test and try out new models and then we also go to the press. We have had an extraordinarily good response from the media and I think it is because we say things which are outrageous and not expected and that we are talking about the interests of society and of the young people coming after us.

Finally, we in the Gray Panthers are trying to promote the idea of interdependence instead of independence and dependence for older (and younger) people. We say that we cannot be human all by ourselves; we need each other. I have arthritis and I have failing vision and the two conditions are very complicated; they complicate my life and they could make me a housebound cripple. But I try to conquer my fears. I say to people: 'Help me, may I take your hand up this step or down this kerb.' I have learnt not to feel diminished by asking for help. Instead, I feel a new kind of reward from human love: I touch your arm and something happens, something that is warming and affirming. The person who helps you feels good and the person who is helped also draws strength and encouragement. We need to develop this interdependency in all our services. We need also to work together rather than compete with each other. And we must strive for intergenerational contact in all activities. These are some of the goals and priorities in our search for a peaceful and more equal society.

PART ONE : THE SOCIAL CONSTRUCTION OF DEPENDENCY

PART ONE : The Social Construction of Dependency

Chapter One

CHALLENGES AND OPPORTUNITIES OF AN AGEING SOCIETY

Gunhild O. Hagestad

Introduction : The Three Revolutions

My paper will explore challenges and opportunities presented by an ageing society.[1] I want to stress that we live in a watershed era. How we handle it will shape lives for young and old in a new century. Building on work by my colleague George Maddox (1985), I shall discuss three revolutions:

- the demographic revolution;
- the revolution of knowledge about ageing;
- the revolution of possibilities and hope.
The first two have already taken place; the third is up to us.
     For some time, we have observed western societies go through what we call the demographic transition: reduced mortality and reduced fertility, resulting in altered age composition of the population. Lately, I believe we have come to realise that it is more than a transition. It deserves the label revolution, because of the enormity and rapidity of change.

- Lives are not what they used to be.
- Families are not what they used to be.
- Society is not what it used to be.
     THINGS WILL NEVER BE THE SAME.

The Revolution in Mortality

When the demographic revolution is discussed, it is common to point out that reduced fertility was a more powerful force than reduced mortality in the greying of populations. In other words, ageing occurred more at the base than at the apex of the population pyramid. Nevertheless, there are some recent changes in mortality patterns which deserve our attention. We know that most western societies have had

1

their general life expectancy doubled during this century, due to dramatic reduction in mortality. The average age at death in the United States is now 73, and 80 per cent of all deaths occur after the age of 60 - in the seventh decade of life. In the first part of this century, the average age at death was in the fourth decade of life. Death has become more predictable, and the meaning of the phrase 'an untimely death' has become much clearer. I like to quote one of your countrymen who captured the dramatic realities represented in demographers' life tables: '.... We place dying in what we take to be its logical position, which is at the close of a long life, whereas our ancestors accepted the futility of placing it in any position at all' (Blythe, 1979, p.4).

Death has not only become more predictable - it also appears to provide some predictors. Now that most members of a birth cohort tend to die within a limited time period in their later years, it is easier for researchers to study the last phase of life in longitudinal research. Some fairly remarkable findings are beginning to emerge and converge from some research. As I will discuss when I turn to the knowledge revolution, recent research has found a good deal of stability in individual functioning across the adult years, including the latter part of adulthood. In other words, if we plot 'performance curves', they are relatively flat across age. However, a number of researchers have found sudden and dramatic declines across a number of dimensions. It turns out that the predictor of the decline - be it in patterns of social interaction, cognitive performance, or the functioning of the immune system - is not age, but distance from death. Such findings were discussed at the recent World Congress of Gerontology (Berg, 1985). As I was reading these research reports, I realised that the Norwegian dialect of my childhood had a word which described what the researchers are now finding. The folk culture had a recognition that individuals who are close to death show it in a number of ways. The word, literally translated, means that a person is 'marked'. This phenomenon, which researchers have referred to as 'terminal drop', seriously challenges age - the distance from birth - as a predictor of decline. Overall, chronological age has not proven itself to be a valuable variable in research (Maddox and Campbell, 1985).

A few more comments may be added on the timing of death. The revolution in mortality has in part been an epidemiological revolution (Bourgeois-Pichat, 1979; Siegal, 1980). In the first phase of mortality change, we conquered infectious diseases, which mostly reduced deaths in the early part of life. In the United States, as in most other western nations, the most dramatic changes came in the period after World War II and lasted until the mid-1950s. Then came a levelling off - a plateau - which lasted until the late 1960s. We have recently witnessed a third era, resulting from a reduction in deaths from what epidemiologists call endogenous diseases (e.g. heart disease, atherosclerosis). These changes affect late-life mortality. Since 1968, there has been a 30 per cent reduction in mortality after the age of 50 in the United States. This trend makes it necessary for us to recognise that we are now witnessing ageing at the apex of the population pyramid. These recent changes have made the very old - those 85 and over - the fastest growing segment of the population. It has also opened up some startling possible scenarios for the next century. If mortality stays at its current level, general life expectancy in the year 2025 will be 80, and 22 per cent of the population will be aged 65 and over. However, if we see the same rate of improvement in mortality between now and then as the one observed since 1968, life expectancy will be 100, and 33 per cent of the population will be 65 and above (Siegal and Taeuber, 1986). It can certainly be argued that we seem to have a levelling-off in mortality decline, which makes it doubtful that the next two decades will repeat the patterns since 1968. There are also a number of biologists who would be sceptical about the prospect of centenarian status becoming average. However, demographers have given us food for thought and showed the need for dialogue between scholars from biology, epidemiology, and demography. As part of such a dialogue, we may need to reassess the concepts of life span and life expectancy, as well as how the two are related.

We all know that the demographic revolution has altered the age composition of society. The number of children and youths has decreased; the number of aged has increased. In the western industrialised world, we are now approaching a situation where we have more individuals over the age of 60 than we have children under the age of 15. Between 1980 and the year 2000, the number of people aged 80 and over will increase by one-third in Europe and North America. In most countries, the world of the very old will be the one of women (U.S. Bureau of the Census, 1984).

The final aspect of mortality change which has to be recognised is the 'gender gap' in life expectancy. In many of our western industrialised nations, there is a seven to eight year difference in the average length of life for men and women. In the Soviet Union, it is approximately ten years.

To summarise the discussion so far: the revolution in mortality has given us more than seven decades of life years. Furthermore, it has made death much more closely associated with advanced old age, and it has been an important factor in shaping the age composition of our population. Before we take a look at societal consequences of these changes, let us focus attention on an intermediate level - the family.

Families in an Ageing Society

In the family arena, the combination of altered mortality and fertility has produced a number of striking new trends. Five such trends will be briefly discussed here:
(1) An unprecedented duration of family bonds;
(2) Clearer patterning of family deaths;
(3) The emergence of a new grandparenthood;
(4) A widening gap between the family worlds of men and women;
(5) A growing importance of vertical family ties.

In the beginning of this century, young couples considered themselves lucky to have parents present at their wedding. Currently, many couples expect to have their grandparents among their wedding guests. This is but a simple example of how demographic change has reshaped kinship in our society.

In the United States, loss of a young child was experienced by nearly two-thirds of parents in the early part of this century. In the late 1970s, the probability of such a family event was .04 (Uhlenberg, 1980). Losing a child is now an unexpected crisis. On the other hand, death of parents has become a more 'normal and predictable' adult transition, which typically occurs when individuals have grown children themselves. A person's first encounter with death in the family context is likely to be the loss of a grandparent. Again, this typically occurs in adulthood, and may become more recognised as a life course marker, because it ends a relationship of considerable duration.

American television has yet to discover the revolution in grandparenthood. In televison commercials, we still see a silver-haired lady who serves lemonade to toddlers and worries about slipping dentures. If that woman is real at all, she would certainly have to be the youngster's great-grandmother. Their grandmother - most likely - is off working, playing tennis, or taking a course. Most grandparents who are in advanced age have grandchildren who are adults. I believe this is a relationship to watch. By that age, the grandchild is likely to have the wisdom to appreciate how special grandparents are. Researchers who have examined relations between young adults and their grandparents have found accounts of strong and personally significant ties, especially when grandchildren are interviewed (e.g. Robertson, 1976; Hoffman, 1979-1980). The most important functions of grandparents at this stage may be symbolic ones (Hagestad, 1985). The old represent an important presence, a potential comfort. As one author put it, grandparents may 'provide the final validation of life itself' (Taylor, 1948, p.829).

In recent American research, there is growing evidence that for the family system, grandparents serve critical stabilising functions: they are catalysts for family cohesion by bringing members together; they bolster the next generation's ability to parent; they help younger generations understand one another; they provide 'a place to go' in times of trouble (Tinsley and Parke, 1984). A number of authors have argued that one major social trend which activates grandparents in a variety of support functions is the high rate of divorce.

Patterns of marital endings and remarriage show marked contrasts between men and women. Most older women are widows and living alone; most older men live with their wives. Contrasts in life expectancy and marriage patterns of men and women have strong implications for the rest of their families. The oldest members of a family are likely to be women, and women more often than men have great- and great-great-grandchildren. Men typically have a significant horizontal, intragenerational relationship in the later phase of their lives - women do not. As a result, women's intergenerational relationships become more important sources of help and support in old age. Throughout their adulthood, women invest more time and energy in intergenerational ties and serve as their families' kin-keepers.

Ageing societies are often divorcing societies. The year 1974 was the first time in the history of the United States that more marriages were terminated by divorce than by death. Again, new contrasts are emerging between the experiences of men and women. Research on divorce tends to paint a picture of serious financial hardship for women; of impoverished family networks for men. Not infrequently, divorce means the loss of a 'kin-keeper' since the wife facilitated contact and communication to the husband's kin. Recent research also suggests that divorce may lead to increased matrilinearity in kin relations. The marital break-up often intensifies bonds to grandparents on the 'custodial' side, but leads to a weakening of ties with 'non-custodial' grandparents. As is well-known, the mother is the custodial parent in the vast majority of divorce cases. A growing number of paternal grandparents may face the loss of active grandparenthood as a consequence of their children's divorce (Hagestad et al., 1984).

Modern societies are currently facing a socio-cultural paradox. At a time when ideology stresses convergence between family roles of men and women, demographic and social changes may have produced growing chasms between their family worlds. While women's intergenerational ties are more varied and durable than ever before in history, a growing number of men have only precarious vertical family ties.

As populations age, kin networks take on new shapes. Multigenerational families are more common; families are more 'top-heavy', and family members have a growing number of relationships which bridge generational lines. Both in Great Britain and the United States, it has been found that many grandparents are also great-grandparents, i.e. members of families with four generations or more (Townsend, 1968). Recent American research estimates that nearly half of all grandparents are members of such multigenerational units (Shanas, 1980). We have good reasons to believe that five-generation families have become more common, but lack estimates of how common they are (Lehr and Schneider, 1983). The number of generations in a family line gives us an indication of the web of relationships it contains. A four-generation family has three 'tiers' of parent-child ties and two sets of grandparent-grandchild ties. In five-generation families, we find grandparents who are also grandchildren.

Under earlier demographic conditions, individuals were likely to have a variety of intra-generational, horizontal ties. Under current conditions, many family ties are vertical, i.e. they cross generational lines. An extreme example of such a shift would be in China's recent one-child policy. If it is successful, Chinese in the coming century will have only vertical family ties outside the marital role. In the western world, families are becoming increasingly 'top-heavy'. This is the first time in history that married couples have more living parents than children (Preston, 1984).

The Knowledge Revolution

So far, our attention has been focused on the first revolution: demographic changes and their consequences. Has the generation of knowledge kept up with these changes? Most likely not, but we have seen research which should challenge us to rethink the meaning of age. Two key trends in recent research deserve our attention: A common past trend to associate age and decline is being seriously challenged, and research is providing a picture of impressive variability in the later phases of life (Baltes and Willis, 1978; Baltes and Reese, 1984).

When George Maddox was recently asked to review decades of ageing research in the United States, one of his key messages was: 'the good news is that some of the bad news has been wrong.' Especially during the last decade, we have seen substantial evidence which challenges the common view that ageing inevitably leads to decline in physical functioning, cognitive abilities or problem-solving capacity. Furthermore, we have learned to test what Maddox (1985) calls 'the limits of modifiability'. He reminds us that 'if you want to understand something, you try to change it.' Schaie and Willis, along with numerous other investigators (Baltes and Willis, 1978; Schaie and Willis, 1986) have shown that old dogs can learn new tricks, if they are only given the opportunity, and that often, decline is due to disuse. When it comes to cognitive functioning, the same rule applies as holds for other aspects of our humanity: 'use it or lose it!' Clearly, the issue of individual plasticity is related to the issue of variability. When we are now concluding that development in later life is more malleable than we have earlier assumed (Brim and Kagan, 1980), we are also allowing for a wide range of possible outcomes. Indeed, the great interindividual variability in patterns of ageing may reflect sharp differences and inequalitiies in access to resources which maintain or enhance functioning (Baltes and Willis, 1978; Maddox, 1985).

Both in research on intellectual functioning and in studies of mortality and morbidity, we have gained new appreciation for the importance of social environment and lifestyles. A recent study in the United States (U.S. Public Health Service, 1978; Clogg, 1979) estimates that one quarter of mortality from heart disease, cancer, cerebrovascular disease and atherosclerosis can be attributed to genetic factors. The other three-quarters are accounted for by lifestyles, living environment and health care delivery systems. Another study focused on 45 year old men and concluded that men who practice seven health habits gain several life years over those who practice three or fewer of the habits (Belloc and Breslow, 1972; Wiley and Camaco, 1980). The list includes regular exercise, maintaining moderate weight, limiting snack foods, eating breakfast, no smoking, moderate drinking and getting seven hours of sleep. Research such as these two studies should lead us to question why 'We prefer to think of ageing as a biomedical problem with social implications, rather than ageing as a social problem with biomedical implications' (Maddox, 1985, p.22).

Gerontology in an Ageing Society

How have gerontologists responded to the revolutions in demography and knowledge? I am not sure we have always kept up. All too often, the word 'ageing' has been associated with the word 'problem'. The old are and have problems. I believe we have contributed to the popular image of old age as a period of inevitable decline, senility and dependency. At the World Congress in New York this summer, a participant could have spent the entire Congress listening to papers on Alzheimer's disease and senile dementia. On the other hand, a participant wanting to attend sessions on the old as a resource would have had a lot of free time. In discussions of the family, the recurrent theme in recent gerontological literature has been the burden of parent care. There is growing concern over the strain experienced by families who provide care for impaired elderly members (e.g. Brody, 1985). Many of the discussions focus on women

7

in the middle generations, who tend to be the main providers of care. It is frequently argued that today's families face more of a careload than was the case before societal ageing. Unfortunately, we do not have the historical data to judge the accuracy of such claims, but I believe it is very important to keep in mind that before our society had rectangular survival curves, illness and death were experiences which were encountered in all phases of family life. Families have always been caregiving units. The most significant differences between today's families and families of the past is not likely to be in the total amount of care they provide, but in the focus of care. On a societal level, there is talk of burden again, the burden of economic dependence and the service burden. We blame the survivor, says Robert Butler (1985).

In no way do I want to belittle the massive problems which confront ageing societies and their families. But when are we going to look at the positive sides? When are we going to discuss the old as societal and interpersonal resources? When are we going to shift from discussing ageing to discuss age? When are we going to recognise that dependence and neediness requiring time, attention and resources are found in all age categories? (Neugarten, 1982). When will we recognise that many discussions of 'problems of the elderly' could substitute the word 'young' for the word 'old' in the text, and still make good sense?

There are some ways in which gerontology has fundamentally missed the challenges of an ageing society. First, by concentrating on old age in isolation, we have segmentalised phenomena which should be treated as integrated wholes. We have also taken a static view of dynamic realities. We have disregarded the integrity of lives, across life phases. We have neglected to note that lives are interwoven, and different age groups share problems and challenges. Very often, obstacles to a full life in old age are also obstacles for youth. Strengthening families has positive effects for the young and the old. In a society which severely underutilises both the old and the young, gerontologists should be part of a vanguard, saying: At this unique point in history, let us redefine the meanings of age! Let us not discuss dependence, but interdependence! We need to look at interdependence among phases of life; among individual lives; among age groups and generations.

The Revolution of Possibilities and Hope

We are now getting to the third revoluton - one which needs to be brought about. Gerontologists should take a lead in a search for the art and science of the possible. Let me briefly mention three frontiers: education, work and the lives of men and women.

Education

In an ageing society characterised by rapid cultural and technological change, we need life-long education in two meanings of the word. We need education for and throughout a long life. Modern education is doing extremely little to educate people for eight decades of life. Indeed, children and youth are still socialised as if life expectancy were 35. We still have the cultural expectation that if you have not made it by your thirties, you will never make it. In the decade of history when the eight-decade life became a statistical reality, we had books and public concern focused on 'the hurried child'. Studies of life course have repeatedly shown that the early part of adulthood is currently more compressed and hectic than ever before in recent history. I recently reviewed a book on the Norwegian pension system (Hatland, 1984). Under this system, everyone gets a basic pension. However, in order to qualify for maximum additional retirement income, a person must have been in the workforce for 40 years. The level of this extra pay is determined by the 20 years of continuous employment when the person had the highest income. In Norway, as in most other western countries, women's work patterns are characterised by exits and entrances, reflecting their involvements in family responsibilities. As I was working myself through the rather technical discussion of how the final retirement income reflects 'the 20 best years', it struck me that for young adults, particularly women, there is a distinct need for help with life course planning, for instance in the timing and sequencing of paid employment and family care work. Such planning, and the co-ordination of the work of husbands and wives, can have profound effects on income in late life. To my knowledge, such assistance is not available anywhere in the educational system.

Facing the challenge represented by eight decades of life, young people and adults need to be reminded that the quality of life in later years is the product of a lifetime; that today's behaviour can become tomorrow's risk factor or tomorrow's strength. A few years ago, Swedish society switched all traffic from the left to the right side of the road. There was considerable apprehension that total chaos would ensue, but things went remarkably well. In preparation for the change, the Swedes launched a public information campaign which is likely to become a classic example of how one can produce change in thinking and behaviour. Prior to the change, there were signs and banners everywhere, reading 'Think right!' I believe many modern societies are overdue for a lifespan campaign. Over and over again, people should be reminded to 'Think 80!'

It is extremely difficult to understand why, in our ageing society, education is our most narrowly and rigidly age-segregated social institution. It is for the most part reserved for the first two decades of life, because we still seem to have the outdated notion that preparation for life in society can be accomplished once and for all. We are never going to get rid of stereotypes of the old as outdated and not with it if we expect them to function in today's society with knowledge and skills acquired half a century ago, in a totally different society. But the old are not the only losers. We know from classical social psychology that prejudice and stereotypes emerge under conditions of incomplete knowledge and acquaintance. That goes for relationships 'up' and 'down' age lines.

Of course, if we are discussing socialisation across age groups, we must not forget the family. In this social arena, cultural and social changes are interpreted and buffered, as family members from different generations construct a common reality. A good deal of my own research has explored intergenerational socialisation (Hagestad, 1984). I have been repeatedly impressed with how older family members help the young build bridges to the past, and how the young often help make a startling present manageable and understandable to those in generations above them. Not long ago, a colleague, who is a grandmother, got a new computer to help her writing. She had some trouble figuring out the machine, until her six year old grand-nephew gave her a tutorial session. I believe many lessons could be learned from the family realm as to how age-integrated social settings can help members of all age groups take some of the edges off social change.

Work

Issues of education are closely related to issues of work. As Sarason (1977) has noted, we can no longer think in terms of 'the one life - one career alternative'. Rapid changes in the world of work make re-tooling necessary, and education and work no longer follow a lock-step pattern (Hirschorn, 1977). If we were better able to integrate work and education across the course of life, it might reduce discontinuities for the young as well as the old (Riley, 1978). It has often been commented that youth is deprived of experience in the workaday world, only to be suddenly confronted with its demands in early adulthood. In old age, there is similar discontinuity through a sudden departure from the work sphere. It is time that we consider some radical proposals, using the solid actuarial knowledge currently available to us. Why not make work careers much more flexible? Why not allow individuals of different ages part-time work? Why not create 'time out' - sabbaticals, at chosen points in adulthood?

Men and Women

In his presidential address to fellow demographers on the demography of ageing, Siegal (1980) devoted a good deal of time to the imbalanced sex ratios and stated: 'I would like to send you a clear message that I am seriously concerned about the physical and emotional isolation of older women.... Even though I anticipate increased economic independence of women, this change will not greatly affect the situation' (p.348). I believe Siegal was identifying a highly significant and much neglected social issue.

We seem to have been all too ready to accept 'the feminisation of old age' as a given - a phenomenon to which we adjust, rather than seek to change. As a result, old women live in an impoverished social world; families experience strain, and societal supports are overloaded.

When are we going to see serious discussions of how the ratios might be more balanced? Part of Siegal's original speech had a somewhat lighthearted discussion of how such a goal might be accomplished, but it also identified social programmes which could be created with a recognition that men are, in a sense, 'an endangered species'. Not all such programmes would be overtly discriminatory, but would benefit men and women. We could, for example, implement some of our recent knowledge on the importance of life style and environmental factors. We could fund more mobile units, sponsor health examinations, educate men to seek medical help for lesser ailments at the same rate women do (Verbrugge, 1976), start a national campaign to keep men healthy. In the family realm, men could, for example, be encouraged and supported to follow the seven health habits identified in the study discussed above (Wiley and Camaco, 1980).

Conclusion

Demographic change and break-throughs in knowledge have put us at a watershed in history. We should let things slide so that only demographic and structural factors change in our society. We need to grasp this historical movement and move towards a new social contract. This is the time to recreate the meaning of age - for young and old - women and men.

Notes

(1) Many of the thoughts expressed here were developed while I was writing a paper (Hagestad, 1986) for a project on 'The Aging Society', sponsored and organised by the Carnegie Corporation. A number of colleagues associated with this venture have ·had profound influence on my thinking. A collection of some of the papers appeared in a special issue of Daedalus in the winter of 1986.

References

Baltes, P.B. and Reese, H.W. (1984) 'The Life-Span Perspective in Developmental Psychology' in M.H. Bornstein and M.E. Lamb (eds.), Developmental Psychology: An Advanced Textbook, Erlbaum, Hillsdale, NJ.

Baltes, P.B. and Willis, S. (1978) 'Life-span Developmental Psychology, Cognitive Functioning, and Social Policy' in M.W. Riley (ed.) Aging from Birth to Death (Vol.I), American Association for the Advancement of Science, Washington, DC.

Belloc, N.B. and Breslow, L. (1972) 'Relationship of Physical Health Status and Health Practices', Preventive Medicine, Vol.1, pp.409-421.

Berg, S. (1985) Distance from Birth or Distance from Death?, Invited Roundtable on Decline in Old Age, 13th World Congress of Gerontology, New York.

Blythe, R. (1979) The View In Winter, Harcourt Brace Jovanovich, Inc., New York.

Bourgeois-Pichat, J. (1979) 'Future Outlook for Mortality Decline in the World', United Nations Prospects of Population: Methodology and Assumptions, pp.227-266. (Paper of the Ad Hoc Group of Experts on Demographic Projections, United Nations, New York, November, 1977), Population Studies, Series A, No. 67, United Nations, New York.

Brim, O.G. and Kagan, J. (1980) 'Constancy and Change: A View of the Issues', in O.G. Brim and J. Kagan (eds.) Constancy and Change in Human Development, Harvard University Press, Cambridge, MA.

Brody, E. (1985) 'Parent Care as a Normative Family Stress', Gerontologist, Vol.25(1), pp.19-29.

Butler, R.N. (1985) 'The Longevity Revolution', in M.T. Coleman, B.K. Smith and C. Warren (eds.) Looking Forward: Texas and its Elderly, Hogg Foundation for Mental Health, University of Texas, Austin.

Clogg, C.C. (1979) 'The Effect of Personal Health Care Services on Longevity in an Economically Advanced Population', Health Services Research, Vol.14, pp.5-32.

Hagestad, G.O. (1984) 'Multi-Generational Families: Socialization, Support, and Strain', in V. Garms-Homolova, E.M. Hoerning and D. Shaeffer (eds.), Intergenerational Relationships, Lewiston, New York; C.J. Hogrefe Inc., Toronto.

Hagestad, G.O. (1985) 'Continuity and Connectedness', in V.L. Bengston and J. Robertson (eds.), Grandparenthood, Sage, Beverley Hills, CA.

Hagestad, G.O. (1986) 'The Aging Society as a Context for

Family Life', Daedalus, Vol. 115, no.1, pp.119-140.

Hagestad, G.O., Smyer, M.A. and Stierman, K.L. (1984) 'Parent-Child Relations in Adulthood: The Impact of Divorce in Middle Age, in R. Cohen, S. Weissman and B. Cohler (eds.), Parenthood: Psychodynamic Perspectives, Guildford Press, New York.

Hatland, A. (1984) Folketrygdens Farmtid, Universitetsforlaget, Oslo.

Hirschorn, L. (1977) 'Social Policy and the Life Cycle: A Developmental Perspective', Social Service Review, Vol.51, pp.434-450.

Hoffman, E. 1979-1980) 'Young Adults with their grandparents: An Exploratory Study', International Journal of Aging and Human Development, Vol.10, pp.299-310.

Lehr, U. and Schneider, W.F. (1983) 'Funf-Generationen-Familien: einige Daten uber UrurgroBeltern in der Bundesrepublik Deutschland', Zeitschrift fur Gerontologie, Vol.16, pp.200-204.

Maddox, G.L. (1985) 'Constructing the Future of Aging', in M.T. Coleman, B.K. Smith and C. Warren (eds.), Looking Forward: Texas and its Elderly, Hogg Foundation for Mental Health, University of Texas, Austin.

Maddox, G.L. and Campbell, R.T. (1985) 'Scope, Concepts, and Methods in the Study of Aging', in R.H. Binstock and E. Shanas (eds.), Handbook of Aging and the Social Sciences, (2nd Ed.), Van Nostrand Reinhold Company, New York.

Neugarten, B.L. (ed.) (1982) Age or Need?, Sage, Beverley Hills, CA.

Preston, S.H. (1984) 'Children and the Elderly in the United States', Scientific American, Vol.251(6), pp.44-49.

Riley, M.W. (1978) 'Aging, Social Change, and the Power of Ideas', Daedalus, Vol.107(4), pp.39-52.

Robertson, J.F. (1976) 'Significance of Grandparents: Perceptions of Young Adult Grandchildren', Gerontologist, Vol.16, pp.137-140.

Sarason, S.B. (1977) Work, Aging, and Social Change, Free Press, New York.

Schaie, K.W. and Willis, S.L. (1986) 'Can Decline in Adult Intellectual Functioning be Reversed?', Developmental Psychology, in Press.

Shanas, E. (1980) 'Older People and their Families: The new Pioneers', Journal of Marriage and the Family, Vol.42(9), pp.9-15.

Siegal, J.S. (1980) 'On the Demography of Aging', Demography, Vol.17, pp.354-364.

Siegal, K.W. and Taeuber, S. (1986) 'Demographic Perspectives on the Long-Lived Society', Daedalus, Vol.

115, no. 1., pp.77-118.

Taylor, K.W. (1948) 'The Opportunities of Parenthood', in H. Becker and R. Hill (eds.), Family, Marriage, and Parenthood, D.C. Heath, Boston.

Tinsley, B.R. and Parke, R.D. (1984) 'Grandparents as Supports and Socialization Agents', in M. Lewis (ed.), Beyond the Dyad, Plenum, New York.

Townsend, P. (1968) 'The Emergence of the Four-Generation Family in Industrial Society, in B.L. Neugarten (ed.), Middle Age and Aging, (pp.255-257), University of Chicago Press, Chicago.

Uhlenberg, P. (1980) 'Death and the Family', Journal of Family History, Vol.5, pp.313-320.

U.S. Bureau of the Census (1984) J.S. Siegal, and S.L. Hoover. International Trends and Perspectives: Aging, International Research Document No.12.

U.S. Public Health Service Center for Disease Control (1978) Ten Leading Causes of Death in the United States, 1975, Atlanta, Georgia.

Verbrugge, L.M. (1976) 'Sex Differentials in Morbidity and Mortality in the United States', Social Biology, Vol.23, pp.275-296.

Willis, S.L. (1985) 'Towards an Educational Psychology of the Older Adult Learner: Intellectual and Cognitive Bases', in J.E. Birren and K.W. Schaie (eds.), Handbook of the Psychology of Aging, Van Nostrand Reinhold.

Acknowledgement

My research and writing are supported by a Research Career Development Award from the National Institute on Aging.

Chapter Two

THE POLITICS OF AGEING IN AMERICA

Carroll L. Estes

Introduction

The central challenge of a political economy of ageing is to move beyond a critique of conventional gerontology, to develop an understanding of the character and significance of variations in the treatment of the aged, and to relate these to polity, economy and society in advanced capitalism (Estes et al., 1982). This requires an examination of society's treatment of the aged in the context of the national and world economy, the role of the state, conditions of the labour market, and class, race, gender and age divisions in society. At base, this requires examination of the relationship of capitalism to ageing (Myles, 1984). It also begins with the proposition that the status and resources of the elderly, and even the experience of old age itself, are conditioned by one's location in the social structure and the local to global economic and social factors that shape that location (Estes et al., 1982).

The themes that characterise and frame contemporary American debate over policy for the ageing are inextricably linked to the major issues of the economy, and the respective roles of the state, the for-profit (market) and the not-for-profit sectors. Of growing importance is the struggle between the rights of citizens versus the rights of property (Myles, 1984), or in O'Connor's (1973) terms, the struggle between the citizen state and the class state.

The decade of the 1980s is characterised by economic uncertainty and political ambiguity regarding the direction of American public policy for the elderly. Analysis of policy trends during the past decade suggests that four forces have been and will continue to be central in shaping American policy: austerity, federalism, deregulation and the medical-industrial complex.

First, Austerity: Inflation, recession, unemployment, tax cuts for the wealthy, reductions in social spending, increases in defence spending, high interest rates, and other fiscal and monetary policies portray, in vivid economic terms, the impact of austerity and its political processing.

Austerity is both objective and subjective. The objective basis of austerity is a worldwide economic crisis that has resulted in less 'slack' in the economic system and increased efforts to foster the conditions for renewed capital expansion (in O'Connor's (1984) terms, it is an 'accumulation crisis'). A noteworthy result in the United States, beginning about 1978 and continuing to the present, has been the generation of an objective fiscal crisis at both state and local levels resulting from a combination of successful and conservatively organised state taxpayer revolts, federal budget cuts, and a recession engineered in the face of a profit squeeze, increased corporate bankruptcies and decreased competitiveness of large industrial sectors. Although these impacts have not been equally felt in the different states, states and localities are experiencing serious financing problems for their increasing programme responsibility.

The subjective basis of austerity lies in the socially constructed notion that federal spending on the elderly and on the poor is the cause of the problems in the American economy. Blaming the ageing obscures the origins of problems stemming from the capitalist economic system and the subsequent political choices that are made – choices that dramatically increased the federal deficit (i.e. the $750 billion tax cut; the 57 per cent increase in expenditure for defence; the trebling of American interest on the debt, from $50 to $150 billion annually, all since 1981) as well as the continuing flight of American capital around the globe in search of new investments and profits.

That such 'social constructions' of reality become a force of their own is evident in the current ideology that austerity (now coined as 'deficit reduction') and not social need is to be the determinant of social policy. Needless to say, both symbolic and material consequences flow from such definitions (Edelman, 1977).

It must be observed here that the content of the defined crises that necessitate austerity, as well as the remedies invoked are not so much related to the objective facts of the situation as to the capacity of strategically located groups and classes to press their views into public consciousness and law. In other words, the resulting sacrifices will be apportioned according to inequalities in the power to define and design the 'solutions'. Thus, class, race and gender will tend to differentiate the distribution of the consequences of the sacrifices to be made.

Secondly, Federalism: Federalism denotes the relationships among different levels of government, raising the fundamental question of politics: Who will decide? In the 1970s, President Nixon introduced new federalism policies designed to increase state and local responsibility, to reduce the federal role, and to stem the proliferation of categorical programmes in the 1960s. A number of such categorical programmes had developed in health and ageing services. Under the Reagan Administration, new federalism continues to be vigorously pursued through block grants, the abolition of federal revenue sharing and other federal budget reductions to the states and localities, under the rhetoric of returning more autonomy and discretion to the states. In its most extreme form, new federalism challenges the idea that there is a national responsibility for meeting basic human needs in health, income, housing or welfare.

Two fundamental questions concern contemporary new federalism and the decentralisation fostered by it: First, do state and local governments have the fiscal and other capacity to deal effectively with their traditional responsibilities and to assume greater responsibility for programmes in welfare, education, transportation, social services and health, particularly when the broad economic policies that necessitate these programmes do not lie in the hands of decentralised governments, but are the result of federal policies and actions? Secondly, how uniformly committed can (or will) states be to equity, social justice and racial equality, particularly under conditions of austerity (Estes, 1979; Estes and Gerard, 1983)?

Thirdly, Deregulation: A hallmark of Reagan Administration policy is deregulation, both in bureaucratic practice and ideology. Its effects are evident in the new discretion that state government have received to cost-cut, to relax (i.e. tighten) eligibility, to eliminate their matching for federal funds, to eliminate services, and to relax affirmative action and civil rights requirements. The most profound impact of deregulation is the eradication of federal restrictions against the entry of proprietary for-profit firms in many governmentally financed programmes that previously barred such firms, and the efforts to promote 'market competition' that have accompanied these deregulatory moves.

Fourthly, the Medical-Industrial Complex: Finally, and of growing importance to the elderly, is what has come to be known as the medical-industrial complex, and particularly the growing proprietary ownership of hospitals, of systems of medical care delivery, and of other businesses related to medical goods and services (Relman, 1980; Wohl, 1984).

With American personal health care expenditure approximating $400 billion per year (almost eleven per cent of the gross national product), the importance of the for-profit markets in medical care is obvious. Intensified by the pro-competition and deregulation policies noted above, a perennial issue in the politics of American health care has been unearthed - whether health care should be provided as a 'market good' (i.e. purchased as a commodity primarily by

17

those who can afford to pay) or whether health care should be treated as a 'merit good' (i.e. as a right or collective good that should be available regardless of ability to pay)(Estes et al., 1984).

The medicalisation of ageing via a robust medical-industrial complex is entirely consistent with the predominant American image of ageing as a process of individual physiological and biological decline that requires biomedical research and medical interventions for its treatment. Consistent with the liberal philosophical emphasis on individual responsibility, American public policy has been predicated largely on a conception of ageing as an individual problem (and thus an 'apolitical' problem of inexorable biological decline). Public policy has emphasised treating individuals via services with a medical character, placing power largely in the hands of service providers who receive reimbursement (Estes, 1979), and raising questions of socially generated dependency (Walker, 1981).

The resulting policies also have the core characteristics of being largely separatist in nature - that is, of separating the aged from other groups in American society on the basis of their special need. In 1979, I described the consequence of this problem formulation and policy prescription as the creation of an 'ageing enterprise' of programmes, organisations and professionals to serve the elderly. The concept of an 'enterprise' was employed in order to call attention to how the aged and their needs are processed and treated as a commodity, and to the fact that the age-segregated policies that fuel the enterprise are, I believe, socially divisive solutions, in contrast to those policies that do not single out and separate the aged from the rest of society (Estes, 1979).

In addition, current American old age policy reflects a two-class system of welfare where benefits are distributed on the basis of legitimacy (Tussing, 1971) rather than on the basis of need. Old age neither levels nor diminishes social class distinctions. As is the case in the United Kingdom, resources in old age are largely determined by lifetime conditions and labour force participation established prior to retirement age (Walker, 1981). In the United States, income, health and social service policies reflect different classes of 'deserving-ness' in old age (Nelson, 1982). Deservingness in old age is predicated upon the principle of differential rewards for differential lifetime achievements in the labour market (see Figure 1).

The 'deserving' (nonpoor) aged have the resources to permit access to public and private services without the necessity of government intervention. They also receive a disproportionate share of the benefits of the largest federal programmes for the aged (e.g. Social Security, Medicare and retirement tax credits), estimated at $43 billion in 1982 (Nelson, 1983). Most social service policies tend to favour

Figure 1

Class Basis of Ageing Policies

	Deserving Elderly (1 Federal Policy)	Undeserving Elderly (50 State Variable Policies)
	SOCIAL SECURITY (SS)	
Income	Regressive Taxation - No SS Tax After $35,700 Salary Level	Minimum Social Security Benefit Eliminated for All Future Eligibles
	PRIVATE PENSIONS TAX POLICY Individual Retirement Accounts	Unlikely to Supplement with Private Pensions SUPPLEMENTAL SECURITY
	(IRA) Tax Credits - Economic Economic Recovery Tax Act of 1981	INCOME (SSI)* Payment Levels Below Poverty Means-Tested for the Poor Only
	MEDICARE PROGRAMME	
Health	Expenditures are High for this group Greater Capacity to Pay Deductibles and copayments	Lower Access to Physicians and Hospitals For Blacks and Other Minorities and Poor MEDICAID PROGRAMME* Means-Tested for the Poor Only - Approx 50% of Persons Below Poverty Not Covered
	PRIVATE INSURANCE	
	More Capacity to Afford Coverage	Little or No Capacity to Purchase Coverage
	SOCIAL SERVICES BLOCK GRANT* (Formerly Title XX of the Social Security Act)	No Federally Mandated Priority To Low-Income Eligibles
Social Services	OLDER AMERICANS ACT* Services Needed by Middle Class e.g. Information and Referral: Transportation	No Federally Mandated Priority

* State variable policies emerge primarily from state-federal programmes in which states have much discretion over eligibility and scope of available services. State discretionary programmes are fiscally vulnerable, uncertain, unstable and highly vulnerable to swings in state level political and economic factors.

the 'newly poor' in old age, largely because they are thought
of as both deserving and threatened with impoverishment in
later life. These services (e.g. congregate meals and Older
Americans Act services) were designed to assist this
potentially downwardly mobile group to maintain their
lifestyles, rather than to provide the more crucial life-support
services (e.g. income or housing) most needed by the
'undeserving' aged.

Those 'undeserving' life-long poor aged are assisted
largely through increasingly stringent and inadequate
income-maintenance policies such as Supplemental Security
Income (SSI), which has different eligibility and payment
standards across the states; and through Medicaid, the
medical-welfare programme for the extremely poor (which is
highly variable from state to state and so stringent that only
46 per cent of the below-poverty population is eligible) (U.S.
Senate, 1985).

In the past, those individuals who had been casually (or
sporadically) employed or who had very low lifetime earnings
covered by Social Security (mainly women and minorities)
were entitled to a minimum Social Security benefit that
guaranteed a basic monthly payment of $122.[1] However, the
Reagan Administration eliminated even this meagre minimum
benefit for new retirees after January 1981 (U.S. Public
Legislature, 97-35, 1981) successfully removing these
'undeserving' aged from receiving Social Security trust funds
that they had not earned.

In sum, policies that deal with the 'undeserving' aged
are 'state discretionary policies' carried out by 50 states with
programme eligibility and benefits largely dependent upon the
states' variable political willingness and fiscal capacity.
These programmes are both more economically and politically
vulnerable and variable than uniform federal programmes.
Thus, the most economically disadvantaged aged (the
'undeserving' aged) do not have the security of stable,
uniformly administered federal policies (like Social Security
and Medicare) that apply to those considered more deserving.

Even Medicare, the American national health programme
for its ageing, benefits the 'deserving' more than the
'undeserving'. First, research has shown that there are
significant benefit inequities based on income, race and
religion. For example, in the southern region of the United
States, where 56 per cent of the nation's aged non-whites
reside, the disparities between benefits received by white and
non-white Medicare beneficiaries persist (Ruther and Dobson,
1981). These inequities are noteworthy when controlling for
illness, since the lower income and minorities tend to
experience disproportionately ill health. Secondly, the higher
income aged can better afford the rapidly rising co-payments
and deductibles increased since 1981 to discourage service

utilisation.[2] Thirdly, the well-off elderly can supplement these benefits by purchasing private health insurance, in contrast to the lower income ('undeserving') aged who cannot afford to do so. Fourthly, the flat-rate copayments and deductibles (e.g. currently $400 for the first day of hospital care in a year regardless of income - and rising to $492 on January 1st, 1986) and other out-of-pocket costs are particularly onerous since they exceeded $1,500 per capita in 1984 (Davis, 1983). Estimates by the Congressional Budget Office are that in 1984, those with incomes above $58,000 would pay only about one per cent for their out-of-pocket medical costs (U.S. Congressional Budget Office, 1983).

The lesson is clear. For all of the public veneration of ageing, it is not federal policy to formally address the needs of the most disadvantaged with a national policy that is uniform for all low income - either aged or non-aged across the country. Thus, decisions about services to the poor are located at the state and local level, precisely where pressures to control social expenses are greatest and where it is most difficult to increase corporate taxes for fear of business threats to relocate. (This phenomenon has been described as the structural segregation of policy by Friedland et al., 1977).

Major Current Trends

An important effort in the United States' public policy debate has been the attempt to 'de-legitimate' the ageing by reinstating the dominance of ideologies of individualism and self-help to reaffirm the belief that individuals create their own conditions and opportunities and thus are to blame for their predicament. Attacks on Social Security and Medicare share the characteristic of blaming the elderly for the problems of the economy.

The blame for 'impending bankruptcy' of Social Security (of course, an impossibility with publicly financed programmes) has not been placed on the fiscal, monetary and other factors that produced the recession, nor on other pressures for early retirement such as unemployment (that reduce payments into Social Security) and inflation (that increase payments out by Social Security through cost of living adjustments, (COLAs)).[3] Instead, Social Security's problems have been portrayed as the product of 'mistaken' generosity in domestic programmes, of demographic ageing - ignoring health status, age discrimination and structural unemployment problems that significantly contribute to early retirement (Estes et al., 1983).

Probably most important in stimulating the socially produced Social Security crisis was the need for new sources of investment in the context of profitability problems of corporate America (Myles, 1982). Conservative economists argue that Social Security reduces public reliance on the market; it increases individual dependency on government; and it reduces incentives for personal savings that are needed in the private sector for capital investment and economic growth (Rahn and Simonson, 1980). The needs of private capital have fuelled the political attempts to drastically weaken American commitment to its Social Security programme and to privatise the bedrock programme that keeps an estimated 60 per cent of the elderly in poverty.

Although the re-privatisation scheme for Social Security failed, big tax subsidies were enacted to encourage private saving through Individual Retirement Accounts (IRAs), imposing: (1) the definition of Social Security as an unstable 'flim flam' public programme; (2) constraints against raising future Social Security payments to adequate levels (because the middle class can now privately buy their increments in old age income through IRAs); (3) a new source of investment capital to banks and stockbrokers who invest in IRAs; and (4) a continuance of a class-biased old age income policy where those able to afford a $2,000 a year tax-free IRA investment will be subsidised by the rest of us, while those dependent on public programmes (e.g. women and minorities) will fall further behind.

A similar scenario is being played out regarding Medicare - a programme that pays only 44 per cent of the elderly's medical bill and that does not cover physical examinations, out-of-hospital drugs, dental or eye care or custodial in-home or institutional long term care. As socially 'constructed' and 'produced' by powerful opinionmakers in the United States, the dual symbols of a Medicare hospital trust fund bankruptcy[4] and the resurgent ideologies of individualism and market competition, support the tendency to blame the elderly for Medicare's problems (for using too many services and, of course, for living too long). The solutions promoted under this construction of reality are the corporatisation and the further (or complete) privatisation of medical care.

In addition to significant increases in the amount of patient cost-sharing already described, a new reimbursement scheme for hospitals has been introduced under Medicare to control costs. Under this scheme, hospitals are paid on a prospective, fixed price basis per diagnosis (DRGs), creating major incentives for hospitals to reduce in-patient hospital days and encouraging the discharge of elders 'sicker and quicker'. In fact, the average length of hospital stays for those aged 65 and older declined 7.5 per cent in 1984, attributed largely to this new policy. It also appears to be generating an accelerated demand on the community-based service delivery systems and on women caretakers (Wood et al., 1984). In addition, deregulation and tax laws are encouraging the entry of proprietaries into medical markets (both hospital and home health).

Among the 'solutions' offered, but not yet adopted, for Medicare's problems are: (1) increasing the age of eligibility for Medicare to 67 years of age (in spite of the fact that those poor and minorities with higher rates of chronic illness and lower life expectancy would be severely disadvantaged); (2) making Medicare a voucher programme, giving elders vouchers to privately purchase their own medical care, to hopefully force them to behave rationally in a (theoretically competitive) market under-insuring themselves and paying higher costs out of pocket; and (3) instituting a completely private medical insurance system through 'Health Bank Individual Retirement Accounts', or IRAs. The latter two approaches (medical vouchers and IRAs) are likely to encourage the now familiar phenomena of 'dumping' the sickest, most costly elderly, and 'creaming' (enrolling) those who are most healthy and 'profitable'. Not only is the government not likely to save costs under these schemes, costs could actually increase significantly since the state will probably have to pay for the highest cost, sickest elderly under either programme.

Health care advocates and the elderly are caught between the dual interests of government and the for-profit sector. Each is attempting to constrain and reduce its own direct expenditures, while neither is seeking to assure or enhance access to needed services. Simultaneously, physicians, hospitals and proprietary corporations are seeking to ensure the availability of a growing and highly profitable market in medical care.

Regrettably, the hope that medical cost containment pressures might result in the financing of <u>alternatives</u> to costly acute hospital care has not come to pass. In spite of much rhetoric calling for chronic care and social supportive services, paradoxically, the United States appears to be moving further away from - not closer to - that heralded continuum of care. Our research is documenting several potentially ominous trends. First, since 1981 there has been a significant reduction of federal funding for non-hospital community social, health and mental health services, and particularly to non-profit sector agencies delivering these services (Salamon and Abramson, 1985). Secondly, a restructuring of the community care delivery system appears to be resulting from recent federal policies that are promoting:

(a) the <u>recommodification and privatisation</u> of the most profitable areas of human services (e.g. expansion of proprietaries into areas of medical and social services) through de-regulation and other policies (e.g. tax subsidies) favouring their entry;

(b) the <u>de-legitimation</u> of both non-profit sector and state sector services through ideological attacks on their efficiency and 'unfair competition'. This is important since, historically, both the state and non-profit sectors have served the low income population;

(c) the expansion and diversification of organisational forms (auspice, tax status) of agencies that deliver community services, including their vertical and horizontal integration (Starr, 1983);

(d) the absorption of non-profit community agencies by for-profit entities;

(e) the medicalisation of social service due largely to United States' Medicare and Medicaid reimbursement schemes, and the inherent advantages of medical over social services in terms of publically financed reimbursement (and profitability);

(f) the further fragmentation of services ('unbundled' services where primarily those single services are offered by providers that are reimbursed by the state while other important services are dropped). The result is a change in the scope and nature of the services that are available;

(g) the polarisation of services in favour of the 'old old' versus the 'young old' (frail versus non-frail), and a class-linked polarisation between those agencies serving clients who can afford to pay privately versus those serving clients who cannot afford to pay for their services;

(h) a growing disparity between medical services provided in the home and social services provided in the community. With hospital cost containment, the 'newest institution' is becoming the home, where extremely sick elders receive minimal medically-oriented services for a finite time period; and

(i) a process of informalisation, wherein functions of hospital and community agencies are being transferred out of the formal delivery system and into the family and home (mainly to women).

Political economists have described the search for profits and ever new sources of capital investment as a driving force of capitalism (O'Connor, 1984). What the austerity of the 1980s shows is that, in the United States the search for new sources of capital investment, new markets and profits is not confined to the pursuit of foreign markets or to the internationalisation of capital. There is a re-invigorated pursuit of such potential sources of profitability within the United States' borders itself via the corporatisation of virtually every aspect of medical care and the profitable areas of social care (e.g. meals on wheels and in-home medical services).

Given the contemporary social, economic and political crises of the capitalist system, there is heightened debate among political theorists: Is the welfare state compatible with, or necessary for, capital accumulation? (A long line of welfare state theorists have argued this one). How compatible or essential is the not-for-profit voluntary sector with the needs of capital at this historical juncture and under the current ideology and practice of austerity? It will be important to distinguish between those functions that the state and the non-profit sectors perform (separately or in combination) in the provision of old age benefits, which various segments of capital need but cannot perform itself and those activities that in some way 'infringe' on capital. Equally important questions concern how social movement, class and other political constellations will obstruct (or facilitate) the transformations of the state and the non-profit sectors that appear to be underway, and what these transformations will mean for the existing patterns of inequality.

The Future of Ageing

The future of ageing in the United States will be profoundly shaped and altered by the economic, social and political crises of capitalism and the ensuing struggles around them.

A deeply political process of crisis naming, blaming, sorting and shifting has occurred. For the ageing, the potential implications include greater social inequalities; the private purchase of more and more needed health and social care by individuals rather than entitlement to it; increased corporatisation of services; the medicalisation and disaggregation ('unbundling') of services to increase profitability; and the transference of a growing number of public responsibilities to private families (informalisation).

Two American observers have raised central and basic questions: Kuttner (1984) asks: What are the limits of the welfare state in countering the inequalities of the laissez faire capitalist system? While S.M. Miller (1985) calls us to a broader outlook, saying that:

> welfare state adherents have to address the issues of macroeconomic policy and economic structure so that the original distribution of income is less unequal, reducing the task confronting the welfare state.
> (Miller, 1985, p.64)

The challenge for students of social gerontology is to meet the promise of a political economy of ageing - to do the serious intellectual work that will compel others to understand and act, based on the knowledge that ageing is part of the whole; that is, part of the capitalist economy and society within which redundancy is declared and imposed and within which power struggles are waged and won that shape the ageing experience. In the process, we must learn much more about the power of the human agency to resist and to de-construct, as well as construct reality - and particularly such 'realities' as fiscal crisis and the notions of who is to blame and who is to sacrifice.

For those working for social change, two immediate challenges are presented. One raises a question of class. There is a need for ageing interest groups, organisations and professionals to identify and work on the basis of the commonalities existing between the socially and structurally induced problems of the aged and non-aged. For example, in the United States a health 'system' that costs $400 billion; that is eleven per cent of the gross national product (GNP) that produces more than $60 billion annually in private profit; that is 42 per cent government financed; that does not cover (or insure) more than 35 million Americans (almost 20 per cent) for their health care, including 389,000 elders; and that costs older Americans 19 per cent to 27 per cent of their annual income (not covered by Medicare), calls for a major reorientation and re-structuring based on an intergenerational agenda. In the United Kingdom the preservation of the National Health Service against its privatisation and the erosion of public entitlement is a comparable issue. The class question concerns whether (and how) the middle class aged (who are highly dependent on the state benefits of Social Security, Medicare and tax credits) can be persuaded to understand the commonalities between their interests and the survival of a welfare state that contains re-distributive purposes benefitting their less advantaged age cohort members.

Tough issues must be raised, including those of rights to work, to retire, to subsistence and to health, as well as issues of tax equity (including tax subsidies to the rich and the virtual abolition of corporate taxes in the United States), labour control of pension funds (Olson, 1982), and the unparalleled militarisation of the American economy.

Notes

(1) Since some estimated three million beneficiaries receive a higher monthly payment than would be payable under the regular benefit formula, critics have pointed to the alleged welfare character of the minimum social security benefit.

(2) Measures already implemented to reduce Medicare costs are: significant increases in patient costs for hospital care through Medicare Part A hospital deductible (up 96 per cent since 1981), for medical treatment by doctors throughout Part B annual deductibles for physician services (up 25 per cent since 1981) and the annual Part B premiums (up 62 per cent since 1981), as well as new co-payments on certain equipment.

(3) For every one million unemployed workers, Social Security loses $100 million in contributions per month, and each per cent of inflation is estimated to cost Social Security $1.5 billion annually.
(4) 'Medicare's success in reducing its own costs. The date for Medicare bankruptcy keeps being postponed. The Congressional Budget Office now says ten years as compared to 1989 or 1990 a short time ago, and if one takes seriously the optimistic economic projections of the 1986 budget estimates, the date would move to sometime in the next century' (Ball, 1985).

References

Ball, R.R. (1985) 'Health and Social Policy for an Aging Society', Unpublished paper, University of Texas Health Science Center, Houston, Texas.

Davis, K. (1975) 'Equal Treatment and Unequal Benefits: The Medicare Program', Milbank Memorial Fund Quarterly/Health and Society, Vol.53, No.4, pp.449-488.

Davis, K. (1983) 'Health Implications of Aging in America', Unpublished manuscript, Johns Hopkins University, Baltimore.

Edelman, M. (1964) The Symbolic Uses of Politics, University of Illinois Press, Urbana, Illinois.

Edelman, M. (1977) Political Language: Words That Succeed and Politics That Fail, Academic Press, New York.

Estes, C.L. (1979) The Aging Enterprise, Jossey-Bass, San Francisco.

Estes, C.L., Gerard, L.E., Zones, J. and Swan, J. (1983) 'Social Security: The Social Construction of a Crisis', Milbank Memorial Fund Quarterly/Health and Society, Vol.61, No.3, pp.445-461.

Estes, C.L., Gerard, L.E., Zones, J. and Swan, J. (1984) Political Economy, Health, and Aging, Little, Brown and Sons, Boston.

Estes, C.L. and Gerard, L. (1983) 'Governmental Responsibility: Issues of Reform and Federalism', in Estes, C.L. and Newcomer, R.J. (eds.) Fiscal Austerity and Aging, Sage, Beverly Hills, California.

Estes, C.L., Swan, J. and Gerard, L.E. (1982) 'Dominant and Competing Paradigms in Gerontology: Towards a Political Economy of Ageing', Ageing and Society, Vol.2, No.2, July, pp.151-164.

Friedland, R., Alford, R.R. and Piven, F.F. (1977) 'The Political Management of the Urban Fiscal Crises', Paper presented at the annual meeting of the American Sociological Association, Chicago, September.

Kuttner, R. (1984) The Economic Illusion: False Choices Between Prosperity and Social Justice, Houghton Mifflin, Boston.

Miller, S.M. (1985) 'Welfare State Revisited', Social Problems.

Myles, J.F. (1980) 'The Aged, The State, and the Structure of Inequality', in Harp, J. and Hotley, J. Structural Inequality in Canada, Prentice-Hall, Toronto.

Myles, J.F. (1982) 'Population Aging and the Elderly', in Forcese, D. and Richer, S. (eds.) Social Issues: Sociological Views of Canada, Prentice-Hall, Toronto.

Myles, J.F. (1984) The Political Economy of Public Pensions, Little, Brown and Sons, Boston.

Nelson, G. (1982) 'Social Class and Public Policy for the Elderly', Social Services Review, Vol.56, No.1, March, pp.85-107.

Nelson, G. (1983) 'Tax Expenditures for the Elderly', Gerontologist, Vol.23, No.5, October, pp.471-478.

O'Connor, J. (1973) The Fiscal Crisis of the State, St. Martin's Press, New York.

O'Connor, J. (1984) Accumulation Crisis, Basil Blackwell, New York.

Olson, L.K. (1982) The Political Economy of Aging, Columbia University Press, New York.

Rahn, R.W. and Simonson, K.D. (1980) 'Tax Policy for Retirement Programs', in Retirement Income: Who Gets How Much and Who Pays? (National Journal Issues Book), Government Research Corporation, Washington, DC.

Relman, A.S. (1973) 'The New Medical-Industrial Complex', The New England Journal of Medicine, Vol.303, No.17, 23 October, pp.963-970.

Salamon, L.M. and Abramson, A.J. (1985) 'Nonprofits and the Federal Budget: Deeper Cuts Ahead', Foundations News, March/April, pp.48-54.

Starr, P. (1982) The Social Transformation of American Medicine, Basic, New York.

Tussing, A. (1971) 'The Dual Welfare System', in Horowitz, L. and Levey, C. (eds.) Social Realities, Harper and Row, New York.

U.S. Congressional Budget Office (1983) Changing the Structure of Medicare Benefits: Issues and Options, Washington, DC.

U.S. Senate, Special Committee on Aging (1985) Developments in Aging: 1984, Vol.1, Government Printing Office, Washington, DC.

Walker, A. (1980) 'The Social Creation of Poverty and Dependency in Old Age', Journal of Social Policy, Vol.9, No.1, pp.49-75.

Walker, A. (1981) 'Towards a Political Economy of Old Age', Ageing and Society, Vol.1, Part 3, pp.73-94.

Wohl, S. (1984) The Medical-Industrial Complex, Harmony,

New York.
Wood, J.B., Estes, C.L., Lee, P.R. and Fox, P.J. (1984) <u>Public Policy, the Private Nonprofit Sector and the Delivery of Community-Based Long Term Care Services for the Elderly</u>, Final Report, 1983; Year 2 Report, 1984. Aging Health Policy Center, University of California, San Francisco.

Chapter Three

THE POLITICS OF AGEING IN BRITAIN*

Alan Walker

Introduction

Contemporary accounts of the social impact of ageing usually
dwell on the expansion of the elderly population, past and
projected, and the implications of this growth for both formal
and informal support services. Growth in the numbers of
elderly people is linked with increases in need and, in turn,
demand for social services. Often underlying this sort of
analysis is the functionalist assumption that changes in
population produce changes in policy. In fact, as a detailed
historical analysis of demographic change shows, expenditure
on health and social services has not been particularly
sensitive to increases in population and need (Ermisch, 1983,
p.283). The deciding factors in the allocation of resources to
the elderly are not demographic but political. It is
remarkable, therefore - and indicative of the
underdevelopment of political gerontology in this country -
that very little attention has been paid to the potential
political consequences of population ageing. Indeed the
prospects for a fully fledged political gerontology have been
daunted by the functionalist pluralist paradigm that has long
dominated social gerontology. As has been argued at length
elsewhere (Walker, 1980, 1981) this paradigm has disguised
the deep divisions of interest and power both among elderly
people and between the elderly and younger adults. Like the
now burgeoning political economy of old age, political
gerontology must address itself to these social divisions -
forged over the whole life course - and their implications for
political consciousness and action, rather than the party
political arena, if it is to adequately explain the politics of
old age and, thereby, enfranchise itself into the study of
gerontology.
      The purpose of this chapter - a more modest precursor
to the major task facing political gerontologists - is to outline
the current state of the politics of old age in Britain. Has
the ageing of British society altered its political

decision-making? How far has political advocacy for the old developed? Has it become a divisive force? How far are the interests of older people represented in the British political system? Have recent changes in demography and policy produced militancy or acquiescence among Britain's elderly?

Demographic change has been the second major 'external' pressure operating recently on the policy-making processes of all advanced industrial societies. It is, however, the combination of this and the primary pressure, created by change in economic ideology and policy which has proved irresistable. Thus the government has acted recently to curtail increasing public expenditure on elderly people and has made plans for further cuts. The major changes in policy on ageing represent a fundamental break with the post-war party political consensus on elderly people, enshrined in the welfare state, as well as a fissure in the all-party consensus on pensions over the last decade. They might also signal the start of overt conflict in the political arena over policy on ageing, as did similar changes in France (Guillemard, 1986). The causes of this new conflict are examined here and some general lessons are drawn for the study of political gerontology.

Ageing and the Political Process

There is no need to document the ageing of the British population over the course of this century and the projected continuation of the trend into the next century (see, for example, Wicks, 1982; Henwood and Wicks, 1984). What has been the impact of this major structural change on the political arena?

If we are looking for indications of a direct impact on the decision-making process in terms of increased representation of elderly people's interests in the political system or the exercise of political muscle by elderly people or those advocating for them, there are no significant ones.

There are few signs, as yet, of heightened political awareness on the part of either politicians or elderly people themselves of the potential power of older citizens in the political arena. There are no new national pressure groups of older people formed in the last 10 years, in the wake of increasing population numbers, although existing groups have increased in size and there are several important examples of local initiatives taken by groups of pensioners. This might be contrasted with the growth in recent times of groups comprising or working closely with people with disabilities (the Disability Alliance, for example, has more than eighty organisational members).

The absence of a parallel growth in ageing advocacy groups is surprising because political organisation on a national scale among elderly people in Britain dates back to the 1930s. The Scottish Pensioners' Association and the National Federation of Old Age Pensions Association were both formed in 1939, primarily to campaign for improvements in old age pensions (Phillipson, 1982, p.131). Although the National Federation grew substantially over the post-war period, to some 250,000, dissatisfaction from within about its lack of militancy led to some groups breaking away in 1973 to form, along with the Scottish Pensioners' Association, the British Pensioners Trade Union Action Association (Phillipson, 1982, p.138). The Association has strong links with the trade union movement and, in conjunction with the TUC, has organised several recent national conventions of pensioners' associations and Senior Citizens Days of Action, most notably in September 1985 when 10,000 pensioners gathered in London to protest against government cuts in benefits and services.

Apart from several local pensioners' action groups, including the Greater London Pensioners' Trade Union Association - the long-term importance of which may far outweigh their seemingly local focus - these are the main examples of collective pensioner militancy. Although a summary cannot do justice to the range of campaigns undertaken by pensioners associations and action groups - which demonstrate, in contrast to popular stereotypes, that there is political activity and militancy among elderly people - this activity is on a limited scale both in terms of the numbers involved and the impact on the political system.

The other main participants in ageing advocacy - Age Concern, the Centre for Policy on Ageing and Help the Aged - have concentrated on establishing all party support for moderate policies rather than militant action. As a result the form of their lobbying has tended to be exclusionist, based on expert activity and geared towards policy-makers, rather than collective and popularly orientated. In short there is, as yet, no sign of widespread political action on the part of pensioners in Britain. There is no sign of the emergence, on the national stage, of a more activist population of elders challenging traditional stereotypes of ageing of the sort predicted for the USA (Neugarten, 1974, pp.196-7). Moreover reference to a pensioners' movement is premature: age-advocacy groups differ widely in their goals and methods and have not shown consistently the unity of purpose necessary to constitute a single social movement. The reasons for this lack of activism and unity and the prospects for a more militant tendency in old age are discussed later. Before doing so it is important to examine the factor which has had a much more direct bearing on old-age policy than population ageing itself, change in economic ideology and official attitudes towards the role of the state. In other words analysis must be directed to the nature of the <u>response</u> to population ageing as well as to the demands created by population ageing or age advocacy.

The Political Economy of Population Ageing

Policies towards elderly people have been characterised by consensus between the two main political parties over the whole of the post-war period. The system of pensions and other benefits introduced following the Beveridge Report has survived largely unchanged for 40 years (Shragge, 1984). Both espoused, though never committed sufficient resources to, a policy of community-based care (Walker, 1982). True there was competition over pensions policy, with each party vying for electoral supremacy in the pledges they made to pensions about increases in pensions and the specific benefits of the new pensions structure they were proposing. During the 1970s this competition was reminiscent of the similar one over house building during the post-war reconstruction in the 1950s, with each one bidding up the other's offer of higher pensions. It was during this period, under the Labour government of the mid-1970s, that the pensioner lobby had its greatest impact in the form of significant real increases in pensions. Here was a sympathetic government engaged in corporatist power sharing with the trade union movement and, partly because of the newly forged links with trade unions, pensioners were able to lobby effectively for better pensions. It was during this period too that the new State Earnings-Related Pension Scheme (SERPS) was initiated with all-party support. This represented a compromise between Labour and Conservative policies – with Conservative opposition being bought-off by a guarantee of state inflation-proofing for private pensions – and promised a substantial number of pensioners retiring towards the end of this century and into the next a significant increase on top of their basic retirement pension.

This broad political consensus on policy towards the elderly was accompanied by the consolidation of a conventional wisdom about politicians' sensitivity to the potential power of the pensioner vote. No government, it was argued, would dare to challenge the position of elderly people as the most deserving of all minority groups. But in the 1980s that apparent political commitment to the elderly has been gradually whittled away and recently the longstanding consensus on ageing policy has been shattered.

A series of measures introduced since 1980 have significantly reduced both the total amount of public resources being spent on the elderly and the incomes of substantial numbers of elderly people. There have been cuts in supplementary pensions, housing benefits, heating additions and other benefits affecting elderly people. One change alone – the substitution of a prices index for an earnings index in the uprating of pensions – has resulted in a pensioner couple losing £4.80 per week or 12 per cent of what the pension would have been if the government had not changed the method of uprating. This cut in pensions will be progressively increased over the next 50 years as the incomes of those in employment increase and pensions fall further and further behind.

This and other similar reductions in pensions and other benefits are dwarfed, however, by the government's plans for SERPS. The original intention, announced in the Green Paper on the reform of social security in June 1985, was to phase out SERPS completely for men under 50 and women under 45 (DHSS, 1985a). But the public outcry which greeted this proposal and particularly the weight of influential opinion ranged against it - including the Confederation of British Industry, the Engineering Employers Federation and the private pensions industry itself in the form of the National Association of Pension Funds and insurance companies - caused the government to modify its plans. Thus the White Paper, published in December 1985, contained proposals to cut the projected costs of SERPS in half by reducing the pensions paid under it and providing generous incentives to encourage the take-up of private pensions (DHSS, 1985b). Because of their political sensitivity these changes to SERPS have been deferred until 1988, after the next election. It is clear though that the consensus on which the 1975 earnings-related scheme was based has been abandoned and pensions are once more a political football (Walker, 1986). The implementation of other major proposals in the Green and White Papers on social security has not been delayed, and the main measures were contained in the Social Security Bill which was before Parliament during the first part of 1986. According to the government's own figures the average reduction in disposable income resulting from the implementation of the White Paper's proposals will be 80p a week for those age 60-79 and 20p for those 80 and over. The government is actually planning to reduce the incomes of 2.2 million of the poorest pensioners in the country (including 350,000 aged 80 and over) (DHSS, 1985b, Technical Annex).

In order to explain these recent changes and the emerging conflict over pensions it is necessary to look beyond demographic changes to the political economy of ageing and other social policies. In other words it is only in conjunction with other more influential socio-economic factors that demographic change has an impact on policy formation.

The key factor was the fiscal crisis of the state which occurred in the mid-1970s in the wake of the world oil crisis, this was followed by the unprecedented twin scourge of inflation and unemployment and a series of crises in the British economy which culminated in the election of the first Thatcher administration in 1979 (Walker, 1982b). This was, and remains, a government based on the values of neo-liberalism and one pledged to rolling back the frontiers of the state (Bull and Wilding, 1983; Bosanquet, 1983). In the place of the post-war (Butskellite) consensus on the welfare state has been put hostility towards the public sector and a cost-effectiveness imperative. The equity goals of social policy have been wholly subordinated to the efficiency goals of economic policy and public services are expected to meet the same cost-benefit criteria as private industry (Walker, 1984, pp.45-68).

Two interrelated policies follow from this ideological change in government.

In the first place, the government is committed to reducing the size of the public sector and hence public expenditure. The first sentence of the Thatcher administration's first White Paper on public expenditure in 1979 asserted that 'Public expenditure is at the heart of Britain's economic difficulties' (Treasury, 1979, p.1). Similar assertions have been made regularly since then.

The significance of the elderly to public expenditure can be gauged from the fact that only 9 per cent of the incomes of those aged 65 and over derive from wages and salaries (compared with 82 per cent of the incomes of those under 65), only 22 per cent from private pensions and over half (60 per cent) from social security benefits (DHSS, 1984, p.16). The largest public expenditure programme in Britain is social security (around one-third of total expenditure) and elderly people receive 49 per cent of that budget. In the words of the recent government Green Paper on public expenditure and taxation:

The main factor affecting the social security programme is the provision which has to be made for the elderly ... they remain the major source of pressure on social security expenditure (Treasury, 1984, p.14).

Greying of the budget in the future

The main worry for the government was the rising long-term cost of the SERPS. Although the cost of the basic retirement pension - by far the largest element in the social security budget - is not set to rise much over the next 40 years or so, the SERPS element, because it is a new scheme in the process of development, is due to increase by 2,300 per cent by the year 2025. Even so, it is only one-fifth of total pension costs and the total national cost of pensions is expected to rise only very slightly (4.7 per cent to 4.8 per cent of GDP) over the next 40 years. Moreover both the Government Actuary, and the Social Security Advisory Committee, in warning the government against abolishing SERPS, dismissed fears about the rising cost of pensions as alarmist and argued that action on the all-party pension scheme would be premature.

That the government has chosen to act is a matter of

ideology rather than the effect of demographic change. Further evidence of this is provided in the Beveridge Report itself. The population projections underlying Beveridge's original national insurance pension scheme 40 years ago, predicted that people over pension age would be 21 per cent of the population by 1971. That figure had still not been reached in 1981 - when the proportion stood at 18 per cent (Beveridge, 1942, p.91).

Secondly, there is the government's ideological commitment to privatisation (Walker, 1983). A considerable boost has been given to the occupational and private pensions industry, in the hope that more and more of the cost of pensions can be shifted from the public to the private sector. Unlike Beveridge the government apparently has not considered any of the evidence about the private pensions industry. This suggests that private occupational schemes are more expensive, less efficient, more discriminatory and administratively more cumbersome (James, 1984; Reddin, 1984). The unemployed, single parents, people with disabilities and women are particularly disadvantaged with regard to private schemes. Again, policy is not a planned response to population change, although it is frequently expressed in those terms, but primarily a matter of ideology. The provision of earnings-related pensions will continue even though, as a result, we will spend more as a nation on such pensions (Reddin, 1984).

It is not only in the pensions field that privatisation has been taking place. Elderly people are major consumers of public health and personal social services. For example 90 per cent of residential accommodation goes to those aged 65 and over, as does 87 per cent of home help support. Privatisation of the health and personal social services - particularly residential and nursing services - has been proceeding rapidly as a result of government encouragement in the form of small business and social security subsidies.

In sum, the ageing of the British population has not, as yet, produced significant changes in the pattern of ageing advocacy or the political process itself. Furthermore recent policy changes have stemmed primarily from ideology rather than either direct political advocacy for the old or indirect pressures created by an ageing population. It seems probable that these changes in policy are themselves more likely to produce reactions on the part of sections of the elderly population than any changes resulting from the ageing of the population, and this prospect is pursued in the next section.

The Political Sociology of Ageing: from Acquiescence to Dissent?

Why has the politics of old age in Britain been characterised by acquiescence rather than positive action and the growth of age advocacy groups as in the USA? The answer helps to explain why, despite conventional wisdom, the current government has been able to cut benefits and services going to the elderly without creating a significant backlash on the part of elderly people themselves. There are five main factors to be considered.

First there is the political economy of old age. It is mistaken to regard elderly people as a homogenous group which might coalesce around a single politics of old age. In other words there is not one but several politics of ageing, depending not on age as such but on socio-economic status, race, gender and religion.

I have written at length previously about the tendency for policy-makers and social gerontologists alike to regard the elderly as a distinct social group, in isolation from the rest of the social structure and especially from their own status and class position at earlier stages of the life-cycle (Walker, 1980, 1981, 1986). In similar vein Carroll Estes has argued that a largely classless view of old age has been incorporated into public policy (Estes, 1983; Minkler and Estes, 1984). Moreover this stereotype of elderly people as a homogenous group with special needs has been legitimised by narrow theries of need based partly on age and narrowly functionalist theories of ageing. But, in addition, pluralist analyses have tended to assume a common interest among elderly people by virtue of their age. Thus the labels 'age interest groups' or 'age advocacy' suggests the common exercise of pressure around the issue of ageing (Nelson, 1982). This obscures more than it reveals. In particular the exercise of power on behalf of the dominant class through hegemonic relations, and the deep divisions between elderly people and the rest of society, but also among the elderly, are hidden by pluralism's concentration on issue politics.

In fact, as an analysis of the political economy of old age shows, elderly people are just as deeply divided along class and other structural lines as younger adults. While both functionalist and pluralist analyses suggest a common interest among elderly people, with age acting as a leveller of class and status differentials, a political economy perspective shows that the social construction of old age is a function of two separate sets of relations. On the one hand older people carry into retirement inequalities created and legitimated at an earlier phase of the life cycle, particularly though not exclusively through the labour market. On the other hand the process of retirement imposes a reduced social and economic status on a large proportion of older people in comparison with younger economically active adults (Walker, 1981; Townsend, 1981). Social gerontology and especially political gerontology has put too much emphasis on the latter and too little on the former. Although the process of retirement results in an average fall in income of about one-half, it has a differential impact on elderly people depending primarily on prior socio-economic status. For the majority (two-thirds) - some 5.9 million people - retirement means living in or on the margins of poverty (compared with one-fifth of the non-elderly). Just over one million elderly people are living on incomes below the official poverty line, often in the most abject conditions with insufficient nutrition and heating. At the same time one-fifth of pensioners are to be found in the middle quintile of the income distribution and one-fifth in the top two quintiles (Walker, 1986). Moreover there has been a significant improvement in the income status of retired households over the last decade. In 1971, almost half of all married couples and single pensioners were in the bottom quintile of the income distribution, and more than a quarter of each were in the second quintile. By 1982 the proportions of each in the bottom had been almost halved to around a quarter. Whilst some of this shift is reflected in the second quintile, much of it goes higher up the income distribution: the proportion of retired couples in the top three quintiles increased from 28 per cent in 1971 to 41 per cent in 1982; the figures for retired single adults are 26 per cent and 36 per cent (Walker, 1986). Arguably the relative improvement in the living standards of some, newly retired, pensioners has weakened further the basis for a unified politics of old age.

The main reason for the growth of inequality in old age is the spread of private and occupational pensions. They are the primary stimulus to the emergence of the 'two-nations' in old age forewarned by Richard Titmuss some 30 years ago (Titmuss, 1963, p.74). Two forms of inequality derive from this private sector of welfare. First, there is unequal access to occupational pensions according to employment status. Similarly the amount and quality of occupational pensions differs considerably, with, for example, the mean level of pensions for professional and managerial workers exceeding that of unskilled manual workers by five times. Women and other groups with incomplete employment records are particularly disadvantaged. Thus only one-third of lone women receive income from an occupational pensions compared with over one-half of lone men and nearly two-thirds of couples (DHSS, 1984). (SERPS was intended to partially redress this inequality by crediting women for time spent on home responsibilities).

Second, there is inequality between generations of elderly people arising from newly emerging pension opportunities. Fewer pensions are paid to the very elderly and those that are paid are relatively low. Again very elderly lone women are much less likely than either younger women or very elderly men and couples to receive an occupational pension.

Another important source of inequality between elderly people is in labour-force participation. Those who continue in paid employment after retirement age are much less likely than the retired to experience poverty. Yet again very elderly people and especially lone women are the least likely to have access to employment or self-employment income. Only 4 per cent of lone men age 75 and over receive such income and only 1 per cent of lone women; compared with 21 per cent and 6 per cent of those aged 65-69 (DHSS, 1984).

While age-barrier retirement and the assumption that public pensions will be lower than wages is the dominant factor in the creation of reduced social and economic status in old age (Walker, 1980, 1986), the growth of early retirement in the wake of mounting unemployment has again distinguished two unequal groups of older workers (Walker, 1985). On the one hand there are those who are able to make a free choice about early retirement, based on secure employment and command over sufficient resources to ensure an adequate income. On the other, there are those who are forced into early retirement by social processes of exclusion - redundancy, unemployment or ill-health - usually from a position of economic insecurity, with inadequate incomes, who therefore face an extended period of poverty in old age.

There is no need to labour the point further: old age is associated with major social and economic inequalities, including differences in power and influence. It is mistaken to regard social divisions as coming to an end on retirement and, thereafter, elderly people sharing a common purpose. The inaccuracy of this view can be demonstrated by the complete absence of evidence of elderly people operating as a voting bloc. For example, 38 per cent of men aged 65 and over and 47 per cent of women are identified with the Conservative Party and 36 per cent and 30 per cent with the Labour Party (Jowell and Airey, 1984, p.39).

It is not surprising, therefore, that campaigning and militancy among pensioners has tended to reflect these political and class divisions and differences in economic experience. Few national issues have forged coalitions across party lines. Militant campaigns for improved pensions have comprised those primarily reliant on state pensions and with earlier life cycle experience of collective action: relatively poor working class men. There are no examples of national campaigns on age specific issues among middle class pensioners.

Even in the face of public welfare state provision elderly people do not share common interests. In his seminal essay on the social division of welfare, written 25 years ago,

Richard Titmuss distinguished between three sectors of welfare provision: social, fiscal and occupational (Titmuss, 1963). All of which are subsidised forms of welfare provided by the state. This social division of welfare is crucial to an understanding of the differential status of public beneficiaries - the approved status of the fiscal welfare recipient and the disapproved status of the public welfare claimant. Thus we might contrast elderly people wholly or predominantly reliant on public welfare, in the form of pensions and social services, whose interests lie in increased expenditure on those pensions and services; with those depending on occupational and fiscal welfare and private sector services, who may be more concerned to limit the size of the public sector in order to reduce the taxes they pay. Because this social division of welfare reflects a division in power those in the public sector have lower incomes, attract more stigma and have lower quality services than those in the fiscal and occupational sectors. Public welfare recipients have their interests represented, inadequately, by some trade unions and claimants groups. Ranged against them pressing for occupational and fiscal benefits are powerful financial interests: the City of London, stockbrokers, pension funds, insurance companies and so on.

All this suggests that as well as there being a conflict between those under and those over retirement age there is an intra-generational conflict among the elderly which militates against a unified politics of ageing. A few words of explanation may be necessary. The conflict between young and old (or more specifically those under and over retirement age) is not overt but buried within the political and policy-making processes. It is a conflict over resources and is one largely constructed by the state and state policies, for example, retirement and the social creation of dependency on low public pensions. It surfaces only rarely but glimpses of the underlying conflict can be seen in occasional outbursts of alarm at the 'burden of dependency', the cost of pensions and the worsening dependency ratio (Phillipson, 1982).

Conflict among the generations of elders takes a similarly covert form. As we have seen it is a conflict over resources distributed primarily through the agencies of the state. Both forms of conflict are likely to heighten as public expenditure comes under increasingly tight restrictions and, if present policies continue to enhance the position of the better-off at the expense of the worse-off, they might become open conflict.

Secondly there is the relative powerlessness of the elderly. The main source of political power for working class people is their economic base in the workplace. For elderly people the social process of exclusion, that retirement and early retirement represent, not only removes them from the major source of income but also from collective activities and political influence through the trade unions. The process of exclusion itself is likely to encourage conservatism, because it detaches older people from collective workplace activities and potential sources of political information and promotes privatisation and individualised home-centred activities. Thus elderly people face a variation of Catch-22: being effectively, excluded from both economic activity and the political means to challenge their low social and economic status (de Beauvoir, 1977).

This disengagement effect of the retirement process can be seen clearly in a recent study of British Social Attitudes. Using a similar approach to Almond and Verba's Civic Culture this survey found the lowest propensity for collective action among the retired and, in contrast to the employed and other groups in the labour market, a preference for personal over collective action. Two measures were used - a Personal Action Index (PAI) and a Collective Action Index (CAI) - to provide an indication of the level of potential activism in different groups in relation to eight possible courses of protest action (for example, contact MP, sign a petition, form a group of like-minded people). The PAI score for the retired was 0.57 compared with 0.70 for the full time employed and 0.64 for the self-employed. The CAI scores were 0.50, 0.75 and 0.54 respectively (Jowell and Airey, 1984, p.24). The explanation for the remarkable degree of acquiescence displayed by retired people was attributed to a sense of powerlessness or non-competence reflecting the individual's circumstances and their lack of real resources for political influence. This was closely related to social class. It was also a reflection of subjectively measured power and this was associated with past education.

Thirdly there is the relative lack of formal political organisation for the elderly. The main political parties have almost totally failed to gear their organisational structures and campaigns towards pensioners and to include them in their machinery. This is particularly noticeable in the labour movement, which has tended to concentrate on issues identified with the interests of trade unions, particularly in the industrial sector and has thereby excluded those, including pensioners, who are outside of the labour market. The fact that the working class movement is fragmented horizontally (among groups of similar age and status) has been commented on widely, but as Chris Phillipson (1982) has pointed out, very little attention has been paid to vertical fragmentation (across the life-cycle). Clearly as the size and potential influence of the elderly population increases political parties which ignore this vertical fragmentation and do not attempt to overcome it will be severely disadvantaged at elections.

Fourthly there are barriers to political participation. Disabling later life-course events help to explain the relatively low level of political activity on the part of the elderly people. They suggest that as well as individually based explanations of acquiescence in old age the social construction of ageing for large numbers of, particularly working class, elderly people creates considerable barriers to positive action and participation. These include poverty and low incomes, ill health and disability, ageism and the negative stereotypes of old age that still remain firmly entrenched in British society despite the wealth of research refuting them. Many elderly people too, particularly women, are themselves actively engaged in caring for other elderly people. It is unreasonable to expect active participation in political activities in the face of such considerable economic and social barriers. Equally when a major characteristic of the experience of ageing is social exclusion – whether from the labour market as a result of retirement, from the social services as a result of marginalisation by professionals, or from the polity as a result of their dismissal by the political parties – it is unreasonable to expect elderly people to volunteer for participation in political activity.

Finally there is the issue of conservatism. It is not that people become more conservative as they grow older – despite the commonplace nature of that assumption (Hudson, 1980). Although there is evidence that older people are more conservative than younger ones – certainly voting patterns suggest this. The reasons, again, are largely unrelated to age. Some have been mentioned already, including the removal from sources of potential influence and activity. But, in addition, the present generation of elders have completely different historical and political reference points to younger generations. Many of their formative years occurred during and between the two world wars.

One way in which this generational effect shows itself is in the experience of relative deprivation revealed by some elderly people. The gap between objective and subjective deprivation is an important feature of research on the material circumstances of Britain's elderly population (Walker, 1986). An important factor in explaining this phenomenon is the reference group and reference point used by this generation to judge their standards of living. One important effect of this is the failure of some 900,000 elderly people to claim the supplementary pensions they are entitled to. Moreover pensioners are the least likely of all age groups to say they believe that real poverty exists in Britain today (Jowell and Airey, 1984, p.39). Again because of their particular reference point and experience of inter-war poverty they are more likely than younger people to express conservative opinions on this sort of social issue.

Conclusion

For much of the post-war period in Britain there has been no politics of old age in the sense of major party political conflict over ageing issues. A surface party political consensus has ruled over pensions and services for the elderly. Similar to the 'sacred' character of the interests of the elderly in American political dialogue, identified by Nelson (1982), and the bipartisan approach towards this group in the US, the main political parties in Britain have vied with each other to espouse the deserving cause of elderly people. Not surprisingly, therefore, this sense of priorities is widely shared in Britain. For example, when asked in a recent national survey which was their highest priority for extra government spending on a list of social benefits, two-thirds ranked retirement pensions first or second (Jowell and Airey, 1984, p.79). This finding is the latest in a long line of similar ones. So there is no sign of open, interest-group based inter-generational conflict in the political arena.

But, the apparent policy consensus between the political parties has disguised major differences in interest between different groups of pensioners, especially those who rely primarily on the public sector and those who rely primarily on the private sector of pensions. The aspirations of the former have been successfully contained by the factors outlined above and the tendency for politicians to patronise the elderly and exploit their acquiescence. This has helped to prevent potentially more productive conflict relations from asserting themselves. Moreover bipartisanship over the welfare state for elderly people has papered over the deficiencies in public sector provision, while state subsidies to the private sector have expanded continually. More importantly there is the failure of the welfare state to provide incomes sufficient to lift the majority of elderly people out of poverty. There are also the related problems of stigma and inadequate services associated with the social services.

What of the future? The consensus has broken down. When he announced his review of pensions two years ago the Secretary of State for Social Services assured Parliament that its purpose was 'not to call into question the fundamental pension structure that was established in the 1970s with all-party agreement and to which I was a party'. That pledge has been broken by the planned reduction in the scope of ↧'S and the further expansion of the private sector. Furthermore, in doing so, the government has engaged in a great deal of alarmism over the growing numbers of older people and the cost of pensions (DHSS, 1985a). This might backfire in the form of a surge of resentment at pension provision - which is always a danger in a pay-as-you-go scheme which rests on a social contract between successive generations. There is unlikely to be a reaction on the part of existing pensioners to the changes in SERPS because it is only future generations that will suffer. But the government is assuming that these future pensioners will be prepared to accept successively lower incomes. The evidence for this is shaky. True, there is a linear relationship between age and support for pensions: only 18 per cent of 18-24 year olds give them first priority compared with 55 per cent of the retired (Jowell and Airey, 1984, p.79). But as they near pension age the former are bound to change their tune!

The operation of state social policies in creating and managing dependency and acquiescence in old age has remained obscured by the veneer of consensus politics. Now that period in the politics of old age is over these policies are likely to come under increasing critical scrutiny as sources of inequality and dependency. The result is likely to be more open conflict over the welfare state budget, with different groups of elderly people, particularly those with a working class base being forced to enter the political arena to contest attacks on their incomes and services.

References

Almond, G. and Verba, S. (1963) The Civic Culture, Princeton University Press, Princeton N.J.
Beauvoir, S. de (1977) Old Age, Penguin Books, Harmondsworth.
Beveridge, W. (1942) Social Insurance and Allied Services, Cmnd 6404, HMSO, London.
Bosanquet, N. (1983) After the New Right, Heinemann, London.
Bull, D. and Wilding, P. (1983) (eds) Thatcherism and the Poor, CPAG, London.
DHSS (1984) Population, Pension Costs and Pensioners' Incomes, DHSS, London.
DHSS (1985a) Reform of Social Security, Cmnd 9517, HMSO, London.
DHSS (1985b) Reform of Social Security, HMSO, London.
Ermisch, J. (1983) The Political Economy of Demographic Change, Heinemann, London.
Estes, C. (1983) 'Fiscal Austerity and Ageing', in Estes, C., Newcomer, R. et al., Fiscal Austerity and Ageing, Sage, London, pp.17-39.
Guillemard, A-M. (1986) 'Social Policy and Ageing in France' in Phillipson, C. and Walker, A. (eds) Ageing and Social Policy, Gower, London.
Henwood, M. and Wicks, M. (1984) The Forgotten Army, Family Policy Studies Centre, London.
Hudson, R. (1980) 'Old-Age Politics in a Period of Change' in Borgatta, E. and McCluskey, N. (eds) Ageing and Society, Sage, London, pp.147-189.
James, C. (1984) Occupational Pensions: The Failure of

Private Welfare, Fabian Society, London.

Jowell, R. and Airey, C. (1984) (eds) British Social Attitudes - The 1984 Report, Gower, London.

Minkler, M. and Estes, C. (1984) (eds) Readings in the Political Economy of Ageing, Baywood, New York.

Nelson, D. (1982) 'Alternative Images of Old Age as the Bases for Policy' in B. Neugarten (ed) pp.131-170

Neugarten, B. (1974) 'Age Groups in American Society and the Rise of the Young Old', Annals of the American Academy of Political and Social Science, Vol. 415, pp.187-98

Phillipson, C. (1982) Capitalism and the Construction of Old Age, Macmillan, London.

Reddin, M. (1984) 'Cost and Portability' in Fabian Society, Social Security: the Real Agenda, Fabian Society, London, pp.11-14.

Shragge, E. (1984) Pensions Policy in Britain, Routledge and Kegan Paul, London.

Titmuss, R.M. (1963) Essays on 'The Welfare State', (second Edition), Allen and Unwin, London.

Treasury (1979) The Government's Expenditure Plans 1980/1, Cmnd 7746, HMSO, London.

Treasury (1984) The Next Ten Years: Public Expenditure and Taxation into the 1990s, Cmnd 9189, HMSO, London.

Walker, A. (1980) 'The Social Creation of Poverty and Dependency in Old Age', Journal of Social Policy, Vol. 9, no.1, pp.45-75

Walker, A. (1981) 'Towards a Political Economy of Old Age', Ageing and Society, Vol. 1, no. 1, pp.73-94

Walker, A. (1982a) (ed) Community Care, Basil Blackwell and Martin Robertson, Oxford.

Walker, A. (1982b) (ed) Public Expenditure and Social Policy, Heinemann, London.

Walker, A. (1983) 'The Political Economy of Privatisation' in J. Le Grand and R. Robinson (eds.) Privatisation and the Welfare State, Allen and Unwin, London.

Walker, A. (1984) Social Planning, Basil Blackwell and Martin Robertson, Oxford.

Walker, A. (1986) 'Pensions and the Production of Poverty in Old Age' in Phillipson, C. and Walker, A. (eds) Ageing and Social Policy, Gower, London.

* A version of this paper was originally presented to the XIIIth International Congress of Gerontology, New York, July 1985 and in summary form to the British Society for Gerontology Annual Conference, Keele, September 1985.

Chapter Four

POLITICAL ECONOMY AS A PERSPECTIVE

IN THE ANALYSIS OF OLD AGE

John Bond

Introduction

Political economy has emerged as the fashionable perspective
of social policy rhetoric and debate in the analysis of old age.
In Britain Phillipson (1982), Townsend (1979, 1981) and
Walker (1980,1981, 1982) among others have stressed the
importance of inequalities throughout the economic, political
and social structures which have fostered the growth of
'structural dependency'. Rooted firmly in the sound tradition
of Fabian sociology they have amassed substantial evidence
justifying their hypotheses and suggested a variety of social
policies intended to reduce inequality in old age. This
structural perspective has also been undertaken in Europe
(Guillemard, 1982) and North America (Estes, 1979; Dowd,
1980; Myles, 1980) but within the context of the differing
welfare systems operating in these countries. This kind of
analysis has become known as the political economy of old
age.
    Political economy has also been an important perspective
in the analysis of health and health care. However, as will
be apparent through the reading of Illich (1975), Navarro
(1976), Doyal and Pennell (1979) or McKinley (1984) among
others, the political economy of health and health care is
fundamentally, although not exclusively, Marxist in approach.
Although the political 'right' may not see any real difference
in these two approaches they each offer a distinctive
perspective on political economy as a method of analysis.
    The purpose of this paper is to review these two
perspectives with a view to providing an explicit statement of
the political economy of old age.

Definition

That the political economy perspective actually encompasses a
variety of sociological perspectives is apparent from one of
the few attempts to define political economy. Estes quoted

Walton as providing the following definition:

> Political economy is understood to be the study of the interrelationships between the polity, economy and society, or more specifically, the reciprocal influences among government ... the economy, social classes, strata and status groups. The central problem of the political economy perspective is the manner in which the economy and polity interact in a relationship of reciprocal causation affecting the distribution of social goods. (Walton, 1980, quoted by Estes et al., 1982, p.154).

As a description of political economy this definition is not unhelpful. However, like definitions of other sociological perspectives such as structural functionalism, Marxism, symbolic interactionism or ethnomethodology, definitions can be manipulated unless more explicitly stated. The purpose of this paper is to provide a more explicit statement of political economy as a perspective in the analysis of old age.

Structural Dependency

Walker (1982) has argued that structural dependency describes the development of a dependent status resulting from the restricted access to a wide range of social resources, particularly income. This is reflected in the large numbers of disabled and elderly people who live in poverty (Townsend, 1979). A review by Walker (1980) of secondary data on earnings, incomes and assets, housing circumstances and benefits in kind show that about one in four elderly people have incomes which are equal to or below the State Poverty Line - the supplementary benefit rate appropriate to each family or household. It has long been recognised that older people feature in the lower levels of the income distribution because they are usually not in so called 'productive' work. Society tends to reward present work; it does not reward past work and therefore it does not reward old age. Older people are discriminated against by economic and social policies which benefit the young employed and the well off. Thus poverty in old age and the dependent status of the elderly are related to low resources and restricted access to resources throughout the life cycle.

We can illustrate this relationship by considering the effects of retirement on a person's access to resources. Prior to retirement manual workers - the majority of elderly men - experience reduced socio-economic status (Townsend, 1979). Increasingly early retirement schemes are pushing elderly workers into less skilled and lower paid jobs and into unemployment. After retirement the inequalities resulting from low pay, unemployment, disability and ill health, and for

women sex discrimination, are carried through into old age.
The decline in the real value of savings and pensions means
that the worse off are the very old. In addition, retirement
also restricts access to social resources in the form of a
reduction in social relationships once a person is away from
the world of work (Phillipson, 1982).

In old age the inequalities experienced throughout the
life cycle are exacerbated. The elderly widow of a manual
worker was probably never in 'productive' work, except
perhaps for the few years before marriage, and is therefore
likely to be dependent on state benefits. If she did work it
will probably have been part time, and poorly paid, and
without any occupational pension rights. The chances of her
accruing any significant savings will have been very small
(Townsend and Wedderburn, 1965; Townsend, 1979).
Physical and mental impairment will increase the likelihood of
her becoming dependent on the state.

In contrast the retired executive or doctor, who will
more often be a man, will have accrued throughout his life
considerable assets as a result of house ownership,
investment of savings and occupational pension rights. He
will be less dependent on the state. If physically or mentally
impaired he may be able to draw on his not inconsiderable
resources in order to maintain his social and political
independence. However, the presence of these resources
does not always sustain long-term independence. Long-term
independence may only be the reward of the wealthy and
healthy.

Thus this approach to the political economy of old age
provides an analysis of the interrelationship between the
economic, political and social structure of modern society
which leads to structural dependency. How does society
create and sustain independence in old age? The majority of
social policy options suggested by these analyses have been
incorporated into A Manifesto for Old Age (Bornat, Phillipson
and Ward, 1985). These have been summarised as follows:
1. Challenge ageism within society.
2. Ensure that older people become directly involved in
    planning and running the services they receive.
3. Establish imaginative social policies for retirement.
4. Establish more generous levels of financial support.
5. Tackle inequalities in health and promote positive
    attitudes towards health in later life.
6. Develop new policies for elderly people from ethnic
    minorities.
7. Secure greater choice and freedom for people in the area
    of residential care.
8. Campaign for a major programme of investment in areas
    such as housing and transport.
9. Establish education as a major right and resource for
    older people. (Bornat,Phillipson and Ward,1985, p.106).

If we were to judge the usefulness of the political economy perspective in the analysis of old age on this list of prescriptions we would probably be well satisfied. No doubt other proposals will emerge and it is unlikely that we all agree with every item on this list. It is also unlikely that we could agree on priorities for action. Nevertheless, it provides a useful and important contribution to the evolution of social policies for old age. However, using a medical analogy, does this list do any more than just treat the symptoms? How do we eradicate the disease?

Before attempting to suggest answers to these questions I will turn to the analysis of health and health care.

Political Economy of Health and Health Care

The social policy approach has also been widely used in the analysis of health and health care. It has made a useful contribution to the development of a more critical understanding of health and health care by generating statistical data concerning inequalities in health - in terms of differences in morbidity and mortality rates between social groups, the differential utilisation of health care facilities and regional inequalities (Townsend and Davidson, 1982). Its major value has been in the way it has identified ways to minimise environmental threats to health, methods of providing health care to a greater number of people and how to determine priorities within the limits of the scarce resources available to health care.

The fundamental limitation of the social policy approach is its failure to consider in any depth the broader role of health care in modern society. As a result it continues to support and reinforce widely-held beliefs about the role of health care in society.

A political economy of health and health care takes a more radical view than this. It comprises essentially a critique of the logic of advanced capitalism. (Capitalism is used not just to define the economic system of Western democratic societies but to describe the economic system, which predominates world wide, including Eastern bloc countries).

The Logic of Advanced Capitalism

Central to an examination of this perspective is an understanding of the logic of advanced capitalism. Profitability as we are continuously told is the defining characteristic of capitalism. Almost all institutions are driven by this fundamental requirement. McKinlay (1984) has characterised the logic of capitalism in the following way:
(1) Some form of competition forces 'capitalists' to expand

productive output and sales irrespective of questions concerning the use or values of the commodities produced. Thus we can observe the evolution of 'junk food' as a means by which the food industry can expand profits once society's nutritional needs have been met. Similarly, we can see the over expansion of private nursing home places for older people beyond the 'need' for such provision.

(2)   Increased output and sales result in expanded profits and the accumulation of capital. Failure to expand profits leads to eventual extinction of the organisation in its present form.

(3)   The presence of accumulated capital necessitates its reinvestment in even more enterprises or in the development of more technologically efficient enterprises. Failure to reinvest again leads to the eventual extinction of the organisation in the present form.

(4)   Since profits must also be realised on these new investments, and a falling rate of profit avoided, even greater productive output and sales are required.

(5)   The resulting pressure to find new buyers leads to increased penetration of the domestic market and ultimately, through sometimes deceptive advertising, the creation of a commodity fetishist culture. The whole culture surrounding 'The keeping up with the Jones' is clearly a central process here.

(6)   When the domestic market is eventually saturated, attention is directed toward susceptible foreign markets, either through expropriation of resources in less developed countries to reduce costs and risks or through the capture of foreign markets through direct investment. This is characterised by the explosion in the number of multi-national companies.

(7)   Finally the resulting capital from the profit of this expanded output and sales must once again, be reinvested and the whole cycle is repeated albeit on a more escalated scale.

The key feature of this whole process is not so much the essential characteristic of profitability but the lack of social control over the usefulness of the goods or services being produced. More importantly the key decision-making under advanced capitalism such as where to invest or where emerging technology should be applied is seldom influenced by any awareness of collective needs of society or of the social costs likely to be entailed, except perhaps at a time of war. Thus under advanced capitalism the most socially needed activities cannot be given priority unless meeting the criteria of profitability.

It is currently difficult to judge whether the advantages of the capitalist system are now outweighed by the disadvantages implied by McKinlay's description. Perhaps

only future historians will be able to make that judgement.
Clearly capitalism has brought social benefits throughout the
world. The emergence of capitalism and an accompanying
revolution in agriculture produced a vastly increased
agricultural output, which was the cause of major health gains
through improved nutrition and environmental control
(McKeown, 1979) and which has subsequently helped create
our ageing population. Of course, the social costs of this
agricultural revolution were the uprooting of stable
communities and subjugation of all areas of life to constantly
changing demands of the market for labour. And, one
outcome that we are all aware of, has been the denigration of
'non-productive' people, the majority of them older people, to
the level of second and even third class citizens.

Critiques of the political economy of health and health
care discount it because of the essentially Marxist orientation
of the theory. Yet, if we examine different aspects of the
health care industry we shall see that McKinlay's logic has
been closely followed. The most documented example of a
health care industry adhering to McKinlay's logic is the
multi-national pharmaceutical industry. It is generally argued
that the activities of the pharmaceutical industry are, on
balance, beneficial to the average National Health Service
patient. Certainly competition has led to a variety of safe
drugs being available in Britain for both major and minor
ailments. Medical nemesis does exist (Illich, 1975) but most
people appear to support the level of safeguards set up to
prevent the misuse of drugs. Because the demand for certain
drugs is limited in Britain and other advanced industrial
societies the pharmaceutical industry has expanded and
invested in the Third World. This will have been beneficial
to many Third World inhabitants. However, whereas
expenditure on health care in Third World countries is much
less than in the developed world, expenditure on drugs is
proportionately very much greater (Doyal and Pennell, 1979).
Third World countries often pay considerably more for the
same products than do European countries. More worrying
has been the reported use of specific antibiotics such as
streptomycin for general use so that specific diseases such as
tuberculosis have become resistant to the only available cure.
This description has been accounted for as the 'unacceptable
face' of capitalism by defenders of advanced capitalism. Yet
the disregard of social costs further exemplifies the
appropriateness of McKinlay's logic.

Towards a Political Economy of Old Age

In this paper I have briefly explored the political economy
perspective in the analysis of old age and health and health
care. I have suggested that the political economy of old age
is essentially a social policy approach in the tradition of

Fabian sociology, while the political economy of health is essentially a Marxist critique of advanced capitalism.

Structural dependency in old age is analytically useful and has helped initiate new social policies and encouraged us all to think about the position of old people in our society. Specifically the approach has led to a practical manifesto for old age. If just one of the nine items on this agenda were achieved the quality of life for many older people would be substantially improved. However, in answer to the questions posed by our medical analogy, this manifesto only touches the surface of the problem and provides a treatment for the symptoms. The disease for which there may be no known treatment is advanced capitalism. A political economy of old age should be focused squarely on an analysis of the interrelationship between the economic, political and social structures of capitalistic societies. An acceptance that advanced capitalism is the underlying cause of structural dependency may encourage greater pressure toward change in the system. However, I have little cause for optimism unless in the future the democratic rights of older people can be motivated to act in their own collective self-interest, or in Marxist terms older people and other similar deprived groups develop their own brand of 'class consciousness' which would be a necessary condition for any major changes in the economic, political and social structures of modern society. Unfortunately, class divisions extend into old age (Townsend, 1979; Walker, 1980; Phillipson, 1982) and the aged are therefore unlikely to unite to change the nature of advanced capitalism.

References

Bornat, J., Phillipson, C. and Ward, S. (1985) A Manifesto for Old Age, Pluto Press, London.

Dowd, J. (1980) Stratification Among the Aged, Brooks/Cole, Monterey, California.

Doyal, L. and Pennell, I. (1979) The Political Economy of Health, Pluto Press, London.

Estes, C.L. (1979) The Aging Enterprise, Jossey-Bass, San Francisco.

Estes, C.L., Swan, J.S. and Gerard, L.E. (1982) 'Dominant and Competing Paradigms in Gerontology: Towards a Political Economy of Ageing', Ageing and Society, Vol.2, pp.151-164.

Guillemard, A-M. (ed.) (1982) Old Age and the Welfare State, Sage, New York.

Illich, I. (1975) Medical Nemesis: Expropriation of Health, Calder and Boyan, London.

McKeown, T. (1979) The Role of Medicine. Dream, Mirage or Nemesis?, Basil Blackwell, London.

McKinlay, J.B. (1984) Issues in the Political Economy of Health, Tavistock, London.

Myles, J.F. (1980) 'The Aged, the State, and the Structure of Inequality' in J. Harp and J. Haflay (eds.) Structural Inequality in Canada, Prentice Hall, Toronto, pp.317-342.

Navarro, V. (1976) Medicine Under Capitalism, Prodist, New York.

Phillipson, C. (1982) Capitalism and the Construction of Old Age, Macmillan, London.

Townsend, P. (1979) Poverty in the United Kingdom, Penguin Books, Harmondsworth.

Townsend, P. (1981) 'The Structured Dependency of the Elderly: Creation of Social Policy in the Twentieth Century', Ageing and Society, Vol.1, pp.5-28.

Townsend, P. and Davidson, N. (eds.) (1982) Inequalities in Health. The Black Report, Penguin Books, Harmondsworth.

Townsend, P. and Wedderburn, D. (1965) The Aged in the Welfare State, Bell, London.

Walker, A. (1980) 'The Social Creation of Poverty and Dependency in Old Age', Journal of Social Policy, Vol.9, pp.49-75.

Walker, A. (1981) 'Towards a Political Economy of Old Age', Ageing and Society, Vol.1, pp.73-94.

Walker, A. (1982) 'Dependency and Old Age' Social Policy and Administration, Vol.16, pp.115-135.

Walton, J. (1980) Economic Crisis and Urban Austerity: Issues in Research and Policy in the 1980s. Paper presented at the conference on Economic Crisis and Urban Austerity, Columbia University, New York, May 21-24.

Chapter Five

STRUCTURED DEPENDENCY REVISITED

Graham Fennell

Introduction

Social gerontology, as a developing field of study, has to advance on a number of fronts. One constant need is for new substantive field studies. No less important is the need for conceptual refinement and theoretical advance. Writers on the elderly frequently make use of concepts such as 'dependency', 'morale' and 'loneliness', but these are only infrequently subject to discussion and clarification. The relationships between concepts and their operational definition - the way in which they are actually measured in the field - are seldom reviewed. Here I hope to make a contribution to our understanding of the concept of 'dependency' and, most crucially, to sketch an approach to a theory of independence, by a sympathetic critique of the important article with which the journal Ageing and Society was launched: Peter Townsend's, (1981) 'The Structured Dependency of the Elderly: a Creation of Social Policy in the Twentieth Century.'

Peter Townsend's Sociology

1. Locating Sociology

Townsend begins his paper with the assertion that:

> If we are able to develop better methods of integrating elderly people into society then above all we need a better sociology of the ageing and the aged.
> (Townsend, 1981, p.5)

What would this mean? Let us first locate sociology by references to Galtung's (1967, p.15) helpful matrix.

Figure 1

Locating Sociology, Following Galtung

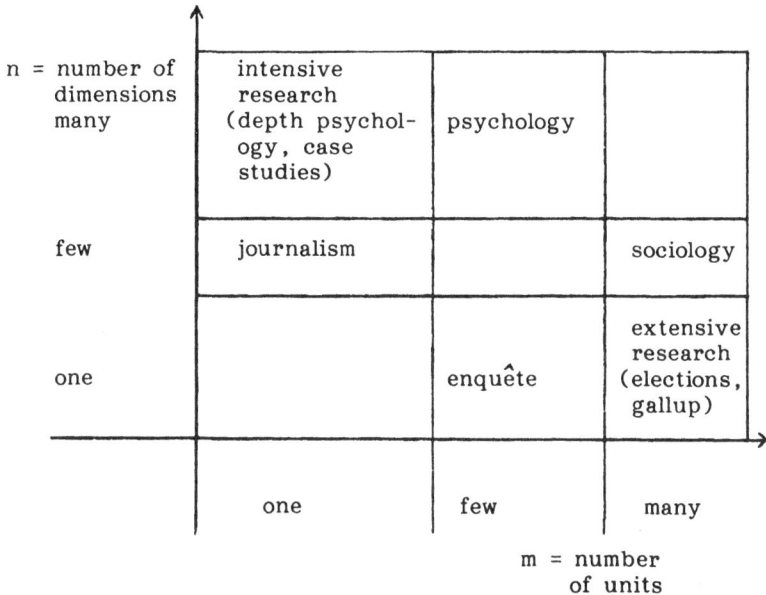

n = number of dimensions			
many	intensive research (depth psychology, case studies)	psychology	
few	journalism		sociology
one		enquête	extensive research (elections, gallup)
	one	few	many

m = number of units

Galtung argues that if we consider together the number of units studied (in our case these are usually individual elderly people) and the number of dimensions (or variables) which are examined, sociology is typically characterised by aiming to study a large number of units in respect of relatively few variables. The reason for taking large samples is to bring out patterns and ensure representativeness, to minimise sampling bias; the reason for examining relatively few variables is to ensure that the inter-relationships are explored in the search for meaning. Sociology is an interpretative discipline, aiming to explain and make meaningful to us the patterns which are observed. It can be distinguished then, from what Galtung calls extensive research, or the compilation of social statistics; although sociology will naturally draw on and could not operate without the existence of statistics, collected for instance by the Census or General Household Survey.

What distinguishes sociology from journalism, in Galtung's view, is the number of units studied and hence the drive for truth and representativeness. The sociologist is not ultimately interested in good copy, but in truth, and while much can be learned from small samples or the detailed

examination of one individual, sociologists are always going to
be doubtful about the conclusions drawn and will seek to test
them against wider samples as part of a programme of
scientific advance.

In this context, Peter Townsend has written:

> I work as a sociologist. I should like this to mean that
> I explore, and write about, present-day society so that
> others may understand it better. I should like it to
> mean that I spend a good deal of time observing and
> interviewing small cross-sections of the population before
> writing detailed reports which aim to keep human beings
> to the forefront. Above all, I should like it to mean
> studying very carefully the life of the poorest and most
> handicapped members of society.
> (Townsend, 1958, p.103)

2. Better Field Studies

One of Townsend's great strengths as a sociologist of old age
has been his patient and sensitive fieldwork. One route to a
'better sociology of ageing and the aged' would be for more
researchers to follow his lead and engage in what Douglas
(1970, p.200) has called 'personal involvement studies' of
elderly people. This both helps to produce authentic, as
opposed to spurious, knowledge, and is a caution against
over-facile generalisation and simplification. Some sample
quotations show what this means in the context of Townsend's
work. In an autobiographical fragment he gives a
sympathetic and ironic account of his first contact with the
field.

> I could avoid the hardest job no longer. The first
> address I had chosen at random proved to be a dark,
> terraced house.... Twice my courage failed me and I
> walked past without knocking. My hands were thrust in
> my raincoat pockets and I can still remember fumbling
> with some scraps of paper and tearing them into minute
> pieces while I stood at the corner of the street and
> pretended to be looking for a bus.

> I knocked hesitantly and when the door opened explained
> myself rather abjectly to a woman in her early twenties.
> She was friendly and showed me into a rather bare
> sitting-room where her two-year-old son was romping
> around.... My questions were bad, my manner worse,
> and I felt a complete charlatan - a bungling amateur with
> no right to scientific pretensions. Yet somehow she
> patiently coached me through my interview, tactfully
> answering the really important questions which it had
> not occured to me to ask. (Townsend, 1958, p.106)

This insight, that social investigators, for all their learning, know very little, whereas the so-called 'subjects' know a great deal about the social world under investigation has long been recognised by anthropologists; the need for this 'patient coaching' and exchange of information by the subjects is increasingly being recognised and formalised in survey research as well (Wax, 1972; Bateson, 1984).

When he moved on, from studying unemployment in Lancashire cotton towns, to studies of elderly people living at home and in institutions, Townsend gained sufficient confidence and maturity to write what could still be a programme for today's enquirer:

> The task of interviewing old people was treated as the most important single task of the research. It proved extremely difficult to plan the content and scope of the interviews and lengthy pilot inquiries were carried out.
> (Townsend, 1962, p.11)

This focus on interviewing, and the need for proper pilot investigations, is too often neglected. He also devotes special care to the 'hard-to-reach' respondent, and to confirming data gained from one source by observation and by comparison with other sources, the technique we now call triangulation.

> Some of our methods had to be adapted as we went along. A number of mentally and physically handicapped persons were able to answer only some of the questions. Rather than weaken our conclusions by leaving them out of the final analysis we sought every means possible of getting information about them. We wrote out our questions for those who were stone deaf. We talked to mentally handicapped persons quietly on their own and often were delighted to get patchy responses when they had not been expected either by the matron or by ourselves. We were able to check certain details, for example about mobility and special disabilities, by personal observation.
> (Townsend, 1962, p.11)

A clear plea for 'personal involvement' is made in The Last Refuge, some years before Douglas (1970) in America took up the same theme:

> Those in charge of much recent research seem not to have given sufficiently high priority to 'participant' observation and interviewing, even though they have been keenly aware of the importance of accumulating statistical evidence as a basis for generalization.

Instead, they have tended to separate interviewing and
reportage from the activities of administering, analysing
and writing up social surveys, involving themselves only
in the latter tasks.... We believed that those engaged on the research should
be as few in number as possible and that they should all
be continuously involved in each stage of the field-work.
Thus the person or persons in charge of the interviews
and the analysis should not be isolated from the actual
job of talking to people and observing life. In the
event.... two people [Robert Pinker and Peter
Townsend] did 80 per cent of the interviewing. We hope
to have shown that an extensive survey can be carried
out without losing too many of the advantages normally
claimed for localized or intensive research.
(Townsend, 1962, p.15)

3. Conceptual and Operational Development

To create a scientific discipline, to lift the field studies above
the level of ordered common sense, analytical concepts have
to be created, defined, refined and operationalised.
Townsend has always made notable contribution here, for
instance in the development of his social contact scoring
system, his work on the Capacity for Self Care Index (1962),
and his analyses of loneliness, isolation and desolation (1968).
Most recently it is the concept of structured dependency with
which Townsend has made his major contribution to the
development of a 'better sociology of ageing and the aged.'
If we are to build upon his contribution, we must engage
in critical discussion of this concept. Kaplan (1964), in his
methodological classic The Conduct of Enquiry, gives us some
hints on how conceptual work can be advanced: in particular
he indicates mistakes we should avoid. It is no real
criticism, for instance, to say that one finds the concept of
dependency vague and undefined. Conceptual vagueness is a
matter of timing and judgement. Kaplan argues that a degree
of vagueness in the definition of concepts is necessary at
early stages of enquiry: above all one must avoid what he
calls 'premature closure'.

There is a certain kind of behavioural scientist who, at
the least threat of an exposed ambiguity, scurries for
cover like a hermit crab into the nearest abandoned
logical shell. But there is no ground for panic. That a
cognitive situation is not as well structured as we would
like does not imply that no enquiry made in that
situation is really scientific.... The scientist is in no
hurry for closure.

> The demand for exactness of meaning and for precise
> definition of terms can easily have a pernicious
> effect.... It results in the premature closure of our
> ideas.
> (Kaplan, 1964, p.71)

Kaplan also advises us to beware of the 'principle of the
drunkard's search' (i.e. looking for a lost doorkey under the
streetlight, where it is easier to see, rather than looking in
the dark where the key was actually lost). The streetlight
equivalent for dependency would seem to be all the numerous
dependency scales and operational field indicators; the dark
side of the moon, varying the metaphor slightly, is surely the
concept of independence, to which so little attention is given.
It is that concept about which I hope to generate more
discussion.

Structured Dependency Revisited

The concept of structured dependency, unveiled in 1981, was
instantly recognisable as an important addition to the
analytical armoury of the social gerontologist. The 1960s had
seen the creation of what Jones (1975) has called the
'literature of dysfunction' concerning residential care. We had
become familiar with the concepts of total institution,
institutional neurosis and institutionalisation. Later,
Seligman's (1975) concept of 'learned helplessness' had begun
to penetrate English academic discussions.
    'Structured dependency' fitted into place like the missing
piece of a jigsaw puzzle. It was obviously the sociological
counterpart to the psychological concept of learned
helplessness. Various concepts could now be fitted together
to form a satisfactory pattern. For instance, industrial
societies create total institutions. In them, the residents find
themselves in a situation of structured dependency; people in
situations of structured dependency learn helplessness. The
result is institutionalisation or institutional neurosis.
Furthermore, the great attraction of the concept of structured
dependency for the sociologist is that it can be applied to any
structured situation, whether at the micro level of the
individual elderly person dependent upon a 'carer'; or at the
macro level of categories of elderly people dependent upon
particular pension systems.
    Despite its instant appeal, I have always found some
features of Townsend's argument problematic, particularly the
taken-for-granted or unspelled-out aspects of it.
    One of the clearest and least ambiguous terms among the
article's keywords, for the sociologist, is the concept of
'structure'. For the non-sociologist, an easy route to
understanding is to contrast it with an opposite notion,
randomness. Random dependency occurs unpredictably. A

spouse might become demented, for instance, and require your continuous presence, or you might be the victim of some other sudden random event - a road accident which transforms you from mobility to immobility, a fire which destroys your home and possessions and makes you dependent on others for help. This type of dependency arises episodically and unpredictably and lies outside the sociologist's notion of structure. Structured dependency, by contrast, affects identifiable categories of people according to predictable probabilities.

While this is crystal clear I am less sure what Townsend means by dependency and, in this context, by social policy. Particularly I puzzle over the suggestion that the structured dependency of the elderly is a creation of social policy in the twentieth century. What does 'creation' mean here, I wonder?

It raises questions of the type, 'if the structured dependency of the elderly is a creation of social policy in the twentieth century, was there no structured dependency in former times?'. Alternatively, if there was, 'by what mechanisms was structured dependency previously created, and is it correct to associate the creation of dependency so directly with twentieth century policy?'. Also, while clearly social policy creates structures, 'does it invariably structure dependency, can it not also create independence - which is after all an avowed aim?'. This leads inevitably to more cosmic questions of the type, 'what does one mean by independence in old age and is an independent old person a theoretical possibility?'.

I am uneasy about our use of the terms dependency, independence and independent in our discussions of elderly people. 'Who is independent?', I wonder, in any society, let alone a complex, high-energy technological society such as our own. Surely what we see is a very complex interdependency, a highly specialised division of labour, a total vulnerability (even among those who pride themselves on their 'independence') to systems failure?

These ruminations always lead me to the conclusion that one should begin, not with the taken-for-granted concept of dependency, but with a theory of independence (a concept I find equally dubious and problematic) and locate the creation of structured dependency within that. In my conclusion I will sketch a possible approach to doing so.

The Pensions Case

Townsend outlines his argument by reference to two main areas, the development of pensions and of residential care. He argues that the twentieth century has seen the development of progressively more embracing pension schemes. Inevitably this creates or alters a structure of opportunity. But is it inevitable that it structures dependency?

The argument would seem to have two component parts. One is that, while the manifest function of the benefit system is to help the needy and make resources available to those who otherwise did not have them, the latent function of the existence of this welfare structure is to legitimate excluding people from other resource systems. Once a concept of 'retirement pension' exists, it becomes possible to retire people more easily: the process of categorisation which has allegedly seen the creation of childhood and indisputably has seen the creation of the teenager, is matched at the other end of the life-span in the social construction of the retirement pensioner. Rather than being a progressive social policy, this might amount to the legitimate creation of unemployment and redundancy among people who might otherwise wish and be able to continue work.

The other component of the argument must be to do with pension levels, and here I wonder if Townsend is confusing a historical accident with a general necessity. Undoubtedly the Beveridge-based pension system in the United Kingdom has been associated with the structured creation of poverty in old age for many people. But was this true of the original 10/- Lloyd-George pension? Is it true for the superannuated pensioners of Sweden? Is it possible to combine a pension system with flexible retirement age? These thoughts suggest to me that the poverty of the elderly in the United Kingdom might be attributable less to social policy, rather more to the peculiarities of the British political system and the inability (given what might be regarded as a bias towards inertia in the way the political system operates) actually to develop a progressive social policy. The poverty of UK pensioners might be attributable, in other words, not to social policy but to the lack of it.

The Residential Care Case

Apart from pensions and the creation of poverty and redundancy in old age (a term I return to in an entirely different sense at the close of this paper), the other main strand in Townsend's argument is his work on residential care.

Within the general context of sociological argument, it is easy to understand what he is doing here. While few elderly people spend substantial portions of their retirement in residential care, it might still be supposed to have something to tell us about the total social construction of old age. Sociologists often argue that the normal workings of the social order can be exposed by examination of deviant cases and, in this instance, entering residential care might be regarded as a form of deviance. Despite the small numbers involved, the way in which elderly people are treated in residential care might exemplify in microcosm the structured dependency of the elderly in the wider society. Admissions are seldom self-initiated, decisions are taken for people, autonomy is sapped, petty restrictions are enforced.

Is this, however, a fair test? Is the example not rather more like an engineering test-to-destruction than the classical 'deviance' test of the sociologist? An engineer might expose the wing of a plane to constant stress, to determine the point at which it breaks down. A car might be crashed into a concrete wall, to test how safe it is. Is not residential care (or at least the sort Townsend has so powerfully in mind) more that sort of test of our social policy?

The reason I would argue this is because of the concept of relativity. Townsend has done more than anyone, through his poverty studies, to impress upon us the relativity of needs, the relativity of resources to requirements. Arguably, some of the dysfunctions of residential care are relative to the needs of the elderly entrants. To quote just one example: suppose yourself to be a confused old lady who lives alone. During the day the kindly ambulance men (you do not know who they are) come and take you to the day centre (you do not know what it is), where you are fed, and kept warm and safe. In the evening, kindly men take you back to your empty house. You are afraid to go upstairs, because you once caught your sleeve on a nail (you did not realise this) and thought there was an intruder in the house. You have forgotten that your social worker has brought the bed downstairs, so you settle down for the night in your armchair, remembering to put your shoes in the refrigerator before turning off the light.

If you are a lady like this, to talk of preserving your independence by keeping you out of residential care is nonsense: residential care is a safe haven and is increasingly catering (or at least the local authority sector is) for people whose dependency is extreme. It does not, in other words, create, magnify or exemplify the structured dependency of the elderly, but represents a response to a dependency which arises from a variety of other sources.

Towards a Theory of Independence

If the task is to examine dependency in the elderly, and if we initially assume that the meaning of the term is unproblematic, we have two continuous variables to plot against one another. We can collapse them for the purposes of illustration into a 2 x 2 table as in Figure 2.

Figure 2

Independence

		Low	High
	High	(a)	(b)
Age			
	Low	(c)	(d)

It is imperative to examine, or at least to be aware of, the four cells in the table. If we simply examine dependency in the elderly [cell (a)], ignoring the independent elderly [cell (b)] and the behaviour of the variable in other age groups [cells (c) and (d)], we stumble into a classic methodological pitfall and are likely to try to prove what we believed to be true in the first place, rather than testing some form of null hypothesis, which might yield more fruitful insights. This is the self-same problem which besets investigations of, say, loneliness in the elderly, rather than loneliness or the lack of it in the population at large. As well as being poor scientific practice, it also helps to perpetuate negative stereotypes of old age and emphasises the differences between elderly people and other age groups, rather than regarding these differences as a matter which has first to be established.

How do we recognise an independent person - supposing such a being exists in human society? What is independence and how are people more or less independent? The way I would approach this initially would be to look metaphorically around the sociologist's workshop to see if there are any oddments and offcuts with which an approximate model could be constructed. If so, the model could be refined in due course.

Following the parsimony principle, one would want to use as few of these oddments as possible. The necessary components which suggest themselves to me are needs, resources, relativity and redundancy, and possible sources for elaborating them would be Sklair's (1970) Sociology of Progress, Townsend's (1979) work on poverty, particularly as developed in the recent study by Mack and Lansley (1985). For the concept of redundancy, we refer to Frankenberg's (1966) book on Communities in Britain.

Needs

We start with human needs on the assumption that the most independent person is the most able to satisfy his or her needs. What are human needs? Considerable work has been done on the conceptualisation of human needs, particularly in the search for 'basic' ones.   A convenient starting point is Sklair's typology (1970, p.191).

Figure 3

Sklair's Typology of Human Needs

	Primary	Secondary
INDIVIDUAL	Nutrition; shelter sleep	Stability of personality; cognition
SOCIAL	Reproduction; Communication; socialisation; motivation	Role differentiation; preferences; institutionalisation

From this highly schematised list, concrete indicators (a winter coat, an underblanket and two overblankets per person, a week's holiday away from home per six months, etc.) could be developed.

Relativity

However, the same general argument about human needs can be applied here as Townsend has shown us should be applied in the case of the poverty studies.   We should not assume that these needs are permanent and universal, but culturally and socially specific, or relative to time and place.   Needs vary from society to society and change as social conditions change.

The best way to develop a 'needs inventory' would be to use a variant of Mack and Lansley's method, that is, starting with a schematic list of needs derived from Sklair, public opinion samples might indicate what these needs actually are (or are defined as being by some modality of public opinion) at a given moment in time.   Having begun to establish what needs are, we would next consider how people meet them.

Resources

Presumably people meet needs by deploying resources.   For a conceptualisation of resource systems to which people have variable access one could go initially to Townsend's (1979) work on poverty and then add to it, building on social resources such as kin, friends and other sources of social support; personality resources such as courage, love, ingenuity; and other personal resources such as health, strength and what, following Bourdieu (1984), we might call intellectual capital. An extended typology of resources, following Townsend for items 1 - 5, with suggested additions (6 - 8) is presented in Figure 4.

Figure 4

An Extended Typology of Resources, Based on Townsend

1. **Cash Income**
   (a) Earned
   (b) Unearned
   (c) Social Security

2. **Capital Assets**
   (a) House/flat occupied by family, and living facilities
   (b) Assets (other than occupied house) and savings

3. **Value of Employment Benefits in Kind**
   (a) Employer's fringe benefits; subsidies and value of occupational insurance
   (b) Occupational facilities

4. **Value of Public Social Services in Kind**
   Including government subsidies and services, e.g. health service, subsidised education and housing but excluding social security

5. **Private Income in Kind**
   (a) Home production (e.g. of smallholding or garden)
   (b) Gifts
   (c) Value of personal supporting services

6. **Social Resources**
   (a) Kin
   (b) Friends
   (c) Others (neighbours/strangers)

7. **Personality Resources**
   Including courage, love, resourcefulness etc.

8. **Physical and Intellectual Personal Resources**
   Including the individual's health, strength and intellectual capital (following Bourdieu)

The most independent person is perhaps the one who has access to most alternative resource systems when it comes to meeting needs. We have come to think of financial resources as the most flexible and liquid, but we must remember that there are some needs which, despite the fact that they can be satisfied only by reciprocal exchange, involve a currency other than money.

Redundancy

The notion of alternative systems is brilliantly captured by Frankenberg's concept of redundancy, which he borrows from telecommunications:

> If it is wished to send an electrical impulse from point A to point B, it is only necessary to connect them by a single channel. If the channel is in good order the signal will arrive, if not it will not. A negative result at B therefore may mean that no signal has been sent or it may mean the channel is out of order. The would-be receiver cannot judge which is the case. A way out of this difficulty is to provide alternative pathways, and this is in fact what telecommunication engineers do. These extra, in one sense, unnecessary additional channels create <u>redundancy</u> in the network. <u>The reliability of the components now becomes less important than the number.</u>
> (Frankenberg, 1966, p.281) (my emphasis)

So, finally, we might argue that the most independent person is he or she who has the greatest total redundancy in his or her total resource system, that is, the person who has the most alternative ways of meeting such needs as arise, given that needs change over time.

Let us take a homely rural example to give a concrete illustration. Suppose a child's bicycle gets a puncture. Suppose the child has neither strength, competence nor tools to mend it. Let us admit the child <u>needs</u> the puncture repaired (clearly a 'relative' need). How dependent is that child? Let us assume a lack of liquid assets to buy a puncture repair kit on the open market. But there may always be Dad to help, or possibly an older sibling or friend: there is a certain redundancy in the network already. Perhaps Dad can mend it, perhaps he has not got the time. Perhaps Dad has more money than time, so he can pay someone else for the repair, having his own alternative means of meeting needs. Suppose no money. Suppose no Dad. Well, there may be an older neighbour who could help. Help requires reciprocity. Can the child reciprocate? This will partly depend on the child's ingenuity or intellectual capital. Perhaps the child can pick a bunch of wild flowers for the neighbour, or prevail upon Mum to make a cake for the neighbour. Perhaps Mum can be prevailed upon to mend the puncture.

We see that, even considering what at first sight may look like a hopelessly dependent situation, the child may be a more independent agent than we at first supposed; and it is always open to the child to redefine the need, decide to discard the bicycle for the time being.

If this argument is accepted it follows that, if we admit the concept of independence at all, an ageing person is likely to lose some or all of it because of the exhaustion of resources and the depletion of redundancy in access to resource systems; but this may occur slowly and with great individual variability. Some needs may increase with age, but some may equally diminish; and, while access to some resource systems may be closed (such as remunerative work) others (such as pensions and maturing insurance policies) may open. Hence our overall conclusion, working this exercise through, might be more complicated than Townsend's starting point, that the structured dependency of the elderly is (a) a twentieth century phenomenon, and (b) a creation of social policy.

References

Bateson, N. (1984) Data Construction in Social Surveys, Allen and Unwin, London.

Bourdieu, P. (1977) Outline of a Theory of Practice, Cambridge University Press, Cambridge.

Douglas, J.D. (ed.) (1970) The Relevance of Sociology, Appleton Century Crofts, New York.

Frankenberg, R. (1966) Communities in Britain, Penguin, Harmondsworth.

Galtung, J. (1967) Theory and Methods of Social Research, The University Press, Oslo.

Jones, K. (1975) 'The Development of Institutional Care' in Butterworth, E. and Holman, R. (eds.) Social Welfare in Modern Britain, Fontana, London.

Kaplan, A. (1964) The Conduct of Inquiry, Methodology for Behavioural Sciences, Chandler Publishing, San Francisco.

Mack, J. and Lansley, S. (1985) Poor Britain, Allen and Unwin, London.

Seligman, M.E.P. (1975) Helplessness, on Depression, Development and Death, W.H. Freeman, San Francisco.

Sklair, L. (1970) The Sociology of Progress, Routledge and Kegan Paul, London.

Townsend, P. (1958) 'A Society for People', in Mackenzie, N. (ed.) Conviction, MacGibbon and Kee, London.

Townsend, P. (1962) The Last Refuge, Routledge and Kegan Paul, London.

Townsend, P. and Tunstall, S. (1968) 'Isolation, Desolation and Loneliness' in Shanas, E. et al., Old People in

Three Industrial Societies, Routledge and Kegan Paul, London.

Townsend, P. (1979) Poverty in the United Kingdom, Penguin, Harmondsworth.

Townsend, P. (1981) 'The Structured Dependency of the Elderly: a Creation of Social Policy in the Twentieth Century', Ageing and Society, Vol.1, No.1, pp.5-28.

Wax, R.H. (1972) Doing Fieldwork, Warnings and Advice, The University Press, Chicago.

Chapter Six

WHAT DO DEPENDENCY MEASURES MEASURE?

CHALLENGING ASSUMPTIONS

G. Clare Wenger

Introduction

A higher proportion of the UK population is over 80 than ever before and projections suggest that both this proportion and the real numbers of over-eighties will continue to increase up to the end of the century. This paper looks at the question of dependency of people in this age-group living in the community - and even after 80 most people are in the community. It (1) briefly considers the implications of the interpretation of longevity as a social problem; (2) examines the measures of dependency most commonly used in UK studies; (3) provides evidence to suggest that some of these measures are misleading and (4) discusses some of the implications of these hypotheses.

The discussion is based on the survivors of a 1979 study of the elderly in North Wales (Wenger, 1984). In 1983 those who had been 75 or older in 1979 and who were still living in the community were reinterviewed. They were then in their eightieth year or beyond. In the intervening four years, 32 per cent had died and 6 per cent were in 1983 in long-stay residential care. Of the survivors, 9 per cent were in institutional care. The research was based on a population sample (N=125 in 1983) and included an intensive study of thirty old people.

Longevity as a Social Problem

Longevity is something which has always been sought after. A good long life is what we wish for ourselves and for those that we love. The parents and siblings of today's over-eighties frequently died in early and middle adulthood from a variety of causes including: tuberculosis, childbed fever, infectious diseases and the results of poor housing or industrial working conditions. These causes of death have been eradicated or substantially reduced and the prospects of long life for subsequent generations are correspondingly

69

better.
Increases in the number over eighty, however, far from being hailed as an accomplishment of which society can be justly proud, are more commonly perceived as a social problem. Longevity is being viewed with anxiety because a high level of dependency is expected among the over-eighties. The fact that survival into the eighties is classed as a problem is worrying because a logical extension of this line of reasoning could be that the more old people who die the better for society because the costs will be less. Bearing in mind that service innovations are currently being evaluated on an accountancy basis, any improvement in a service which results in longer life could reduce unit costs in the short-term but may in the long run be more expensive. Hence policy-makers are confronted with a dilemma. It behoves us, therefore, to make sure that measures of dependency are as reliable as possible, since any over-measuring of dependency can result in fiscal or policy panic!

Measures of Dependency

The dependency measures usually used in service policy planning concentrate on physical or mental dependency. There is a tendency to play down emotional, structural, political and economic dependency, despite the fact that all these aspects may interact with physical dependency and make demands on statutory services, families and private and charitable provision.
Table 1 looks at the familiar measures of dependency which have been used in a number of surveys (e.g. Abrams, 1978; Hunt, 1978) and which were used by the author in both the 1979 and 1983 surveys mentioned above. The advantages of the fact that these measures have been widely used is that replication makes comparison possible.
All of these measures are based on self-assessment. They ask the respondent: to evaluate their overall state of health; whether or not their activities are limited by their physical condition; whether or not they need help with a range of self-care tasks; and whether or not they are housebound.
Given that the respondent population were 80 or over the figures in Table 1 represent a fairly low level of dependency. But let us look more closely at what these measures measure. So far as self-evaluation of health is concerned, we know that the elderly tend to over-estimate their clinical good health (Anderson and Judge, 1974). We also know that there is a high correlation between morale and health (Lawton, 1975; Toseland and Rosch, 1979-80; Wenger, 1984) and loneliness and health (Isaacs et al., 1972; Brown and Harris, 1978; Wenger, 1984). It is, therefore, not clear

Table 1

Dependency Measures based on Self-Assessment (%)
(Figures from author's 1983 survey of those who
had reached their eightieth year)

1.Self-assessed health	Good/Excellent	40
	All right for age	39
	Fair	15
	Poor	6

| 2.Whether or not activities are limited by physical condition | Yes | 78 |
| | No | 22 |

3.Whether help is needed
with a series of personal
care tasks (listed in
order of problem frequency,
proportion needing assistance)

Cutting own toenails	58
Taking bath or all over wash	23
Getting out of doors alone	22
Getting up and down steps	11
Putting on shoes and stockings	11
Taking own medication	10
Doing up buttons and zips	6
Dressing self (other than above)	6
Shaving or (for women) doing hair	6
Getting to and using W.C.	5
Getting in and out of bed	4
Washing hands and face	4
Getting around the house	2
Feeding self	1

| 4.Housebound | 17 |

whether good health maintains high morale or if the causal relationship is the converse, that high morale or absence of loneliness leads to a positive perception of one's health status. It has also been found that the elderly seek to project a positive self-image by rejecting the sick role (Tinker, 1981).

On the other hand, we might ask what does 'all right for my age' mean. This response tends to be used by older respondents. It was clear from my intensive study that old people frequently compare themselves with others worse off than they are. If a neighbour cannot get out of the house and they can at least walk to the shop, albeit with difficulty, they can consider themselves lucky. Since there is a tendency to look for someone worse off, 'all right for my age' may very well be a comparison with peers who are at the more impaired end of the continuum. It all depends on what the respondent's expectations were on reaching 90! Self-assessed health is likely, therefore, to be an extremely subjective measure if used as an indicator of dependency.

The same is true of respondents' answers as to whether or not their activities are hampered by their physical condition. I suspect that all of us over 30 might realistically answer that question in the affirmative! But, how limited does one have to be to answer 'Yes'? A high level of acceptance of restricted mobility is found among the elderly (Williamson et al., 1964). I find heavy digging in the garden limited by my own strength – is that a limitation by physical condition? If gardening is important to a respondent are they more likely to answer positively than those whose favoured activities are sitting with their feet up in front of the television set? It may also be that personality plays an important part. Determination may override physical problems in some instances. Limitation in itself may not make one dependent on help. This measure also is unlikely to be a realistic indicator of dependency.

Similar objections can be raised about the need for help with personal care tasks. What does needing help mean? Does it mean that the task could not be accomplished without help even to save one's life, or does it mean that it is nice to have help because it removes the fear of falling or accomplishes the task more quickly? Does it mean that formal or informal care-givers feel more secure if they provide help and that subsequently, because help is provided, the respondent comes to believe that they cannot manage without help? Some dependencies are learned. Examples of cultural dependency are not difficult to find: a newly widowed or divorced woman may think she cannot change a fuse because she has never done so, while a man in the same situation may be convinced that he cannot cook a 'proper' meal. Responses here may measure the availability of help more accurately than levels of dependency.

Dependency Measures

Even those who are housebound represent a wide range of dependency from those who are bedfast and unable to take care of even bodily functions to those who live alone severely impaired by arthritis but mentally alert and dependent on others only for essential supplies and some housework. Many in this situation continue to maintain a range of social contacts.

Obviously, after 80, there are more people who are ill and impaired. There are some who are incapable of doing things. There is no intention here to underplay the fact that some old people are very dependent or severely impaired. The measures discussed obviously pick up such people but do they overmeasure dependency? What these measures do not do is to differentiate between different levels of dependency or between physical and mental impairment. One question which they do not even attempt to answer is, given that we are all dependent on others, at what level does dependency become a social problem? The questions, however, remain, how accurate are these measures, what do they describe and what is their relationship to levels of dependency?

One way of checking their accuracy might be to compare self-assessments with assessments made by other people. The Pfeiffer dependency measures developed by Duke University (North Carolina) (Pfeiffer, 1970) are a set of explicit measures which are available for use by interviewers. These measures were used in the 1983 survey and it was found that the self-assessments considered above have very high correlations with the Pfeiffer measures for physical health, mental health and activities of daily living. The Pfeiffer measures, however, are more precise in their descriptions of health and differentiate between levels of dependency or impairment.

If we look at Table 2 which measures physical health, it can be seen that the categories on the left hand side of the table define more precisely the state of health of the subject. Categories 1 and 2 are comparable with the 40 per cent who assessed themselves as being in excellent or good health. Those in category 4 were suffering typically from diabetes, arthritis or some other chronic but not immediately life-threatening condition. Categories 5 and 6 are comparable to the numbers of those who said their health was poor. Note that more of those living with relatives (mainly daughters, some siblings) were assesed to be in excellent health. Those 6 per cent who were totally physically impaired were living with a relative.

Self-assessments of health do not discriminate between physical and mental health. Table 3 shows the Pfeiffer assessments for mental health. Here again distinctions are made between different levels of impairment. The 20 per

Table 2

Pfeiffer Physical Health Resource Scale. (%)

	All	(p = <.05)		
		Living Alone	With Spouse	With Relatives
	(124)	(52)	(38)	(34)
1. In excellent physical health Engages in vigorous physical activity, either regularly or at least from time to time.	20	17	21	24
2. In good physical health No significant illnesses or disabilities. Only routine medical care such as annual check ups required.	18	25	11	15
3. Mildly physically impaired Has only minor illnesses and/or disabilities which might benefit from medical treatment OR corrective measures.	25	25	26	24
4. Moderately physically impaired Has one or more diseases or disabilities which are either painful Or which might require substantial medical treatment.	32	29	42	26
5. Severely physically impaired Has one or more illnesses or disabilities which are either painful or life-threatening, OR which require extensive medical treatment.	2	4	0	0
6. Totally physically impaired Confined to bed and requiring full time medical assistance OR nursing care to maintain vital bodily functions.	3	0	0	(N=2) 6

Table 3

Pfeiffer Mental Health Resource Scale (%)

(p = <.005)

	All	Living Alone	With Spouse	With Relatives
	(124)	(52)	(38)	(34)
1.Outstanding mental health Intellectually alert and clearly enjoying life. Manages routine and major problems in his life with ease and is free from any psychiatric symptoms.	39	33	53	32
2.Good mental health Handles both routine and major problems in his life satisfactorily and is intellectually intact and free of psychiatric symptoms.	41	46	32	44
3.Mildly mentally impaired Has mild psychiatric symptoms and/or mild intellectual impairment. Continues to handle routine, though not major, problems in his life satisfactorily.	16	21	11	15
4.Moderately mentally impaired Has definite psychiatric symptoms and/or moderate intellectual impairment. Able to make routine commonsense decisions, but unable to handle major problems in his life.	2	0	5	3
5.Severely mentally impaired Has severe psychiatric symptoms and/or severe intellectual impairment, which interfere with routine judgements and decision-making in everyday life.	0	0	0	0
6.Completely mentally impaired Grossly psychotic or completely impaired intellectually. Requires either intermittent or constant supervision because of clearly abnormal or potentially harmful behaviour.	2	0	0	(N=2) 6

cent falling in categories 3 - 6, mildly mentally impaired to completely mentally impaired, is comparable with the 22 per cent of over-eighties which Kay et al. (1964) identified as suffering from dementia. Note, however, that only 4 per cent were judged to be more than mildly impaired. Again those who were completely mentally impaired were living with relatives. However, 76 per cent of those living with relatives were in good or outstanding mental health.

Challenging Assumptions

It might be assumed that dependency increases with age. Using the self-assessment measures however, only self-assessed health, being housebound, being unable to take a bath, medicine, food or to shave or brush hair were related to age at a significance of p=<.01. Other measures were less clearly related to age. Household composition, however, is related to age. Those who live with a spouse only tend to be younger than those who live alone or with relatives, while the very old are more likely to live with relatives. It seems logical to assume that the most impaired will be unable to live alone. We also know that women live longer in poor health, while men tend to pre-decease their wives. Those living with spouses, as well as being younger, are therefore for the most part in better health. Those living alone or with relatives are more likely to be women.

Concern about the burdens placed on carers by elderly relatives (Finch and and Groves, 1980; Nissell and Bonnerjea, 1982; Walker, 1981; Wright, 1983) has become a rallying cry for reformers and the need for services is often supported by the numbers of elderly people receiving help from relatives with the range of personal care tasks. But do these figures reflect the incidence of dependency or the incidence of helpers? Tables 2 and 3 suggest that with the exception of a small minority those living with others are not significantly more impaired than those living alone.

In Table 4 the commonly used dependency measures are broken down by household composition. Looking first at help with personal care tasks, what is striking is the high levels of help provided to those living with relatives. If we compare these figures with those for health, however, we find that more of those living with relatives consider themselves to be in good or excellent health. More in this category also assess their own health as poor but the proportions receiving help are considerably higher than those. One explanation of this may be that the figures represent the availability of help rather than dependency or the need for help. These outcomes may, therefore, reflect an induced or false dependency - if you always receive help you come to believe that you need it.

To check out if these figures reflect available help

Table 4

Self-Assessment Dependency Measures
by Household Composition (%)

	All	Living: Alone Only	With Spouse	With Relatives
	(125)	(51)	(35)	(35)
Health				
Good/excellent	40	39	37	46
All right for age	39	40	53	23
Fair	15	15	11	20
Poor	6	6	0	11
Activities Limited (yes)	78	77	84	74
Housebound	17	21	5	23
Personal Care (in order of prevalence of help)				
Cutting own toenails	58	55	47	71
Bathing	23	12	16	46
Getting out of doors	22	21	11	37
Getting up and down steps	11	10	0	26
Putting on shoes/stockings	11	0	11	26
Taking medicine	10	4	0	29
Doing up buttons/zips	6	0	0	23
Dressing self (other)	6	0	0	23
Shaving or brushing hair	6	2	0	20
Getting to/using W.C.	5	0	0	17
Getting in/out bed	4	0	0	14
Washing hands/face	4	0	0	23
Getting around house	2	0	0	9
Feeding self	1	0	5	20

Table 5

Help with Personal Care by Health
and Household Composition (%)

Cannot do or needs help with:

	Bathing	Washing	Shoes/Stockings	Buttons/Zips	Dressing	W.C.	In/out bed	Feeding	Shaving/hair	Toenails	Up/down steps	Around house	Out doors	Take medicine	Housebound	Activities limited by health
In good health																
Lives alone	0	0	0	0	0	0	0	0	0	35	0	0	0	0	0	55
Spouse only	0	0	0	0	0	0	0	0	0	29	0	0	0	0	0	57
Relatives	13	0	6	0	6	6	0	0	0	44	6	6	6	6	6	44
All right for age																
Lives alone	14	0	0	0	0	0	0	0	5	71	5	0	29	10	24	86
Spouse only	20	0	20	0	0	0	0	0	0	50	0	0	20	0	10	100
Relatives	100	25	38	50	25	13	13	13	25	100	50	13	88	38	38	100
Health only fair or poor																
Lives alone	30	0	0	0	0	0	0	0	0	60	36	0	46	0	55	100
With spouse	50	0	0	0	0	0	0	0	0	100	0	0	0	0	0	100
With relatives	55	27	46	36	46	36	36	0	46	100	36	18	46	55	36	100

rather than need, we can compare the figures for help broken by self-assessed health as shown in Table 5. This table should be self-explanatory, although interpretation should be cautious since the numbers in some cells are very small. However, the distribution indicates that those living with relatives are more likely to receive help even when they perceive themselves to be in good health. There are suggestions that gender may also affect the provision of help. While women generally are more impaired, men are more likely to receive help with bathing. Although this finding corresponds with findings for household help, it is surprising inasmuch as most carers are women and it might be imagined that cross-sex intimacy constraints would lead to the opposite result when bathing is at issue.

Other findings seem to demonstrate that the old person's perception of what they can do is affected by the availability of help. Table 6 shows that those living with relatives are more likely to perceive themselves as unable to do a range of housekeeping tasks, despite the finding that fewer of them claim that their activities are limited by their physical condition! A similar pattern as that discussed for personal care tasks exists when household management tasks are considered on the basis of self-assessed health. Perceived ability was more closely correlated with household composition than with either health or age. Do these patterns have something to do with believing that they cannot do such tasks because they never need to do them?

For those living alone, only shopping was affected by activities being limited. Most were able to do their own cooking except for two-thirds of those few who considered themselves to be in poor health. Only those over 90 experienced a significant level of difficulty in the management of heating systems. Most restrictions were related to health problems. Those living with their spouse only followed a similar pattern except that under 85 only men claimed they could do no cooking and 80 per cent of those who could do no laundry or ironing were men, despite the fact that the women generally are in worse health. Again most limits were health related. In contrast to those living alone or with their spouse, limits on household tasks experienced by those living with relatives were more directly related to age than to health.

Despite a lack of statistical significance, it is interesting to note that higher proportions of men than women claimed they could do no shopping, cooking, laundry and ironing and higher proportions of women claimed they could not manage heating systems. While there was no overall correlation with gender this was accentuated amongst those living with relatives. This reinforces the impression that in addition to measures of levels of dependency being affected by the availability of help, they are also affected by cultural

Table 6

Perceptions of Competence by
Household Composition

Can do:	All easily	With Difficulty	Some	None
Living alone (N=50)				
Shopping	44	18	6	32
Cooking	82	10	4	4
Laundry	53	16	20	10
Ironing	70	11	6	13
Manage heating	79	9	0	13
Living with spouse only (N=38)				
Shopping	47	11	26	16
Cooking	63	16	5	16
Laundry	58	11	5	26
Ironing	53	21	0	26
Manage heating	79	5	5	11
Living with relatives (N=35)				
Shopping	20	9	0	71
Cooking	29	11	9	51
Laundry	29	6	3	63
Ironing	29	6	3	63
Manage heating	29	6	9	57
All (N=125)				
Shopping	38	13	11	38
Cooking	61	12	6	21
Laundry	48	12	11	30
Ironing	53	13	3	32
Manage heating	64	7	4	25

All items correlate with household composition at $p = <.0001$
                              health $p = <.001$
                              age $p = <.003$

No overall correlation with gender.

dependency related to conventional gender roles and stereotypes. Qualitative data from the intensive study which formed part of the 1983 study support this hypothesis, although further testing is indicated. Those who lived alone placed great stress on maintaining their independence. Anxieties were most often expressed in terms of threats to health and autonomy. They went to great lengths to overcome limiting conditions and played down their infirmities. Great pride was taken in accomplishments which demonstrated their continued competence. Most of these traits were also true to some extent for most of those who lived with others but in the give and take of shared residence, compromises had to be reached. In general, two styles of caring can be identified. Obviously, these are ideal types and the reality of the situation is probably closer to a bimodally biased continuum. Relatives tend to adopt either a protective style which in the extreme could be described as infantilising, or an enabling role. Both styles may be motivated by the desire to do the best for the person for whom they are caring. The first offers, or more frequently insists on providing help, restricting mobility and allowing the old person to do very little for themselves. The second follows a hands-off approach, allowing the old person to do as much as they can, encouraging, assisting and praising as they see the need. Daughters it seems are more likely to adopt a protective style, while siblings seem more likely to favour the more encouraging style. There were few married carers in the study but discussion with those who were and with those who had been widowed suggests that spouses experience conflict between the intellectual desire to promote independence and the fear of risk. This, of course, is likely also to be a factor for adult children and siblings.

The interaction between physical and to a lesser extent mental impairment, the availability of help and the prevalent caring style in an old person's environment and the resultant level of functional or psychological dependence constitute an area where further research might profitably be conducted. The effect of gender stereotyping and other cultural factors affecting dependency might also be explored in this context.

It has been suggested in this paper that self-assessed measures of dependency are affected by: the availability of help as measured by household composition; self-perceptions of competence related to available help and gender roles; and by caring styles. Questions have been raised about the reliability of self-assessment measures of dependency. At the same time, it has been demonstrated that such measures have a high correlation with dependency measures which are assessed by others. Self-assessed dependency measures obviously do measure acute dependency in those cases where there is no question about ill-health and/or the inability to perform certain tasks. However, the evidence in this paper indicates that self-assessment measures over-measure dependency. The more discriminant Pfeiffer measures indicate that the number of highly dependent old people who place burdens of strain on carers represent very small proportions.

Implications

Ever since I heard a senior lecturer in social work tell a British Association of Social Work meeting that two-thirds of elderly people were isolated because one-third lived alone and one-third were childless, I have had anxieties about the way in which statistics and measures are interpreted and used. Concern about carers carrying heavy burdens of total or near total care, especially where dementia is involved, is increasing. Often, the fact that 20 per cent of over-80s live with relatives is interpreted to mean they are being <u>cared</u> for in some way which is unacceptably burdensome for the carer. In fact, very few need frequent supervision. By the same token, the finding that over 20 per cent of the over-80s demonstrate symptoms of dementia is interpreted as acute dependency, when as Table 3 shows most of that 20 per cent are only mildly impaired and 'continue to handle routine problems.... satisfactorily.'

By demonstrating that levels of dependency may be lower than numbers receiving help, I do not wish to undermine demands for more help for carers. At present, those old people living with relatives find it most difficult to get help. However, much of the reluctance of social services planners to make a concentrated commitment to support for carers seems predicated on a belief that to provide adequate domiciliary support would lead to service being overwhelmed by demand. The fact that at any one time the incidence of very dependent people in the community is small means that there is no cause to throw up our hands in despair at growing numbers over 80 - rather it is to demonstrate that given goodwill the problem is one of manageable proportions. Most old people do not become totally dependent and a large proportion continue to live relatively independent lives until death.

The findings discussed in this paper raise important questions about caring styles and suggest that with the best will in the world relatives and residential care workers in seeking to help and protect try to eliminate risk and may unwittingly be reinforcing dependency. While more research is indicated in this area, it has been shown elsewhere that morale is higher and survival prospects enhanced where independence can be maintained (Abrams, n.d.; Harel, 1979) and that mental health is closely related to self-esteem (Levin, 1964).

Ageism in our society is endemic, so much so that

gerontologists and service practitioners whose main concern is for old people often do not recognise it in themselves. The stigma of impairment is a central image of the negative stereotype. It is, therefore, important to challenge the image of old age which stresses increasing dependence and burden on younger generations. An 85 year old man in my intensive study recently decided against undergoing surgery because he said he had read in the papers that the burden of old people was a drain on society and did not choose to prolong his life. Obviously, with increasing longevity the numbers of dependent over-80s will increase as the number of over-80s increases. But it is important to recognise that acute dependency affects a small proportion at any one time. Some are affected for a short period only; others are never acutely dependent. Most of the over-80s are competent and relatively independent even though impaired.

References

Abrams, M. (1978) Beyond Three-Score Years and Ten: A First Report on a Survey of the Elderly, Age Concern, London.

Abrams, M. (n.d.) People in their Late Sixties: A Longitudinal Survey of Ageing, Part 1, Survivors and Non-Survivors, Age Concern, London.

Anderson, W. Ferguson and Judge, T. (eds.) Geriatric Medicine, Academic Press, London.

Brown, G.W. and Harris, T. (1978) Social Origins of Depression: A Study of Psychogeriatric Disorder in Women, Tavistock, London.

Finch, J. and Groves, D. (1980) 'Community Care and the Family: A Case for Equal Opportunities', Journal of Social Policy, Vol.9, Part 4, pp.487-511.

Harel, Z. (1979) 'Discriminators Between Survivors and Non-Survivors among Working Class Aged Living in the Community', The Gerontologist, Vol.19, No.1, pp.83-89.

Hunt, A. (1978) The Elderly at Home: A Study of People aged 65 and over living in the Community in England in 1976, HMSO, London.

Isaacs, B., Livingstone, M. and Neville, Y. (1972) Survival of the Unfittest: A Study of Geriatric Patients in Glasgow, Routledge and Kegan Paul, London.

Kay, D.W., Beamish, P. and Roth, M. (1964) 'Old Age Mental Disorders in Newcastle-upon-Tyne: Part I, a Study of Prevalence', British Journal of Psychiatry, Vol.110, p.668.

Lawton, M.P. (1975) 'The Philadelphia Geriatric Center morale scale: a Revision', The Gerontologist, Vol.30, pp.85-89.

Levin, S. (1964) 'Depression in the Aged: The Importance of External Factors', in E. Kastenbaum (ed.) New Thoughts on Old Age, Springer, New York.

Nissell, M. and Bonnerjea, L. (1982) Family Care of the Handicapped Elderly: Who Pays?, Report No. 602, Policy Studies Institute, London.

Pfeiffer, E. (1970) 'Survival in Old Age', Journal of the American Geriatric Society, Vol.18, No.4, pp.273-285.

Tinker, A. (1981) The Elderly in Modern Society, Longmans, London.

Toseland, R. and Rosch, J. (1979-80) 'Correlates of Life Satisfaction and AID Analysis', International Journal of Aging and Human Development, Vol.10, No.2, pp.203-211.

Walker, A. (1981) 'Community Care and the Elderly in Great Britain: Theory and Practice', International Journal of Health Services, Vol.11, No.4, pp.541-557.

Wenger, G.C. (1984) The Supportive Network: Coping with Old Age, George Allen and Unwin, London.

Williamson, J.W. et al. (1964) 'Old People at Home: Their Unreported Needs', The Lancet, Vol.i, pp.117-120.

Wright, F. (1983) 'Single Carers: Employment, Housework and Caring', in Finch, J. and Groves, D. (eds.) A Labour of Love: Women, Work and Caring, Routledge and Kegan Paul, London.

Chapter Seven

NEW LIFESTYLES IN OLD AGE?

Mike Featherstone and Mike Hepworth

Introduction : The Stigma of Ageing

It is almost impossible nowadays to read the literature of
ageing without coming across some reference to the
stigmatisation of ageing. The most recent published attack on
prejudice against age in the United Kingdom can be found in
Bornat, Phillipson and Ward's Manifesto for Old Age. In this
they draw attention to the necessity of challenging the
negative images of ageing in our society in order to help lift
the burden of prejudice from the shoulders of many of our
ageing men and women. They argue, for example, that there
is:

> prejudice in the language we use about older people, in
> the way they are portrayed in the media, in our
> adoption of myths and fallacies about ageing (for
> instance, that the elderly are sexually inactive; or that
> they are unable to learn as well as the young; or that
> senility is an inevitable part of growing old).
> (Bornat et al., 1985, p.11) (our emphasis)

In this book and elsewhere it is argued that the lives of
many of the elderly are needlessly restricted by outworn and
inaccurate beliefs about the ageing process which, effectively
disbar them from 'full social acceptance.' As a consequence,
the process of growing old is accompanied by the progressive
experience of 'disengagement' (to use that controversial term)
and ultimately loss of independence. In other words, the
stigmatisation of ageing and the dependency of the elderly are
closely related social constructs.

Before we explore the sociological implications of this
apparently pervasive situation further, it will be useful to
give brief consideration to the concept of stigma as it was
originally developed by Erving Goffman (1968).

Goffman defines stigma not as a personal condition but
as a social situation. There are, he says, three kinds of
stigma: (i) 'abomination of the body'; (ii) blemishes of

individual character; (iii) tribal stigma of race or nation. What they all have in common, and we can add, what is more important from the point of view of ageing, is in his words, 'the situation of the individual who is disqualified from full social acceptance' (Goffman, 1968, p.9).

For Goffman the central issue of 'the stigmatised individual's situation in life.... is a question of what is often, if vaguely, called "acceptance".' And this is particularly the case in situations of 'mixed contacts' where the stigmatised (the 'discredited' as he calls them or the 'discreditable' - those who may be discredited if found out) find themselves in the company of each other.

As one of the fundamental processes of social life, stigmatisation is a language of relationships in which categorisation or stereotyping (whether it be negative or positive) plays an indispensible part. In his sociological analysis of stigma Goffman is more concerned with the social functions of stigmatisation in the creation of boundaries between deviance and normality than with the cultural origins of particular stigmas. Two factors have to be taken into account here: (i) visibility and (ii) obtrusiveness. It is primarily, says Goffman, through our sense of sight that 'the stigma of others frequently becomes evident' (Goffman, 1968, p.65) but in addition, it is the inability of an individual to prevent a stigma from intruding into interaction that causes the gravest offence. The ability of individuals to manage their stigma or even completely conceal it is the foremost criterion of admission to normal interaction.

The poignancy of the stigmatised individual is that he or she can play both parts: that of 'normal' person and that of deviant. Stigmatisation is, in the last analysis, what Goffman calls a 'normal-deviant-drama': 'a two-role social process in which every individual participates in both roles, at least in some connections and in some phases of life'. Goffman also suggests that:

> the painfulness of sudden stigmatisation can come not from the individual's confusion about his identity, but from knowing too well what he has become.
> (Goffman, 1968, p.168)

And this brings us on to the problem of the ageing body.

The Ageing Body

At the beginning we noted that it is not the physiological processes of ageing as such which provoke concern amongst students of ageing, but the social and personal consequences of negative stereotypes of ageing which apparently continue to bedevil the elderly and cramp their lives. In line with Goffman's concept of stigma it is assumed that changes in an individual's physical appearance and physical competence can hamper social interaction and thus lead to imputations of less than full acceptability. Empirical investigations such as the work of Joyce Stephens (1980), Jules Henry (1972), Liz Patterson (1978) and Charles Stannard (1973) suggests that the major problem faced by the elderly can be traced to the inability of our culture to identify with the aged. This characteristic is considered by Norbert Elias to be an endemic feature of the modernisation of western society which he has defined as 'the civilising process'.

In his most recent book, The Loneliness of Dying, Elias (1985) argues that cruelty towards the elderly, whether male or female, has been manifest throughout history but has, in the contemporary world, now assumed a very specific configuration:

> It is closely connected to a very characteristic change in interpersonal relations that takes place when people grow old or are on their death bed: as they grow older they grow potentially or actually less powerful in relation to younger people. They become visibly more dependent on others.... it is perhaps useful to remember that some of the things old people do, in particular some of the strange things, have to do with their fear of losing power and independence and especially of losing control over themselves.
> (Elias, 1985, p.13) (our emphasis)

As a result of the civilising process - the increasing role of manners and etiquette in the regulation of social relations; and in particular the pronounced development of the 'disgust function' - it is not surprising that loss of control over bodily functions is seen as a shameful and embarrassing loss of control over the body and thus the self.

One of the central emphases in the Elias thesis of the civilising process is that the gradual refinement of the disgust function over the last four hundred or so years has produced a social climate in which displeasing odours; incontinence; farting and soiling have become increasingly unacceptable. In other words, the threshold of self-control has been raised to the degree that such physical processes are now regarded as barriers to social interaction especially in respectable circles. It is thus now possible for Erving Goffman to describe such natural functions as 'bodily betrayals'. Failure to control 'nature' is an interactional offence and as such likely, unless remedied, to lead to personal stigmatisation. Individuals who are for physical reasons unable to exercise complete 'self-control' as we call it, must either become adept at apologising or manipulating their behaviour in such a way that their physical shortcomings do not intrude. The only other alternative is, of course, to withdraw from 'mixed contacts'.

Here, of course, we are referring to what Bromley has labelled 'the aversive properties of the aged person'. Many people, he suggests, and especially those who have had little contact with the elderly, experience a sense of physical revulsion 'on encountering a physically and mentally deteriorated aged person' (Bromley, 1978, p.52). The reason for this reaction may be found in the way we become conditioned to perceive and understand human beings. Bromley goes on to argue that:

> Throughout childhood we acquire a notion of what is normal and expected in relation to the appearance and behaviour of human beings. Close contact with any marked deviation from the norm tends to elicit anxiety, hostility and rejection....
> (Bromley, 1978, p.63) (our emphasis)

At the same time, sociologists and gerontologists who have taken up the issue of the 'aversive properties of the aged person', point out that the tendency is not entirely irreversible. It is subject to restraint or even elimination under certain conditions, because the aversive properties of old age are associated with the relative powerlessness of certain individuals or groups to escape the stigmatisation ageing can produce. It is for this reason not particularly useful to talk about the ageing body but more valuable to refer to specific groups of the elderly in terms of their access to strategies for combatting or confronting the stigma. The relative power to escape stigmatisation becomes visibly inscribed on the bodies of the elderly and thus open to social recognition. To borrow again from Goffman, the irony is that such heroes of ageing become no longer representative of the ageing population as such.

The Sociology of the Body

It is not therefore simply with the fact of physiological change as such that the elderly have to contend, but with the interactional implications of visible evidence of the fact of growing older. Whilst this is the most obvious aspect of any consideration of ageing, what is remarkable is that the body as a social phenomenon has until recently received remarkably little consideration (Turner, 1984).

In the last decade or so a sociology of the body has emerged which emphasises that the body is of central importance when it comes to understanding social processes. According to this approach, the human body can best be understood as a social construct created through processes of social control whereby codes of knowledge and schemes of classification are produced and inscribed on human bodies.

A central feature of the sociology of the body is the concept of the embodied person. The notion of the embodied person means that it is impossible to talk about belief and consciousness, power, social control, superiority and inferiority, without reference to the body. In short, when we speak about the body, we speak about society.

We have already referred to the view of Norbert Elias that western culture, as a result of the civilising process, makes it very difficult for younger members to identify with the elderly. A social distancing which is closely linked to the cultivation of delicacy and shame and contemporary versions of the fear of death. The feeling of shame, he argues:

.... is a specific excitation, a kind of anxiety which is automatically reproduced in the individual on certain occasions by force of habit. Considered superficially, it is the fear of social degradation, or more generally, of other people's gestures of superiority. But it is a form of displeasure or fear which arises characteristically on those occasions when a person who fears lapsing into inferiority can avert this danger neither by direct physical means nor by any other form of attack. (Elias, 1982, p.292)

The ways in which we manage shame are a reflection of our access to material and other resources: in other words, our social class. For the sociologist Pierre Bourdieu, the body, and therefore the ageing body, is an immediate betrayer of social class.

In his book, Distinction (1984), Bourdieu provides a complex analysis of the ways in which social class structures taste, consumption, and lifestyle. Taste, which is often popularly regarded as a matter of personal preference - an expression of essential individuality - (for example, taste in food; clothing; sport; body-maintenance; holidays; furniture; art; music; restaurants; newspapers; cars; films etc - in short the entire range of lifestyle activities, bodily practices and high or popular cultural pursuits) can all be mapped out and correlated with the class structure within which different groups compete to maintain and increase their own interests. Thus, for Bourdieu, cultural capital (the possession of or knowledge about valued cultural goods) is as important a source of distinction, and hence a means of classifying the bearer, as economic capital. The value an individual places on his or her body, for example, is not simply a matter of personal choice or taste but is determined by what Bourdieu describes as the class habitus.

Class habitus comprises the unconscious dispositions, taken-for-granted preferences, and attitudes towards the world which are displayed in the individual's natural sense of the correct behaviour and bodily order; taste for cultural goods e.g. holidays; view of morality; sense of time and so on. These together are the product of his or her social group, class or class fraction's relation to other groups, classes or class fractions which inhabit the social space.

With regard to the body, Bourdieu makes the following observation:

> It follows that the body is the most indisputable materialisation of class taste, which it manifests in several ways. It does this in the seemingly most natural features of the body, the dimensions (volume, height, weight), and shapes (round or square, stiff or supple, straight or curved) of its visible forms which express in countless ways a whole relation to the body, i.e. a way of treating it, caring for it, feeding it, maintaining it, which reveals the deepest dispositions of the habitus. It is in fact through preferences with regard to food which may be perpetuated beyond their social conditions of production (as, in other areas, an accent, a walk etc.), and also, of course, through the uses of the body in work and leisure which are bound up with them, that the class distribution of bodily properties is determined. (Bourdieu, 1984, p.190) (our emphasis)

It is important to stress that the social forces to which Bourdieu refers are effective precisely because they 'function below the level of consciousness and language, beyond the reach of introspective scrutiny or control by the will' (Bourdieu, 1984, p.466). They are subtly revealed to us in apparently trivial and insignificant bodily movements, in gestures, in 'ways of bearing one's body, presenting it to others, moving it, and in making space for it' (Bourdieu, 1984, p.474).

Thus our relationship with the social world and our place in it are expressed in our bodies and the relationship of our bodies in space and to other people. Therefore knowledge of the social world has to take into account practical knowledge: that is, a system of embodied practical schemes which are used by members of the social world.

What are the implications of Bourdieu's sociology of the body for the lifestyles of ageing and stigmatisation? If we follow Bourdieu's analysis we can see that the class habitus provides an individual with a sense of positive or negative feelings towards the body, thus governing his or her self-perception and the ability to insulate these perceptions from the effects of the appraisals of others. So, for example, the possession of an upper class habitus as in the case of royalty and the aristocracy may enable the individual to distance him or herself from the aversive properties of ageing through a disposition to deny their relevance or efficacy. The social bearing of such a person will tend to downplay physical ageing by overlaying any negative traits with other more socially acceptable ones which indicate and reinforce the superior status of the bearer. In this respect it may not be income as such which is used to finance the war against bodily decay (since this tends to be more characteristic of the new bourgeoisie) but rather the disposition to deny the need for such remedies stemming from a consciousness of symbolic power, and this is visible in specific forms of bodily display, gestures and so forth. The case of the Queen Mother is valid here: she is, it can be argued, a specific instance of the more general tendency to perceive chronological age as an apparent social disadvantage in persons of high social status. She is not simply 'wonderful for her age' but in terms of Goffman's theory of stigma, not in social terms at any rate an old person at all.

Bourdieu argues that it is possible to 'begin to map out a universe of class bodies.... which tends to reproduce in its specific logic the universe of the social structure' (Bourdieu, 1984, p.193). Amongst the salient characteristics he identifies we find:

> degree of assurance
> self-consciousness
> instrumental attitudes towards the body.

And it is in his view the petite-bourgeoisie who are the most concerned with body maintenance; and who experience the imperfect, alienated body. Such people are consequently the most likely social class to experience embarrassment and self-consciousness because their social position relative to other classes and class fractions has accustomed them to observe their bodies from the outside 'through other people's eyes, watching, checking, correcting' themselves. Such a person will tend 'by his desperate attempts to reappropriate an alienated being-for-others', expose 'himself to appropriation, giving himself away as much by hypercorrection as by clumsiness' (Bourdieu, 1984,p.207). Hence the attraction of the array of cosmetics, exercises and body-maintenance techniques which are ostensibly designed to deliver the ideal body: the body which is, as in the case of the aristocracy, at ease with itself.

Bourdieu asserts that the upper class or bourgeoisie experience a sense of ease with their bodies:

> .... a sort of indifference to the objectifying gaze of others which neutralises its powers, presupposes the self-assurance that comes from the certainty of being able to objectify that objectification, appropriate the appropriation, of being capable of imposing the norm of apperception of one's own body, in short, of commanding all the powers which, even when they reside in the body

New Lifestyles in Old Age?

and apparently borrow its most specific weapons, such
as 'presence' or charm, are essentially irreducible to it.
(Bourdieu, 1984, p.208)

Conclusion

As sociologists concerned with ageing we really need to ask
two interrelated questions: (1) who are the advocates of the
'new age', the new lifestyles in old age?   (Hepworth and
Featherstone,   1982),   and   (2)   what   interests   do   they
represent?   Following   Bourdieu,   we   would   see   the   new
petite-bourgeoisie as playing a key role here.   As he puts it:

> The new petite-bourgeoisie comes into its own in all the
> occupations   involving   presentation   and   representation
> (sales, marketing, advertising, public relations, fashion,
> decoration   and   so   forth)   and   in   all   the   institutions
> providing symbolic goods and services.   These include
> the   various   jobs   in   medical   and   social   assistance
> (marriage   guidance,   sex   therapy,   dietetics,   vocational
> guidance,   paediatric   advice   etc.)   and   in   cultural
> production   and   organisation   (youth   leaders,   play
> leaders,   tutors   and   monitors,   radio   and   television
> producers and presenters, magazine journalists) which
> have expanded considerably in recent years; but also in
> established occupations such as craftsmen and nurses.
> (Bourdieu, 1984, p.259)

In attempting to answer the question concerning how
widely the message is circulated and received by different
fractions of the market, we would assume that people from
different habitus will perceive and decode the message in a
variety of ways.   An interesting point of comparison is the
different reception of the fitness and health messages put out
by the Health Education Council or a number of research
findings which have discovered a class and of course a
gender factor in dieting and slimming.

According to Bourdieu's analysis, the working class are
not   aspiring   pretenders   like   the   petite-bourgeoisie   and
therefore would probably largely ignore the message because
their habitus tends to support preferences for certain types
of food; belief in the naturalness of overweight as one gets
older; and the general view that the body naturally runs
down with age.   Interestingly, Bourdieu does not mention the
privatised working class whom, it would be expected, would
be more receptive to the new age lifestyle message.   It should
also be noted that when members of this stratum make use of
the message, goods and lifestyles they may not be accepted
as legitimate by others who do not allow the pretenders to
pass.   In this case while the out-groups refuse to accept the
status move, within local groups of the stratum, or within the

private sphere of family relationships, the adoption of new bodily practices aimed at combatting the aversive properties of ageing may succeed and represent a move which enhances the relative status of the individual. This of course does not mean that the meaning of the messages and the way in which goods are used coincides with those intended by their originators, but does point to the fact that certain groups may find them useful strategies to adopt as moves within their local and interpersonal power-balances.

Overarching these variations in social practice is the Elias message that the civilising process which is responsible for our sensitisation to the aversive properties of old age (the disgust function) has no forseeable end. In this context the two major strategies for confronting the stigma of old age have certain built-in weaknesses:

(1) **The partial redistribution of income and resources to favour the elderly.** The problem with this social-democratic reformist strategy is that by granting previously denied goods, services and cultural strategies to underprivileged groups, the existing social matrix is destabilised and the groups and class fractions which occupy higher positions in the social space will consequently adopt new practices, endorse new goods and strategies which are designed to re-establish and maintain the original social distance between groups. In effect, all that the reformers and cultural entrepreneurs will have achieved will be inflation, which increases the pace of the social dynamic, but results in the same distance.

(2) **The technological fix.** Specifically: the search for drugs to delay the process of ageing. In the first place they are accessible to advantaged groups before being marketed to the general population, and in the second, it is more likely that they will be inscribed into the existing social space and used to maintain the existing set of differences and distinctions between strata, than that they will be used in a democratic way to reduce differences.

All this leads us to believe that the stigmatisation process is alive and well though subject to some of the variations we have outlined. And the scenario that we envisage is one of continuing competition and social differentiation as a central aspect of social life: those very processes which help unfortunately to perpetuate the stigma of ageing. Everything that this entails takes place against a background of the continuing expansion of the caring professions and in particular the 'ageing enterprise'. In addition the continuing influence of the new petite-bourgeoisie described by Bourdieu who produce the new age strategies within consumer culture, will also grow as they promote the new market in pre-retirement and retirement lifestyles.

In terms of the social space described by Bourdieu, a

key element which accounts for the relative power which social groups can draw upon to impose their particular cultural practices as legitimate, is their relative social trajectory. Changes in the division of labour mean that certain groups will have a declining trajectory (e.g. farmers and peasants) and therefore an increasingly limited influence, whereas other groups such as the new petite-bourgeoisie will have an upward trajectory as they increase numerically, and increase their relative social power. Therefore those who advocate and define the consumer culture lifestyles, the 'new age', the caring professional, marketers, advertisers, media people etc. are part of an expanding class fraction with an accelerating upward trajectory within the social space. They will relatively expand their economic and cultural capital, and be in a stronger position to legitimise their view of the body and its uses and the acceptability of their own particular habitus.

References

Bornat, J., Phillipson, C. and Ward, S. (1985) A Manifesto for Old Age Pluto Press, London.
Bourdieu, P. (1984) Distinction: A Social Critique of the Judgement of Taste, Routledge and Kegan Paul, London.
Bromley, D.B. (1978) 'Speculations in Social and Environmental Gerontology', in Carver, V. and Liddiard, P. (eds.) An Ageing Population: A Reader and Sourcebook, Hodder and Stoughton/Open University Press, London.
Elias, N. (1982) The Civilising Process: Volume 2: State Formation and Civilisation, Basil Blackwell, Oxford.
Elias, N. (1985) The Loneliness of Dying Basil Blackwell, Oxford.
Goffman, E. (1968) Stigma: Notes on the Management of Spoilt Identity, Penguin, Harmondsworth.
Henry, J. (1972) Culture Against Man, Penguin, Harmondsworth
Hepworth, M. and Featherstone, M. (1982) Surviving Middle Age, Basil Blackwell, Oxford.
Patterson, L. (1978) 'A Suitable Case for Care', Health and Social Service Journal, 24 February.
Stannard, C.I. (1973) 'Old Folks and Dirty Work: The Social Conditions for Patient Abuse in a Nursing Home', Social Problems, Vol.20, No.3, Winter, pp.331-342.
Stephens, J. (1980) Loners, Losers, and Lovers: Elderly Tenants in a Slum Hotel, University of Washington Press, Seattle and London.
Turner, B.S. (1984) The Body in Society: Explorations in Social Theory, Basil Blackwell, Oxford.

Chapter Eight

TOWARDS AN ANATOMY OF AGEISM : SOCIETY,

SOCIAL POLICY AND THE ELDERLY BETWEEN THE WARS

Andrew Blaikie and John Macnicol

Introduction

Over the course of the 1918-1948 period in Britain, the elderly emerged as a distinct, identifiable group that was beginning to attract the attention of social commentators. The late-Victorian and Edwardian debate on the elderly had primarily been about their poverty, and whether the Poor Law was the appropriate instrument for dealing with them. Although the elderly were increasing in numbers over the 19th century, and their plight becoming more visible, as a proportion of the population they showed little growth: between 1851 and 1911 the proportion of the United Kingdom population aged over 65 only rose from 4.7 per cent to 5.3 per cent. But after 1911 a massive rise took place, caused primarily by the post-1870s decline in the birth rate and consequent shift in the population age-structure: by 1951 there had been a 160 per cent rise in the number of over-65s, and as a proportion of the population they doubled, to 10.9 per cent. It is quite mistaken, therefore, to see - as some writers have done - the very recent rise in the proportion of elderly as unprecedented and alarming (Shegog, 1981). By the late 1940s, in fact, there was emerging a discussion of issues that have been on the 'old age agenda' ever since, such as low take-up of social security benefits or the urgent need for more sheltered housing (Nuffield Foundation, 1947, pp. 15, 96). As will be shown in this paper, the development of the elderly's separate status was a complex process, full of tensions and contradictions - a product of changes in the economic and social structure and expressed in an intriguing dialectic between 'expert' categorisations and popular perceptions of old age.

The Marginalisation of the Elderly

Some historians of old age have argued that with the transition to late industrial capitalism and an increasingly

An Anatomy of Ageism

technological mode of production, the elderly become 'marginalised': they are shaken out of a labour market that is becoming more competitive and specialised, they lose their authoritative role in the extended family, and they become increasingly reliant on social security provided by a paternalistic state. Many reservations have been expressed about the implications of such an interpretative model: Peter Laslett has found no convincing evidence that family and kinship support has weakened (Laslett, 1977); Richard Smith has argued that the elderly's structured dependence is not exclusive to the 20th century and industrialisation (Smith, 1984) - though, of course, the qualitative features of that dependence may have altered significantly; and anthropological studies such a Nancy Foner's point to the complexity of the 'old age experience' in all types of societies, with status being affected by factors such as social class, wealth, culture, family support, and so on (Foner, 1984).

Again, marginalisation may not have been exclusive to the elderly. It may simply have been part of a wider process of classification that was being applied to other groups in society (for example, children, the unemployed, the mentally retarded) - a consequence of a more specialised division of labour and an increasingly interventionist state with better techniques of classification, identification and surveillance (Armstrong, 1983). And there is a danger that marginalisation theory can lead on to a rather anodyne functionalist model, in which old age is invested with a suspiciously appropriate social necessity. For example, Carole Haber's excellent study of old age in American history concludes that the increasing tendency to perceive old age as a problem by the end of the 19th century was part of a general imposition of age-related classifications as a consequence of 'the growing bureaucratisation of America'. 'The reliance upon chronological age', she writes:

was not directed solely at the old, nor did it indicate a sudden decline in their prestige. The age restrictions written into these plans were simply part of a rational attempt by professionals to solve myriad national problems. In an era when urban and industrial growth seemed to magnify the complexities of society, age as a determining factor eliminated many uncertainties. It became an acceptable barometer of one's position in the world (Haber, 1983, p.127).

However, it is obvious that by the late 1940s the elderly were being marginalised into a state of measurable relative deprivation: it is in this sense that structured dependence was novel, and could be expressed as a combination of social disadvantages - poverty, low health status, poor housing, isolation, and so on - as Nicholas Bosanquet has shown

(Bosanquet, 1978). The inter-war years saw an increasing
tendency for old age to be defined in terms of retirement
from the labour market: between the early 1900s and the
1950s the proportion of men aged over 65 who were working
fell from about two-thirds to just under one-third. There
was a gradual shake-out of the elderly worker consequent
upon technological change, assisted by the pressure of mass
unemployment and by the growth of private pension schemes;
this was institutionalised by the 1946 National Insurance Act's
stipulation that receipt of the state pension should be
conditional upon retirement. The late 1940s also saw the
emergence of geriatric medicine, the publication of the first
social surveys into old age, and the realisation that the
elderly were going to be a major category of social security
claimant: by 1951, in fact, out of 1.46 million claimants to
national assistance at any one time, roughly 970,000 were
over retirement age. The 'population panic' of the 1930s, in
which there had been expressed great concern over the social
and economic consequences of an ageing population, had given
rise to a new ageist vocabulary in which the elderly were
portrayed as an unproductive burden on the rest of society:
for example, Richard and Kay Titmuss warned that 'there will
be an increasingly higher proportion of older persons who will
hold appointments by virtue of their seniority.... society
will lose the mental attitude that is essential for social
progress', and implied that an increasingly geriatric House of
Commons (with 214 M.P.s out of 558 who revealed their ages
being aged over 60) was an example of this (Titmuss, 1942,
pp. 42,47). By 1947 the Nuffield Survey could assert
crudely that 'the burden of maintaining the aged may become
so great as to result in a lowering of the national standard of
living'. (Nuffield Survey, 1947, p.2). These sentiments
were, of course, tempered by a rhetoric of 'deservingness', in
which the elderly were seen as having a strong 'social
contract' claim to decent treatment by the state, and by a
tendency to distinguish the 'young old' from the 'old old' with,
as Chris Phillipson has pointed out, the former being seen as
a reserve army of labour, to be utilised (as, indeed, they
were in the 1950s) in times of economic growth (Phillipson,
1982, Ch.3).
    However, the debate that accompanied this process of
marginalisation was complex. A curious feature of it was that
concern about the elderly as such was often peripheral to
much wider social issues. One can see that the inter-war
discussion of pensions, which clearly equated old age with
retirement and economic uselessness, was but a small part of
a general debate on mass unemployment. For example, the
1925 Widows', Orphans' and Old Age Contributory Pensions
Act introduced a contributory pension of 10s.0d. per week
for those insured workers (and their wives) between the ages
of 65 and 70, and pensions for life (with dependants'

benefits) for widows of insured men. Yet if we look at the impulses behind the Act, we see no specific attention on the elderly as such. First, there was concern in the early 1920s over the overlaps, inefficiencies and administrative muddle of existing insurance schemes, and calls for a system of 'all-in insurance' to replace them (basically, an amalgamation of health and unemployment insurance with workmen's compensation and pensions). Secondly, with the break-up of the Lloyd George coalition in October 1922 each of the three main political parties began to look around for policies that might be electorally appealing. The Labour Party had shown a long-standing interest in mothers' pensions; at its 1925 Annual Conference it eventually adopted a resolution for old age pensions of £2 per week, financed solely out of taxation. In response, the Conservatives were evolving their alternative based on the insurance principle – a cardinal tenet of conservative social reform. Their aim was to 'peg out our claim to the ground before the others have had time to get in', as Neville Chamberlain admitted (Macleod, 1961, p.106). Finally, the 1925 Act was more than anything else a product of the growing realisation that mass unemployment was going to be long-term, and that persuading the elderly worker to retire was a relatively easy way of tackling the problem by redistributing available jobs. As Chamberlain put it, 'what we want is a workable scheme which will give us a pension sufficiently high to make it worth while for the old men to come out of industry' (Public Record Office, 1924). Similarly, in the 1930s there was much discussion on the need for better pensions for the elderly: 'The ideal of an honourable retirement, not later than 65, on an adequate pension, should be the aim of social policy', declared the research organisation Political and Economic Planning (P.E.P., 1934, p. 12), but this laudable goal was set in the context of a plan to lower unemployment and reflate the economy.

Surveying Social Standards

The complexity of emerging attitudes to old age can be illustrated by examining social surveys. Shortly after the Second World War, the survey group Mass-Observation produced a Bulletin summarising these attitudes (Mass-Observation 1948). Panel members talked of 'a very real fear of senile decay; two in five dread mental debility.... And others prefer death to a decay in life'. There was anxiety too about institutionalisation: one woman, who regarded the new Rest Homes as no better than Mr Bumble's workhouse, remarked that' while I had six pennies and the gas laid on, I would take that way out before entering one'. The pamphlet closed by stating that 'Aesthetically, too, old people sometimes offend. They cannot help their physical failings, 'double chin, wrinkles, knobbly, misshapen limbs', but there is no need to disregard the aesthetic properties. As one 36 year old housewife writes:

> I shall see to it that I smell nice and dress in pastel shades, keep flowers always by me and not be, as one old lady who terrified me as a child, an old lady always dressed in black, who smelt musty like the grave, and always reminded me of a fat spider ready to grab me.

By contrast with the plethora of postwar studies, the inter-war decades had been curiously deficient in research into issues of ageing. Poverty surveys using or adapting Rowntree's family cycle model saw old age as largely peripheral to the nuclear family with children and it was not until the later 1940s that Rowntree himself turned his full attention to the subject (Nuffield Foundation, 1947). In 1930, nevertheless, Priscilla Dodds, research assistant to the New Survey of London, interviewed several dozen pensioners in their homes in East London with a view to obtaining information about living conditions, daily budgets and attitudes towards various forms of support.[1] As the Departmental Committee on Old-Age Pensions had revealed, many subsisted on low-protein diets (Departmental Committee, 1919). Most knew few other old folk and some were visited only by sons and daughters, on whom they were part-dependent; many had bought no new clothes in ten years or more; some were 'inclined to plead poverty to all enquirers', frightened that any disclosure might disqualify them from receiving a full pension. This latter was rarely deemed satisfactory although many stated they 'would rather starve' than rely on the parish for support.

The flavour of Miss Dodds' remarks, meanwhile, resembled that of a Relieving Officer in their weighing up of motives and indexing of approval and disapproval. On the one hand, there were those who caused no moral qualms. Often they were ex-domestics, like Miss A., who was 'very superior and kept everything about her spotlessly clean'. But, on the other, we have:

> Miss S. [who] seemed to be rather a grubby woman. Her clothes were very, very untidy and not too well cared for. She said, however, that she always took care to go out looking neat and that I must not judge her by her morning clothes.... She said that she always buys a 1s.8d. bottle of Guinness each week, as when you get old you must have nourishing things: I rather wondered whether she drinks, as when I went in in the morning there was a large bottle of beer on the table.

Like many, however, this woman would not apply for help from the Public Assistance Committee whilst she had any savings (Llewellyn Smith, 1932). Indeed, such ordered ambiguities could find striking resonance amongst the elderly. One interviewee protested:

> There ought to be a system where the deserving poor get enough money to live on without having to go to the Public Assistance Committee with the thriftless part of the community.... those who really deserve more money rarely get it. The people who have been thoroughly hard-working all their lives find it very hard to swallow their pride and have to go down to the parish just as the lower types do. They are often told they do not need it [relief] as they are neatly dressed.... it is the better types of poor that suffer.

Popular Perceptions: Cartoons as Unwitting Testimony

Society at large appears to have stayed aloof to such niceties, popular press coverage tending to confirm Fielding's dictum that 'the suffering of the poor are, indeed, less observed than their misdeeds; not from any want of compassion but because they are less known' (Fielding, 1753). In 1909, the News of the World ran a story under the banner 'Pension Fraud - First Conviction Under New Act' (Golding and Middleton, 1982), whilst reviews of the New London Survey devoted at best a token paragraph to the chapter on old age. When 1,275,000 applications were lodged for the new supplementary pensions of 1940 (within the first three months of availability) instead of the expected maximum of 400,000, The Times leader thus talked of 'a remarkable discovery of secret need' (Deacon, 1981).

For the most part the tabloids represented old age as a phase characterised by infirmity, forgetfulness and semi-idiocy. A scan over Joe Lee's work for the Evening News illustrates how cartoonists codified the fears and resentments of the non-aged. For example, a 1934 sketch has a stooped old man with inordinately long beard and a stick peering over his spectacles at an ape behind bars. The caption reads, 'Excuse me, Sir, can you direct me to the chimpanzee's cage?'[2] Another shows an octogenarian in a bathchair being wheeled past Waite's statue 'Physical Energy' in Kensington Gardens. Wartime images, meanwhile, pillory Dad's Army and geriatric postmen on Penny Farthing bicycles. One has a vision of the artist's bottom drawer, labelled 'Old Fogeys' and filled with a series of cut-out stencils for rapid reference. Such caricatures do not exactly suggest a sublime gerontocracy. However, there were more sympathetic penmen, such as the Daily Mirror's Vicky, who parodied the minister in the likeness of Marie Antoinette, saying 'If they can't afford bread, why don't they eat statistics?' - a reference to the Radio Doctor's claim that the elderly ate increasingly more food. In another cartoon a bedraggled elderly couple huddle over a backdrop of slum tenements. The caption read 'We've got one consolation, dear, our plight's always on the mind of the Chancellor' [Parliament will debate old-age pensions on Wednesday]'. Vicky's messages come from the early 1950s and reflect an awakening concern. Nevertheless, the elderly are still presented as generally ravaged, shabbily-clad and undignified.

The Politics of Discontent

Clues to the pervasiveness of such a negative iconography may be found by studying the campaign literature of the two main pressure groups for the elderly, the National Conference on Old Age Pensions (which developed during the First World War) and the National Federation of Old Age Pensions Associations (which began just before the Second)[3] At the 1922 Conference, the secretary intimated that, 'there would have been considerably more OAPs present were it not for the fact that they had not respectable clothes to enable their attendance....they had no means to purchase them'. The plea for higher pensions nestled alongside the fight to abolish the means test, an inquisitional procedure and affront to self-respect, rendered yet more iniquitous by disentitlement to a full pension for those whose union or friendly society benefits exceeded the weekly limit. Their slogan ran 'Penalties on Thrift Must be Abolished. The Thrifty Aged Britishers Must be Protected'. Here, the morality of thrift and deservingness could be used as a weapon in the mobilization of moral outrage against Governmental hypocrisy. They canvassed their own constituents and produced Facts and Figures compendia. Postcards were sent to sitting members citing starvation statistics beneath the heading 'Does this mean anything to you?' The Federation later cited the weekly budgets of Miss Hope Less and Mr and Mrs Art Broke in their Open Letter to Parliament from John Pensioner. Their proverb read:

> The MP who shall use his endeavours to ease the lot of the old will be called blessed, but he who fails to take notice of their misery shall lose his seat and be cast into the outer darkness.

Thus, when the Blackburn Branch advised its members to vote for Barbara Castle and John Edwards in the 1945 General Election it was 'not because they are Labour candidates, but because they will support you'.

Stoddard makes the point that we can analyse popular conceptions of women, which treat all women alike, although we cannot effectively study the experience of women themselves as a group (Stoddard, 1983). The point bears repetition with regard to the old. If, as we have seen, the elderly sought to maintain lifelong class divergences and social distances amongst themselves, such fragmentation was, nonetheless, counterbalanced by solidarities which endeavoured to abolish rather than sharpen the boundaries of stigma. Alternatively, again, marginalised status itself provided a rallying point for negotiation. If the cartoons one discovers in The Pensioner - forerunner of today's Pensioners' Voice - continued to portray old people as raggedly impoverished, the visual shorthand operated in a context which used biting invective and political reasoning to explain it. In one sketch, from 1943, an emaciated old lady stands barefoot before the plump Means Test Man, smoking cigar and carrying a case monogrammed 'Snooper, Esq'. She is holding a pair of heavily patched bloomers while he retorts 'Rot woman! You don't want new ones - they won't show underneath - it's extravagance'. In another, a tousled old man is picking a dog-end from a gutter - the caption, 'Can the Brains Trust explain?' Such graphic statements clearly mocked the assumption that it was the fault of the elderly themselves, that they were degraded or dissolute.

Redrawing the Margins

In terms of the claim for adequate aid on the basis of want, old people had to legitimize their case. In stipulating the injustices which State doctrine perpetuated against 'thrifty aged Britishers', the National Conference were demanding recognition for the providential habits of a lifetime. It would be fallacious, then, to separate the old (or the young) from their own history. Victorian values such as thriftiness appear to have been less a legacy than a set of moral and material guidelines which they themselves had grown up with. The distinction between mass circulation press cartoons and pressure group propaganda lay in attitudes: on the one hand, we are presented with a social stereotype - a visual myth - on the other, a reworking of this negative symbolism to make a political point. Both drew on popular perceptions held by the non-aged.

It was more than mere ideology, however. The National Federation had the perspicacity to remind their leaders that 'one of the greatest mistakes an elector can make is to regard an MP as an expert'. They were by no means willing to grant power to those who could not further their cause or deliver the goods.To this extent, the active engagement of the elderly in shaping their own - and our future - destinies serves to illustrate that the social construction of old age is a process involving negotiation over rights and resources and not just a function of political economy or consensus management which assumes that all over 60 or 65 necessarily suffer in silence or isolation.

Notes

(1) Material drawn from The New Survey of London Life and Labour MSS Archive at the British Library of Political and Economic Science.
(2) All cartoons examined are housed in the Centre for the Study of Cartoons and Caricature, University of Kent.
(3) N.C.O.A.P. Reports and Pamphlets, 1916-1928, are available in the British Library; N.F.O.A.P.A. Miscellaneous material and The Pensioner (from February 1940) from Headquarters, Melling House, Blackburn.

References

Armstrong, D. (1983) Political Anatomy of the Body: Medical Knowledge in Britain in the Twentieth Century, Cambridge University Press, Cambridge.
Bosanquet, N. (1978) A Future for Old Age, Maurice Temple Smith, London.
Deacon, A. (1981) 'Thank You, God, for the Means-test Man', New Society, 25 June.
Departmental Committee on Old-Age Pensions (1919) Minutes of Evidence, Parliamentary Papers, Vol. 27.
Fielding, H. (1753) A Proposal for Making an Effectual Provision for the Poor, A. Miller, London.
Foner, N. (1984) Ages in Conflict: A Cross-Cultural Perspective on Inequality Between Old and Young, Columbia University Press, New York.
Golding, P. and Middleton, S. (1982) Images of Welfare: Press and Public Attitudes to Poverty, Blackwell, Oxford.
Haber, C. (1983) Beyond Sixty-Five: the Dilemma of Old Age in America's Past, Cambridge University Press, Cambridge.
Laslett, P. (1977) 'The History of Ageing and the Aged', in Family Life and Illicit Love in Earlier Generations, Cambridge University Press, Cambridge.
Llewellyn Smith, Sir H. (1932) The New Survey of London Life and Labour, Vol.III, Appendix, P.S. King and Son, London.
Macleod, I. (1961) Neville Chamberlain, Muller, London.
Mass-Observation (1948) Bulletin, New Series No. 21, Letchworth.
Nuffield Foundation (1947) Old People: Report of a Survey Committee on the Problems of Ageing and the Care of Old People, Oxford University Press, London.

Phillipson, C. (1982) Capitalism and the Construction of Old Age, Macmillan, London.

Political and Economic Planning (1934) P.E.P. Civic Division, An Outline of a Planned Employment Report, Political and Economic Planning Archives, WG 3/4 (British Library of Political and Economic Science).

Public Record Office (1924) file PIN 1/4, Neville Chamberlain to Duncan Fraser, 20 May.

Shegog, R.F.A. (ed.) (1981) The Impending Crisis of Old Age, Oxford University Press and Nuffield Provincial Hospitals Trust, Oxford.

Smith, R.M. (1984) 'The Structured Dependence of the Elderly as a Recent Development: Some Sceptical Historical Thought', Ageing and Society, Vol.4, Pt.4, December.

Stoddard, K. (1983) Saints and Sinners: Women and Aging in American Popular Film, Greenwood Press, Westport, Conn. and London.

Titmuss, R. and K. (1942) Parents Revolt, Secker and Warburg, London.

PART TWO : RESPONSES TO DEPENDENCY

PART TWO : Responses to Dependency

Chapter Nine

AGEISM, ENCOURAGEMENT AND REASSURANCE

IN PRE-RETIREMENT EDUCATION

Alastair Weir

Introduction : Some Early Examples of Ageism?

Robert Butler's term 'ageism' (Butler, 1969) has become all too familiar to us over the years – somewhat unfortunately, because as usually interpreted it refers exclusively to those prejudices held by the younger amongst us against the older. At least as important are the negative feelings held by the older against the younger, and against the youth culture in general. If indeed there is a valid generalisation which can be made about people over fifty, it is that virtually all of us detest the output of Radio 1!

If we revert to the more usual sense of the term ageism, we must recognise that not only are depressed and negative feelings about old age very general at the moment, but they almost always have been. Let me quote a few examples from some of the world's earliest literary traditions. Of uncertain date, but probably not as early as the almost five thousand years ago sometimes claimed for it, we find the Chinese source called 'The Yellow Emperor's Classic of Internal Medicine' (Veith, 1966), in which the following rather chilling comment appears:

> At the age of forty the emanations become smaller, he begins to lose his hair and his teeth to decay. At forty-eight his masculine vigour is reduced or exhausted; wrinkles appear on his face and the hair on his temples turns white. At fifty-six the force of his liver deteriorates, his muscles can no longer function properly, his secretion of semen is exhausted, his vitality diminishes, his kidneys deteriorate and his physical strength reaches its end. At sixty-four he loses his teeth and his hair.

And as if that weren't enough, later in the same study we find:

At the age of fifty the body grows heavy and the ears no longer hear well, nor is the vision of the eyes clear any longer and again At the age of sixty ... impotence sets in.

Is this to be regarded as an early example of rampant ageism - it certainly seems to have rather a smell of sexism clinging to it? And if not ageism, then what? The folk wisdom of the ancients? Let us turn for some shred of comfort to one of China's main competitors for the prize as the world's senior intellectual tradition - Egypt. Some 2600 years B.C., we find the chamberlain Ptah-hotep (Gunn, 1906), commenting to his Pharaoh as follows:

Oh Prince, my Lord, the end of life is at hand; old age descendeth upon me; feebleness cometh and childishness is renewed. He that is old lieth down in misery every day. The eyes are small; the ears are deaf. Energy is diminished, the heart hath no rest. The mouth is silent, and he speaketh no word; the heart stoppeth, and he remembereth not yesterday. The bones are painful throughout the body; good turneth into evil. All taste departeth. These things doeth old age for mankind, being evil in all things. The nose is stopped and he breatheth not for weakness, whether standing or sitting.

Even worse, isn't it? But surely if we turn to a tradition rather closer to our own, that of Classical Greece, we must turn up something a bit more encouraging ... and sure enough, in the beginning of Plato's Republic (Hamilton and Cairns, 1961), we find a conversation reflecting a more positive view of old age; material which Cicero was to plagiarise shamelessly in his De Senectute (Falconer, 1922). However, the depressed view was still active as well, as shown by the following, from Xenophon's account of the trial of Socrates (Fielding, 1910), in which he has the prisoner say:

... if my years are prolonged, I know that the frailties of old age will inevitably be realised, - that my vision must be less perfect and my hearing less keen, that I shall be slower to learn and more forgetful of what I have learned. If I perceive my decay and take to complaining, how.... could I any longer take pleasure in life?

A Comparison with the Present Day

So much for ancient Greece - but after all, that was two-and-a-half millenia ago, and even if today's general public hasn't altogether grown out of that kind of attitude, at least our professional gerontologists and geriatricians have - haven't they? There now follow two quotations, of which the first comes from a publication of the American Association for the Advancement of Science (Handler 1960) and the second from a paper in the Journal of Gerontology (Weber et al., 1983). The first defines ageing as follows:

> Ageing is the deterioration of a mature organism resulting from time-dependent, essentially irreversible changes intrinsic to all members of a species, such that, with the passage of time, they become increasingly unable to cope with the stresses of the environment, thereby increasing the probability of death.

Even as recently as 1983, the definition doesn't seem to have cheered up all that much. Now it runs:

> Ageing is a multifactorial phenomenon. It is characterised by a progressive deterioration in physical performance and an increasing tendency toward the development of degenerative diseases, including coronary heart disease, hypertension, stroke, diabetes and cancer.

Depressing Topics in Pre-Retirement Education

By this time, a question has surely raised itself in your mind - the question 'why?' Why rehearse this melancholy catalogue of afflictions? Why all these quotations, and above all, why in the context of pre-retirement education? After all, I presume that none of us in pre-retirement education would ever dream of using any of these sources when talking to one of our groups - I certainly have never done so. But the question which now raises itself in my mind is the converse one - 'why not?'

Perhaps it seems ridiculous even to ask this. After all, the obvious reason why we don't use this kind of material is that its effect is likely to be quite depressing, and we don't want to have that effect on the people in our courses. But this in turn raises the whole issue of what we are in fact trying to do to and for these people. As educators, we must learn continuously from our groups, but we must also give to them, and the problem is - give what? What are we trying to tell them about the post-retirement stage of life into which they are about to move? Simply as a basis for discussion, let's try an obvious solution - the truth, the whole truth and nothing but the truth.

Even at first sight, it is obvious that it will not work. For one thing, the whole truth is clearly impossible, even if we knew it, which we don't. We have to be selective, even from the material which we are sure of, and which we feel could be useful. Which of course raises in turn the problem of our criteria of selection - on what basis do we include or exclude material from the content which we wish to present? As we have already hinted, usefulness to the course member is one important consideration, and as research in this area suggests (see Phillipson and Strang, 1983) this involves an understanding of the particular needs and interests of the specific group of people with whom we are dealing. If we now proceed to the question 'usefulness for what?', the issue becomes rather more complex. People's earlier attitudes to retirement and old age may well have conformed to the depressing tradition of our initial quotations - it is clearly useful to them if they can be helped to modify these attitudes in favour of more positive ones. In such an effort, we are attempting to overcome the effects of thousands of years of woeful contemplation of the common phenomena of old age. The quotations with which we started have a strong factual basis; we can seek to combat the depression which these facts may produce, but we must never ignore them.

Reassurance Versus Encouragement

It is at this point that I feel that some writers on retirement and old age are in danger of confusing encouragement with reassurance. By reassurance I mean the bland, cosy suggestion that our troubles are all illusory and will melt away with little or no intervention on our part. By encouragement I mean literally the fostering of courage - helping people facing retirement to reach the conclusion that while post-retirement living will have its problems, a closer inspection shows that they are not so insuperable as they might appear, that a number of methods can be suggested for coping with many of them, and that individuals possess the personal resources to devise further techniques to suit their own lives.

As is obvious, I am pleading that pre-retirement educators should be more concerned with encouragement and spend less time on reassurance. In this context, a problem-centred approach to pre-retirement education seems not only feasible but actually preferable. How can we be encouraged to cope with the problems of later life unless they are clearly and unambiguously described? If we play down the problems and content ourselves with too much simple reassurance, our course may well look highly successful in terms of changed attitudes on the part of the participants. However, this attitude change may be highly fragile; when one of the problems which we have minimised or ignored crops up in the lives of our participants, they may not only find themselves unarmed against it, but may lose confidence in all the rest of the reassuring course content as well.

And worst of all, if we play down the problems and rely too much on simple reassurance, it seems to me that we are committing against older people the one unforgivable sin - that of infantilisation. We are treating them as people who, like young children, have to be protected and shielded from the harsh realities of life because they are incompetent to deal with them.

Dealing with Depressing Topics

If we accept that reassurance is not enough and that we should rely more on encouragement based on a clear statement of the problems, then obviously there can be no taboo topics. It may be that here, in the past, I personally may have gone rather too far. Largely at my instigation and with the aim of showing our participants of post-retirement life warts and all, the Scottish Retirement Council's courses included for many years a visit to a psychogeriatric ward. I think I am now about ready to stop apologising for this. It was predictably the most frequently criticised part of the course and attracted (if that is the right word) the highest rate of absenteeism. Yet I retain the strong suspicion that its failure, and mine, were due mainly to the fact that I was unable to ensure an appropriate preparation of the group for the visit. Even without such preparation, a sizeable minority of the group extracted from the visit precisely the kind of positive encouragement which I had intended.

To return to the main line of the argument, if I have set up the problem correctly, it is how to deal with what look like intrinsically depressing topics without inducing depression. This is clearly a difficult one, which I must confess I find myself rather more able to cope with orally than in writing. In the cold layout of the print, the more negative aspects of the situation seem to loom up more ominously and to be more difficult to exorcise.

Nevertheless, spoken or written, it should be possible to attain our aim. Let us take one of the seemingly most difficult topics to handle, and see how we might go about it. As part of my regular talk on mental health in retirement, I find it essential to say something about senile dementia. Suppose we attempt to list some of the encouraging things we can say on this topic, while of course also including an accurate description of the main symptoms:

(1) Senile dementia is not an inevitable accompaniment or result of growing old - it is an illness.

(2) Although it is age-related, it is possible to be senile at 30, or completely non-senile at 100.

(3) It has been estimated that only 4-5 per cent of the population will at any stage in their lives contract senile dementia.

(4) Even among those dying after the age of eighty, only

about one in three shows significant signs of brain deterioration.

(5) Although one of the main symptoms of senile dementia is a gross loss of immediate memory, this must not be confused with the increasing problem of memory retrieval which is a general, normal change in middle-aged people.

(6) Many or most cases of mental confusion in later life are not indicative of senile dementia, and are indeed reversible.

(7) This is true even when admission to a psychogeriatric hospital has taken place - the average time elapsing between admission to and discharge from many such hospitals is only a few weeks.

Persuasion and 'Knowing Better'

All of these statements can of course be supported by evidence. Nevertheless, in the context of a pre-retirement course with limited time at its disposal, they have to be presented inevitably as assertions to be accepted on the basis of authority. Making such statements involves two basic assumptions which seem rather dubious when stated explicitly. One is that the exercise is largely persuasive in nature, while the other is that we know what is good for people better than they do themselves. To which I can only reply that on the authority of the great linguist Karl Buhler (Buhler, 1934), all communication involves some element of persuasion, while (on no authority but my own) all education presumes that the educator knows more about something than do the people to be educated, and may as a result be able to reach conclusions which the course participants should know about, but which are different from those which they may have drawn for themselves. It may be undesirable for the educator to advocate the conclusions directly, but it seems irreproachable to place before the group the evidence on which the conclusions were based, and let them draw what inference they wish.

Conclusion

After all, in pre-retirement education, we do have the explicit aim of bringing about some change which we regard as improvement in the attitudes towards retirement held by our course participants. I have urged that we do so by means of encouragement rather than simple reassurance - encouragement based on a clear statement of the problems and difficulties involved. To work effectively on this basis is by no means easy, but I believe that we owe it to those in our pre-retirement groups to try; for if we rely unduly on reassurance, we are in danger of infantilising our groups, and that above all is to be scrupulously avoided.

References

Buhler, K. (1934) Sprachtheorie, Fischer, Jena.
Butler, R.N. (1969) 'Age-Ism', Gerontologist, 9, 243-246.
Ferguson, W.A. (transl.) (1923) Cicero: De Senectute, De Amicitia, De Divinatione, William Heinemann, London.
Fielding, S. (transl.) (1910) 'Apology, or the Defence of Socrates' in Socratic Discourses: Plato and Xenophon, J.M. Dent, London.
Gunn, B.G. (transl. and ed.) (1906) The Instruction of Ptah-Hotep and the Instruction of Ka'Gemni: The Oldest Books in the World, John Murray, London.
Hamilton, E. and Cairns, H. (eds.) (1961) The Collected Dialogues of Plato, Princeton University Press, Princeton.
Handler, P. (1960) 'Radiation and Aging' in N.W. Shock (ed.) Aging, 199-223, American Association for the Advancement of Science, Publ. No.65, Washington, D.C.
Phillipson, C. and Strang, P. (1983) The Impact of Pre-Retirement Education: A Longitudinal Evaluation, Department of Adult Education, University of Keele, Keele.
Veith, I. (transl. and ed.) (1966) Huang Ti nei ching su wen: The Yellow Emperor's Classic of Internal Medicine, University of California Press, Berkeley.
Weber, R., Bernard, J. and Roy, D. (1983) 'Effects of a High-Complex Fat Diet and Daily Exercise on Individuals 70 Years of Age and Older', Journal of Gerontology, 38, 2, 155-161.

Chapter Ten

AGEISM AWARENESS TRAINING : A MODEL FOR GROUP
WORK

Catherine Itzin

I. Ageism : The Theory

The purpose of this paper is to provide enough information
about the nature of ageism - what it is and how it affects
individuals - so that its effects can be eliminated as
systematically as they are acquired. It includes an
abbreviated account of the theory and practice used by the
author in ageism awareness workshops.

What is Ageism?

As with every other form of oppression - such as sexism or
racism or anti-semitism - ageism involves the systematic
mistreatment of individuals as members of groups (women,
blacks, Jews), reinforced by the structures of society. The
reasons for oppression are always (directly or indirectly)
economic - one group having access to money and power at
the expense of another group. But the capacity to maintain
oppression is primarily psychological. As with every other
form of oppression, ageism is therefore both institutionalised
in the structures of society (legal, medical, welfare,
educational, political and other such structures) and
internalised in the attitudes of individuals.
    Ageism is usually regarded as being something that
affects the lives of older people. Like ageing, however, it
affects every individual from birth onwards - at every stage
putting limits and constraints on experience, expectations,
relationships and opportunities. Its divisions are as arbitrary
as those of race, gender, class and religion. Thus the
chronology of ageing becomes the hierarchy of ageism.
    Ageism is a system in which nobody can be seen to
benefit because everyone is, or once was, a child, and
everyone (who survives) will eventually be an old person.
And yet the system - in which adults have rights and
privileges which are denied to young people and old people -

continues to the detriment of everyone.

Connections Between Ageism and Adultism

There are many parallels between the position of old people and young people in society. These serve to demonstrate the similar ways in which ageism is institutionalised and internalised both at the beginning and the end of the life-span.

Institutionalised ageism takes a variety of forms, but always includes the denial to old people of personal rights and the power to control one's own life. As part of this process of subordination, old people as a group are systematically treated as insignificant, unintelligent, incapable, inadequate, inferior: they are isolated, invisible and ignored. They are often regarded as stupid, boring, useless, helpless, pathetic - a burden on society, their lives less valued than those of adults. Feelings associated with old people include disgust, exasperation, embarrassment, anger. These are typical of the attitudes held about old people and which old people hold about themselves which constitute the internalised oppression.

The ageism institutionalised at the early (childhood) end of the life-span - which I refer to as adultism - involves a similar denial to children of rights and power to control their own lives. Like old people, children also are often regarded as difficult, boring, stupid, inferior, insignificant, helpless, a nuisance if not a burden. This is the internalised adultism - the attitudes people hold about children and that children come to hold about themselves. Both adultist and ageist attitudes are learned by everyone when they are members of the subordinate social group - children.

How Ageist Attitudes are Acquired

The process of learning any oppressive attitude is likely to be distressing. It is accomplished through the experience of invalidation (which is painful), receiving incorrect information or not receiving correct information (which is also painful), and through violence or threats of violence or the possibility of violence (even more obviously painful). Children themselves are invalidated, given misinformation about themselves and their world, and intimidated. They also see members of other oppressed groups treated in the same way. The process is painful because it hurts to be invalidated and misinformed. It hurts to be forced to give up and believe lies about oneself and other people. No-one would 'willingly' acquiesce in this process if they had any other option at the time. Children do not have the 'power' to resist because of their economic and emotional dependency on adults and the power of adults in their small lives.

115

Information is given through stereotypes, incorrect or biased history or demonstrations of violence against certain groups (women, blacks, Jews, working class people) in ways that persuade members of both the privileged and powerful (oppressor) groups and the under-privileged groups (oppressed and without power) that they deserve their position in society. This process creates low self-esteem, confusion and fear in everyone. These feelings - together with the feelings of hopelessness and powerlessness that would inevitably have also been internalised as a result of the giving up - are the glue that hold oppressive attitudes in place, and which prevent most people from taking action to change or eliminate the structures of oppression.

But what is learned can be unlearned. This is the premise of awareness training or 'unlearning oppression' work with individuals. Eliminating internalised oppression is (and always has been) an essential part of the process of ending institutionalised oppression.

II. Unlearning Ageism - The Practice in Theory

'Unlearning oppression' is not an intellectual or academic exercise. It involves an individual examination of personal experience and feeling - 'going back' to early years, remembering the incidents and events connected with acquiring the misinformation and 'reclaiming' the correct information, reliving the experience of invalidation and re-learning an appropriate sense of positive self-esteem, and 're-claiming the power' that was diminished or denied. It is an exciting and empowering process. It is a great relief to unburden oneself of attitudes, beliefs and feelings that were originally taken on unwillingly anyway, but it is also a process that inevitably involves 'facing feelings' that were uncomfortable and painful - and still are. It requires a considerable degree of 'safety' (i.e. freedom from any further possibility of invalidation, criticism, humiliation or intimidation) for people to be prepared to make themselves vulnerable to feeling those feelings again. Ageism awareness work therefore depends on a group agreeing certain working assumptions and making certain agreements.

Assumptions and Agreements

(1) The first assumption that is required in order to unlearn oppression is that all human beings are born 'fine'. I usually suggest that people adopt the point of view that human beings at birth are reasonably intelligent, loveable, eager to love, communicate with, be close to and co-operate with other people. The implication is that, whatever else happens to them, everyone remains essentially like this or retains the potential of being like

this.
(2) The second assumption is that everyone has always done
the best they could given their circumstances at any time
in their lives. This assumption draws on the theory
outlined above: namely, that the oppressive systems that
have operated in everyone's life will have influenced them
negatively against their will and better judgement;
therefore, negative attitudes and inappropriate behaviour
will have been acquired not only under pressure, but
with as much resistance as it was in the person's power
to muster at the time; and, finally, that no-one would
have succumbed without a 'struggle'.
(3) The third assumption follows on from the second: that it
is not the fault of any person that they acquired ageist
(or sexist or racist and anti-semitic) attitudes and
behaviour any more than it was their fault that they were
victims of adultism in the first place. Neither self-blame
nor being blamed is helpful or appropriate. It reinforces
the original hurt, and actually makes it more difficult to
take responsibility for holding (through no fault of one's
own) oppressive attitudes and eliminating them.
(4) The fourth and final assumption is that everyone is now
and always has been acting with the best possible
integrity. People often take objection to this assumption
and offer a lot of persuasive evidence of the people who
do not act with integrity. Hitler is one example most
frequently mentioned. But the assumption is based on
the belief that no matter how assaulted by invalidation,
misinformation and intimidation, and no matter how
irrationally and oppressively a person may behave, there
was, in the beginning, and still is at least the core of
inherent goodness or its possibility.
Anyone who would not be prepared to operate on these
assumptions, at least for the period of the work together as a
group, would find it difficult to participate.
     The safety required for an individual to unlearn
'oppressive' attitudes in a group also requires everyone
participating in a workshop to make certain basic agreements.
These are:
(1) **Confidentiality.** No-one ever repeats anything heard
from anyone else's personal disclosures during or after
the workshop unless they have received the prior consent
of that person.
(2) **Listening.** Everyone agrees to listen to each other with
complete respect and with good 'attention':
i.e. non-judgementally, with approval of them as a person
as distinct from their attitudes or behavioural patterns.
(3) **No Ridicule or Banter.** Though we have grown
accustomed to regard the 'lightness' of banter or ridicule
as trivial, it was a key element in the original childhood
experience of invalidation and humiliation. Safety

117

requires an agreement not to indulge in this or to subject anyone to it.

(4) **No Criticism or Critical Attacks.** Everyone agrees to refrain from criticising anyone else for what they say or do and from attacking anyone for their beliefs or behaviour, however 'wrong' we may know or feel them to be.

(5) **No 'Guilt Trips'.** Everyone must agree to forego blame and self-blame on the assumption of the fundamental integrity of every individual and also on the assumption that guilt reinforces inappropriate behaviour rather than alleviating it.

(6) **No Defence of Positions.** In addition to agreeing to refrain from any personal attacks, people must agree not to try to defend or justify their beliefs and behaviour.

(7) **Share Personal as well as Professional Selves.** This can feel difficult if people have come together as professionals or around an issue or area of work, but it is essential to eliminating oppressive attitudes because these are held by people personally. Just making the decision to do this is usually sufficient for it to happen with safety.

(8) **Hold the Aim or Goal to Change Beliefs, Attitudes and Practices.** It helps if everyone has agreed in advance on the need and value to change beliefs and behaviour and has the purposeful intention of changing personal and professional practice.

Having made these assumptions and agreements, an individual will be in an excellent position to relieve themselves of the burden of prejudice and collusion with discrimination with which their lives have been weighted. With the assistance of the group leader (who ideally should have some training or experience), they will be able to go through a process of:

- remembering the early, sometimes previously obscured, hurtful experiences;
- releasing the long-stored feelings and emotions that went with the experience (embarrassment, humiliation, grief, anger);
- re-evaluating the incident or experience and what was 'mis-learned' from it;
- revising their beliefs and behaviour in the light of new insights and understanding;
- deciding on different behaviour and practice (both personal and professional) for the future.

III. An Ageism Awareness Training Session - The Practice in Practice

The format of the group work is simple. Each participant is given the opportunity to think about and answer a series of questions which the workshop facilitator puts to each person in turn. It is essential that others in the group listen attentively and do not interrupt. The group leader needs to give particularly good 'attention' to the person 'thinking out loud' in front of the group and to make no comment about the answers. The 'correct' answer is whatever comes into the person's mind in response to the questions, and each participant needs full support and eager encouragement to 'trust their thoughts', to give them voice and to 'pursue' their thoughts - whatever they are and however irrelevant or trivial they may at first seem. The job of the group leader is therefore to draw out the person's thoughts in a direct and specific way - with questions like 'What was that thought? What were you thinking? What happened? What happened next? How did you feel about that?' or 'What was that like for you?' People always need assistance in 'catching' their first thoughts, 'trusting' them and feeling confident enough to 'speak' them.

It is essential that every person in the group has the opportunity to be asked each question with approximately equal time and attention to respond (even if much of their time is spent 'not knowing' or 'thinking of nothing').

Starting with the Age We Are

Question 1: How old are you?

The place to begin ageism awareness work is focussing attention on the age we are. The reason for this is that ageism makes people either want to forget their age or want to be some other age. Children are offered the carrot of more and more 'privileges' as they get older. They see older children and adults with opportunities denied to younger ones. They are often told 'When are you going to grow up and behave better?' or to 'Stop acting like a baby' - meaning they would be treated more respectfully if they were older or 'acted' older. As a consequence, it is almost universal for children to wish they were older than they are - to be looking forward to or longing for the next birthday, rather than relishing and delighting in the age they are.

In the 'middle' years, between twenty and forty, it is not uncommon for people to 'lose track' of the age they are. From the forties onwards, it is also common for people to wish they were younger or to conceal or lie about their age (especially women who are hit hardest by the combination of ageism and sexism). And, not only are the sheer numerical 'abundance' of years in the period from 65 to 90 lost in the catch-all category of 'elderly' but the very concept of quality of life has little meaning in much of this period. So simply to ask someone to state their age - with delight and pride of voice and physical posture - is an effective contradiction to the weight of ageism. It creates an opportunity to begin to unburden - in a fairly light way - the emotional tension people carry as a consequence.

The group leader will almost certainly need to demonstrate or to model how to do it. 'I'm 41' - spoken in a pleasant, self-satisfied tone of voice, with a smile, head 'held high'. Participants will need regular repetitions to remind them of the appropriate tone and posture. Doing this usually produces a lot of embarrassed laughter from everyone in a group. It is an 'ice-breaker', brings a sense of relief, and also a sense of connection with oneself. In some cases it has produced tears: for example, from older women who have the opportunity to let go of the 'worry' about people knowing their age and judging them negatively. And if someone finds it too difficult or impossible to say their age, as sometimes happens, that's fine. The point is to persist and continue to ask the question so people have the chance to put their attention on themselves and feel whatever feelings they have acquired in connection with their age. The point is not to go through the motions or to give a correct answer. The real point is to value ourselves as we are now whatever age we may be, and to recognise the value of doing so.

Question 2: What's good about being the age you are now?

Because of the way ageism operates, most people have never thought about themselves in this particular way. The reality is that even though we go round unaware of our age and what is good about it, there are many, many good aspects to being 7 or 17 or 27 or 37 or 47 or 57 or 67 or 77 or 87 or 97.

It is important that the group leader persists with repeating the question in an interested tone and with a look that communicates eagerness to hear the answer, assisting people to put words to anything that 'pops' into their heads until the thoughts start coming. They will. They always do - with patience, interest and good attention. Sometimes people start with 'nothing' i.e. saying they can think of nothing good, and then there is no stopping them. Everyone benefits from the mere opportunity to think in these terms, and most people start to beam and blossom with positive thoughts about themselves and their age which they have never thought of before.

Working on Adultism

The next stage of the awareness work - after everybody has had the chance to participate in the first stage - is to focus directly on childhood experience. The reason is that it was in childhood that everyone learned their ageist attitudes as well as negative attitudes about themselves. It was also the time when people internalised the feelings of powerlessness that stop them them now from feeling able to change themselves or social structures.

Question 3: What did you most enjoy about being a child?

Often it is not easy for people to be able to think immediately of what they enjoyed – they say 'nothing', or 'I can't remember'. Again the key is persistence, repeating the question and expecting to hear the details eventually. The reality is that everyone will have enjoyed something even from a very unhappy or particularly hurtful childhood.

Many people will have enjoyed much but, because of the way ageism operates, forgotten a lot. Each person should have- the opportunity to remember several things. Assistance in 'catching' first thoughts is important. This context of pleasant memories of positive experiences creates the basis from which people can be asked to remember, recall and reclaim the experiences which hurt them.

Question 4: What did you most hate about being a child?

People love this question in this context. At last someone wants to listen to what was hard for them as children. And what people say always paints the picture as it is experienced by children. 'I hated having to go to bed before my brothers and sisters, being talked down to, not being allowed to be angry with my parents, having to do piano lessons because my mother wanted it, being shouted at, being beaten, being ridiculed or made fun of, being criticised, having no privacy etc.' People automatically describe 'the oppression' of adultism when asked, what was difficult or hurtful about being a child.

Question 5: How did you manage, as a child, to 'outwit' the adults and to maintain your integrity?

The point is to remind people of the power they really did have as children (however limited), and the strategies they devised to survive. Again, the answers are usually quite accessible at this stage in the session and in the 'safety' of the context that has been established. 'I used to read in bed under the covers with a torch', 'I'd sit on the stairs and listen to the grownups talking about the things I was 'too young' to hear'. 'I locked my door and wouldn't let anyone in'. 'I had a secret place in the garden I'd go to'. 'I ran away from home'. 'I pulled the wings off butterflies'; 'I bullied my little brother'; 'I wouldn't let my father see me cry when he beat me'; 'I'd cry in my room under the pillow'; 'I had a fantasy world of best friends and heroic deeds', etc. These are typical of the 'powerful' things that people remember doing as children. They are often long-forgotten.

People love the experience of remembering all this, especially when encouraged to take real pride in how 'clever' they were. It is not uncommon for people to cry in safe groups while remembering these events – from grief about the distress they experienced in having to survive under such pressures when they were so small. But 'feeling feelings' – laughing away the old embarrassment and humiliation, and crying out some of the grief – are important parts of becoming 'aware' and are always a great relief when there is the safety to do so.

Question 6: What would you like to say now – with what you know from your position as an adult – to the little 'you' then?

The session on adultism ends with an invitation to each person to speak to their 'little selves'. It can seem an odd question, but people always respond easily and often with considerable release of emotion. The responses are sometimes in the vein of appreciations: 'Well done. Weren't you clever to have done that. What an amazing child you were.' These communications come with a surge of feeling of previously unappreciated self-appreciation. 'I had no idea how clever I really was. I didn't know how strong I really was'. Another vein is of great sympathy. 'Poor you. How awful it must have been for you. How lonely you must have been.' There are insights into just how 'hurt' we often were and they can come with considerable grief.

Another typical vein of response is real indignation. 'How dare they do that to you. How could they! What were they trying to do? Couldn't they see how lonely/frightened/confused/ you were?' And the feelings that come up here are usually the deep, long-suppressed anger that would have been felt at the time. The job of the group leader is to encourage people to feel the anger and to reassure them that it is all right to raise their voices and actually say – how dare you! – in an angry tone of voice, and even to shake and tremble and perhaps even sweat a bit in the process. 'Cathartic' is a good word to describe the effect of these sessions – and 'catharsis' is precisely what is needed given the 'hurts' people have experienced and the hold the suppressed feelings and obscured memories have had on their lives.

Working on Ageism

Question 7: What do you like about old people?

The aim of this question is to assist people to think about the reality of being old and of old people which is obscured by the stereotypes. Because the stereotypes have such an overwhelming influence, people usually find it difficult to think of anything in response to the question in this form. So I fairly quickly go onto the same question in another form.

Question 8: Tell us about an old person you have been close to and what you have liked about them.

This is easier. People usually have no trouble in thinking of members of their family or of friends who are old whom they like and love and are close to. They should be given plenty of time and encouragement to describe one of the relationships in detail, describing the person and what they have liked and valued about them and their relationship.

Question 9: What can't you stand about old people?

In the context of the 'reality' of old people and our relationships with them, established in the previous questions and answers, it is vital to have the opportunity and safety to bring out the oppressive 'junk' we have all accumulated and internalised - the misinformation, the stereotypes, the negative feelings and our fears. In a good session, I have seen people able to admit the feelings of distaste, disgust, exasperation, fear and anger that everyone will inevitably have acquired. In the process, it is possible to get rid of some of these feelings, and also the feelings of shame and humiliation people feel for having been forced to adopt these attitudes in the first place. It is very important to remind people at this stage that it is not their fault they have acquired these attitudes and to reassure them that it is fine to acknowledge the negative feelings. The real fear that people have of old people and their fear of themselves growing old becomes apparent at this stage, and leads to the next question.

Question 10: What is your greatest fear about growing old (or older) or being old?

At this point, this is the easiest question of all. People usually have easy access to their fears by this stage in the session, and are relieved to be able to voice them. What people fear is what they despise. They fear the loss of looks and vigour, sexuality and sexual activity, degenerative disease and ill health, being helpless, pathetic, a burden, a nuisance, getting in the way, loss of independence - being despised in their turn. The relief of getting all this out in the open is tremendous.

Question 11: How should it be, for you, when you are old?

If this is difficult, the group leader can ask people to imagine how it should be in an ideal world. The following is a list of comments that came from an Ageism Awareness Workshop with a group of Health Workers who worked with elderly people: 'We should have exercise, outings, clubs to meet people, friends, family, good health, wealth, respect, work. We should be part of the community - be able to help other people as well as be helped by them. Be active, to be able to get around, independent, financially independent, have a decent standard of living, do what we want to do, do things for ourselves. Dignity'. A picture of possibilities begins to emerge: a vision of the way life would be without the oppression of ageism.

Question 12: What would you like to say to your older 'future self' from where you stand now?

The aim is to continue to connect people with the possibilities and their power to change the system. Answers are often in the vein of - 'It doesn't have to be as bad as you fear. I'll make it better for you. Don't worry. You can make sure it's what you want. It's not going to happen to you'. This leads directly on to the final questions in the awareness work, directed at changing practice and structures - the 'what are you going to do?' questions.

Question 13: If there were no adultism or ageism, if you were confident and without fear, how would your relations with old people be different now?

People love this question and they imagine lots of old people for friends, being open, friendly, making contact, asking old people how they feel, asking them about their lives, being physically close and affectionate, visiting old people in homes and hospitals, visiting old people in their own families etc. There are often feelings of excitement and hopefulness.

Deciding to Change

Question 14: What specific changes in a relationship with one or more old people would you like to make from this point on?

People not only need the opportunity to become aware of themselves and their attitudes, and to acquire new insights, but assistance in making decisions about changes and in acting on those decisions. This is one kind of question that helps people to make decisions: 'To visit elderly Mrs.

so-and-so next door, to spend more time with parents or grandparents, to move nearer to an elderly parent, to invite an elderly parent to move in or nearer, to talk to the old man in the park' etc. The internalised oppression always pulls people to mean well but leaves barriers to action (the powerlessness) , so I ask people to be specific: Who? How? When? Where? How often? Starting when? I then ask them to make a commitment to act on their decision.

Question 15: What is one thing you are going to do to change ageist practices in your workplace and the structures of ageism in your profession or in society?

The goal of any 'oppression awareness' work must be to change policy and practice. Changing oppressive structures and assisting others to change the oppressive conditions of their lives is inter-dependent on changing attitudes. Ageism awareness work can and should be used as the basis for deciding on different, less oppressive ways of working. And, as eliminating internalised ageism is an essential stop in eliminating institutionalised ageism (they go hand in hand), awareness work should also be used as the basis for deciding on goals, working out strategies and then acting on them, individually and collectively.

Conclusion

The last question is not one for a group necessarily, but for ourselves: Why bother? People's initial response to doing this kind of work varies, though it is often much the same whether it is racism, sexism or ageism. 'Oh no, not something else we have to think about and feel bad about', 'I have never been aware of it before, why should I start now?' Or, 'I get on just fine with old people - or men or black people. It's not a problem for me. I am happy as I am. What difference will it make? It won't change anything 'out there'. I might change myself, but society will never change.' Or, 'What do feelings and attitudes have to do with class struggle or women's or black liberation? What we need to do is 'fight the enemy' (i.e. men, whites, middle/ruling class)'.

My answer is simple. There is the 'enemy without' (the oppressive system) and the 'enemy within' (how the oppressive systems have affected individuals from birth onwards). Tackle the enemy within and we become increasingly effective at tackling the enemy without.

Oppression (whether racism, sexism, classism or ageism) is big and overwhelming. Pretending it is not there - or even being 'unaware' of it - does not mean it is not there, hurting us all the time, limiting our lives daily. Becoming increasingly aware may be uncomfortable and as we move from numbness to awareness (taking care to avoid the trap of guilt), we may well feel some of the hopelessness ('it is all too much') as well as the powerlessness ('there is nothing I can do'). But these feelings are not the best measure of the value of the exercise, for the oppression is there regardless of what we do or do not feel about it. Awareness is knowledge and knowledge is power. The difference that awareness makes (the discomfort does not last) is to put us in a position to choose to change the oppressive system and how it affects us and others. That cannot be bad!

Chapter Eleven

'BY' THE COMMUNITY : AN IDEOLOGICAL RESPONSE
TO THE CRISIS IN THE WELFARE STATE?

Janet Henderson

Introduction

This paper attempts to provide a Marxist approach to the
welfare state. It considers the welfare state's function as a
mechanism of social control and the main political, economic
and ideological dimensions. This paper tries to go beyond
traditional Marxist perspectives on welfare, highlighting the
way in which the state prescribes particular patterns of
responsibilities and dependencies within the family. Specific
examples are given, from the author's own research, of family
care for older people.

The Welfare State in Crisis

At a time of economic recession, the welfare state faces major
contradictions. The provision of goods and services is being
challenged by a growth in consumption which is out-stripping
supply; at the same time there is a growing public awareness
that the increase in provision of services is not resulting in a
commensurate improvement in the area of health and social
services (Crawford, 1977; Navarro, 1978; Doyal and Pennel,
1979; Graham, 1979; Iliffe, 1983). In the words of Crawford:
'These contradictions produce a crisis which is at once
economic, political and ideological, and which requires
responses to destabilising conditions in each of these spheres'
(Crawford, 1977, p.663). Although Crawford is discussing
the provision of health services, his analysis is applicable to
the field of social care generally. In this paper, I assess
how governments in Britain have responded to the crisis,
focusing, in particular, on community care policy.

State Responses to the Crisis

With the end of the expansionary period of the 1960s and the
growing economic crisis of the 1970s and 1980s, an ideological

response emerged which attacked the notion of 'rights' to welfare and focused instead, on notions of individual and community responsibility. Initially, this response was based upon an ideology of prevention, particularly applicable in the field of health where the promotion of the concept of individual responsibility for one's state of health linked strongly with the predominant medical model. This model assumed causality and solution on an individual basis rather than in terms of socio-enonomic determinants of health and disease (Doyal and Pennel, 1979). In social care generally, the preventive ideology promoted a concept of individual behaviour which directed attention away from structural determinism to individual causality; it emphasised personal responsibility and, further, implied that the individual had the power and autonomy to take and to carry out decisions which affected his/her life-style. In emphasising individual responsibility, the preventive ideology legitimised and enabled an economic response in the 1970s in the form of reductions in social expenditure, for it followed that if individuals could do more, the state could do less.

But this represented a devaluation of the existing role of families, and particularly women, within the welfare state. For the welfare state has been developed and directed on the basis that families assume primary responsibilities for their members based upon a gender division of labour. As Moroney states: 'The entire structure of the 'Welfare State' as it has evolved depends on a set of implicit and explicit assumptions concerning the responsibility which families assume, or are expected to assume, for their members and the conditions under which this responsibility must be either shared with or taken over by society through its public or voluntary organisations' (Moroney, 1976, p.4).

With the emergence of Thatcherism, came a basic questioning of the provision of social care services. Unlike the older form of Conservatism, this philosophy challenges the very concept of a welfare state and regards this form of state intervention in the family as damaging to individual liberty; it reaffirms the objections to provision of services first stated by nineteenth century Liberals (Jordan, 1976; Rose and Rose, 1982). This ideology not only encourages belief in causality and solution of social care problems on an individual basis, but actively seeks to reinforce assumptions that social welfare provision is morally unacceptable. As a result, the dismantling of the welfare state and the concomitant increased cuts in expenditure are presented as a virtue rather than a necessary vice: the government is provided with an economic and political response to the crisis which is justified by an ideology to which it is already committed.

The new right do not acknowledge the welfare state as necessary for the maintenance of capitalist society; instead, they see such expenditure in terms of 'social consumption' rather than 'social investment' (O'Connor, cited in Gough, 1979, p.51) and ignore the return flow of state benefits and services to the private or market sector (Gough, 1979). Ideologically, the need for the welfare state's function of maintaining social harmony is obviated both by an increase in coercion (Navarro, 1976; Rose and Rose, 1982), and by the reinforcement and reproduction of assumptions regarding women's responsibilities within the family. The latter is achieved by a focus on the informal economy of welfare, relying on the notion of the family as the 'natural' unit of protection. The new right focus thus denotes a break with the apparent consensus on the need for welfare provision which had existed among the major political parties since the 1940s. However, Moroney (1976) questions whether there really was a consensus on welfare in the post-war period. He suggests that fundamental differences were regarded as relatively unimportant in an expansionary period, or that consensus was held together by a tenuous bond that only began to come apart when the economic situation was reversed. Thus he states that the pattern up to the 1970s (and, I would argue, the 1980s) would suggest that ideological disagreements have a tendency to become more important in times of economic crisis and are used to defend or attack existing or proposed courses of action.

'By' the Community : An Ideological Response?

Certainly this has been the case in the re-emphasis of the concept of community care which has provided an ideal context for the ideological responses of governments in the 1970s and 1980s, particularly of the new right. As Walker indicates, community care is not in itself of course a recent development, but has been a main focus of policy interest for successive governments since the immediate post-war period (Walker, 1982, pp.14-15). It can be argued that the principle of shifting care from long-stay institutions to the community has been a feature of post-war social policy and 'community care' a well-established priority.

But the ideology of prevention emergent in the 1970s gave a new significance to the concept of community care. This period brought a plethora of discussion and consultative documents and white papers (Priorities for Health and Personal Social Services in England, 1976; Prevention and Health: Everybody's Business, 1976; A Happier Old Age, 1978; Care in the Community: A Consultative Document on Moving Resources for Care in England, 1981; Growing Older, 1981; Report of a Study on Community Care, 1981; Care in Action: A Handbook of Policies and Priorities for Health and Personal Social Services in England, 1981). These publications on community care differed from earlier ones in that they epitomised the translation of preventive ideology into policy statements. To some extent, this shift has been recognised in debate and much attention has been concentrated upon progression from care 'in' the community to care 'by' the community (Bayley, 1973). The former, basically, is described by Abrams (1978) as services provided in residential, but relatively open settings - the deliberately constructed 'caring community' and services provided through the placing of professional and specialist personnel 'in the community'. This is contrasted with 'community care' which, as defined, corresponds with care 'by the community' and consists of services provided in their own locality by lay/non-specialist persons on a voluntary and quasi-organised basis. It is these latter definitions which appear to have been officially accepted, at least over the last decade. For example, in Growing Older it is stated '.... the primary sources of support and care for elderly people are informal and voluntary. These spring from the personal ties of kinship, friendship and neighbourhood. They are irreplaceable. It is the role of public authorities to sustain, and, where necessary, develop - but never to displace - such support and care. Care in the community must increasingly mean care by the community.' (DHSS, 1981, para. 1.9). Similarly, the Barclay Report (1982) emphasised partnership between the personal social services and the 'community' in which the latter is equated with 'informal care'.

But to a large extent the product of the continuing debate would appear to be no more than identification of the family as increasingly having primary responsibility for community care. The definition of what constitutes community care in terms of its nature and content or practice of care remains ambiguous and vague. This is acknowledged even by the DHSS, which refers to 'the need to specify what is meant by 'community care' on each occasion rather than using it as an easy catch-all phrase' (DHSS Report of a Study on Community Care, 1981, para.2.1). So the DHSS are aware of and acknowledge differing definitions and their uses; the result is the publication of documents and recommendations of policies without properly defined terms.

Implications for Community Care

I would argue that the significance of the debates over meaning is that, first, to a large extent they concentrate attention upon economic and political issues of resources in terms of identification of needs and quantification of resources to meet those needs, and secondly, by doing so obscure and divert attention from the ideological reasons underlying the process of a shift from 'in' to 'by'.

(a) Economic and Political Issues of Resources

The resource issue in itself seems a reasonable exercise, except for the fact that it both ignores the underlying question concerning viability of transfer of resources, and restricts the focus of costing to the direct and viable costs to the formal economy in the form of the social care services.

To take the issue of viability first, it could be argued that even were resources to be increased, it would serve only to reinforce the existing pattern of class and professional controls which determine the priorities in social care systems. This has obvious implications for the economic and political response to the crisis in terms of the distribution of resources, and the determination of priorities in relation both to allocations of public expenditure and within public expenditure. With regard to the health services, for example, resources are concentrated in major investment areas such as high technology medicine and the pharmaceutical industry. Given the background of previous policy statements of the DHSS regarding transition of resources to the 'cinderella' services, there is little evidence to indicate that these are being translated into action. The consultative document Priorities for the Health and Social Services was an attempt to establish expenditure priorities and to denote promotion of services for the elderly, the mentally and physically handicapped and 'preventive' services. But at the time, expenditure in those areas was actually decreasing and the proposed change in emphasis away from general acute hospital services would have had 'little effect on the people who are presently in receipt of the poorest services' (Radical Statistics Health Group, 1976, p.4).

More recently, Walker has demonstrated that targets for the provision of domiciliary services have never come even close to being achieved. On the contrary, statistics indicate that within local authority personal services over the period 1974-81, the proportion of expenditure provided to residential as opposed to community care actually increased slightly (Walker, 1982, pp.20-21).

On the second issue of the true nature of costs, community care has been presented as a method of reducing expenditure by redistributing resources from hospital services towards cheaper primary care services, and at the same time making the use of resources more cost effective by concentrating services to where benefits are likely to be greater (Graham, 1979). For example, the Consultative Document on resources referred to 'good reasons for believing' that transference of people from hospital results in lower cost and better value (Care in the Community: A Consultative Document on Moving Resources for Care in England, 1981, para. 3.7). But low cost is only feasible if based upon the direct and visible costs to the social care services. Evidence indicates that there is a failure to assess the real costs of community care. These problems have not been addressed in policy-making. They are, however, increasingly being raised by women themselves and by academics with a feminist approach and awareness (Macintyre, 1977; Finch and Groves, 1983; Green, Creese and Kaufert, 1979; Nissel and Bonnerjea, 1982). They have indicated that the costs of care should include the cost to families in economic, social, emotional, psychological and physical terms. It is also argued that in emphasising the importance of families' responsibility for care, policies are reinforcing assumptions, not only about the primary responsibility of the family, but also about the gender division of labour in caring. Studies have shown that the prescription of particular patterns of gender responsibilities and dependencies within the family has meant that women have always played the major role in caring (Hunt, 1968, 1970, 1978; Shanas, 1968; EOC, 1980, 1982a, 1982b; Nissel and Bonnerjea, 1982; Family Policies Centre, 1984).

(b) Ideological Issues in the Shift from 'In' to 'By' the Community

As argued above, political and economic debates around resources obscure the ideological rationale behind the shift in emphasis from 'in' to 'by' the community. Increasingly, for example, the debate on resources is tied up with official concern to stimulate 'family care'. In earlier community care publications, resources were seen in terms of social care services provided through the placing of professional and specialist personnel and institutions in the community. For example, the Ministry of Health in 1963 stated 'where illness or disability nevertheless occurs, their [the health and welfare services] aim is to provide care in the community - at home, at centres or where necessary, in residential accommodation - for all who do not require the types of treatment and care which can be given only in hospitals. Care in the community provided through the health and welfare services supports, and is supported by the medical care given by the general practitioner (Ministry of Health, 1963).

But since the 1970s, government publications have increasingly made explicit the ideology of individual responsibility in respect of community care and made crucial to the viability of such care the role of families and support networks within neighbourhoods and voluntary agencies. The general principles on which the White Paper on Better Services for the Mentally Handicapped (DHSS, 1971) were based, referred specifically to 'understanding and help from friends and neighbours and from the community at large' to help the family (para. 40, (xv)), although there was still emphasis on 'the availability of someone, usually the social worker, from whom they can expect understanding and help to meet any situation' (para. 145).

In the documents published in the post-1979 era, the relative emphasis on formal/informal services has been somewhat altered. The principle is no longer one of formal services supported by individual/neighbourhood responsibility, but one which envisages a peripheral role in certain restricted spheres for the health and social services. 'By the community' is a definition promoting community care as a lay alternative to formal services 'in the community', and is grounded in a philosophy which promotes the merits of individual and neighbourhood responsibility. When community care is defined in this way and no longer regarded as integral to the welfare state, it can be used on an ideological level to legitimise the reduction or absence of state support, and on a political and economic level to justify public expenditure cuts in areas of least resistance whilst maintaining expenditure where the interests of capital are paramount. In line with this, the White Paper 'Growing Older' asserts that:

> The Government sees the primary role of the public services as an enabling one, helping people to care for themselves and their families by providing a framework of support. Only a small minority of elderly people is in receipt of these services at any one time. This could not be otherwise, since it would be quite unrealistic for them to assume responsibility for total support, and unwelcome to most elderly people. Some kinds of help can only clearly be provided by appropriately trained staff, but it is essential that scarce professional skills should be reserved for the circumstances in which they can provide care and treatment not otherwise available (DHSS, 1981.)

Community care – or Women's Care?

To promote an ideology which encourages the reduction of state support is to ignore the fact that families, and particularly women, are already assuming primary responsibilities for their members. Even with the inception of the post-war welfare state, the primary responsibility for caring has always been rooted in the family. As Walker indicates in relation to informal care: 'The state has done very little actively to support these caring efforts by families. For the most part it has been content to remain passive, while legitimating this course through the ideological assumptions that it is 'natural' for family members to provide care to dependents, and especially 'natural' for women to do so' (Walker, 1982, p.25).

The net result of community care policies of the late 1970s and 1980s may be regarded as essentially the explicit acknowledgement and approval of the furtherance of women's responsibility in caring for family members. Their viability rests upon the promotion of a fundamental ideology that families, as the primary 'natural' unit of society, provide the 'best' form of care, and have a moral responsibility to do so. Studies show that carers in many cases respond to this ideology. (Green, Creese and Kaufert, 1979; Sinclair, Levin, Neill and Williams, 1983).

My own research[1] supports these findings: women do in many cases articulate the assumptions regarding family responsibility which are contained in community care documents. They accept an ideology of the family which defines gender-specific responsibilities and dependencies in relation to family members and which dictates that through those responsibilities and dependencies women assume the primary role in caring. Carers could not perceive an alternative. In the words of one carer 'People will [care] because they like to think that their own won't be like that and who is going to say 'no' to their own?' As another carer stated in relation to her mother: 'It's just that I've never left, even at the worst moments, because I've felt that certain amount of responsibility and I still feel that'. Another carer, who had suffered from a major disease for several years and was really caring for her sick husband, said of taking on the responsibility of caring for her father 'What else could I have done? I think if you've been in my position you'd have done the same'. And yet another stated 'I don't know how anybody else copes but it's just something you've got to do'. Caring responsibilities were focused upon daughters rather than sons on the assumptions that sons were unable to care and daughters-in-law were not blood kin and therefore not 'eligible' to care. One dependent woman who lived next door to her son and a few doors away from her daughter remarked 'It's a good job my daughter lives so near as I don't know how I'd go on without her'. Another woman said of her two sons who had lived locally: 'They come when they can, you can't expect them to come regular though'. This same woman also had a son living with her, but in relation to caring she mentioned only her daughter who lived a few streets away.

But carers' acceptance of this ideology does not in itself provide that ideology's justification. I would challenge the ideology on two grounds: first, that whilst carers accept caring as their responsibility, they do not always do so willingly. In this situation, the ideology of individual responsibility simply reinforces feelings of guilt and failure, whatever the reasons for refusal or inability to care. One carer, despite saying that 'We cannot live like that with rows every day and tears' suffered from sleeplessness at agreeing to intermittent care. Another stated in relation to having a week's break 'If I made her go [into a home] I'd feel so guilty it would make me poorly, that's what I think'. One carer said 'I know I shouldn't be doing it, I don't even enjoy doing it.... It wouldn't bother me if he had to go now because I've got used to not feeling guilty'. But she still could not make the final decision not to care in her own home despite the justification she identified in her own health problems. Secondly, for several carers and their dependents, caring is an isolated and isolating relationship. My research suggests that invariably one child emerges as the obvious carer, often because of a particular tie with her mother relating back to a significant event in childhood such as serious illness; the carer is often caring in relative isolation or with the aid of a spouse. Where there is additional support, it comes from families, or exceptionally as in the case of an unmarried child caring, from friends and neighbours. But such support, from whatever source, is marginal: the core of caring is the responsibility of one person. Such absence of support has obvious implications for a policy which acknowledges the need for relatives, friends, neighbours and voluntary organisations as a mainstay of carers. It challenges the concept of 'natural support networks' (DHSS, 1981d) as corollaries to family units and thus begs the question of viability of care 'by' the community.

The explanation of isolation may be simple - if someone is identified as responsible, others do not perceive the caring task as theirs. I would suggest a further element which has not been recognised in policies - the issue as to whether support networks would in fact be acceptable to the carer and the recipient of the care. For even among families where there is conflict over the lack of support received, it is evident that judgements are made by the principal carer on other members' competence to care. Comments were made such as 'She's not homely like V....' and 'She's too fussy and my mother would have interrupted her timing and routine of things'. With regard to friends, neighbours and voluntary services, there are additional implications, although the outcome - the isolation of the carer - is the same. There either is a very real reluctance to involve others except on a crisis/peripheral basis, or the absence of consideration of this point, for there is a strong articulation among carers of the principle that the family (and usually a woman) should be the primary source of care and responsibility for dependent members.

Conclusion

Both carers and cared for are locked into an existence over which they have little control or choice. As one carer in a recent television programme expressed it: 'It's rather like house arrest, like being a prisoner of conscience' for 'far too

By' the Community

much is expected of individual carers' ('From the Cradle to the Grave', Yorkshire Television, 5 August, 1985). Yet women do care and will no doubt continue their 'labour of love' (Finch and Groves, 1983).

Caring presents both practical and moral dilemmas: practical in that much of caring involves intimate tasks and relationships onto which it is problematic to superimpose support. The dilemma is moral in that carers and cared for have an engrained sense of the family's responsibility for caring; as a result they have an implicit reluctance to request and receive help on a basis other than reciprocal. Ideologically, social policies have been based upon an implicit model of the family as private and in need of protection of its present pattern of gender responsibilities and dependencies. This has enabled the presentation of social policies as non-interventionist and protectionist in relation to the family. Community care policies, in emphasising individual responsibility reinforce notions of self-reliance and privacy within the family and reflect the dominant ideology within social policies. But in reality social policies, including community care policies, directly interfere in the family and represent a form of social control and sanction over women by pushing them back within the domestic sphere and discouraging or preventing their labour market activities (Land, 1978; Land and Parker, 1978; Finch and Groves, 1980; Walker, 1982, 1983; Ungerson, 1983). Community care policies, in shifting the emphasis from 'in' to 'by' the community serve as an indication and reflection of the state's response to the crisis, which is to shift the burden of care towards women. There is an implicit recognition of the state's dependency on women to bolster its limited caring activities. This dependency is justified by assumptions of wider networks of friends, neighbours and relatives to give support to women. These assumptions can only be rationalised in terms of identifying the 'natural support networks' as extensions to the family. But such a rationalisation is paradoxical to an ideology which stresses privacy and protection of families. As Judith Oliver has stated 'Community goodwill is not the answer' (From the Cradle to the Grave). The solution must surely rest with some form of state action, yet community care as envisaged currently by policy-makers does not offer even a palliative.

Notes

(1) My current research arises from concern with the attempt in current community policies to legitimise the care of the intergenerational elderly within families and the consequences of this for the carers. I am attempting to develop the conceptualisation of caring to clarify whether carers articulate

the assumptions contained within policies, and whether family
care is, ipso facto, 'better' for elderly people.

References

Abrams, P. (1977) 'Community Care: Some Research Problems
    and Priorities', Policy and Politics, Vol6(2), pp.125-151.
Barclay, P.M. (Chairman) (1982) 'Social Workers: Their Role
    and Tasks', Report of a Working Party set up by the
    National Institute for Social Work, Bedford Square Press
    of the National Council for Voluntary Organisations.
Bayley, M. (1973) Mental Handicap and Community Care,
    Routledge and Kegan Paul.
Crawford, R. (1977) 'You are Dangerous to your Health: the
    Ideology and Politics of Victim-Blaming', International
    Journal of Health Services, Vol.7, No.4, pp.663-680.
Curtis, M. (Chairman) (1946) The Report of the Care of
    Children Committee, Cmnd. 6922.
Department of Health and Social Security (1976a) Prevention
    and Health: Everybody's Business, HMSO.
Department of Health and Social Security (1976b) Priorities
    for Health and Personal Social Services in England,
    HMSO.
Department of Health and Social Security (1978) A Happier
    Old Age, HMSO.
Department of Health and Social Security (1981a) Care in
    Action: A Handbook of Policies and Priorities for the
    Health and Social Services in England, HMSO.
Department of Health and Social Security (1981b) Care in the
    Community: A Consultative Document on Moving
    Resources for Care in England, HMSO.
Department of Health and Social Security (1981c) Growing
    Older, Cmnd. 8173, HMSO.
Department of Health and Social Security (1981d) Report of a
    Study of Community Care, HMSO.
Department of Health and Social Security and Welsh Office
    (1971) Better Services for the Mentally Handicapped,
    Cmnd. 4683, HMSO.
Doyal, L. and Pennel, I. (1979) The Political Economy of
    Health, Pluto Press, London.
Equal Opportunities Commission (1980) The Experience of
    Caring for Elderly and Handicapped Dependents, a
    survey report, EOC, Manchester.
Equal Opportunities Commission (1982a) Caring for the Elderly
    and Handicapped: Community Care Policies and Women's
    Lives, EOC, Manchester.
Equal Opportunities Commission (1982b) Who Cares for the
    Carers? Opportunities for those Caring for the Elderly
    and Handicapped, EOC, Manchester.

Family Policy Studies Centre (1984) The Forgotten Army: Family Care and Elderly People, Family Policy Studies Centre.

Finch, J. and Groves, D. (1980) 'Community Care and the Family: A Case for Equal Opportunities', Journal of Social Policy, Vol.9, No.4, pp.487-514.

Finch, J. and Groves, D. (eds.) (1983) A Labour of Love: Women, Work and Caring, Routledge and Kegan Paul, London.

Garmikov, E., Morgan, D., Purvis, J. and Taylorson, D. (1983), The Public and the Private, Heinemann Educational Books, London.

Goffman, E. (1968) Asylums: Essays on the Social Situation of Mental Patients and Other Inmates, Penguin.

Gough, I. (1976) The Political Economy of Welfare, Macmillan, London.

Graham, H. (1979) 'Prevention and Health: Every Mother's Business', in Harris, C. et al. (eds.) The Society of the Family: New Directions for Britain, Sociological Review Monograph 28.

Green S., Creese, A. and Kaufert, J. (1979) 'Social Support and Government Policy on Services for the Elderly', Social Policy and Administration, Vol.13, No.3, Autumn, pp.210-218.

Hunt, A. (1968) A Survey of Women's Employment, OPCS, HMSO.

Hunt, A. (1970) The Home Help in England and Wales, HMSO.

Hunt, A. (1978) The Elderly at Home, OPCS, HMSO.

Jordan, B. (1976) Freedom and the Welfare State, Routledge and Kegan Paul. London.

Land, H. (1978) 'Who Cares for the Family?', Journal of Social Policy, Vol.7, No.3, pp.357-384.

Land, H. and Parker, R. (1978) 'Implicit and Reluctant Family Policy - United Kingdom', in Kamerman, S.B. and Kahn, A.J. (eds.) Family Policy: Government and Families in Fourteen Countries, Columbia University Press, New York.

Macintyre, S. (1977) 'Old Age as a Social Problem', in Dingwall R., Heath, C., Reid, M. and Stacey, M. (eds.) Health Care and Health Knowledge, Croom Helm, London.

Mental Health Act (1959) Chap.72.

Ministry of Health (1963) Health and Welfare: The Development of Community Care, Cmnd. 1973, HMSO.

Moroney, R. (1976) The Family and the State, Longmans.

Navarro, V. (1976) Medicine under Capitalism, Croom Helm, London.

Navarro, V. (1978) 'The Crisis of the Western System of Medicine in Contemporary Capitalism', International Journal of Health Services, Vol.8, No.2, pp.179-211.

Nissel, M. and Bonnerjea, L. (1982) Family Care of the Handicapped Elderly: Who Pays?, Policy Studies

Institute, No.602, London.

Public Expenditure to 1975-76 (1971) Cmnd. 4829, HMSO.

Report of the Royal Commission the Law Relating to Mental Illness and Mental Deficiency, 1954-57 (1957) Cmnd. 169, HMSO.

Rose, H. and Rose, S. (1982) 'Moving Right out of Welfare - and the Way Back', Critical Social Policy, Vol.2, No.1, pp.7-18.

Rossiter, C. and Wicks, M. (1982) Crisis or Challenge? Family Care, Elderly People and Social Policy, Study Commission on the Family.

Shanas, E. et al. (1968) Old People in Three Industrial Societies, Routledge and Kegan Paul, London.

Sinclair, I., Levin, E., Neill, J. and Williams, J. (1983) 'Part III - Who Applies and Why?' National Institute for Social Work, Seminar on Residential Care for Elderly People, Background Papers and Synopsis of Research, DHSS.

Townsend, P. (1962) The Last Refuge, Routledge and Kegan Paul, London.

Ungerson, C. (1983a) 'Why do Women Care?', in Finch, J. and Groves, D. (eds.) op.cit.

Ungerson, C. (1983b) 'Women and Caring: Skills, Tasks and Taboos', in Gamarnikov, E. et al. op.cit.

Walker, A. (ed.) (1982) Community Care: The Family, the State and Social Policy, Martin Robertson/Blackwell, Oxford.

Walker, A. (1983) 'Care for Elderly People: A Conflict Between Women and the State', in Finch, J. and Groves, D. (eds.) op.cit.

Chapter Twelve

COMMUNITY CARE AND ELDERLY PEOPLE :

ONE WAY TRAFFIC?

John Harris and Des Kelly

Introduction

Community care has emerged as the antidote to long-stay
institutions. In the context of services for elderly people, it
is a policy ostensibly aimed at attacking the dependency
associated with institutions; dependency which has been the
subject of detailed documentation in empirical studies of both
health and social services (Townsend, 1962; Robb, 1967).
The assumptions behind the policy of community care for
elderly people have much in common with those encountered in
everyday life about the desirability of promoting
community-based services as an alternative to 'putting people
away'. Our contention is that this convergence of
assumptions resulted in community-based services becoming
equated with independence and residential provision with
dependence, both in policy development and in the public
mind.
    Sally MacIntyre (1977) argues for a very different
analysis of community care as a social policy. She suggests
that although community care has been presented as a deeply
humanitarian policy, the humanitarian rhetoric has run
parallel with economic concerns, so that the social costs of
ageing to the individual have been balanced against the
economic costs to the State. She argues that the
double-edged character of the policy has rested on
assumptions which have remained remarkably consistent over
time, with the emphasis merely shifting back and forth
between humanitarian and economic considerations. We can
illustrate this briefly:

    In recent years there has been a considerable awakening
    of public interest in the problems of old age, an
    awakening that has manifested itself in a sympathetic
    attitude to old people and in a widespread desire to be
    generous to them. The Committee are in full sympathy
    with this attitude, but they have felt bound to take into

account another point of view, based not on any lack of sympathy with the aged but on a recognition of the country's strictly limited resources of wealth and labour, and on the rapidly growing proportion of old people in the total population. This attitude is best summed up in Lord Beveridge's words ... 'It is dangerous to be in any way lavish in old age' ...
(Rowntree, 1947, p.95)

The provision of direct social service is regarded by many as something that the family should undertake.... elderly parents and relatives, for example, who cannot manage on their pension.... are the responsibility of the next of kin to help. The logical action to take is therefore for such responsibilities to be made legally mandatory ... Neglect of these family responsibilities would be actionable by the State ... In these cases of neglect, social services will be necessary, just as police are necessary to maintain law and order.
(Minford, 1984, p.2)

These quotations, which are separated by 37 years, echo with similar sentiments. They support our view that the policy within which professionals operate contains tensions and contradictions, which cannot be reduced to the simple dichotomy of 'good' comunity-based, independence-promoting practice and 'bad' residential, dependency-creating practice.

The Care Continuum

The implementation of the policy of community care has resulted in the notion of the care continuum; an approach to the provision of services which is based on discrete forms of care suited to certain categories of elderly people. This results in a continuum along which elderly people progress, so that as their basic needs change they move from one form of care to another (see Figure One).

Referral forms, Part III forms and other applications for services tend to reflect this model of defined stages which involve incremental consumption of domiciliary services. The continuum of care model is essentially and progressively 'one way'. Once an elderly person has begun a career on the care continuum the offer of services will depend on the position of the individual along the conveyor belt. The care continuum epitomises inflexibility and an inability to respond innovatively. It creates situations in which intervention is frequently either too late or inappropriate, a consequence of which is to create fatalism amongst social services staff about working with elderly people.

Our research shows that this is the dominant model of practice used by staff (Harris, 1979; Kelly, 1980). In our

Figure 1

Continuum of Care

INDEPENDENCE

FAMILY SUPPORT
Or other informal support
or isolated but coping

COMMUNITY CARE

including:
home help
mobile meals
laundry service
lunch club
telephone

Sheltered   PARTIAL RESIDENTIAL CARE   Assisted
Accommodation   Lodgings
Day Care
Short stay, respite care

PERMANENT RESIDENTIAL CARE

LONG-STAY WARD, GERIATRIC HOSPITAL

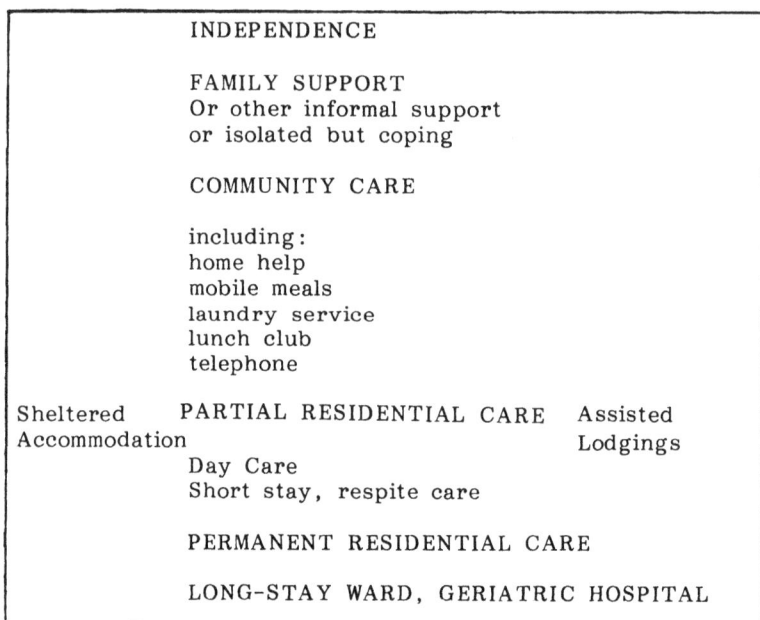

discussion of social work practice, we will highlight the routine judgements made by social workers in order to show the effect that these judgements have in creating dependency in community-based services. At this point, we merely wish to note that the double-edged nature of the assumptions, humanitarian and economic, underlying the policy of community care forms the context within which local authorities construct their services. These assumptions also shape elderly people's experiences of community care policies. We would argue that, ironically, the services provided on the care continuum, which were set up ostensibly to combat dependency in institutions, are now services in which dependency is institutionalised. Many of the services engage with elderly people in ritualised ways which determine the content of the service received. The DHSS funded study of social services teams (Stevenson and Parsloe, 1979) demonstrated that elderly people were considered to require the application of routine procedures.

We stress this point because many welfare professionals explain the dependency they encounter in elderly people in terms of this generation's experience of hardship and deprivation, which is seen as rendering them, for the most part, grateful and acquiescent to the support given by staff such as social workers (Townsend, 1968; Elder, 1977; Harris, 1979). We readily acknowledge the importance of this individual and collective biography. However, we regard this as a necessary but not sufficient explanation of the encounters between social workers and elderly people. We are, therefore, attempting to redress this imbalance, which places a disproportionate emphasis on elderly people themselves and renders social workers in the guise of neutral helpers.

Referral - Entering the Care Continuum

We have chosen the referral as our point of departure in order to demonstrate the transition of policy into practice. The referral form starts the process, which marks the designation of an elderly person as a client. Our fictitious referral (see Figure Two) illustrates what local and national policies can actually mean to individuals about to enter social service systems. It is not easy for someone to secure help from a Social Services Department. The process of reception is carefully controlled by social work agencies, referral and allocation performing gate-keeping and rationing functions. As in any organisation information is collected in particular ways, potential clients are coded, categorised and labelled (Hall, 1974; Foster, 1983). As access to services is generally determined at this early stage the point of referral to a Social Services Department can be regarded as a critical period in relation to the development of a case. It is critical in so far as it will inevitably represent the fusion of available services with local demand. It is a fusion brought about in a particular way, representing the attempted match of demand to the services, not the reverse. In these early encounters at the point of referral, social workers appear to interpret demand in a knowledge of what can be selected from the 'continuum of care', which, as we have seen, has certain identifiable features (see Figure One).

An elderly person is introduced to the continuum of care by a social worker. In effecting the introduction, the social worker experiences the contradictions between the rhetoric of community care policy and the reality. The encounters which result can become a vicious circle of low expectations of the services, few demands from the elderly person and a low priority ranking from social workers. These encounters are not a random series of events in which disinterested social workers meet disheartened old people. They are part of the marginalisation of elderly people by Social Services Departments. According to one critic:

... from its inception, social work attached marginal significance to work with the elderly. These trends were to continue, however, during the period of

expansion in social services during the mid-1960s to the mid-1970s.
(Phillipson, 1982, p.106)

Experiencing Social Work

We can illustrate the foregoing discussion in the case of Mrs C. set out in the form of a fictitious referral form (see Figure 2). Most Social Services Departments have a referral form which invites two sorts of information; reasons for referral and comments after investigation. The intention in having such a form appears to be to encourage a two-stage process. First, for the social worker to take note of the specific nature of the request for help, and secondly, for the social worker to stand back from the specific request and to offer an assessment of the pertinent circumstances.

In approaching this request for help from the daughter-in-law of Mrs C., the social worker is already tidying it up so that it will be a recognisable type of referral, which can be slotted into the care continuum. The information is being coded by her into pre-existing categories of service delivery. These are carried around in her head as representing the correct response, or combination of responses, to elderly people's problems. We can almost hear her ruminating: 'Is this a Part III? A telephone? A Day Care? ...'

Figure 2

Referral 1

REASONS FOR REFERRAL

Possible Need for Day Care

S.W. COMMENTS FOLLOWING INVESTIGATION

Mrs C. (Junior) to office. Her husband has a heart condition. He can't look after his mother, and Mrs C. (Junior) has a part-time job. Mrs C. (Senior) is neglecting herself. She is lonely and confused. The neighbours keep ringing her daughter-in-law whose 'nerves' are beginning to suffer.

ASSESS FOR DAY CARE?

It is the familiar short-hand of Social Services Departments; the language by which elderly people become synonymous with the services they consume. One social worker summed up this experience of working with elderly people:

What the Corporation provides is a kind of tramlines. It
doesn't matter what you need, that is what we provide
sort of thing, so you'll have to slot into what we
provide.... more so with the elderly because we're so
unenlightened about what we do provide for the elderly.
(Harris, 1979, p.145)

In this referral, through the substitution of the
anticipated solution for the reason for referral, the social
worker has also sorted out the identity of the client - Mrs
C. The response is in terms of services constructed for her,
and for her alone. The anguish of her daughter-in-law is
discarded as so much gloss on the plot. So the social worker
regards herself as having discovered the 'real' client, the
'real' problem, and the correct response.

Following up the Referral

The ordering of reality established in this initial interview
will usually be confused when Mrs C.'s case is put forward
for allocation to a social worker. Given the low priority of
work with elderly people in most social work teams, Mrs C.
may have to wait a considerable time for further attention.
This sort of case would drop like a stone in most allocation
meetings. Our research, in one Social Services Department,
showed that elderly people had the lowest chance of allocation
to a social worker of all client groups (Harris, 1979, p.68).
Given this resistance to following up referrals on elderly
people, when Mrs C. is eventually contacted the social
worker may be visiting under duress. It is not difficult to
develop the case still further: agitation from neighbours,
intervention from a local councillor, a chance admission to
hospital, discussions in supervision or any number of
circumstances may keep Mrs C. moving along the care
continuum.
    We would argue that it is the existence of the continuum
of care as a central and consistent feature of state social
policy and its local translations which generate such
scenarios, so that only the individual characters change.
Although the continuum of care appears to have the potential
for movement in either direction, in day-to-day practice the
continuum simply reinforces the notions of progressive decline
and inevitable dependency by legitimising a model of service
provision and service delivery which is unilinear. The result
is a form of 'professionalised' dependency in the relationships
between elderly people and social service staff across the
range of services.
    Economic constraints have exacerbated this situation by
creating a climate in which service options are burdened by
cost-effective criteria which operate to divert, delay or deny
demand. In consequence a range of schemes have been

developed such as adult fostering, very sheltered housing, respite care, and private and voluntary agencies have been encouraged to absorb any surplus demand. Nevertheless the essential framework of provision has remained unchanged. If anything the conveyor belt model of the care continuum has become more explicit outside professional vocabularies and as a means by which elderly people themselves make sense of the 'reality' of the welfare state.

Not Practice Perfect, But ...

All this can sound like a counsel of despair. We wish to counter such pessimism by suggesting some points of departure for improving practice. The referral form can, for example, be re-run, (see Figure 3).

The social worker's response to this request for help is not presented as an idealised form of perfect practice, but it does contain some distinct improvements on the first interview. The social worker is not squeezing the problem into the available services. She is listening to the daughter-in-law's account and respecting it, while remaining conscious of the fact that it is her account. It is an account of her anxieties. The social worker is trying to find out what she wants and what is at stake for her. The social worker is aware that this viewpoint does not represent the totality of the situation and suggests that this is remedied by hearing the daughter-in-law's account. It is important to note that the social worker has not assumed that Mrs C. needs to be 'assessed', in terms of her individual pathology. The assessment will be of the total situation, and only then, the social worker suggests, should joint action be taken to alleviate whatever problems are uncovered. At the point of the request for help the social worker is struggling to stay open to what emerges, rather than offer conclusive pointers to how the 'case' can be finished off.

The subsequent response of the social work team to the referral is crucial. However good the initial interview is, the social worker's efforts will be thwarted if the referral encounters resistance at allocation. It is, therefore, vital to give careful thought to team organisation. This is merely an extension of a practice which is common in relation to other areas of work. Teams commonly give time to deciding criteria for Section I payments for children; for providing a crisis service under the Mental Health Act; for developing a consistent response to children at risk. In some teams groups of workers pursue the interests of particular consumer groups. In the case of elderly people, the group could consist of social worker, home help organiser, voluntary help organiser and occupational therapist. Such a group contains the necessary expertise to analyse the extent of support currently provided and to work out a 'contract' with those

Figure 3

Referral II

REASONS FOR REFERRAL

Breakdown in the arrangements for care and support of Mrs C.

S.W. COMMENTS FOLLOWING INVESTIGATION

Mrs C. (Junior) came to the office. She was distressed, describing her mother-in-law as lonely and confused. She instanced night time wandering as evidence of this confusion. Mrs C. (Senior) was wandering in the street three times last week, for between half an hour and an hour, on each occasion. Mrs C.'s neighbours telephoned Mrs C. (Junior) on each occasion and she says that this is affecting her 'nerves'.
Mrs C. (Junior) says that up to the present time, she and her husband have been able to respond to any occurrences like this, which have arisen about once a fortnight over the last five years, but Mr. C. has been diagnosed as suffering from angina and has been advised to rest. Mrs C. (Junior) has a part-time job in the evenings which she does not want to lose. I tried to discuss with Mrs C. (Junior) what the problem was from her viewpoint. It seems to centre on feeling totally responsible for Mrs C. (Senior), and having no respite from the anxiety about her safety.

Recommend:
(1) Visit to Mrs C. (Senior) to ascertain her view of the situation.
(2) Following (1), to hold a meeting with Mr and Mrs C. and Mrs C. (Senior) and any other significant figures who emerge to discuss what services should be provided.

---

involved. Duplication could be avoided by delegating to each group member the power to offer any of the services available from the team. As well as dealing with individual cases, such a group could develop resources, for example the possibility of day care in people's own homes, a relative support group, researching the needs of elderly women, evaluating patterns of domiciliary support.

In beginning to develop a form of practice which aims to combat dependency a basic principle needs to be asserted. Elderly people are adults. As such we should respect their right to choose, including their right to choose to take risks. This may involve advocacy on their behalf including challenging the inevitability of the unilinear continuum of care. We consider that the biographical approach of collecting information from elderly people, which seeks to understand their own interpretations of their lives and life events, is fundamental to good practice (Johnson, 1978). We recognise that even this limited improvement in practice can only be defended if there is a collective response to the definition of need and services provided to meet need. It would take a remarkably strong individual to resist the force of societal pressure and the day-to-day denigration of work with elderly people which produce a familiar pattern of priorities down which elderly people sink. In addition to defending the standard of individual practice, a greater collective consciousness of elderly people's needs encourages the development of a more collective, consumer-oriented response in which the marginality of elderly people's position in the service system can begin to be overcome. For a team attempting to combat dependency, the next stage might be to meet with consumers of the team's services and representatives of elderly people's organisations to receive feedback on the services provided and proposals for their development.

Conclusion

We have tried to demonstrate that there is no simple equation between community services and good practice, by examining the processes at work when elderly people are referred, or, more rarely refer themselves, to generic social work teams. The current reorganisations of service provision either towards greater specialisation or the more concentrated genericism of 'patch' teams (Challis and Ferlie, 1986), will have a minimal impact on the quality of services provided for elderly people unless these issues are addressed.

The struggle to defend community services against cutbacks, has led practitioners to regard them in an uncritical light. Understandably, demands have concentrated on increasing the quantity of existing provision, rather than scrutinising the content of what is offered to individual elderly people. Our contention is that the lack of scrutiny has resulted in an essentially inflexible, unilinear model of service provision, which has placed elderly people in a vulnerable and dependent position in relation to the social workers who guide their careers along the care continuum.

References

Challis, D. and Ferlie, E. (1986) 'All Change - But Which Way?' Community Care, 15 February, pp.19-21.

Elder, G. (1977) The Alienated: Growing Old Today, Writers and Readers Cooperative, London.
Foster, P. (1983) Access to Welfare: An Introduction to Welfare Rationing, Macmillan, London.
Hall, A.S. (1974) The Point of Entry: A Study of Client Reception in the Social Services, Allen and Unwin, London.
Harris, J. (1979) More Than Going Grey: A Preliminary Examination of Gerontological Theory and Social Work Practice with Elderly People, Unpublished M.A. Thesis, University of Warwick.
Johnson, M. (1978) 'That was Your Life: A Biographical Approach to Later Life', in Carver, V. and Liddiard, P. (eds.) An Ageing Population, Hodder and Stoughton, Kent.
Kelly D. (1980) Long-Term Care of Elderly People: An Essentially Human Tragedy? Unpublished M.A. Dissertation, University of Warwick.
MacIntyre, S. (1977) 'Old Age as a Social Problem', in Dingwall, R. et al. (eds.) Health Care and Health Knowledge, Croom Helm, London.
Minford, P. (1984) 'State Expenditure: A Study in Waste', Supplement to Economic Affairs, Institute of Economic Affairs, April/June.
Phillipson, C. (1981) Capitalism and the Construction of Old Age, Macmillan, London.
Robb, B. (1967) Sans Everything: A Case to Answer, Nelson, London.
Seebohm Rowntree, B. (1947) Old People: Report of a Survey Committee on the Problems of Ageing and the Care of Old People, Oxford University Press, Oxford.
Stevenson, O. and Parsloe, P. (1979) Social Service Teams: The Practitioners' View, DHSS, London.
Townsend, P. (1962) Last Refuge: A Survey of Residential Institutions and Homes for the Aged in England and Wales, Routledge and Kegan Paul, London.
Townsend, P. (1968) The Family Life of Old People: An Inquiry in East London, Penguin, Harmondsworth.

Chapter Thirteen

WHO CARES FOR THE ELDERLY? : FAMILY CARE

PROVISION AND RECEIPT OF STATUTORY SERVICE

Maria Evandrou, Sara Arber, Angela Dale and G.Nigel
Gilbert

Introduction

This paper examines, through the use of nationally
representative data, the roles of formal and informal care
networks in the provision of care for elderly people living at
home.
    Recent research based upon local surveys has
demonstrated that although state services play a role, it is
not the case that families are neither willing nor able to care
for the elderly (Land, 1978; Wicks, 1982:105; Wright, 1983).
The studies document a number of findings. The first is that
it is the family which provides the majority of care given to
older people. Indeed such family care may be more common
now than in the past (Greengross, 1982). Small scale studies
(Nissel and Bonnerjea, 1982) have already shown that the
sexual division of caring tasks means that in practice care is
provided by women. Thus daughters and daughters-in-law
constitute the largest group of carers of elderly people
(Hunt, 1978; Charlesworth et al., 1984).
    The second major finding is that shared care amongst
family members is uncommon. Once someone takes on the
responsibility of caring, and is so identified by relatives,
friends and neighbours as 'the main carer', they subsequently
receive little support from other family members (Townsend,
1957; Gilhooly, 1982; Nissel and Bonnerjea, 1982).
    Thirdly, only a minority of carers receive state services
in support of their work, and then, usually only at a time of
crisis, rather than as part of a long-term pattern of support
(Walker, 1982; Parker et al., 1984). It has been suggested
that the criteria by which services are allocated reflect the
household composition or gender of the main carer rather than
the levels of 'need' (Harris, 1971; Hunt, 1978; Charlesworth
et al., 1984).
    Finally, the government has continued to advocate a
policy of community care, emphasising the importance of

maintaining elderly persons in their own homes rather than admitting them into institutions. Lip service has been paid to the importance of the role of informal carers in this process, and the necessity of providing support for the carers, yet there has been little strategic planning to 'sustain and, where necessary, develop' services in support of informal and voluntary care provision (Walker, 1982, p.120).

In addition to these issues, the impact of changing demographic and socio-economic trends on the care of the elderly contributes to the widening gap between needs and action (Brody, 1981). The number and proportion of elderly people is increasing and future projections indicate that this will continue, especially with respect to the very old (75 years plus) who are most likely to be in need of care and assistance (OPCS, 1984). Furthermore, there has been an increase in the labour force participation of women - especially married women aged 45 - 59 years (OPCS, 1983) - who tend to be the main care providers for older people. These trends, combined with changes in marriage patterns (e.g. increases in divorce and remarriage and in the number of lone parents) and the tendency for smaller family size, suggest that in the future fewer people will be available to take on caring responsibilities (Parker et al., 1984).

With the aim of complementing the findings of local in-depth studies, this paper investigates some of these trends and relationships at the national level. We shall examine the meaning of community care in terms of who provides care for a range of specific tasks which the elderly person is unable to do unaided. We examine how the balance of care between family members, other community members such as neighbours and friends, and statutory services varies according to whether the elderly person lives alone or in different types of household.

Data Source

The research is based upon a secondary analysis of the 1980 General Household Survey (GHS) which is a continuous annual survey carried out by OPCS. It includes approximately 12,000 private households (over 31,000 individuals) in Great Britain (OPCS, 1982) and provides a sample of 4,553 persons aged 65 years and over.[1] Because the GHS conducts interviews with all persons aged 16 years or more in the household, the data enable relationships[2] to be established between individuals in the same household.[2]

The 1980 GHS is particularly valuable because in addition to the standard demographic and socio-economic variables, it includes a special section for respondents aged 65 years and over. For example, it covers topics such as the ability to carry out personal self-care and housecare activities and, for those who require help, who generally provides it. The GHS

Who Cares for the Elderly?

used the age of 65 years for both men and women to
determine those who should be considered 'elderly'. However,
it is important to bear in mind that individuals do not
suddenly 'become elderly' as they reach their 65th birthday.

The Situation of the Elderly

(1) Household Structure

In the last twenty years the size and composition of
households in which elderly people live has changed
significantly: the number living alone has doubled since 1960
and the number of households with three or more people
containing at least one elderly person has fallen by a third
(OPCS, 1984). This latter type of household usually contains
elderly people living with younger family members.
    Since the provision of formal and informal care has been
found to vary with the type of household in which elderly
people live, it is important to derive an appropriate typology
to understand the relationship between family structure and
support. In constructing such a classification of household
structure[3], distinctions were made between elderly people
living alone, elderly people living with other elderly people,
and elderly couples. The latter category comprised married
elderly people where either one or both of the partners were
65 years or over. Among elderly persons living with younger
(i.e. below 65 years) household members, 'sole' elderly
individuals (including widowed, divorced, separated and
never married) were distinguished from elderly couples.
    The 1980 GHS (Table 1) shows that one third of all the
elderly live alone and 45 per cent live with their elderly
spouse. Eighty per cent of the spouses of those living with
partners are also elderly. About 18 per cent of elderly
people live in households with adults below 65 years, the
majority of whom are single adult relatives of the elderly
individual. It is in these types of households that daughters
and/or sons provide care for ageing parents. One tenth of
the elderly in the GHS sample live in households comprising a
sole elderly person with younger members, and a slightly
smaller proportion, eight per cent, live as elderly couples
with one or more younger household members.

(2) Capacity for Daily Activities

This paper focuses on those elderly people who require help
from others to carry out daily living activities, thereby
enabling them to live in the community, alone or with others.
Before analysing who provides help for the elderly, it is
important to consider what proportion of all the over-65s
require help with various activities. The majority of older
people do not have any limitations on their physical mobility

152

Table 1

Household Structure in which Elderly

Persons at Home Live

		%	n
1.	Sole elderly alone (1)	33.3	(1717)
2.	Two or more sole elderly persons	3.4	(157)
3.	Elderly or semi-elderly couples only	45.0	(2047)
4.	Sole elderly persons living with younger household members (2)	10.2	(465)
5.	Elderly couples living with younger household members (3)	8.1	(367)
	Total	100%	(4553)

Source: GHS, 1980.

(1) Sole elderly persons includes widowed, divorced, separated and those who never married.

(2) Younger household members refers to non-elderly individuals, i.e. aged below 65 years and above 16 years.

(3) Elderly couples comprises couples where one or both of the partners are 65 years and over. This household type also contains some elderly couples living with a sole elderly person as well as younger household members.

and can easily perform tasks such as getting in and out of bed, walking outdoors, cooking main meals and washing laundry, (OPCS, 1982, Tables 10.13-10.44).

Certain activities present more difficulties to some people than others. For example, in our research we have found that cutting toenails provides the most difficulty to the largest proportion of elderly people; 42 per cent of the GHS elderly sample had at least some difficulty cutting their toenails without assistance. Furthermore, twelve per cent either required help or could not manage to go out of doors and walk down the road, and eight per cent needed help or could not manage to bath, shower or wash themselves all over. Extrapolating these figures to everyone aged 65 years and over, we find that more than one million elderly people were unable to go outside and walk down the road unaided, and about 750,000 were unable to bath, shower or wash themselves all over. Furthermore, future projections indicate that this number will increase over the next five years (Henwood and Wicks, 1985).

Formal and Informal Care Networks

In this section, patterns of care are investigated by examining the primary sources of help both within and outside the household, for those who encounter difficulty in carrying out various physical, self-care and domestic tasks for themselves; for example, getting in and out of bed, bathing, cooking, laundry washing, shopping and getting about outdoors. We examine how the household structure of elderly people influences who provides help with these tasks.

Sources of Help

It is clear from Table 2 that the main source of help comes from individuals within the same household, either the spouse of the elderly person (where one exists), or by other household members. Unfortunately, due to the questions asked in the GHS, it is impossible to distinguish who these 'other household members' are. Thus we cannot establish the gender of the principal care provider.

Among elderly people who cannot manage to go out and walk down the road, 61 per cent were helped by other household members (the majority of whom were spouses), 24 per cent by outside relatives (14 per cent by daughters and sons), 14 per cent by friends and neighbours, and one per cent by social and medical services. Household members assist 91 per cent of the elderly who were unable to get in and out of bed, 84 per cent of those who cannot cook for themselves, 71 per cent of those who were unable to do their laundry and 61 per cent who have difficulty in bathing, showering or washing themselves (Table 2).

Table 2

**Who Generally Helps Elderly People with Various Tasks :
For Those Who Require Help**

WHO HELPS	Getting in/ out bed	Bath/ Shower	Walking Outdoors	Cook Meals	Wash Laundry	Unscrews Jars etc.	Shopping	Cutting Toenails
In Household								
Spouse	51	39	38	54	46	43	29	14
Other member of Household	40	22	23	30	25	28	25	7
Outside Household								
Daughter &/or Son	4	10	14	6	11	9	17	5
Other Relative(s)	3	3	10	3	5	4	9	2
Friend/ Neighbour	1	2	14	2	2	10	10	2
Social/Medical Services	1	23	1	4	9	5	8	70
Paid Help	0	1	0	1	2	1	1	0
Totals	100% (91)	100% (331)	100% (198)	100% (439)	100% (483)	100% (531)	100% (821)	100% (1224)

Source: GIIS, 1980.

155

Nearly a quarter of those helping an elderly person with household shopping and walking were family members who were not co-resident with the elderly person. The contribution of statutory services was more limited and generally confined to footcare, although some aid was provided with bathing; 70 per cent of elderly people who cannot cut their toenails and 23 per cent of them who cannot bath/wash themselves receive assistance from social and medical services. Over a range of tasks, the statutory services provided help to very few of the elderly who need it. Only one per cent were given help in getting in and out of bed, or walking outdoors, four per cent were aided with cooking a main meal and eight per cent helped with household shopping.

Thus the vast majority of help with physical, self-care and domestic tasks was provided by spouses or others living with the elderly person. Substantial help was provided by relatives outside the household, especially daughters and sons, although friends and neighbours figured less prominently.

Provision of Care Across Household Structures

Do statutory services provide assistance on the basis of the need of the elderly person or are they influenced by who else lives with the elderly person? In Tables 3 to 7 we examine the variation in the extent of assistance provided within different household structures, and by whom this help is given.

(a) Elderly Persons Living Alone

The main source of assistance to elderly people living alone is relatives living outside the household, especially daughters and sons; Table 3 shows that of lone elderly unable to get in and out of bed, almost all were helped by family members, and 59 per cent of those who could not manage to go out and walk down the road were assisted by relatives (mainly daughters and sons). Forty per cent of lone elderly who had difficulty in laundry washing and a similar proportion of those who needed help with cooking main meals, were helped by daughters and sons.

Elderly persons living alone are also helped by friends and neighbours, especially with walking outside (37 per cent), opening bottle tops and jars (36 per cent) and doing the shopping (20 per cent). Social and medical services assist most with cutting toenails (86 per cent of lone elderly), bathing or washing (52 per cent) and laundry washing (33 per cent). Of those elderly who cannot get in and out of bed, none are aided by these services and only two per cent are helped with walking outdoors.

Table 3

Of Elderly People Living Alone :
Who Helps With Various Tasks

WHO HELPS	Getting in/out bed	Bath/Shower	Walking Outdoors	Cook Meals	Wash Laundry	Unscrew Jars etc.	Shopping	Cutting Toenails
Outside Household								
Daughter &/or Son	50	32	35	40	40	31	38	8
Other Relative(s)	38	12	24	15	14	12	18	3
Friend/Neighbour	12	3	37	14	6	36	20	3
Social/Medical Services	0	52	2	25	33	19	21	86
Paid Help	0	1	2	6	7	2	3	0
Totals	100% (8)	100% (85)	100% (62)	100% (65)	100% (111)	100% (136)	100% (298)	100% (486)

Source: GHS, 1980.

157

(b) Two or More Elderly Persons Living Together

In households consisting of two or more 'sole' elderly people, the elderly persons themselves are the main care providers. These figures are important in counteracting the 'dependent' image frequently attributed to all elderly people, viewing them solely as recipients of care and assistance. It is important to bear in mind that as the older population increase in age, so do their children and other potential care providers. Thus carers are very often in middle age and early old age themselves. For example, all the assistance provided with getting in and out of bed comes from the other elderly people in the household (Table 4). Furthermore, 90 per cent of the elderly in the household requiring help with laundry washing, 78 per cent with shopping and 61 per cent with bathing and washing receive assistance from another elderly person.

Support from relatives living outside the household is generally less important and where it is provided, it is more frequent with tasks such as shopping, walking outdoors and laundry washing. The help provided by social and medical services is again for activities such as toenail cutting (71 per cent) and bathing (31 per cent).

(c) Elderly Couples

As expected, spouses are the main source of help for elderly people living with elderly or non-elderly spouses; 97 per cent of those elderly people who cannot manage to get in and out of bed, 87 per cent of those who cannot bath, shower or wash on their own, and 89 per cent of those who cannot manage to walk outdoors are helped by their spouse (Table 5)[4]. The data shows that very little help is provided by other relatives and friends or neighbours, and social and medical services only provide chiropody care (60 per cent).

(d) Sole Elderly Persons Living with Younger Household Members

Where sole elderly people live with non-elderly household members, care from within the household predominates, with the exception of footcare. This indicates a flow of help and care from younger family members, usually from adult children to elderly parents, which does not accord with some current assumptions about the role of the 'family' where services are assumed to only flow from parents to children. As Brody (1981) points out, the flow changes direction in the later stages of the life cycle.

Assistance from outside the household (from relatives or neighbours) is infrequent, which supports the argument that once a carer is identified - in this case inside the household - help from other sources is limited or non-existent (Parker

Table 4

Of Households Where Two or More Sole Elderly
Persons Reside :

Who Helps With Various Tasks

WHO HELPS	Getting in/ out bed	Bath/ Shower	Walking Outdoors	Cook Meals	Wash Laundry	Unscrew Jars etc.	Shopping	Cutting Toenails
In Household								
Other Member of Household	100	61	64	93	90	78	78	22
Outside Household								
Daughter &/or Son	0	0	9	3	5	4	3	2
Other Relative(s)	0	4	9	4	5	4	16	0
Friend/ Neighbour	0	0	9	0	0	7	3	0
Social/Medical Services	0	31	9	0	0	0	0	76
Paid Help	0	4	0	0	0	7	0	0
Totals	100% (6)	100% (23)	100% (11)	100% (28)	100% (20)	100% (27)	100% (37)	100% (63)

Source: GHS, 1980.

159

Table 5

Of Households With Elderly Couples(1) :
Who Helps With Various Tasks

WHO HELPS	Getting in/ out bed	Bath/ Shower	Walking Outdoors	Cook Meals	Wash Laundry	Unscrew Jars etc.	Shopping	Cutting Toenails
In Household								
Spouse	97	87	89	100	91	98	80	34
Outside Household								
Daughter &/or Son	0	2	1	0	3	1	7	4
Other Relative(s)	0	1	4	0	2	0	5	1
Friend/ Neighbour	0	2	6	0	2	1	6	1
Social/Medical Services	3	8	0	0	2	0	2	60
Paid Help	0	0	0	0	0	0	0	0
Totals	100% (38)	100% (130)	100% (74)	100% (204)	100% (203)	100% (210)	100% (253)	100% (439)

Source: **GHS**, 1980.

(1) Elderly couples where one or both of the partners are 65 years and over.

et al., 1984). For example, 91 per cent of elderly people requiring help with walking outdoors were aided by younger household members and only 9 per cent were assisted by adult daughters and/or sons outside the household (Table 6). Formal support services provide chiropody (60 per cent) and help with bathing (22 per cent), but these are much lower proportions than those for help provided to lone elderly.

(e) Elderly Couples Living with Younger Household Members

Where there is an elderly couple living with younger household members, the majority of care provided with respect to the eight tasks comes from the spouse of the elderly person, who in the majority of cases is also elderly. However, a significant proportion are helped by the other household members; for example, 58 per cent of elderly persons in need of assistance with bathing were aided by their spouse and 38 per cent by other household members (Table 7). Only four per cent were supported by formal agencies. Once more we find that in such households, help from outside relatives and neighbours is limited and confined to activities such as shopping, cooking, laundry washing and help with opening jars and bottle tops. Formal support services were received only for footcare (48 per cent) and bathing (four per cent) - proportions which are far less than for any of the other household types.

Discussion

Relatives living outside the household are an extremely important source of help for elderly people who live alone. This is not the case with households containing two or more sole elderly persons, as the elderly themselves are their own care providers. Of elderly couples living on their own, it is the spouse who provides the main source of help, and relatives living outside the household feature very little. Furthermore, very little outside help is provided by relatives or friends and neighbours when the elderly person is living with other younger household members. The family members living with the elderly are the main source of care and remain even where the elderly person has a spouse.

The support provided by formal agencies was generally very limited, although they did play a more active role amongst the elderly living alone. Where such support was provided, it was more frequent with respect to 'medical' rather than physical or domestic tasks, such as chiropody services and help with bathing. However, concerning these two care tasks, elderly couples living with younger household members who required help with cutting toenails and bathing, received the least support from such agencies. What is

Table 6

Of Households Where Sole Elderly People Are Living With Younger Household Members : Who Helps

WHO HELPS	Getting in/out bed	Bath/Shower	Walking Outdoors	Cook Meals	Wash Laundry	Unscrew Jars etc.	Shopping	Cutting Toenails
In Household								
Other Members of Household	100	74	91	97	96	97	90	34
Outside Household								
Daughter &/or Son	0	3	9	0	2	2	4	4
Other Relative(s)	0	0	0	2	0	0	1	1
Friend/Neighbour	0	1	0	0	0	0	4	1
Social/Medical Services	0	22	0	1	2	1	1	60
Paid Help	0	0	0	0	0	0	0	0
Totals	100% (27)	100% (65)	100% (34)	100% (95)	100% (89)	100% (121)	100% (163)	100% (156)

Source: GHS, 1980.

Table 7

Of Households Where Elderly Couples[1] Are Living With Younger Household Members : Who Helps

WHO HELPS	Getting in/out bed	Bath/Shower	Walking Outdoors	Cook Meals	Wash Laundry	Unscrew Jars etc.	Shopping	Cutting Toenails
In Household								
Spouse	75	58	64	70	63	62	53	28
Other Member of Household	25	38	36	24	32	32	39	20
Outside Household								
Daughter &/or Son	0	0	0	4	3	3	6	2
Other Relative(s)	0	0	0	2	2	3	1	2
Friend/Neighbour	0	0	0	0	0	0	1	0
Social/Medical Services	0	4	0	0	0	0	0	48
Paid Help	0	0	0	0	0	0	0	0
Totals	100% (12)	100% (24)	100% (14)	100% (46)	100% (60)	100% (37)	100% (70)	100% (80)

Source: GHS, 1980.

(1)   Elderly couple here includes couples with one or both partners aged 65 years and over.
Some of the households also include an additional elderly person.

163

evident from the data is the predominance of family members (in and outside the elderly person's household) rather than professionals in providing care services to those who need them.

The lack of support for domestic tasks by statutory services is also clear; for example, only a fifth to a third of all elderly living alone requiring assistance are helped with shopping, cooking and washing laundry (Table 3). This contrasts with no help, or very limited help, from formal services where the elderly person cannot manage these tasks but lives with either other elderly people or with younger household members.

Attitudinal research on family care of the elderly, carried out by Brody (1981), reports that a high proportion (75 per cent) of the grandmothers interviewed preferred paying someone for providing parental care rather than a working daughter leaving employment to take on such responsibilities. The GHS data did not indicate any significant reliance upon paid help, although households such as lone elderly, and two or more sole elderly persons living together purchased a limited amount of help with respect to tasks such as laundry washing and cooking meals.

Conclusion

Community care is a euphemism for family care, and more specifically women, although our data only extend to the former. The view of the 'community' caring for its elderly members is only supported by our research with respect to a particular household type; elderly people living alone. For elderly persons in other household units, it is kin who are the main care providers. The support by formal agencies is generally limited and where it was provided, usually in the form of 'health care', it was found to be influenced by the household structure in which the elderly person lived rather than whether they were able to carry out various activities of daily living without help.

Current social policy on the care of the elderly reflects the present government's ideology of 'self-sufficiency' and individualistic efforts, reasserting the responsibility of elderly care with the family. Policies are based upon the assumption that the 'family network' and in particular women family members, will continue to be available in providing such care in the future. Yet demographic and economic changes indicate that as the potential pool of carers is shrinking, the proportion of elderly people in need of care is increasing. Furthermore, where family members take on caring responsibilities, the lack of sufficient resources made available for personal social services provides them with little hope of being supported in their 'labour of love'. The government has succeeded in drawing the dividing line betweeen formal and informal care very firmly (Walker, 1983).

Notes

(1) The data base management package, SIR (Scientific Information Retrieval), which was designed specifically for the use of hierarchical data sets, was employed for the analysis along with SPSS (Statistical Package for the Social Sciences).
(2) Although it is important to bear in mind that a study of the 1971 GHS sample (OPCS, 1982) found that older people tended to have lower response rates, there is no evidence to suggest that this has unduly affected the results.
(3) Our preliminary classification generated a detailed 25 category typology. However for the purposes of this paper, a collapsed five category variable is employed in order to avoid problems with low cell counts and make crosstabulations less cumbersome. We examine household structure in detail in a forthcoming paper (Dale, A., Evandrou, M. and Arber, S., 1986).
(4) It may be expected that among many of these couples, only one partner needs help with these tasks.

References

Brody, E.M. (1981) 'Women in the Middle and Family Help to Older People', The Gerontologist, Vol.5, No.5, pp.471-480.
Charlesworth, A., Wilkin, D. and Durie, A. (1983) Carers and Services: A Comparison of Men and Women Caring for Dependent Elderly People, Equal Opportunities Commission, Manchester.
Dale, A., Evandrou, M. and Arber, S. (1986) The Household Structure of the Elderly in Britain, Mimeo: University of Surrey.
Gilhooly, M. (1982) 'Social Aspects of Senile Dementia', Current Trends in Gerontology: Proceedings of the 1980 Conference of the British Society of Gerontology, in Taylor, R. and Gilmore, A. (eds.), Gower, Aldershot.
Greengross, S. (1982) 'Caring for the Carers' in Glendenning, F. (ed.) Care in the Community: Recent Research and Current Projects, Beth Johnson Foundation, Stoke-on-Trent.
Harris, A. (1971) Handicapped and Impaired in Great Britain, HMSO, London.
Henwood, M. and Wicks, M. (1985) 'Community Care, Family Trends ans Social Change', Quarterly Journal of Social Affairs, Vol.1, No.4, pp.357-371. Hunt, A. (1978) The Elderly at Home, HMSO, London.

Land, H. (1978) 'Who Cares for the Family', Journal of Social Policy, Vol.7, pp.257-284.

Nissel, M. and Bonnerjea, L. (1982) Family Care of the Handicapped Elderly: Who Pays?, Policy Studies Institute, London.

Office of Population Censuses and Surveys (1982) General Household Survey 1980, HMSO, London.

Office of Population Censuses and Surveys (1983) Social Trends, HMSO, London.

Office of Population Censuses and Surveys (1984) Census Guide 1: Britain's Elderly Population, HMSO, London.

Parker, G., Baldwin, S. and Glendenning, C. (1984) Informal Care and Carers: A Research Review and Recommendations for Future Research, Department of Social Administration and Social Work, University of York.

Townsend, P. (1957) The Family Life of Old People, Routledge and Kegan Paul, London.

Walker, A. (ed.) (1982) Community Care: The Family, the State and Social Policy, Basil Blackwell and Martin Roberts, Oxford.

Walker, A. (1983) 'Care For Elderly People: A Conflict Between Women and the State', in Finch, J. and Groves, D. (eds.) A Labour of Love: Women, Work and Caring, Routledge and Kegan Paul, London.

Wicks, M. (1982) 'Community Care and Elderly People' in Walker, A. (ed.) Community Care: The Family, the State and Social Policy, Basil Blackwell and Martin Roberts, Oxford.

Wright, F. (1983) 'Single Carers: Employment, Housework and Caring', in Finch, J. and Groves, D. (eds.) A Labour of Love: Women, Work and Caring, Routledge and Kegan Paul, London.

Acknowledgement

We would like to thank the Office of Population Censuses and Surveys (OPCS), who carry out the General Household Survey, for allowing us to use the data, and also the ESRC Data Archive for preparing and distributing the data. The analysis was facilitated by the use of SIR files prepared at the University of Surrey by G.N. Gilbert, A. Dale, S. Arber and J. O'Byrne. The research was supported by the ESRC (Grant No. G0125003) as part of the Ageing Initiative. We would especially like to thank Christina Victor, Hazel Qureshi and Karen Johnson for their helpful comments on earlier drafts.

Chapter Fourteen

RESPONSES TO DEPENDENCY: RECIPROCITY, AFFECT

AND POWER IN FAMILY RELATIONSHIPS

Hazel Qureshi

Introduction

This paper draws upon the results of a survey of elderly
people and their informal carers carried out in 1982-1983 in
Sheffield, and funded by the Rowntree Memorial Trust. The
299 elderly people interviewed were a representative
community sample, drawn from the lists of a number of GP
practices. Fifty-eight carers were subsequently interviewed
after they had been identified by the elderly people. Only
carers living outside the person's household were interviewed.
     The definition of dependency which will be used is from
the work of Anderson (1971):

    A state in which actions by others are a necessary
    condition for an actor to achieve his or her own goals.

Power in this context is understood as:

    The capacity to influence others to assist you in the
    achievement of your goals.

The discussion which follows will be mainly the viewpoint of
the carers: first, their views of responses to dependency by
the elderly people to whom they gave assistance, and,
secondly, the factors which influenced them to provide the
help.
     Before focusing on the specific results of the Sheffield
study I should like to put forward two reasons why I feel
that it is sometimes too glibly assumed that independence is
always the preferred state. As I shall illustrate, there are
people who are eager to assume dependency in both practical
and emotional terms. Secondly, there are certain goals which
it is quite impossible for anyone to achieve independently. I
refer here to the distinction which has sometimes been drawn
between emotional, social needs - for company, affection and
the like, and the need for practical tending.   The

independent attainment of social rewards is impossible. In the sense that we all require interaction with others in order to achieve such rewards, a state of interdependence at least is always necessary for their attainment.

However, it cannot be denied that independence has been shown to be tremendously important to many elderly people, particularly in relation to practical tasks and personal care. Many studies have found a large number of people experiencing difficulty with such activities, but not wishing to receive any help (Shanas, Townsend et al., 1968; Hunt, 1978; Abrams, 1978). In the Sheffield study, for example, one in five of the elderly people had difficulty in washing themselves all over. Although just under half of those in difficulty received no assistance, the vast majority (95 per cent) of these elderly people said that they did not wish to receive any help. This illustrates that if one is in a state of dependency then then one may choose to abandon the goal rather than to engage in any search for help. Thus elderly people perhaps preferred to strip wash, rather than take a bath. Another example of abandoning a goal might be the elderly widow who preferred to eat no meat, because there was no local butcher, rather than to receive assistance in shopping from further afield. It may be of course, in any situation where an elderly person experiences difficulty, that other parties may disapprove of the abandonment of the goal and may seek to persuade the elderly person to accept help in order that the goal might be achieved. Thus, the carers described occasions on which they tried to persuade their elderly relatives to make use of aids such as walking sticks or hearing aids when the elderly person showed considerable reluctance to do so. Equally one son commented on his mother's reluctance to accept assistance with bathing:

Well, I can smell my mother, I put it as blunt as that. (Son)

Thus it has to be acknowledged that different people will define different goals as desirable and that conflict may arise in a given situation. However, having acknowledged this, let us suppose that the elderly person does not wish to abandon a particular goal which they find themselves unable to achieve unaided. What bases of influence are there which will induce other people to provide the required assistance? With regard to influences on relatives, particularly children, one may broadly divide them into two kinds of pressures: external and internal. 'External' pressure derives from a general framework of beliefs about the obligations of children, and about appropriate gender roles, which combine to produce sets of expectations that particular relatives will provide assistance. These beliefs are reinforced in general through the media: newspaper articles, television programmes, and so on. Neighbours and statutory workers will also convey these expectation directly to the particular relatives involved.[1] Factors 'internal' to the relationship include the history of the relationship, its quality, and the specific responses to ageing and dependency exhibited by the elderly person. It is contended that these external and internal factors sometimes reinforce each other, but sometimes they do not. The remainder of this paper will concentrate on internal factors, although references will be made to external factors where appropriate.[2]

Abrams (1980) suggests that informal assistance was based on a productive balance of reciprocity, affect and trust that was particular to individual relationships. Certainly the assumed basis of obligation felt by children towards their parents appears to be reciprocity:

> Let's face it. They've brought us up haven't they? They struggled to bring you up so when they get to that age you automaticaly take over.

> I mean, they will have gone without to bring their children up ... it's more or less saying thank you for what they've done.

All carers were specifically asked whether they felt that the relationship was now one-sided compared with the past. Some carers, mostly neighbours, were unable to compare the present relationship with that which obtained in the past, since the relationship was not yet long-term. However, the responses of those who could make this comparison are given in Table 1.

Table 1

**Responses to a Question About
One-Sidedness of the Relationship**

One sided?	n	%
More so now	17	40
Always has been	7	16
Never has been (and is not now)	19	44
TOTAL	43	100

What meaning can be found behind the categories identified in this table? People who said that the relationship was not, and never had been one-sided - just under half of all informal carers - gave responses such as:

169

> She always just seems to be there. When the kids have
> been ill she'll come and sit with them while I go out and
> do the shopping and that. And she's very good with
> them. All the grandchildren are the same with my mum.
> She's very patient.
> (Daughter)

> 'I think she helps me more than I help her at the
> moment.'
> (Daughter)

Carers who felt that the relationship had become more
one-sided explained that their elderly relative or friend could
no longer perform reciprocal services:

> My mother isn't capable of living on her own. She has
> arthritis so badly some days she can't turn her taps on.
> She couldn't lift a teapot up. She couldn't open a milk
> bottle. Simple things like these.'
> (Daughter)

> She used to do ironing for me and this sort of thing and
> she used to wash up. She still keeps a little bit but
> she doesn't do as much. One thing - her eyes aren't
> very good you see.
> (Daughter-in-law)

But by far the majority of these carers made comments
which illustrate that they felt that they personally owed their
parents a debt for past assistance, even if not for present
help.

> Any time I needed her she'd come at the drop of a hat
> so I feel I owe it back, you see, if she needs it. It
> works both ways doesn't it?
> (Daughter)

> They (parents) were always good to us. I think well we
> should be good to them shouldn't we? They've looked
> after us.
> (Daughter)

However, what of those few who considered the
relationship had always been one-sided? Responses
illustrating this would be:

> She's never been a mother as mothers should be, love.
> She was out every day of her life and she didn't want
> anyone, any kids, any daughter's troubles coming to her
> house to upset her routine because at half past six even
> if the King and Queen was in the house at the time she'd

170

be down that path to the Working Men's Club.
(Son-in-law)

He's never lifted a finger for anyone in this family.
(Daughter)

Thus our data suggests that neither current not past reciprocity is a necessary conditon for engaging in helping behaviour since all those relatives interviewed were giving assistance, no matter what their perception of past help. Of course this does not rule out the possibility that some relatives who feel no sense of debt do refuse to provide assistance, but relatives who did not help were not interviewed.

Affect

Consideration is now given to whether people felt emotionally close to the elderly person they were helping. Table 2 gives responses for the children in our sample.

Table 2

Feelings of Emotional Closeness
Reported by Children

Emotionally close?	n	%
Yes	29	72
No	7	18
Other response	4	10
TOTAL	40	100

Those carers who were not children were less likely to report feeling emotionally close to the elderly person. Less than half of them did so. They were more inclined to stress friendly neighbourly helping rather than emotional closeness. What kind of things did those who reported emotional closeness say?

My relationship with my father has never changed since I were born. We have just been good friends all of us lives, kind of thing, you know. It's no use me telling you it changes because it doesn't.
(Daughter)

I took to my mother-in-law when I first met her, well before I was married. I took to her straight away. She was a person you could take to, you know, straight away. (Daughter-in-law)

171

In contrast, those who were not close gave responses
such as the following:

It's difficult if you haven't the same wavelength. It's
very difficult, I must admit. My mother and I aren't on
the same wavelength and I think she gets better
company from other people than she does from me. It's
as simple as that.
(Daughter)

With my mother and I there's usually been conflict. For
instance, she'll cause trouble between my brother and
myself by playing one off against the other. So there is
an element in my mother's character that I know I
couldn't live with.
(Daughter)

He leaned on me a lot and depended on me, but he
didn't like me. He didn't like anybody. I didn't like
him either. At one bit of me life I hated me father.
(Daughter)

Is there any connection between affect and reciprocity?
Those who were close did not necessarily recall past help.
However in general this meant that they had not needed any
help or that the elderly person had not been in a position to
give any. It would seem that what might have a destructive
effect upon liking, would be a situation in which the child
was in need of help which the elderly person appeared to be
able to give but did not in fact give. Naturally numbers are
too small for generalisation, but those children who did not
feel close to their parents recalled neither past nor present
help, and the majority said that the relationship had always
been one-sided.

Although it has been stated that neither liking nor past
help were necessary conditions for practical help in later life,
such factors seem to have an influence on the possibility that
the carer would be willing to form a joint household, should
this become necessary. Of course not all carers gave an
unequivocal response to such a question, although the
majority did so. Responses are presented in Table 3.

These responses are restricted to children. No
non-relatives would have considered the possibility of a joint

Table 3

**Responses of Children to Questions about
The Formation of a Joint Household**

	n	%
would like to now	4	10
would if necessary	16	40
definitely not	11	27
ambivalent response	9	22
TOTAL	40	100

household. Most considered that the care of the elderly person in extremis was not their responsibility. To illustrate the responses of children: firstly, those who said they would form a joint household if necessary:

> If she was ill or something like that I would have her here. I promised her that she will not go anywhere. I will look after her, you know.
> (Daughter)

> 'I suppose if she gets ill or anything, you know, then we'd do more, or I'd have her up here. I've always said that she can live here, and she will.'
> (Daughter)

A more ambivalent response might be:

> I have to be honest and say that I don't want her to come and live here because... I mean... obviously it would disrupt the whole household. But I'd rather her be here than worrying about her down there (at elderly person's own home).
> (Daughter)

This contrasts quite clearly with the definite intention not to form such a household illustrated by:

> 'I would never have her to live with me, ever. You can write that down.'
> (Daughter)

> 'No, it wouldn't work at all. Definitely not.'
> (Son)

With regard to the initial point about emotional closeness, the vast majority of those who were not close said that they definitely would not be willing to form a joint household.

Whereas only five out of 29 (17 per cent) of those who felt emotionally close said that they would not be willing to do so.

The Dynamics of Emotional Closeness

Of course, it is important not to suggest that feelings of closeness are a constant. Certainly dependency and the reaction towards it can change people's feelings towards each other. One helper commented on the difference between her two parents in this respect.

> Yes, it (helping) could have made us less close. I mean, depending on what type they are. As I say my mum and dad - my dad's very, very thoughtful. My mum tends to think I'm her daughter and I've got nothing else to do. 'You should be with me'. My dad will say 'You do your best for us love and we'll be grateful for what you do'. Well my mum will say 'You could come a bit more often'.
> (Daughter)

Bearing in mind our definitions of dependency and power we shall proceed to consider carers' descriptions of responses to dependency and disability.

Responses to Dependency and Disability

At one extreme lies the determined refusal of help:

> If we went up there and said, look we're going to give your house a good clean up. He just follows us round. 'Why don't you leave us alone. House is right enough for us. Why don't you leave it?' You can't work like that.
> (Son-in-law)

> He won't always accept help if you could get it. You know - 'what do you come here for - noseying around?', that's my dad.
> (Daughter)

These kind of instances illustrate the cases in which it is difficult for relatives to accept the wish of the elderly person not to receive help. Of course carers can be over-protective. It is important to recognise the sources of their anxiety, which may be both genuine concern for the health and safety of the elderly person, as well as a fear of condemnation by others should anything unfortunate happen. Carers may have a well justified fear that other people will not understand that their respect for the elderly person's desire for independence led to an acceptance of risk in that person's life, if the risks may lead to the elderly person being discovered in a state which other people will judge to be unacceptable.

However, as has been mentioned, there is an opposite mode of response: the eager acceptance of dependency:

> This was one of the things that put my hackles up. Father was alive when I first moved in here. When she first came to inspect the property she said 'Oh yes, I shall be alright here when your father goes'. I couldn't believe my ears. She not only planned that my father was going to go first, but that she was coming here ... I thought, please dad don't go.
> (Daughter)

Although there were a few parents who insisted stubbornly on independence, in fact such an attitude was more often described by carers who were not the elderly person's children. Indeed a larger number of children complained of being taken for granted rather than of the elderly person's desire for independence.

> The main thing is that she expects me to be there when I'm wanted, and I suppose it's a natural thing that. I only hope I never get like that, but I think that's it, taken for granted I think, you know, you must drop everything and you don't have a life of your own. You get that you've not made any plans so you know nothing can be put off.
> (Daughter)

One general area of conflict over who should expect what, arose in relation to gender role expectations. It seemed that elderly men had been used to a high level of domestic servicing from their wives, and carers certainly felt that their own generation had different attitudes in this respect.

> Well my mother did. She used to wait on him hand and foot, clean his shoes and everything and he thought I were going to be able to do all t' same, but I told him I can't, you know.
> (Daughter)

> My mother used to mollycoddle him, if you have heard that term. I just accept it. I mean I've known him so long I know this is him ... Obviously my husband does a lot more in the home than my father has ever done, you see, and I think it irks him slightly to seem me having to get his (father's) supper ready and that sort of thing. It's a bit of a bone of contention with the rest

of the family that he never does anything when he comes.
(Daughter)

Another carer complained that her mother-in-law became agitated when the carer's husband performed domestic tasks, because she clearly felt that these should be the responsibility of her daughter-in-law. Thus, generational differences in assumptions about appropriate gender roles could occur in a number of ways. Daughters might resent the expectations by their fathers of a high level of servicing which they were not accustomed to provide even within their own households. Secondly, even if daughters were prepared to provide such help their spouse or other family members might resent this. Lastly, elderly women and men might discourage help which crossed traditional gender boundaries. The expectation of service by women seemed to be very firmly rooted in elderly men. Community support workers in Sheffield told of an elderly man of 73 whose wife died. Having no-one to look after him he decided that he must move back in with his mother. She was 95. The Sheffield study did show that elderly women who had difficulty in performing routine household tasks were more likely than elderly men to express frustration or annoyance at this fact.

Strategies for Achieving Control

The remainder of this discussion will concentrate on the various strategies which are reportedly used by both elderly people and carers in attempts to control the situation. Occasionally parents attempted to control by the straightforward assumption of parental authority.

You see, she'd got into her own routine and her own way of thinking, her own way of dishing the orders out. She's not the easiest person to get on with. We had our moments. Anyway, I think I finally got her adjusted to my way of thinking. She would have had me in an asylum - 'get me this' and 'bring me that' - if you went out you were late... I've finished with that.
(Daughter)

The above attempt to assume authority was resisted by the daughter but this was not always the case. One carer, aged 63, reported:

As a child I was terrified of my father and I never ever lost this business of being afraid of him... I'm his daughter and he feels he can hit me when he likes.
(Daughter)

This quote illustrates the general point that whilst care within families can reflect the most warm and affectionate relationships it is also true that members of families can be uniquely badly treated by virtue of their relationship to the elderly person.

Of course relatives did have sources of power. Indeed one might expect that there is a sense in which dependency will confer power upon those whose assistance is necessary.

> I said many a time, you'll be in a home mother, I can never get on with you.
> (Daughter)

> Mother, you're going in a home (you say that to her do you?) Oh yes (what does she say?) Nothing, I think my mother has had enough of going in homes.
> (Daughter)

However a person in a situation of dependency does have a source of control if there are others who recognise an obligation to assist them. In some instances carers clearly felt that they were manipulated into providing assistance which, in the event, was not really necessary.

> She used to try it on really. She wanted a lot of attention. Like we do a lot of work for the scouts ... and when we're sort of busy and involved with them she'd suddenly be ill to get my attention and make me go up there. Like the time we moved in here I got a frantic phone message to say she was ill and I had to go dashing over the other side of Sheffield and when I got there there was nothing wrong with her.
> (Daughter)

For some carers this was often repeated with consequent destructive effects on the relationship.

> I used to be very upset when she used to ring and she wasn't very well. We used to go over, but now I get a bit ... I dont dash straight out of the house. I go, because you can't afford not to go you know, but my attitude is that when I used to go I used to panic, kind of thing. After two years you get a bit... I suppose a bit blasé about it in a way. Of course, this is where I suppose I feel guilty, that I don't get panicky and I don't rush straight away.
> (Daughter)

Responses to Dependency

Of course not all attempts at control through dependency were as overt as a recurring threat of serious illness. A few carers mentioned the development of minor illnesses or depression in their elderly relative just before they were about to take a holiday break.

Consequences of Control Strategies

The feeling of being manipulated was damaging to relationships. Indeed one carer explicitly said that it was less depressing to provide quantities of help when it was obviously needed than to feel that one was being manipulated.

When I rather feel that what I'm doing the running for is not a physical thing but because she's depressed then I get very agitated and I do tend to get a little bit down. (Step-daughter)

Emotional dependency could be as wearing as the need to provide practical assistance.

I feel as though I'm smothered in a way. I can't go out and just do. If she rings up and I'm not there she gets quite upset. (Daughter)

When carers become convinced that their parents' demands were not based on physical disability such experiences could be damaging to the relationships. Of course depression, anxiety and other mental disorders which afflict some people in old age (such as dementia), may all cause elderly people to behave in ways which their relatives perceive as hurtful, or manipulative, and may thus increase strain upon relatives and reduce the possibility of care continuing to be given in the longer term without additional assistance, although these difficulties might be reduced by giving some explanation to the carer of the reasons for the elderly person's behaviour.

However, it was clear that no matter what the past history of the relationship with the elderly person, or the carer's current feelings about that person, other possible helpers for the elderly person (whether from formal or informal sources) all tended to make the prima facie assumption that the elderly person's relatives were the first choice of people to help them. There was in some cases a considerable resentment at the perception that judgements were always initially made in favour of elderly people: in the sense of assuming that they had the right to expect to receive assistance from family members. Carers did try sometimes to enlist the aid of statutory workers, for example in persuading elderly people that it would be best for them to make use of the aids which had been provided. However, it was much easier for relatives to argue for statutory assistance to be given to elderly people if they could put forward their own informal commitments or personal incapacity for the task. For them to choose not to provide assistance would be, they felt, to be seen to be unacceptable and lead to their being subject to social disapproval. Of course most families did care and did provide practical assistance and in many cases this was what they wished to do. Whilst every assistance should be given to those people who wish to provide such help in order to make sure that they do not suffer unreasonable personal hardship, the findings of the Sheffield study also suggest both, that there are some people who may need assistance in resisting dependency demands, and that there are yet other families who should not be expected to care. Indeed, in the case of a few elderly people it would probably be true to say that their children would be the very last people who should be expected to provide them with assistance in old age.

Notes

(1) These external pressures were the subject of my paper given to this conference last year and so are only briefly referred to in this chapter.
(2) Full discussion of all these issues is included in the report of the Sheffield Study (Qureshi and Walker, 1986).

References

Abrams, M. (1978) Beyond Three Score Years and Ten, Age Concern, London.
Abrams, P. (1980) 'Social Change, Social Networks and Neighbourhood Care', Social Work Service, No.22, pp.22-23.
Anderson, M. (1971) Family Structure in Nineteenth Century Lancashire, Cambridge University Press, Cambridge.
Hunt, A. (1978) The Elderly at Home, HMSO, London.
Qureshi, H. and Walker, A. (forthcoming) The Caring Relationship, Macmillan, London.
Shanas, E., Townsend, P. et al. (1968) Old People in Three Industrial Societies, Routledge and Kegan Paul, London.

Chapter Fifteen

AMERICAN EXPERIMENTS TO SUBSTITUTE HOME

FOR INSTITUTIONAL LONG-TERM CARE :

POLICY LOGIC AND EVALUATION

Bleddyn Davies

Introduction

As the paper by the Association of County Councils (ACC)
(1985) shows, the structure of the formal economy of health
and social services depends more than anything else on the
degree to which the central government and the health and
social care agencies are willing to design and single-mindedly
to implement a policy of 'community care' which improves the
quality of life of dependents and defines the role of informal
carers more equitably. The ACC guesstimates suggest that a
policy which successfully attains these goals would be almost
unimaginable without massively more efficient use of
resources; enormous technical progress and achieving
uniformly high performance in pressing against the limits of
the welfare gains achievable from resources.
    Efficiency-improvement in long-term care can be achieved
by one or a combination of the following means:
(1) Mixing inputs in ways which make better use of their
    relative prices and their substitutability in the production
    of welfare. Following the conventions of the production
    of welfare approach, let us call that improving input mix
    efficiency.
(2) Producing a mix of outputs which better reflects the
    relative valuations of increments of them; i.e. improving
    output mix efficiency.
(3) Producing more outputs for any mix of inputs;
    i.e. improving technical efficiency.
(4) Ensuring that a higher proportion of the resources are
    allocated to those who are currently most helped by them,
    and who are therefore defined to be members of the
    target group; i.e. improving vertical target efficiency.
(5) Ensuring that a higher proportion of members of the
    target group receive what is most appropriate for them;
    i.e. improving horizontal target efficiency.
    There are no doubt periods during which the most
dramatic gains in efficiency will take mainly one of these

forms. However, the healthy development of a system must depend on the search for efficiency of all kinds. All can require or result in the substitution of other modes for institutional care. My paper argues that in these experiments the Americans have focused on devices to improve efficiency of kinds relatively neglected in this country, so that efficiency-improvements may be biased in different directions in the two countries.

It has often been argued that even when systems seem to be making a most radical break with their pasts, they are usually reacting against some features while accepting others without question. Above all, the American policy analysts of the mid and late 1970s were reacting against the dependence on nursing home care. Indeed, most were more clearly designed to prevent unnecessary institutional admission than to improve efficiency.

The Crisis in Long-Term Care

Spending on nursing homes increased more than any other heads during the decade after the introduction of Medicare and Medicaid.[1] The increase in spending was due to higher costs per patient as well as to larger numbers.[2] However, the high costs per patient day did not buy the patients high standards of care and a good quality of life. The trickle of nursing home scandals reported in the media from time to time became a deluge, as in 1970. State and federal inquiries like the Moreland Commission in New York, confirmed what journalists had asserted: widespread venality and corruption among providers, fraud committed against patients and the state, sometimes of a breathtaking scale, increasingly expensive but unevenly effective attempts to assure quality, avoid fraud and abuse, and secure value for state money, rapid and apparently uncontrolled escalation in costs. The title chosen for important books and reports summarise the message: Tender Loving Greed (Mendelson, 1974); Unloving Care: the nursing home tragedy (Vladeck, 1979); Entering a Nursing Home: Costly Implications for Medicaid and the Elderly (General Accounting Office, 1979). Though there was massive unmet need in the community, investigations concluded that there was widespread inappropriate placement in hospitals and nursing homes; a Congressional Budget Office Study infering that the rates of over-utilisation of nursing homes varying from 6 to 76 per cent (Congressional Budget Office, 1977).

Policy analysts reacted first by proposing new methods for financing and regulating nursing home demand and supply, and secondly by promoting the development of substitute forms of service.[3] The arguments included the following:

181

(1) **Arrangements for the public financial aid of those in need of long-term care tended to channel demands towards nursing homes from home and day care services.** Medicaid provided a straightforward source of finance for nursing home care of the poor and the near-poor, but there was not a corresponding source of finance for long-term home and day care. Medicaid (and more so Medicare) regulations biased consumption against home and day care services by restricting both the categories of persons eligible for help and the range and duration of services which might be provided. Unbiased mechanisms for financing demand might not alone be sufficient for efficiency; but in the words of the directors of one of the seminal experiments, 'comprehensive assessment of health care needs and coordination and monitoring of care that has no relationship to reimbursement and no control over financial resources is essentially impotent' (Hodgson and Quinn, 1980). Moreover, Medicaid and Medicare were unambiguously health care programmes, and the nature of the conditions which they imposed distorted care objectives; reinforcing what Meltzer and Farrow (1980) called 'over-medicalisation', 'over-institutionalisation', and 'over-professionalisation'.

(2) **Home care services were difficult to assemble, being provided by different agencies and subject to a wide variety of eligibility criteria.** Not only was skilled assessment required. Efficient packaging required highly specialised knowledge of local systems and time, skill and influence. Few agencies had sophisticated arrangements for the thorough performance of each of the core tasks necessary for the efficient management of cases from its perspective. Hardly any had efficient arrangements for the efficient management of cases from the perspective of the system as a whole. Since those who rationed the services on behalf of individual agencies took into account at most the costs of the agency, there could be cases where total home care costs much exceeded the costs of institutional care because they consumed home and day care services from several agencies (Piktialis, 1981). Only some of the costs to their agencies were visible to many of the allocators. In the United Kingdom, the ratio of visible to the hidden costs of a service can vary greatly between recipients (Davies and Challis, 1986), and no doubt the same is so for American agencies. Again there were few incentives to take on cases who were demanding because of their dependency, personality traits or behaviour problems.

(3) **Home care services were available in insufficient quantity and variety to meet the demands of all those who could most beneficially receive them, particularly in rural areas and the centres of cities.** Therefore the costs of a package of home care might be needlessly great because the monopoly service provider might be taking too much

profit, might be inefficient (as it seems are many VNAs) or unscrupulous (like some home care agencies), might not be willing to deliver a less elaborate package or one producing at least cost the mix of outcomes most needed by the client. I have seen several areas in which non-proprietory visiting nurse associations and home health agencies alike impose restrictions on packages whose sole purpose must be to increase their turnover.

I shall now discuss the score or so of major experimental projects set up in the late 1970s and early 1980s in response to these problems. I shall call them the HCFA (Health Care Financing Administration) projects, though HCFA did not finance the evaluations of them all, and HCFA financed evaluations of others. I have chosen them because most embody features intended to tackle all the causes of the excessive use of nursing homes I have listed, all were large; and all were evaluated. The link between the causes and the features constitute the common elements of their policy logics. Most of the strategic features which differentiate between them (like other innovatory American schemes for the substitution of other care for nursing home and hospitals) reflect either differences in perception about the relative importance of the causes, or the relative influence of groups with different interests in the development and implementation of the schemes. Space does not permit me to describe each of them; merely to hazard some generalisations about the logic and success of their design feature.[4]

Logic and Success of the Design Features

Corresponding to each of the causes of the diversion of demand to institutional forms of long-term care are devices which in one form or another were found in each of the experiments.

Mechanisms for Financing the Substitute Forms of Provision

Waivers and a Single Funds Pool

The HCFA projects financed services principally through 'waivers' to some of the Medicaid and Medicare regulations. Medicaid waivers made more equal the access of the poor and near-poor to non-institutional modes of care. Medicare waivers made more accessible non-hospital care for those who would otherwise utilise hospital beds. What was waivered reflected the interests of the states and the federal government as well as differences in logic. So Medicare waivers were associated with project designs intended to provide care which would make less likely repeated hospitalisations; and so reduce federal spending more,

possibly without great reductions in state expenditures.
At first sight, one would expect the range of resources which the waivers permitted managers to tap to be of great importance for efficiency improvement because the greater the extension of the range of options, the greater the potential for substituting lower for higher cost inputs and the more closely adjusted may be the mix of outputs to the circumstances and values of clients and their informal carers; that is, the greater the degrees of input and output mix efficiencies. But this is not necessarily the case. In projects with the most generous waivers, some of the permitted services were consumed by few. It has not yet been established that projects with waivers allowing a long menu of services had great variety of packages and as a result large improvements in efficiency. However, there were examples where apparently small differences in the nature of the waivers seem to affect care planning considerably. For instance, in experiments with waivers which were extensive with respect to services but not to the duration of services, case managers negotiating care plans with the users first exhaust the more generous Medicare waivers and then draw on the less generous Medicaid waivers to produce a less appropriate package of care. The incentives facing case managers and clients were not to make the best use of resources of the system as a whole. The pattern of the resulting inefficiency would seem to be quite predictable.
The simplest arrangements for extending and equalising was the pooling of funds from categorical sources. All funds from federal and state sources were pooled in the financial control model of the channelling projects. In this respect, the financial control model of channelling is the most similar of the American experiments to the community care models we are experimenting with at the PSSRU. However, the effects seem to have been disappointing.[5] It seems that in the areas with the most elaborate service systems, services accounting for a substantial proportion of total expenditure were financed from other resources. So the pooling was insufficient to secure optimisation for the service system as a whole.

Budget Caps

It will be remarked that in most forms of standard provision, those allocating services are either unaware of the opportunity costs of what they provided or had only a partial view of the costs of alternative care modes. Many of the experiments attempted to correct this by setting limits to the value of services which could be allocated to any one client.[6] However, most allowed some discretion transforming the caps from limits to guidelines.
The span of the costs chargeable to the budget in effect determines the range of interests which the case managers

have incentives to take into account. We have seen that in the more advanced service systems, the budgets in even the financial control model of channelling did not cover all the important substitute and complementary services. The evaluation shows that as a result many in the control group received adequate substitutes in some areas. Using data from our community care evaluations, David Challis and I show great variations in the ratio of costs taken into account to other costs with various definitions of the span of budgetary control (Davies and Challis, 1986, Chap. 13). One would expect the same to be so for the systems for which the American experiments collected data.

In one respect, the American experiments constrained the use of the budgets more than the PSSRU's community care projects. The waivers were for spending on provision by formal organisations; not for spending on the provision of service by individuals. Therefore the most important of the input substitutions of the British community care projects was not available to the American care managers. Whereas American managers match agency services to needs, British community care workers match resources to needs. David Challis and I have argued that the deployment of paid and unpaid helpers in the British community care projects have contributed greatly to the dramatic successes we have described; to the great increase in outputs as well as to the reduction of the costs of outputs (Davies and Challis, 1981; 1986; Challis and Davies, 1985a; 1985b). The Thanet community care project appears to have achieved better results than any of the American experiments, except perhaps the Los Angeles VA hospital experiment (Rubinstein et al., 1984), and that dealt with a rather different clientele from the Thanet project. Perhaps some mix like the community care cocktail of case manager skill, time and value commitment may be a necessary condition for such results with that target clientele; but the authority to use the budget with the greater flexibility shown by British community care workers may also be a necessary condition.

One would also expect such resources to affect the degree to which the provision of more home care services would result in the reduction of inputs from informal carers. American policy analysts greatly feared this. However the experimental results there (as in British community care projects) show that where (as in South Carolina), case managers directly involved informal carers in planning and provision, the result was not a massive reduction in their inputs but a change in the tasks performed. Where however, informal carers were not involved in care planning and middle management did not monitor and seek to influence these outcomes (as in the New York Home Care Project), informal carers did indeed reduce their inputs despite the effort made to ensure their continuing commitment.

American structures made the use of the budget more difficult in another respect: the complex combinations of quality price and availability facing case managers.[7] Without such sophisticated aids as computer-based information and optimising algorithms showing the price, quality and other characteristics of what was actually available and showing the cost consequences of alternative care plans, case managers must have found it impossible to make the best use of resources. However in itself, the complexity presents opportunities for greater diversity of substitutions, and so the better matching of services to needs.[8]

So the creation of implicit or explicit budgets made input substitutions possible. How much they contributed to efficiency depended on their precise form. However it also depended on other aspects of arrangements for the performance of the core of case management. Therefore at this stage we must return to the second argument of the policy analysts: that many were admitted to institutions for long-term care unnecessarily because of the difficulty of assembling adequate and economic home care services.

Case Management and the Assembly of Packages

All the experiments attempted the closer tailoring of services to individual needs by the better performance of at least some of the following core tasks of case mangement: case finding (securing the referral of all those who would be best helped by the range of services offered and who in other ways satisfied the need criteria defined) and screening (ensuring that those referred did in fact satisfy the eligibility criteria); assessment of client circumstances; the planning of care packages with the recipient and others and the negotiation and arrangement of services with providers; and the monitoring of provision (checking the quality and appropriateness of what is provided and ensuring the adaptation of the care plan to changing circumstances). 'Basically, case management means a single worker dealing with multiple client needs and mobilising a range of services from intake until service goals are met ... case managers can be seen as an intervention structure between the individual and the complex array of bureaucracies providing programmes' (Goodman, 1981).

Indeed, many of the experiments were primarily in the creation of a system for the more thorough performance of these tasks. Taken with other devices, some perceived the case management systems to create a hidden hand which would mould the whole development of the long-term care system by channelling demand to some services more than to others and within services, to efficient and high quality providers, and by identifying gaps in and creating mechanisms for filling them.

The experiments did not operate the same arrangements for performing case management tasks. A detailed analysis of the way in which the experiments differed in their case management is given in Chapter 3 of Davies and Challis (1986). Two sets of differentiating characteristics seem to have had substantial efficiency effects: the caseloads and range of tasks of case managers in relation to the complexity of the situations of target clients and the providing system; and the targetting intended and achieved.

Caseloads and the Range of Tasks Performed

At least one experiment (Access) seemed to have improved efficiency although it operated with high caseloads and saw itself as providing a mainly administrative brokerage service. It delegated the performance of most case management tasks directly to providing agencies. However, the Wisconsin Community Care Organisation (CCO) concluded that the direct model permitted greater control, and that this improved efficiency; and preliminary results of the attempt to replicate the intensity and style of the British community care projects in an experiment using the cases of the main Access project as a control group suggests that a more direct and intensive service can achieve greater gains.

Targetting Intended and Achieved

The general descriptions of target groups differed: for instance between persons at risk of institutional admission within a certain period of time, persons in the community refered for nursing home entry, persons at the point of discharge from hospital or nursing home, persons living in institutions who had spent down to Medicaid eligibility, and persons for whom continued institutional stay seemed inappropriate.

The targetting achieved as much reflected the procedure which programmes had been able to negotiate as targetting intentions. As one might expect from the inadequacy of functional capacity as a predictor of admission to institutions for long-term care, the most successful in demonstrating reductions in the costs of care, and so efficiency improvement by one or more criteria other than horizontal target efficiency, were those which intervened most directly in the processes leading to admission to care, not the ones which defined the strictest criteria of functional incapacity[9]. Indeed, eligibility criteria which were extremely strict with respect to functional incapacity tended to be self-defeating, since not only did they define the eligible population in a way which was not highly correlated with the probability of admission to institutions, but they also narrowed it so much that the case management agency lost much of the systems impact desired.[10] What was essential was the political will to ensure that the case management agency had the authority and power to negotiate itself into the precedures at key stages for as high a proportion of those at risk of unnecessary admission to institutions for long-term care, and to have sanctions to apply to those who attempted to sidestep its decisions. Failure to establish its domain could lead either to the narrowing of its systematic influence as in channelling or to changing the target population as in one of the sites of the Wisconsin CCO.

An implication is that it may not be possible to set detailed and enforceable criteria of eligibility centrally. Several experiments attempted to do so. Scoring systems were used in several projects, the scores being computed centrally from questionnaires completed by the field personnel. However the scoring systems were sensitive to controvertible judgements. There is evidence that those who complete the questionnaire both overstate the overall level of needs and make the answers to the questions fit their perception of the level of need (Decker, 1982; Seidl et al., 1983; Sager, 1983). So without elaborate checking procedures with hands-on assessment contemporaneous with the assessments by field personnel for a large sample of clients, the collection of data neither allowed the central control of decisions nor prevented the displacement of the targetting goals of the experiments.

The Insufficient Supply of Home Care Services

This was a pervasive and in many circumstances necessary feature of most experiments.[11] However, gap-filling was not in itself sufficient for much efficiency improvement: one can not expect much efficiency improvement from the coordination of non-existent services.

Evaluation Methodologies

The most elaborate evaluations of these experiments as of experiments in this country have two components: an 'outcome analysis' of costs, service utilisation, targetting and other outcomes, in general heavily statistical, often using multivariate modelling and presenting a vast amount of tabular material from the extremely elaborate data bases collected using sophisticated experimental designs; and a 'process' analysis component, often more ethnographic, focused on 'Type III' error (the translation of experimental intent into actual experimental inputs), and on the relations between features of the implementation and outcomes.

The professional standards of the best work is extremely high. However, it is difficult to obtain from the voluminous reports clear answers to questions about the quantitative

scale of efficiency improvements in general or of each type,
or clear analysis of the causes of the efficiency improvements
and the degree to which they are due to features which may
be replicable. The reason is that although the objective of
the analysis is to describe and explain efficiency
improvements, the evaluators have not seen the design issues
at such a high level of generality. Starting from specific
questions set by their federal research managers, they treat
related issues as separate, and do not answer the special
cases of the general questions begged when the issue is seen
as efficiency improvement: such questions as 'what differences
are made by the experimental inputs to the costs of the
outcomes which most matter to each constituency of persons
or organisation which share a perception of what are the
principal costs and outcomes?'; 'what difference is made to the
costs of outcomes by circumstances of users which care
planners judge to be 'clinically relevant', needs which should
be taken into account in care planning?'; or 'what are the
effects on the costs of outputs of the characteristics of the
systems?' Analyses of costs are kept separate from those of
outcomes. No distinction is made between the interests of
different groups in the analysis of costs and outputs. It is
often unclear which is the precise concept which costs
variables measure. No distinction is made between outcomes
of evaluative importance in their own right and 'intermediate'
outputs, outcomes of interest mainly because they make more
likely some outcome of more direct and ultimate evaluatory
significance. Similarly the process analyses are marred
because of the absence of the more general questions: their
selection of issues to discuss is more arbitrary, and they lack
clear criteria of relevance with which to discipline data
collection and analysis. Americans were attracted by the
production of welfare approach to evaluation because it
appeared to tackle some of these problems, and no equivalents
had been applied in American long-term care research.

Conclusion

These American experiments have much to teach us.

Evaluation Lessons

(1) Some of the giant American experiments draw better on
methodologies for handling evidence: for instance in the
development of indicators and the analysis of design effects.
Also some are extraordinarily effective at the organisation of
large research teams for the collation and sophisticated
handling of data for experiments reporting within periods of
five years or less.
(2) Some well illustrate the importance of using process
evaluations to search for the consequences of disjunctions

between experimental intent and experimental input; process analysis to identify 'Type III' errors.

Lessons for Policy Development

(1) 'Type III' errors often emerged as the implementations responded to pressures from their staff and the outside world. It is worth studying the experiments to understand how management can limit goal displacement without preventing desirable adaptations of function and practice.
(2) During the last thirty years, Great Britain has used its growth in resources mainly to increase quality, and extend the range, of individual services. The American projects are important because they illustrate experiments with devices to secure the better matching of services to the circumstances of clients. The PSSRU census of efficiency-improving innovations in England and Wales showed that such efforts were rare here in 1982 (Ferlie et al., 1983; 1984a; 1984b; Ferlie and Davies, 1984). There were hardly any attempts to make substantial systematic changes which would greatly improve the effectiveness of the performance of most of the case management tasks. There were some led by consultants, supported often from joint finance. Apart from the community care projects, there appeared to be only the most crude and modest attempts emanating from social services departments. An important development has been the creation of teams which combine health and social service research to support in their own homes persons at high risk of admission to institutions for long-term care. However, few perform all the tasks of case management and they do not constitute attempts to set up case management systems for a large proportion of those needing long term care. Every major structural change in the health and social services this century has made more self-absorbed health and social care agencies and each set of field personnel.
The importance of experiments with case management systems is that four out of the five aspects of efficency distinguished in the introduction depend directly on the performance of the core tasks of case management. This is illustrated in Figure 1. Only the technical efficiency of individual services is independent of case management tasks, and this may be affected by effective monitoring with feedback to higher management.
So some of the main lessons are for such areas as field organisation and the relationship between task, skill and training; and the definition of authority and responsibility; the use of devices like budgets and pooled funds; the creation of exchange relationships with the personnel of other agencies; the collaboration and or cooperation of professionals of different backgrounds. Others are about the creation of systems to support field management: devices for quality

Figure 1

Principal Causal Connections Between

Case Management Tasks and Aspects of Efficiency

Case Management Tasks   Aspects of efficiency

Case finding: Offering service
and removing impediments to
uptake by those who should be
recipients ─────────────────→ Horizontal target efficiency

Screening for eligibility:
ensuring that referrals and
recipients are in sufficient
need and are best helped by──→ Vertical target efficiency
the service

Assessment of user circumstances

Care planning and the arrangement
of service and support ──────→ Output mix efficiency

Monitoring ←─────────────────→ Input mix efficiency

Gap filling: mobilisation and
management of community resources
to fill gaps left by services and
existing support networks   Technical efficiency

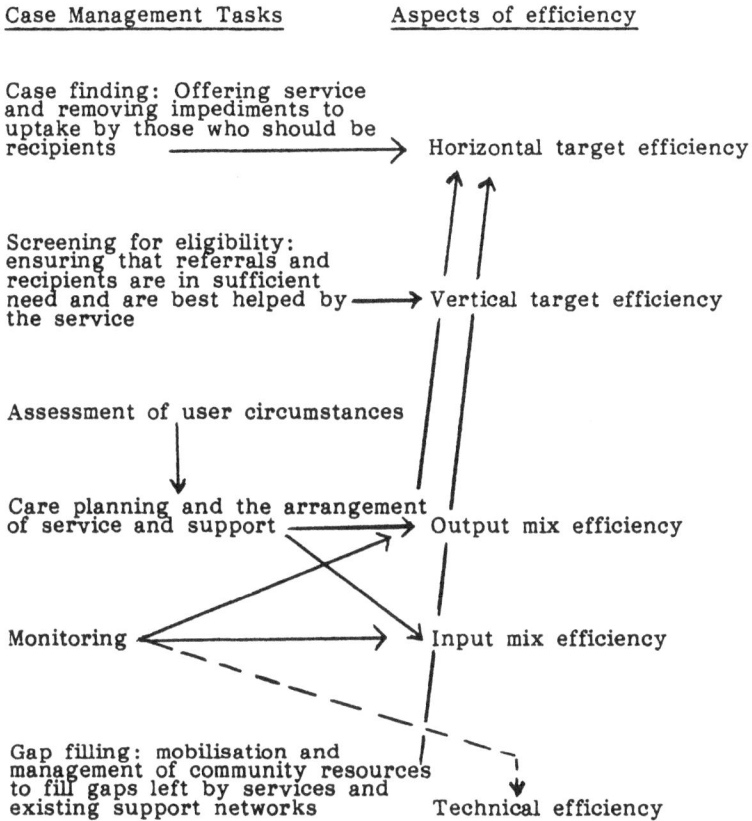

Note: Arrows signify direct causal relationship.   Broken
line signifies an indirect effect.

Matching Resources to Needs in Community Care, Chapter 2.

assurance; the control of targetting, the incidence of costs and benefits, the locus of teams in relation to the input substitutions desired and the other subjects discussed in Matching Resources to Needs in Community Care. This is not to argue that we should ape, even imitate these American projects: merely that we should observe them closely, learn from the analyses of their performance, and think about their implications for home grown British developments.

Notes

(1) In 1966, federal personal health care expenditure for the elderly totalled $8.2 billion of which 15.4 per cent was spent on nursing homes. By 1977, total expenditure had increased five times and 25.5 per cent was spent on nursing homes. The share of publicly financed expenditures financed also grew rapidly. In 1966, only 30 per cent of total health care expenditures were public; in 1977, 67 per cent (Stassen and Holahan, 1980, 6). In some states the rapid development of whose systems seemed to presage the future for the country as a whole, the rate of increase was greater; for instance, in New York, there was an eightfold increase in nursing home expenditure between 1967 and 1975 (Davies, 1981). Much less was spent on home care services. The Congressional Budget Office estimated that of the federal spending on long-term care, 70 per cent was on nursing homes (Subcommittee on Health and the Environment, 79-865 0, 1981, p.2).
(2) For instance, in the State of New York, the Medicaid reimbursement rate for nursing homes increased by 165 per cent between 1967 and 1975, a period during which the consumer price index for the state increased by only 65 per cent (Davies, 1981, p.2).
(3) The first is described in Davies (1981) and such American writings as Vladeck (1979); and the effort to provide more beneficial and effective structure of sanctions and incentives continues though at a lower level since the Reagan cuts. The second was a theme of the White House Conference on Ageing of 1982 and of government reports and congressional hearings and of course, academic writings (US Congress, House of Representatives (1980), US Congress, Senate (1981)).
(4) The experiments on which I have based my argument include Triage-I and Triage-II, Access and its sub-project replicating the PSSRUs community care approach, the Virginia Community-based Care systems for the functionally disabled, the Wisconsin Community Care Organisation, On Lok Senior Health Services, California's MSSP, Georgia's Alternative Health Services, South Carolina's Community Long-Term Care Demonstration project, Texas ICFII, New York State's Long-Term Home Health Care projects, the New York State's

CASAs, Oregon's FIG/Waiver Continuum of Care Project for the Elderly, and the giant channelling experiment with ten sites throughout the United States. Others which I have visited, like the Florida CCE and Pentastar programmes, and to Massachussets Home Care Program, have much in common. I have talked to key personnel in most in 1980 and 1985 and collected material from them all.

All these experiments are large scale by British standards, involving the treatment of a large number of cases. Many have been more thoroughly evaluated than almost any here. The main contract for the evaluation and technical assistance for the channelling projects were to have cost $20 million in 1980 prices - more than the entire DHSS expenditure on non-medical research - and in fact cost far more.

Of course, they are only a small proportion of those who tackle the problems singly or partially. Like the British efficiency-improving innovations in the care of the frail elderly studied by my colleagues Ewan Ferlie, David Challis and I, most American innovations tend to tackle only one or a few causes of efficiency and then only by making very small changes having little effect on the system as a whole.

(5) We must await the definitive reports from the channelling evaluators and technical consultants before we can be sure about this. The financial control activities preoccupied case managers excessively, depriving them of the time they needed to case manage resourcefully and intensively; the demands on their time being all the greater because of the teething troubles of their computer-based financial system. Their caseloads were anyhow twice those of our British community case workers. As a result, some channelling staff argue that case managers might have been more resourceful in the basic than in the financial control sites. Again, our judgement must await the verdict of the technical consultants.

(6) Examples are the financial control model of the channelling demonstration, the New York's LTHHCPs (Birnbaum, Gaumer, Pratten and Burke, 1984), the Wisconsin CCO (Seidl, Applebaum, Austin and Mahoney, 1983), the Georgia Alternative Health Service Programme (Skellie, Favor, Tudor and Strauss, 1982), the South Carolina Long-Term Care Programme (Brown et al., 1983), Oregon's FIG/Waiver project (Special Projects Staff in Long-Term Care, 1981) and Washington State's Community Care Program (Solem, 1979).

(7) For instance, Triage, not operating in a service-rich area, established service contacts with 198 providers, and the Milwaukee site of the Wisconsin Community Care Organisation established 40 provider contacts for 14 services. Case managers in some service-rich areas may have faced an even wider range of combinations of service mix and quality from individual providers, all embodied in inter-agency agreements with the channelling agency, and so part of the menu of

American Experiments

prices.
(8) On Lok adapted a familiar strategy to British observers.
It concentrated a range of service provision in one
organisation. Therefore it was able to exercise more direct
management control and simplify the supply system.
Evaluators have argued that this did indeed enhance
efficiency. It was not clear whether as in the UK, this
biased the incentives to case managers in such a way as to
make highly variable the propensity of field personnel to
refer to independent producers of low cost high quality
services.
(9) Examples of the former were Access, the South Carolina
Long-Term Care Programme and the Virginia Pre-Admission
Screening Program (Carnes and Cook, 1977). Access
provided its case management free of charge to all applicants
to nursing home places irrespective of their Medicaid
eligibility as an incentive to attract those with private means
for whom home care might be an alternative. As the agency
certifying the need for nursing home care and approving
payments to the nursing homes for Medicaid patients, it was
well placed to prevent their unneccessary admission.
    However, the evaluators of the original Access
experiment found that not all at risk of admission to nursing
homes were being assessed by Access and Access argued that
the probability of unnecessary admission clearly reflected the
lack of incentives to the better off to seek home rather than
nursing home care (Price, Ripps and Piltz, 1980). Access
obtained Medicare 222 waivers in 1982 so as to increase the
range of persons to whom it could provide home care services
free of charge (Eggert and Brodows, 1982).
(10) This appears to have happened in channelling.
(11) Gap-filling was accomplished by articulating the needs
for agencies to fill, and by using the budget to create the
demand. Although the Wisconsin Community Care
Organisation found that it could not provide home care for
some because only unnecessarily costly packages of care were
available (Seidl et al., 1983), it seems from the results of
projects which much emphasised the upgrading of home care
packages like the San Diego LTCP and the New York York
City Home Care Program that gap-filling in itself did not
greatly reduce the costs of outputs. Nevertheless, it was
clear from channelling that for the case management agency to
have a budget allowed it to compensate for particular
shortfalls in the local system.

References

Association of County Councils (ACC) (1985.) Strategies for
    Community Care, Association of County Councils,

London.
Birnbaum, N., Gaumer, G., Pratten, and Burke, R. (1984) Nursing Homes Without Walls, Abt Associates, Cambridge, Massachusetts.
Brown, T., Blackman, D.K., Learner, R.M. and Witherspoon, M.B. (1985) South Carolina Community Long-Term Care Project: Report of Findings, South Carolina State Health and Human Services Commission, Columbia, South Carolina.
Carnes, C. and Cook, A. (1977) 'Nursing Home Preadmission Screening in Virginia', Journal of Medicaid Management, Vol.1, No.4.
Challis, D.J. and Davies, B.P. (1985a) 'Long-Term Care for the Elderly: the Community Care Scheme', British Journal of Social Work, Vol.15, No.6, pp.1-17.
Challis, D.J. and Davies, B.P. (1985b) 'Efficiency, Decentralisation and Accountability in Social Care: the Community Care Experiments', Public Money, Vol.5, No.3, pp.21-24.
Congressional Budget Office (1977) Long-Term Care for the Elderly and Disabled,, Government Printing Office, Washington, D.C.
Davies, B.J. and Challis, D.J. (1981) 'A Production Relations Evaluation of the Meeting of Needs in the Community Care Project', in Goldberg, E.M. and Connelly, N. (eds.) Evaluative Research in Social Care, Policy Studies Institute, London, pp.177-198.
Davies, B.P. and Challis, D.J. (1986) Matching Resources to Needs in Community Care, Gower, Aldershot.
Davies, B.P. (1981) A Policy Accident and the Regulatory Response: An Historical Study of the Development of Policy, Procedures, Tools and Practice in the Regulation and Reimbursement of Nursing and Rest Home in the State of New York, 1965-80, Discussion Paper 165, Personal Social Services Research Unit, University of Kent, Canterbury.
Decker, B. (1982) 'The Nursing Home and the Long-Term Care System: A Policy Analysis', The Gerontologist, Vol.22, No.1, pp.39-44.
Eggert, G.M. and Brodows, B.S. (1982) 'Mental Health Patients: A Growing Health System Problem', American Health Care Association Journal, November, pp.24-30.
Ferlie, E., Challis, D.J. and Davies, B.P. (1983) A Guide to Efficiency-Improving Innovations in the Social Care of Frail Elderly, Discussion Paper 284, Personal Social Services Research Unit, University of Kent, Canterbury.
Ferlie, E., Challis, D.J. and Davies, B.P. (1984a) 'Innovation in the Care of the Elderly: The Role of Joint Finance', in Butler, A. (ed.) Ageing: Recent Advances and Creative Responses, Croom Helm, London.

Ferlie, E., Challis, D.J. and Davies, B.P. (1984b) 'Models of Innovation in the Social Care of the Elderly', Local Government Studies, November/December.

Ferlie, E. and Davies, B.P. (1984) 'Patterns of Efficiency-Improving Innovation: Social Care and the Elderly', Policy and Politics, Vol.12, No.3, pp.281-295.

Goodman, C.C. (1981) Natural Helping among Older Adults, Department of Social Work, California State University, Long Beach, California.

Hodgson, J.H. and Quinn, J.L. (1980) 'The Impact of the TRIAGE Health Care Delivery System upon Client Morale, Independent Living and the Cost of Care', The Gerontologist, Vol.20, No.3, pp.364-371.

Meltzer, J. and Farrow, F. (1980) Federal Policy Directions in Long-Term Care, Center for the Study of Welfare Policy, University of Chicago, Chicago, Illinois.

Mendelson, M.A. (1974) Tender Loving Greed: How the Incredibly Lucrative Nursing 'Industry' is Exploiting America's Old People and Defrauding Us All, Knopf, New York.

Piktialis, D. (1981) Notes for the Gerontological Society Annual Meeting, November 12.

Price, L.C., Ripps, H.M. and Piltz, D.M. (1980) Third Year Evaluation of the Monroe County Long-Term Care Program, Macro Systems Inc., Siver Spring, Maryland.

Rubinstein, L.Z., Kane, R.L., Josephson, K.R. and Wieland, C.D. (1985) 'The Effects of Geriatric Assessment and Managed Intervention', New England Journal of Medicine, Vol.312, pp.1066.

Sager, A. (1983) Planning Home Care with the Elderly, Ballinger, Cambridge, Massachusetts.

Seidl, F.W., Applebaum, R., Austin, C. and Mahoney, K. (1983) Delivering In-Home Services to the Aged and Disabled, DC Heath, Lexington, Massachusetts.

Skellie, A., Favor, F., Tudor, C. and Strauss, R. (1982) Alternative Health Services Project: Final Report, Georgia Department of Medical Assistance, Atlanta, Georgia.

Solem, R. (ed.) (1979) Community-Based Systems for the Functionally Disabled: A Project in Independent Living, Department of Social and Health Services, Olympia, Washington.

Special Projects Staff in Long-Term Care (1981) FIG/Waiver Continuum of Care Project for the Elderly: Final Project Report, Department of Human Resources, Salem, Oregan.

Stassen, M. and Holahan, J. (1981) Long-Term Care Demonstration Projects: A Review of Recent Evaluations, Urban Institute, Washington DC.

Subcommittee on Health and the Environment (1981) Report on Experimental Efforts in Long-Term Health Care for the Elderly: 79-865, Government Printing Office, Washington

DC.

U.S. General Accounting Office (1982) Report to the Chairman of the Committee on Labor and Human Resources, U.S. Senate, GAO/IPE-83-1, General Accounting Office, Washington DC.

U.S. House of Representatives (1980) Community-Based Long-Term Care: Obstacles and Opportunities, Government Printing Office, Washington DC.

U.S. Senate (1981) Community Home Health Services Act of 1981: Hearings Before the Committee on Labour and Human Resources.

Vladeck, B. (1979) Unloving Care: The Nursing Home Tragedy, Basic Books Inc., New York.

Chapter Sixteen

HOW EFFECTIVE ARE BENEFITS TAKE-UP CAMPAIGNS

WITH ELDERLY PEOPLE?

Christina R. Victor

Introduction

The basic outline of the British social security system was
created between 1945 and 1948 following the Beveridge report
of 1942. This established a two tier system of social welfare
support. The principal form of social security provison for
old age, unemployment, widowhood and industrial injury was
to be based upon a system of compulsory National Insurance,
entitlement to these benefits being dependent upon the
contributions made by individuals via the National Insurance
scheme. This was complemented by a 'safety-net' of
means-tested National Assistance (now known as
Supplementary Benefit) for individuals not covered by the
insurance system. Eligibililty for National Assistance was
dependent upon the claimant demonstrating, via the
means-test, an income less than a pre-determined level and a
lack of capital assets.
        Beveridge thought that the number of claims made for
means-tested benefits would decrease as the system of social
insurance increased its coverage of the population. The
reality has, however, proved to be rather different. Claims
for means-tested Supplementary Benefit (SB) amounted to
four million in 1982 compared with one million in 1948 (Allison,
1982). Indeed, far from phasing out means-testing successive
governments, in an attempt to allocate scarce resources to
those most in need, have increasingly opted for means-testing
and selectivity in welfare provision. Currently, over forty
selective benefits, which make the provision of help
dependent upon a means-test, co-exist with 'universal'
benefits designed for specific groups of the population
regardless of income such as Child Benefit.

The Take-Up of Welfare Benefits

The success of selective benefits in reaching target
populations is termed the take-up rate. Take-up rates are

198

high for most Insurance based benefits such as the State
Retirement Pension but vary markedly between means-tested
benefits: the take-up of student grants is almost 100 per cent
compared with 75 per cent for Supplementary Benefit and 55
per cent for Family Income Supplement. Within a single
benefit there may also be wide variations in take-up between
different groups of claimants. In 1983, 67 per cent of
pensioners eligible for SB were receiving it compared with
over 80 per cent of single parents.

There are two distinct aspects of the benefits take-up
problem. Beltram (1984) distinguishes between primary and
secondary take-up rates. Primary take-up relates to those
eligible for a benefit but who are not claiming it,
i.e. non-claimers. Secondary take-up relates to those who
are already in receipt of a benefit, such as SB, but who are
not receiving their complete entitlement, i.e. underclaimers.
An example of underclaiming would be pensioners who are
receiving their basic Supplementary Benefit but not the extra
weekly additions (known officially as additional requirements)
for heating to which they are entitled.

These figures on the extent of the low take-up of
welfare benefits by the elderly are focused more sharply when
considered in relation to the problem of poverty in old age.
Social commentators from the time of Charles Booth onwards
have drawn attention to the prevalence of poverty in old age.
Data derived from the 1980 General Household Survey indicate
that 23 per cent of elderly people had incomes at, or below,
the Supplementary Benefit level; an income level which has
been used by previous investigators to define society's notion
of a minimal acceptable income (Victor and Vetter, 1985). A
further 33 per cent had incomes within 40 per cent of this
figure. Thus at least 56 per cent of the elderly population
were classed as poor, or as living on the margins of poverty.

The Reasons for Low Take-Up

The low take-up of means-tested benefits is usually explained
with reference to three factors: lack of information;
difficulties using the service, and stigma. As Hill (1980,
p.135) wrote: 'the general case against means-tested benefits
is that they confuse, deter and stigmatise those who need
help'. This tri-partite explanation has been expanded in
recent years to encompass factors such as perceived need and
utility. However, this more sophisticated explanation of the
reasons for the low take-up of means-tested benefits has not
yet been incorporated into campaigns which aim to encourage
take-up rates. Thus only those factors which have directly
informed such campaigns are considered here. Each of the
major perspectives is now considered briefly below as it is
these explanations of underclaiming which have informed most
benefits take-up campaigns.

The first perspective assumes that underclaiming results, in part, from lack of information by potential claimants. At its most fundamental this argument suggests that eligible claimants cannot procede to make a claim if they are unaware of the existence of a benefit. Taylor-Gooby considered that ' ... survey evidence indicates that simply not knowing what one is entitled to claim is the biggest single obstacle to claiming' (1976, p.17). However, this perspective is rather more sophisticated than just knowledge about benefits, for it encompasses knowledge about eligibility or the method of claiming. For the elderly, a survey by the Ministry of Pensions and National Insurance (1966) suggested that 33 per cent of pensioners entitled to National Assistance did not claim because of lack of information about the benefit and the method of claiming it. Similarly, Broad (1977) suggested that 41 per cent of eligible elderly did not claim benefits because of misconceptions about entitlement or the applications procedure.

The second explanation of the low take-up relates to the difficulties experienced by many claimants (or would be claimants) in using the Social Security service. This may relate to a number of factors, but particularly emphasises the perceived time and effort which has to be expended, such as numerous visits to the offices and the completion of complex forms, in order to make a benefits claim. This may, however, be less of a barrier to claiming to the elderly than for some other groups of claimants. Age Concern observed 'Most elderly who apply for SB, whether the application is successful or not, feel that they have been well treated' (Age Concern, 1974, p.82). In addition, a survey by Briggs and Rees (1980) pointed to the high degree of satisfaction amongst elderly recipients of SB. However, it may be that such attitudes are not characteristic of elderly non-claimants of SB.

Stigma is the third paradigm which has traditionally formed an explanation of the low take-up of means-tested benefits in Britain. Both Engels and Rowntree refer to the reluctance of the poor to seek help. Despite the historical pedigree of this explanation of low take-up, stigma itself has remained a rather ill defined, nebulous concept. It has often been used as a general term to variously describe a sense of pride, personal failure, humiliation, an unwillingness to display private matters for public scrutiny, a desire to be seen as independent and a fear of the loss of personal dignity in claiming. At its most general, this paradigm suggests that potential claimants are deterred by the negative associations that claiming involves. This is thought to be a particularly important deterrent to claiming for the elderly who vividly remember the pre-war household means-test. Some empirical evidence supports this assertion. The Ministry of Pensions and National Insurance (MPNI) (1966) study suggested that a

third of elderly indicated pride/feelings of accepting charity
as a reason for not claiming National Assistance.

Responding to Underclaiming: Take-Up Campaigns

In response to the evidence of extensive underclaiming of
many selective welfare benefits various local authorities and
voluntary agencies have implemented campaigns to encourage
non-claimers (or underclaimers) to claim their full benefit
entitlement. Such campaigns have been mounted in places as
diverse as Strathclyde, Cleveland, Manchester and Harlow.
   The Greater London Council is currently promoting an
extensive project to encourage the take-up of benefits. This
campaign is formulated upon the twin premises that low
take-up is a function of knowledge and negative attitudes
towards claiming. The project consists of several
components: first, a series of local campaigns are being
undertaken within certain districts. Each of the
approximately ten thousand households within each district
receives specially designed publicity material which describes
the main underclaimed benefits and gives the timetable of the
'benefits bus', a mobile advice centre. This also gives the
telephone number of a freephone advice service run by the
Greater London Council, and includes a simple claim form
which can be returned if households think they may be
eligible for any of the benefits described. The local campaign
publicity material also aims to produce more positive attitudes
towards claiming. Thus the whole project operates under the
slogan of 'Claim what's yours!' Secondly, the project has a
'Benefit of the Month' promotion in conjunction with Thames
Television's 'Help' programme. Thirdly, an extensive
campaign involving advertising on television, radio and in the
press took place in Spring 1985.
   Using data from the evaluation of the effectiveness of
the local campaigns, which has been undertaken at the
University of Surrey, this paper considers how effective such
campaigns are for the elderly, compared to the other major
groups with low take-up rates, and examines how pertinent
the explanations of low take-up which underlie such
campaigns are for the elderly.

Method

To evaluate the effectiveness of the local campaigns in
achieving their twin objectives of increasing knowledge about
benefits and promoting a more positive attitude towards
claiming, a series of 'before and after' surveys were
undertaken in six local campaign areas: Wandsworth, Tower
Hamlets, Lewisham, Newham, Greenwich and Haringey. A
sample of subjects were interviewed, prior to the campaign,
about their knowledge of welfare benefits and their attitudes

towards claiming. Six weeks later, at the completion of each local campaign, a second sample was interviewed and the responses of the two groups were compared. The success of the campaigns may then be expressed as differences between the two groups in terms of the major outcome indicators: knowledge of benefits and attitude towards welfare provision.

The campaigns are directed at 'potential claimants' who thus form the study group for the evaluation surveys. This concept is operationalised in terms of the known major groups of underclaimers: the elderly, the sick/disabled, the unemployed and single parents. To give each category equal weight in the analysis a quota sampling strategy was employed. Each 'before and after' survey was set a quota of fifty people per group, giving each local survey a sample of 400 and a study population of 2400. Table 1 describes the sample actually achieved. Both 'before' and 'after' samples show a slight under-representation of the sick/disabled category. Within each household the interview was conducted with the 'pursekeeper', i.e. the person responsible for managing the household finances.

Table 1

Composition of the Samples

	Before Surveys	After Surveys	Total
Pensioners	342	328	670
Unemployed	343	342	685
Single Parents	294	306	600
Sick/Disabled	192	211	403
TOTAL	1171	1187	2359

The DHSS provides the Greater London Council with summary statistics recording the numbers of claims made at local offices during a campaign. These data provided quantitative estimates of the numbers and types of claims generated during the local campaign. This approach is, however, limited. First, the statistics on claims only relate to those which are made on the special Greater London Council forms. Individuals who make a claim as a result of the campaign but who do not use the special form are excluded from the analysis. Secondly, we do not know how many of those who made a claim during the campaign would have done so anyway. Thirdly, the project is only informed of the outcome of claims made for Supplementary Benefit. This, therefore, understates the amount of benefit processed during the campaigns.

Results

The results are presented in four sections. The first examines the DHSS statistics of claims made during the campaign and the second examines the recall of the local campaign publicity material. The effectiveness of the local campaigns in influencing knowledge about benefits is examined in the third section, and section four describes the impact of the campaign upon attitudes towards welfare.

The Analysis of DHSS Returns

The Greater London Council campaigns started in December 1983 with a campaign in the Southwark area. Subsequently there have been nine further campaigns (Table 2). The numbers of claims generated by the campaigns has increased over time from 460 in the Southwark campaign to over 1300 in Greenwich and Haringey. This probably reflects the increased length of the campaigns, improved distribution of the publicity material and improvements in the publicity material itself. In the two most recent campaigns the original campaign leaflet has been replaced by a more extensive campaign pack.

Table 2

GLC Welfare Benefits Project: Local Campaigns

Area	Date	Number of Claims	Number of Claimants	% Claims made by Pensioners
Southwark	Dec 1983	460	333	21
Hackney	Jan 1984	689	473	22
Lambeth	Feb 1984	614	404	19
Brent	March 1984	638	396	24
Wandsworth	May 1984	705	425	22
Tower Hamlets	June-July '84	561	397	27
Lewisham	Aug-Sep '84	654	404	27
Newham	Oct-Nov '84	662	368	27
Greenwich	Mar-April '84	1300+	N.K.	N.K.
Haringey	May-June '84	1400+	N.K.	N.K.

Of the claims made at least 20 per cent have been derived from pensioners. This proportion may be even higher for there are a large number of claim forms for which it has not been possible to identify the claimant type. As with other claimant groups, the majority of claims made by pensioners, approximately 80 per cent, have come from

existing SB claimants; comparatively few new SB claimants
have been generated. Claims from pensioners already
receiving SB have usually been for either weekly additions
for heating or laundry or applications for single payments for
furniture and bedding.

Table 3 summarises the success rates of claims made
during the first nine local campaigns. New SB claims were
more successful for pensioners and single parents than any
other types of claimants: 27 per cent of such claims from
pensioners were awarded, compared with 10 per cent where
the identity of the claimant was not indicated. Pensioners
had the lowest success rate for single payment claims. On
average new SB claims resulted in a payment of £4.62 per
week, compared with £17 for single parents. Similarly, the
average single payment and additional requirements award was
lower for pensioners than other claimant groups.

Table 3

Success Rates and Average Amount
of Benefit Awarded

(A) Success Rates (per cent)

	New SB	Single Payment	Extra Weekly Payment
Pensioners	27	50	42
Sick	23	50	55
Disabled	16	61	46
Lone Parents	27	71	31
Others	10	65	37

(B) Average Amount Awarded in Pounds

	New SB	Single Payment	Extra Weekly Payment
Pensioners	4.62	50.98	0.53
Sick	2.65	87.67	3.57
Disabled	2.40	58.10	1.21
Lone Parents	17.04	113.96	4.43
Others	13.79	103.56	2.76

Response to the Campaign Publicity

Subjects in the 'after' groups of surveys were asked if they remembered receiving the campaign publicity. This analysis is complicated somewhat by a change in the nature of the local campaign publicity material two-thirds of the way through the evaluation. In the first four campaigns, a specially designed leaflet was used; in the last two a more extensive campaign pack was distributed. Thus in the results the 'after' group are sub-divided into leaflet and pack areas. Responses to this question should be interpreted with some caution. Whilst we cannot be sure that all those who stated that they received the publicity material actually did so, it is certain that many of those who did not recall either the leaflet or the pack did receive it.

Given this caveat, over all, 26 per cent of pensioners remembered receiving the campaign publicity as did similar percentages of unemployed and single parents and 29 per cent of the sick/disabled. However recall rates did vary between the leaflet and the campaign pack (Table 4). Recall rates were substantially higher for the pack as compared with the leaflet for all claimant groups. Pensioners were least likely to remember receiving the leaflet but most likely to recall the pack. The majority of subjects, in either group, did not remember receiving the campaign publicity material. Amongst the elderly there were no significant differences in variations in recall rates between the sexes.

Table 4

Recall of Campaign Publicity (per cent)

	Leaflet	Pack
Pensioners	16	44
Unemployed	20	43
Single Parents	25	40
Sick/Disabled	23	41

Changes in Information Levels

Subjects' awareness of benefits was investigated by a simple recognition test. Respondents were asked if they had heard of a series of 23 benefits or pensions. However, where subjects reported knowing about the benefit it was not possible to explore whether they were aware of the rules for eligibility or the method of claiming. Rather than describe the proportions aware of each individual benefit the mean number recognised was computed. The 'after' group was again sud-divided according to the type of campaign publicity material received.

Pensioners had the lowest information levels of any claimant group before the campaigns started (Table 5). In the 'before' group pensioners had heard of an average of 7.4 benefits compared with 10.3 for single parents, the most informed group. Information levels for all groups increased only marginally after the campaign in which the leaflet was used. However the local campaign pack was more effective at increasing benefits awareness amongst all groups. The mean number of benefits recognised by pensioners increased to 9.8 per cent in areas where the pack was used. However this level of awareness was still markedly lower than that characteristic of other types of potential claimants: for example, single parents were aware of an average of 11.5 benefits.

Table 5

Mean Number of Benefits Heard of

	Before Campaign	After Leaflet	After Pack
Pensioners	7.4	7.5	9.8
Unemployed	9.4	9.1	11.1
Single parents	10.3	10.5	11.5
Sick/Disabled	9.0	9.8	10.0

Amongst pensioners, females were more aware of benefits, both before and after the campaigns, than males. There were no differences in levels of awareness between pensioners receiving SB and those not receiving it.

In addition to providing information about benefits, the local campaigns aimed to clarify doubts about entitlement to benefit. Thus subjects were asked if they thought they might be eligible for any benefit/pension they were not currently receiving.

Levels of perceived eligibility were lower amongst pensioners than the other groups of potential claimants (Table 6). Forty-eight per cent of pensioners in the 'before' group felt that they had an underlying entitlement to a benefit compared with at least 65 per cent of the other groups. Perceived eligibility was lower in the 'after' group for all sub-groups with the exception of single parents. This decrease in perceived eligibility was characteristic of both leaflet and pack campaign areas.

Table 6

**Per Cent Perceiving Eligibility for
Benefits Not Currently Received**

	Before Campaign	After Leaflet	After Pack
Pensioners	48	45	48
Unemployed	67	64	64
Single Parents	65	65	66
Sick/Disabled	71	61	61

Amongst the elderly, those females suffering from a long standing illness or disability, and those who had had a claim refused in the previous twelve months, were least likely to report that they thought they might be entitled to a benefit they were not currently receiving.

Another aspect of information is knowing where to seek advice about benefits or pensions. The campaign had little impact upon knowledge of where to seek advice for any of the sub-groups investigated. The DHSS office and the Citizens' Advice Bureau were the two most popular places for seeking advice about benefit entitlement. However 30 per cent of pensioners in the 'before' group, and 31 per cent in the 'after' group, did not know where to go to seek advice. This compares with less than 10 per cent for the other groups of potential claimants.

Attitudes Towards Claiming

Attitudes towards claiming were investigated using a series of Likert type statements. Subjects were asked to agree (or disagree) with three sets of statements relating to general attitudes towards welfare provision, aspects of the claiming process and individual barriers to claiming. Responses to these statements showed no statistically significant differences, for any claimant group, between the 'before' and either of the two 'after' groups. However there were some differences in views between claimant groups and these are described below. The results are based upon the aggregate of the two data sets.

General Attitudes Towards Welfare

The elderly were more ready to agree with the statement that the welfare state was something to be proud of than any other groups (Table 7). However they were also more likely to agree that benefits should be available only to those who had paid in contributions, that benefits reduce independence, encourage dependence and that those receiving such payments should feel guilty at living off taxpayers' charity.

Table 7

General Attitudes Towards the
Welfare State
per cent Agreeing with Statements

	Pensioners	Unemployed	Single Parents	Sick / Disabled
Welfare state something to be proud of	74	54	55	64
Difficult to get full entitlement	75	86	76	75
Help all poor regardless	74	87	86	76
Welfare reduces independence	67	29	44	47
Benefits only to contributors	64	34	24	45
Welfare encourages independence	60	26	36	41
Benefits too generous	26	5	7	8
Poor have only themselves to blame	18	3	3	5

As another method of recording overall attitudes towards welfare, subjects were asked if they thought there were such individuals claiming benefits as 'scroungers'. The elderly were most likely to consider that scroungers existed than other subjects. Eighty-one per cent of the elderly felt that such people existed compared with 61 per cent of the unemployed and single parents.

Those who felt that scroungers existed were asked to estimate what fraction of claimants could be so classified.

The median proportion suggested by pensioners was 50 per cent compared with 20 per cent of the unemployed and single parents. Subjects were asked to nominate the groups that they thought deserved welfare support. Responses to this question showed a remarkable consensus amongst the sample, with the elderly being seen as the major group deserving welfare support by all subjects. Subjects were also asked to nominate the groups that they felt did not deserve welfare support. Again, responses showed few substantial differences between claimant group. Consistently the lazy/workshy or those employed in the 'black economy' were described as not deserving welfare benefits. However at least half of the respondents felt that there were no groups who did not deserve welfare support.

Attitudes Towards the Claiming Process

Overall, attitudes were highly critical of the service provided by the DHSS. However the elderly were much less critical than other groups, and more likely to describe claiming as straightforward; DHSS staff as helpful; leaflets easy to understand; and claims as being dealt with promptly (Table 8).

Subjects were asked if they thought there should be any changes made to the system for claiming benefits. Again, pensioners were less critical of the present system, with 40 per cent agreeing that changes should be made compared with 70 per cent of the unemployed and single parents, and 60 per cent of the sick/disabled.

Those subjects agreeing that changes should be made to the system were then asked to identify the sort of changes they favoured (Table 9). The majority felt that the system should be simplified by cutting down on the number of forms to complete and the number of visits to be made to the DHSS offices. However the elderly were more likely than other groups to suggest increasing the value of benefits and less likely to suggest changes to DHSS offices and staffing.

As another way of investigating barriers to claiming, subjects were asked how they felt benefits take-up could be increased (Table 10). Pensioners were more likely to favour home visits than any other group and less convinced of the power of television advertising, the automatic assessment of entitlement and the provision of an advice service by the DHSS to increase take-up, than other groups.

Benefits Take-Up Campaigns

Table 8

Attitudes Towards the Service
Provided by the DHSS
per cent Agreeing with the Statement

	Pensioners	Unemployed	Single Parents	Sick / Disabled
DHSS staff helpful	78	48	39	52
Claiming is uncomplicated	49	29	25	32
DHSS leaflets explains en-titlements clearly	53	34	37	37
Claiming in-volves filling in a long form	67	88	86	87
Claiming in-volves lengthy waits in offices	76	87	90	81
Claims take a long time to be processed	50	69	73	63

Individual Attitudes Towards Claiming

Subjects were read a series of statements which, they were
told, others had given as explanation for not claiming
benefits. Our sample was then asked to indicate how relevant
these explanations were to them. Table 11 shows that only
three statements ('I would not claim unless I was certain of
my entitlement'; 'I don't feel the need for extra money'; and 'I
would not like to apply and be turned down') showed
differences between our claimant groups; pensioners being
more likely to agree with these statements than other groups.
Rather unexpectedly, the elderly were no more likely to agree
with statements suggesting that claiming benefits threatened
one's pride or independence than were other groups. They
also did not seem to be particularly deterred from claiming by
having to disclose details of their financial circumstances.

Table 9

Proposed Changes to the System of Claiming (per cent)

	Pensioners	Unemployed	Single Parents	Sick / Disabled
Simplify	51	57	53	58
Increase Benefits	16	12	9	12
DHSS staff more helpful	13	32	33	29
Quicker service	12	24	23	14
Simplify leaflets/forms	11	14	14	18
Improve offices	10	22	24	15
More publicity	10	11	12	13

Table 10

Methods to Encourage Take-Up (per cent)

	Pensioners	Unemployed	Single Parents	Sick / Disabled
Home visits	30	24	20	29
TV adverts	17	27	27	24
Leaflets	16	17	23	18
Positive view of claiming	14	12	13	13
Automatic assessment	13	18	23	15
DHSS advice service	11	21	22	13

Table 11

**Individual Barriers to Claiming
per cent Agreeing with Statement**

	Pensioners	Unemployed	Single Parents	Sick / Disabled
Only claim if sure of entitlement	92	76	81	82
Dislike going to DHSS	78	77	83	79
Rather manage without extra money	78	69	78	72
Dislike possibility of refusal	72	63	66	68
Dislike asking for extra money	73	50	56	61
Too much effort to claim	56	48	52	59
Feel loss of independence	57	51	55	52
Feel pride affected	48	41	47	49
Feel it is accepting charity	41	38	36	33
Dislike financial questions	48	45	54	43
Do not need extra money	37	17	17	20

Discussion and Conclusion

In response to the low take-up of means-tested benefits the
Greater London Council has, like other Local Authorities,
promoted a take-up campaign. The twin aims were to
increase awareness of benefits and promote a more sensitive

attitude towards claiming.

Analysis of routine statistics by the DHSS indicated that the majority of claims, from all client groups, were made for Supplementary Benefit and came from existing clients of the SB system. Thus the campaign, whilst reasonably successful at tackling the problem of underclaiming, had very little impact upon non-claimants. This result is typical of take-up campaigns suggesting that a different sort of strategy is probably required to encourage non-claimers to come forward.

Analysis of success rates between groups is hampered by the large number of claims for which the client type could not be identified. New SB claims from pensioners were more successful than those from non-pensioners, however the average weekly payment awarded was higher for non-pensioners. Similarly, additional requirements and single payment awards were lower for pensioners compared with other groups. This may suggest that many of the non-claiming or underclaiming elderly are only entitled to a small amount of extra benefit and therefore do not bother to make a claim.

Compared with other claimants the elderly were less aware of benefits; had lower levels of perceived eligibility and were less aware of where advice about benefits/pensions could be obtained. This suggests that lack of information, in the broadest sense, is a very real barrier preventing the elderly from claiming all the benefits to which they are entitled.

The Greater London Council campaign had some effect upon the awareness of benefits by the elderly. However, for all client groups this effect was confined to the campaigns where the glossy campaign pack had been used. Thus it seems that a very sophisticated level of publicity material is required if this type of mass leafletting of areas about welfare rights is to create any impact.

Levels of perceived eligibility for benefits were significantly lower amongst pensioners as compared with other types of potential claimant. The campaign did not increase levels of perceived eligibility; in fact the reverse trend was observed. However it could be that the decrease in perceived eligibility resulted from the higher information levels brought about by the campaign. Thus far from generating unrealistic claims, a real fear of the DHSS, the campaign enabled subjects to make a better assessment of their own entitlement.

The data indicate that low information levels, as well as uncertainty about eligibility seem to be substantial barriers to claiming for all groups, especially the elderly. However it is difficult to assess just how influential lack of information is in explaining low take-up. Meacher (1972) concluded that 72 per cent of all underclaiming resulted from inadequate information and Taylor-Gooby (1976) reports that two-thirds of his sample gave ignorance as their reason for not claiming rent rebates. However he also reports that two-thirds of these failed to claim when specifically told of the benefit and their entitlement. In the Greater London Council campaign only about one third of those who were told by an advice worker of a specific entitlement to benefit proceeded to make a claim. This proportion was much lower for the elderly at about 20 per cent which is identical to that reported by Scott-Kerr (1982). The simple provision of information about benefits will support about 20 per cent of the elderly to make a claim for benefit. Thus there are obviously many other factors which are influencing the decision to claim.

The complexity of the claiming process and difficulties experienced in using the system seem to be less of a disincentive to the elderly than other groups. The higher degree of satisfaction with the service provided by the DHSS and lower proportions suggesting changes to the claiming system may result from the elderly receiving better treatment in their dealings with the DHSS, compared with other groups of claimants. Alternatively it may be that the elderly are much less critical of the procedures of the DHSS than younger subjects. However as several other studies have reported similar findings (Age Concern, 1974; Briggs and Rees, 1982) it seems that the elderly probably do incur fewer difficulties in their dealings with the DHSS than do other types of claimants.

Despite this, however, the elderly wanted some changes to the system for claiming benefits and particularly favoured home visits from the DHSS. No doubt this reflects the greatly increased mobility problems of the elderly compared with other groups of claimers. However such visits are increasingly being withdrawn in favour of postal methods of claiming. Given the prevalence of sight problems and other disabilities amongst the elderly such a switch in the method for claiming may not produce extra take-up of benefits by them.

The data did not provide much evidence to support the hypothesis that the elderly were deterred from claiming because of feelings of pride or stigma. However the elderly were much less ready to suggest that they might not claim because they did not feel a need for extra money. This could be interpreted as another reflection of the stigma thesis; the desire to be seen as a good manager. However it seems more likely that this low desire for extra money probably reflects the very low levels of perceived need amongst the elderly. Broad (1977) reported that 40 per cent of elderly stated that they did not experience any difficulty in meeting their living expenses. Additionally, Age Concern (1974) reported a high level of satisfaction with their living standard by the elderly. It seems likely that this low level of perceived need seems to derive from the fact that many elderly set their living standards by the criteria of the 1930s rather than the 1980s.

Additional disincentives to claiming were articulated in response to the open-ended questions. A substantial barrier to claiming, for all groups, but particularly the elderly was the uncertainty over entitlement and the influence of a previous refusal. Both elements need to be encompassed into campaigns which attempt to increase the take-up of benefits by the elderly.

The Greater London Council campaign, as many other similar exercises, has tried to increase take-up by providing information to potential claimants and providing a positive image of claiming as a right or entitlement. Whilst the effectiveness of this latter aspect of the campaign is doubtful, there is little doubt that the lack of information is a very real barrier which prevents many from claiming and it is reasonable for take-up campaigns to attempt to combat this. However the lack of information perspective is rather more sophisticated than just awareness of the existence of benefits, for it also implies providing information about entitlement, the process of claiming and boosting the confidence of those who have had a claim refused in the past. These aspects need to be incorporated into any type of take-up campaign. Simple provision of advice will encourage about 30 per cent of clients to claim. It may be that a more sophisticated system of support, advice and encouragement is required to stimulate the remaining 70 per cent to procede to claim.

For the elderly these data indicate that a take-up campaign can have a limited effect in encouraging existing SB claimants to claim their full entitlement. Such campaigns can also have a limited effect upon the awareness of the elderly about benefits and their potential entitlement to them. However it seems that one of the biggest barriers to claiming by the elderly is their very low level of perceived need and it is doubtful that any take-up campaign can have very much impact upon this.

References

Age Concern (1974) The Attitudes of the Elderly and Retired, Manifesto Series, No.34, Age Concern, Mitcham.

Allison, F.M. (1982) The Non Take Up of Welfare Benefits - The Would Be Claimants Obstacle Course, M.Sc. Thesis, University of Bath.

Beltram, G. (1984) Testing the Safety Net, Occasional Papers on Social Administration, No.74, Bedford Square Press, London.

Briggs, E. and Rees, A. (1980) Supplementary Benefits and the Consumer, Occasional Papers on Social Administration, No.66, Bedford Square Press, London.

Broad, P. (1977) Pensioners and Their Needs, OPCS, London.

Deacon, A. and Bradshaw, J. (1983) Reserved for the Poor, Martin Robertson, London.

Hill, M. (1980) Understanding Social Policy, Martin Robertson, London.

Meacher, M. (1972) Rent Rebates: A Study of the Effectiveness of the Means Test, Child Poverty Action Group, London.

Ministry of Pensions and National Insurance (1966) Financial and other Circumstances of Retirement Pensioners, HMSO, London.

Rowntree, B.S. (1941) Poverty and Progress?, Longmans, Green and Company.

Scott-Kerr, A. (1982) 'Deciding about Supplementary Pensions: A Provision Model', Journal of Social Policy, Vol.11, pp.505-507.

Taylor-Gooby, P. (1974) Means Testing and Social Policy, M.Phil. Thesis, University of York.

Taylor-Gooby, P. (1976) 'Rent Rebates and Tenants Attitudes: The Batley Rent Rebate and Allowance Study', Journal of Social Policy, Vol.5, pp.33-48.

Townsend, P. (1957) The Family Life of Old People, Routledge and Kegan Paul, London.

Townsend, P. (1979) Poverty in the United Kingdom, Penguin, Harmondsworth.

Victor, C.R. and Vetter, N.J. (1986) 'Poverty, Disability and use of Services by the Elderly: Analysis of the 1980 General Household Survey', Social Science and Medicine, forthcoming.

Walker, A. (1980) 'The Social Creation of Poverty and Dependence in Old Age', Journal of Social Policy, Vol.9, pp.49-75.

Chapter Seventeen

PHASED RETIREMENT IN WESTERN EUROPE

Frank Laczko

Introduction

The starting point of this paper is the rapid growth in full early retirement that has occurred in recent years. Where early retirement is involuntary and sudden it can be expected to be a particularly stressful event given that in most western societies a strong work ethic prevails and status is closely associated with occupation.

It can be argued that one way in which we can reduce the growing exclusion of older workers from the labour force is by promoting more partial retirement (Laczko and Walker, 1985). Partial or phased retirement means a phased, planned transition from working life to complete retirement involving part-time working; at a certain age the worker ceases to work on a full-time basis and begins to work part-time, by reducing his or her working hours on a daily, weekly, monthly or even annual basis. The case for partial retirement is based to a large extent on Swedish experience which I shall review below. There are also other schemes at the level of the individual firm or industry which exist in a number of European countries, but for reasons of space these will not be discussed here. Instead the public scheme in Sweden will be compared with recent attempts to provide national provision for phased retirement in Britain and France, and to a limited extent Spain. I wish to argue that schemes in the latter countries are unlikely under current arrangements to encourage older people to phase their retirement because unlike in Sweden they are primarily designed to reduce unemployment. But even in Sweden, there are now serious difficulties in promoting phased retirement in the current economic climate which suggests that even if Britain were to adopt a partial pension scheme along Swedish lines a number of obstacles would have to be overcome.

Sweden

The Swedish Partial Pension Scheme was introduced in 1976 for men and women aged 60 - 64. It was hoped that partial pensions would be used to ease the transition between work and retirement whilst also acting as a 'work adjustment' measure for older workers in poor health. Partial pensions were also intended to moderate the growth in involuntary full early retirement which had been particularly rapid in the early part of the 1970s (SOU, 1975, p.81).

Eligibility

An employee wishing to phase into retirement must agree to reduce his working hours by an average of at least five per week and subsequently work part-time for a minimum of 17 hours per week. The level of the partial pension was originally set at 65 per cent of the gross earnings lost as a result of transfer to part-time work. However after the 1st of January 1981 it was reduced to 50 per cent.[1] An important point to make about partial pensions in Sweden is that partial retirement has little adverse effect on pension rights, as the partial pension is assessed as pensionable income for the state earnings-related pension, which is based on the 15 best, rather than the 15 last, working years.

Take-Up

Up until 1981 the number of people retiring early on a partial pension was high. Indeed during the period 1976-1981 slightly more men and women aged 60 - 64 were awarded a partial pension than a disability pension, which provides the most important form of public support for full early retirement in Sweden; (131,910) compared to (120,497). However in recent years the number of new partial pension awards has been declining. By 1984 there were fewer applications for a partial pension than in 1976 (see Table 1).

Impact of Phased Retirement

Evaluation of the impact of partial retirement in the years prior to 1981-1982 suggest that phased retirement offered advantages to both employers and employees. Employers' interest in partial retirement stemmed partly from the fact that they were able to use it to facilitate reductions in manpower. Studies carried out in 1976 and 1979 showed that the principal factor determining variations between the proportions of partial pensioners in different enterprises was the degree to which they needed to shed labour. Firms which needed to reduce personnel were more likely to promote partial retirement (Crona, 1981; Crona and Olson-Frick,

1981). Some research suggests that partial retirement was used to an even greater extent than full early retirement as a means of reducing manpower (Olson-Frick, 1982). However, apart from in small firms, few enterprises reported significant problems in accommodating an increase in phased retirement (Crona and Olson-Frick, 1981).

Table 1

**Take-Up of the Swedish Partial Pension Scheme
1976-1984**

Year	No. of New Awards	Total No. Receiving Partial Pensions	% of Gainfully Employed Aged 60-64 Receiving a Partial Pension	% Share of Women
1976	14,792	14,560	7	30
1977	20,337	31,509	12	30
1978	18,494	41,913	16	30
1979	18,243	48,654	22	31
1980	32,882	67,837	27	31
1981	12,521	64,641	24	33
1982	14,641	61,732	22	35
1983	10,400	58,082	21	36
1984	9,900	47,204	17	N.A.
1985	9,233	37,638	13	N.A.

Source: Swedish National Social Insurance Board (RVF)

The Older Worker

At the individual level there appear to have been few problems associated with phasing into early retirement. Indeed, a comparative study carried out in 1979 of the lifestyles of partial pensioners, early retirees (disability pensioners) and full-time employees suggests that partial early retirement has a number of advantages when compared with full early retirement. In general, partial pensioners expressed a greater satisfaction with their circumstances than full early retirees. However, given that partial pensioners were generally in better health than disability pensioners it might be expected that they would be more satisfied with their circumstances. Nevertheless, partial retirement does seem to have some positive impact on health. Although the health of all three groups deteriorated over time, the rate of deterioration was slowest after partial retirement.

Up until 1981, phased retirement also entailed a relatively small loss of income on average, and in fact the value of partial pensions as they were indexed to the cost of living, rose faster than real wages. The loss of income is now somewhat greater - on average 20 per cent of previous net earnings from full-time work instead of 15 per cent (Crona, 1981).

Until 1981 there was also evidence to suggest that partial pensions were providing a significant alternative to full early retirement on a disability pension, and also an alternative for those who might otherwise have been classified as long-term sick (RFV, 1984, p.188). Among men aged 60 - 64, there was a significant fall in the number of new long-term sickness benefit awards during the period 1976-1982, which it has been estimated was partly due to the introduction of partial pensions.

During the period when partial pension awards were rising, full early retirement as measured by the number of new disability pension awards to those aged 60 - 64 remained stable, although at a relatively high level when compared to the period before 1971 (Laczko and Walker, 1985). Unlike in most of the rest of Western Europe, in Sweden there was no substantial fall in the economic activity rates of male workers aged 60 - 64 during the period 1978-1982, whilst the activity rates of older women continued to rise faster than in other European countries. The relevant figures for men and women aged 60 - 64 over the above period were: 69.7 - 68.4 per cent, and 38.4 - 46.2 per cent, respectively. Although there was a considerable increase over this period in early retirement, it was not reflected in economic activity rates, as a substantial part of the increase was accounted for by partial early retirement.

Recent trends would appear to provide further support for the view that partial retirement played a part in stemming the rise in full early retirement in Sweden. In recent years, whilst partial retirement has been declining, full early retirement has been on the increase for the first time in several years. In 1984, 19,000 disability pensions were awarded to workers aged 60 - 64, compared to 16,300 in 1983. This sharp increase reflects the deterioration in job prospects in Sweden during this period, with almost half those retiring early doing so on labour market grounds (the definition of disability used in assessing entitlement to a disability pension in Sweden includes an assessment of older workers' labour market chances). Another factor is that it is now financially somewhat more advantageous for an individual to opt for a disability pension rather than a partial pension, which until 1981 provided on average the same level of income replacement as a partial pension.

Partial Retirement Schemes with a Replacement Condition

In recent years, against the background of rising unemployment and spiralling pension costs as a result of a rapid acceleration in early retirement, government measures to support gradual retirement have been introduced in Britian, France and Spain. The most recent scheme, the Spanish, introduced in August 1984, will not be discussed here, but a summary table (Table 2) provides an overview and comparison of the British, French, Swedish and Spanish schemes' main provisions. Unlike in Sweden in the latter countries an employer is obliged to employ an unemployed person or priority category job-seeker, when older workers retire gradually. This replacement condition reflects the fact that these schemes are considered to be first and foremost manpower policy measures designed to alleviate unemployment. In Britain, for example, according to the Department of Employment: 'the purpose of the Part-Time Job Release Scheme is to provide more part-time jobs for unemployed people by encouraging such jobs to be created from full-time jobs' (Department of Employment, 1985, p.12). In all three countries partial retirement measures are part of a set of policies that have been introduced to encourage part-time working, and it can be argued that they reflect an approach to tackling unemployment which is in line with conservative economic orthodoxy. Unemployment is to be reduced by sharing existing work and by effectively lowering the wages of those in work as the unemployed and older workers are encouraged to accept part-time work.

The French Solidarity Contracts for Partial Retirement

Under the 'Solidarity Contracts' scheme introduced in 1982, older workers were given the choice between early retirement and partial retirement. Government aid was provided under 'Solidarity Contracts' signed between employers and the Labour Ministry representatives. Employees aged 55 and over in enterprises where contracts were signed could opt for early retirement or partial retirement provided that their employer agreed to recruit on an open-ended contract, a priority category job-seeker.
In order to be eligible for the scheme partial retirees have to have ten years insured employment, and are required to reduce their working hours by 50 per cent. They receive an allowance of 30 per cent of their previous full gross salary, in addition to their normal half-time pay. The vacancies created by an older worker transferring to part-time work do not have to be filled on a part-time basis as employees can combine two part-time vacancies into one full-time position.

The British Part-Time Job Release Scheme

In Britain the Job Release Scheme, which provides a 'bridging allowance' to older employees wishing to retire early, provided that their employer recruits a registered unemployed person

Table 2
Public Provision for Phased Retirement in Four Western European Countries

	France	UK	Spain	Sweden
Form of Regulation	Law permitting conclusion of contracts between enterprises and state	Law	Law	Law
Date of Introduction	1 January 1982	October 1983	August 1984	July 1976
Extent	1,302 private sector recipients 1984. 12,000 public sector 1982-84	242 recipients December 1985	N.A.	152,210 recipients up to 1984
Eligibility	Employees with 10 years insured employment aged 55 and above	Employees working at least 30 hours per week and for present employer at least 12 months. Men aged 62-64; Women 59. Disabled men 60-64.	Employees aged 62-64	Employees and self-employed with 10 years pension contributions paid, aged 60-64.
Size of Worktime Reduction (% or normal work-time)	50%	At least 14 hours. Recipient must work 16-29 hours per week	50%	At least 5 hours below normal full-time. Average 17 per week
Level of Benefit	30% of previous full gross salary and half-time pay. 80% of last gross pay on average	Flat-rate payment. Equivalent to up to 100% wage compensation to low paid	Half-time pay and half state pension	When working half-time approx. 80-85% of last net income
Replacement Condition	Yes	Yes	Yes	No
Effect on Pension Rights	Can be prejudiced	Prejudiced	Not prejudiced	Not prejudiced
Subsidy to Employer	None	Grant to employer from April £840 subject to fulfillment of the replacement condition	50% reduction in social security contributions if the 'replacee' is retained after the full retirement of the partial partner	None

was extended in October 1983 to allow partial retirement. Initially the scheme was open to men aged 62 - 64, women aged 59 and disabled men aged 60 - 61 who gave up at least half their standard working week. Partial retirees can receive a job release allowance at half the full-time rate provided that a registered unemployed or other priority category job-seeker is recruited for the other half of the job. Recipients must have been in full-time employment for at least 30 hours per week. There are four rates of allowance, which are paid at a flat rate.

Take-Up of the French and British Schemes

Despite the somewhat different eligibility requirements of the above schemes neither has had much impact, although in France a separate scheme to the one described above, for civil servants and local government employees, has had a great deal more success than that operating in the private sector.

It was estimated in Britain by the Department of Employment that the Part-Time Job Release Scheme would provide part-time job opportunities for up to 53,000 people by March 1985. But despite an expensive advertising campaign, at the end of December 1985 there were only 242 people taking advantage of the scheme. The main French scheme has hardly had more success, with only 1,169 beneficiaries in 1983. But a separate scheme for civil servants and local government employees has proved more successful attracting 12,000 people between 1982 and 1984, compared to a figure of only 1,650 in the private sector (Ragot, 1985).

Reasons for Low Take-Up

There are several problems which are common to both the French and British schemes. The main factors can be summarised as follows. Firstly, the simultaneous existence of provision for full early retirement and partial early retirement has tended to undermine employees and employer interest in phased retirement. Neither employers nor employees have had much incentive to favour partial retirement. For employees there has been little financial incentive to choose partial retirement rather than full early retirement, whilst occupational pension rights can also be seriously prejudiced. For example in France, the financial benefits of partial retirement compared to full early retirement under the Solidarity Contracts scheme were either negligible or even negative where employers topped up state benefits. Early retirees were granted 70 per cent of last gross income, and partial retirees 80 per cent, but the difference in net income was smaller; 80 per cent of last net income as opposed to 85 per cent (Frank et al., 1982, p.73).

In Britain over 90 per cent of employees who belong to occupational pension schemes (just over half of all employees) are members of final salary schemes. In these the pension is calculated as a fraction of the person's final salary at pension age, multiplied by years of pensionable service. Therefore those who opt for partial retirement with half salary could lose approximately half their pension entitlement on full retirement.

Conversely one of the reasons why partial retirement has been more popular in the public sector in France is because access to full early retirement has been more restricted (Ragot, 1985). Another factor is that although the conditions of the scheme in the public sector are similar to those operating in the private sector, eligibility for partial retirement is not related to any calculation based on previous years in employment. This is an advantage for female workers who tend to have intermittent work records and who make up the majority of partial retirees in the public sector scheme. The high proportion of female partial retirees probably also reflects women's greater willingness to accept part-time work than men, who often tend to regard such work as low grade female work.

From the point of view of employers, partial retirement has been regarded as more cumbersome than full early retirement partly because of the technical difficulty in adapting jobs to part-time work and partly because of the costs and administrative burden of adapting such jobs (Bushell, 1984, p.42). Moreover, because of the replacement condition employers cannot use partial retirement to shed labour as in Sweden. They also have the problem of recruiting suitable part-time workers among the unemployed as replacements. Yet there is not much incentive for the unemployed to fill part-time vacancies, since the wages obtained from part-time work are likely, except for the very young living at home or married women, to be less than the benefits payable if they remain jobless. This was a particular problem it seems in Britain because unlike in France employers are required to recruit two unemployed people for two partial retirees rather than recruit one full-time replacement worker. A recent change in the conditions of the scheme is intended to remedy this problem. The replacement condition has been relaxed, such that part-time vacancies can be filled by unemployed people not receiving unemployment or supplementary benefit. This move is intended to open up part-time jobs to married women who are most likely to be interested in part-time work but who are often excluded from filling vacancies because they are not registered as unemployed. A number of other changes have been made to the British scheme including the introduction of a flat rate subsidy of £840 to employers and a £4 supplement to partial retirees.

In France there have also been further efforts to promote partial retirement. Indeed the full early retirement option under the Solidarity Contracts scheme was withdrawn at the end of 1983 partly in an effort to increase phased retirement which is a much cheaper option from the point of view of the public purse (Laczko, 1985b). However thus far these changes have not proved effective in increasing partial retirement, either in Britain or France.

Conclusion

One of the problems that neither of the reforms in Britain and France address is removing the replacement condition, which restricts employers' personnel policies considerably. Also unlike in Sweden the replacement condition restricts demand for partial retirement among older workers. In particular those working in declining sectors of the economy where there is less likelihood of the replacement condition being fulfilled, cannot choose partial retirement as an alternative to full early retirement or redundancy. There is also the need to protect older workers' pension rights. But even if these reforms were made there is evidence to suggest that there may be problems in promoting phased retirement in a period of high unemployment. In one recent study of a small sample of organisations in Britain, employers expressed a reluctance to encourage partial retirement because controls on overall employment levels were increasingly expressed in terms of headcount; therefore there was generally a preference for one employee rather than two (IMS 1983, p.68). In Sweden it is evident that when unemployment began to rise significantly at the beginning of the 1980s the number of partial retirees fell substantially, although this was also a consequence of a significant reduction in the level of the partial pension.

Notes

(1) For more of the aims and conditions of the scheme see Laczko, 1985a.

References

Bushell, R. (1984) Great Britain, The Job Release Schemes, paper produced for the OECD Panel 'Measures to Assist Early Retirement', mimeo, OECD, Paris.
Crona, G. (1981) Partial Retirement in Sweden, paper presented at the XII International Congress of

Gerontology, Hamburg, July.

Crona, G. and Olson-Frick, H. (1981) Delpensionerades, Fortidspensionerades, och Yrkesarbetandes, Levnadsförhållanden, Swedish National Social Insurance Board, Stockholm.

Department of Employment (1985) The Part-Time Job Release Scheme, Department of Employment, London.

Frank, D. et al. (1982) 'Enterprises et contrats de solidarité de preretraite-demission', Travail et Emploi, July-September, No.13.

Laczko, F. and Walker, A. (1985) 'Excluding Older Workers from the Labour Market: Early Retirement Policies in Britain, France and Sweden', The Yearbook of Social Policy in Britain 1984-5, Brenton, M. and Jones, C. (eds.), Routledge and Kegan Paul, London.

Laczko, F. (1985a) 'Sweden: Trends in Partial Pensions', European Industrial Relations Review, March.

Laczko, F. (1985b) 'Too Old for Work?' Initiatives, August, Longmans.

Institute of Manpower Services (1983) Early Retirement, Institute of Manpower Services Manpower Commentary No.24, Institute of Manpower Studies, Brighton.

Olson-Frick, H. (1982) Förtidspensionärer, Delegationen for Social Forskning, Rapport I, Stockholm.

Ragot, M. (1985) La Cessation Anticipée D'Activite Salirée, Journal Officiel de la République Francaise, No.12.

RFV (1984) Dalpension och rörlig pensionalder en uppföljning och utvardering, Swedish National Social Insurance Board, Stockholm.

SOU (1975) Rorlig pensionsalder Socialdepartementet, Stockholm.

Chapter Eighteen

INSTITUTIONAL REGIMES AND RESIDENT OUTCOMES

IN HOMES FOR THE ELDERLY

Tim Booth

Introduction

This paper reports the findings of a major study of the
effects of institutional regimes on levels of dependency among
residents of local authority homes for the elderly.   The
research was designed to investigate what effects, if any,
differences in the way homes are run have on the creation or
reduction of dependency among residents.

It is a well-attested fact that residential homes are potentially
harmful places in which to live (Hughes and Wilkin, 1980;
Davies and Knapp, 1981).   The apathy, helplessness,
withdrawal and disorientation that research has shown to be
so widespread among their residents have been linked with
the way homes are run and the nature of institutional
regimes.   Broadly, institutional living is seen as having
detrimental effects on the functioning of individuals that
become more severe as the institution becomes more total and
restrictive.
    For example, in a major review of the principles and
practice of residential care, the Personal Social Services
Council (1977) concluded that:

> Both mental and physical deterioration often occurs after
> admission because of lack of the need to do even simple
> tasks like dressing, bed-making or cooking, or to apply
> the mind even to the simplest of decisions, such as
> choosing a menu.

In a similar vein, the Social Work Service in London has
observed:

> There seems little doubt that a loss of expectation,
> independent action, and a removal of the need for
> self-help can cause rapid deterioration, both physically
> and mentally, in relatively active old people. (DHSS, 1979)

227

These same concerns have been echoed in the United States. Lawton and Nahemow (1973), for example, have argued that:

No person is immune to the seductive power of the too-easy life, no matter on what level of competence he is operating. There is no question that it is possible to discourage independent behaviour in the name of service to the elderly.

Similarly, for Tobin and Lieberman (1976), 'an environment that does not encourage full use of potential may cause irreversible deterioration.'

Fears such as these led the Institute of Medicine (1977) to warn of the role of unnecessary services in the development of dependency and of the dangers of divesting individuals of the responsibility for performing daily tasks such as food preparation and personal hygiene. Its report, issued by the National Academy of Sciences, concludes:

Policies that preclude the opportunity for choice among care options, or that fail to recognise the right of individuals to make decisions affecting the quality of their lives, are more likely to produce apathy, hasten disengagement, and accelerate dependency.

As these quotations suggest, the weight of informed opinion now accepts that the process of care may itself induce dependency. In particular, it is believed that homes for the elderly are likely to multiply the problems of dependency they seek to contain unless their routines are flexible, in responding to many different needs, and minimal, in the sense of giving residents as much freedom of action as possible.

From this perspective, homes for the aged are seen to fall somewhere on a continuum of styles and philosophies of care. At one end are those which adopt a generally protective model of care where the emphasis is on doing things for the residents. At the other end are those based on a more supportive model of care where the emphasis is upon enabling residents to do things for themselves. These different types of regime are widely held to produce two distinct kinds of resident: one passive and over-dependent, the other more active and self-reliant. The implication is that many of the detrimental effects of residential living could be avoided by changes and improvements in caring policies and practices aimed at giving residents greater control over their own lives.

Although quite firmly entrenched in current notions about good residential practice, these ideas lack well-grounded empirical support. They are based on professional hunch, and on evidence derived mainly from cross-sectional surveys. Simple cross-sectional designs, however, are not suited to the study of institutional effects because they cannot unscramble the interaction between the inputs and outputs of care. Moreover, they leave many questions unanswered. Are the deleterious effects of residential care really a contingent or, as many of its critics maintain, an inevitable feature of institutional life? Do some types of institutional regime have more damaging effects on residents than others? Do institutional environments affect different residents in different ways?

This study set out to provide some of the missing answers to these important questions using a combination of longitudinal methods and cross-institutional research (Sinclair and Clarke, 1981; Tizard et al., 1975). It was conceived and designed to test the 'induced dependency hypothesis': the idea that the more institutional regimes deny residents control over their own lives, the more they tend to foster their dependency.

Methods

The study comprised three stages. The first stage involved the collection of detailed information about levels of dependency and rates of mortality among residents of 175 local authority homes for the elderly between 1980-1982. Longitudinal data was obtained on changes in the personal functioning of a cohort of 3412 surviving residents over a period of two years in care. The information on residents was aggregated to create four dependency scales each relating to a different area of individual competence and daily living (Booth et al., 1982).

- The self-care scale classified residents according to their mobility and their ability to wash, dress, feed, bath and use the toilet.
- The continence scale classified residents by the frequency of incontinent episodes, treating urine and faeces separately.
- The social integration scale classified residents on the basis of their awareness, standards of behaviour and sociability, as perceived and reported by officers-in-charge.
- The mental state or orientation scale classified residents in terms of their memory, comprehension, orientation, awareness and wandering.

Finally, these four separate scales were combined to produce an overall classification of levels of dependency. Residents whose capabilities were seriously limited in two or more areas of personal functioning were defined as 'severely dependent'. Those rated as competent on at least three of the scales and not less than moderately so on the other were classified as 'independent'. All others were labelled 'moderately dependent'.

Stage two focused on the nature and characteristics of the regimes in these same homes (comprising 178 separate living units). It provided comparative information on the differences in caring routines and management practices between homes on four dimensions of residential life: the opportunities they gave residents to exercise personal choice; the respect they showed for residents' privacy and individuality; the scope they offered residents for participating in the running of the home; and the encouragement they gave to the maintenance of links with the wider community. The aim of this part of the study was to differentiate the homes according to the dependency-producing or dependency-reducing potential of their regimes, conceived in terms of the assumptions of the induced dependency hypothesis.

Cluster analysis was used to differentiate the homes in terms of the character or ethos of their regimes as revealed by the overall pattern of their daily routines (Phillips, 1985). Three clusters were identified which discriminated well between the homes:

Cluster 1 contained those homes (n=37) which tend to allow residents to do or decide things for themselves, leaving them a greater area of freedom of action and individual choice. These homes came closest to showing a positive approach to residents' capabilities. Cluster 2 comprised a group of homes (n=95) which is most accurately described as having 'multiple regimes' in the sense that opportunities on the part of residents for freedom of choice and action in some areas of daily living are counterbalanced by restrictions and controls on others. Also in this cluster are those homes whose overall approach consistently fell between the other two. Cluster 3 contained homes (n=46) which, relative to those in cluster 1, tended to adopt a narrow or restricted view of residents' capabilities, limiting their freedom of action and denying them opportunities for doing or deciding things for themselves.

These three clusters were labelled respectively as 'positive', 'mixed' and 'restrictive' types of regime.

The third and final stage of the study involved relating the data on regimes to the data on outcomes to see if the way homes are run affects the well-being of residents defined in terms of their personal functioning or survival. A full account of the research methods can be found in Booth (1985).

Regimes and Dependency

Substantial variations were found in rates of improvement and deterioration between homes even allowing for differences in the initial dependency of residents. More residents deteriorated, or deteriorated faster, in some homes than in others, and the same holds true for improvement. These worrying variations in the outcome of care, however, were found to be unrelated to the way the homes were run. What differences there were between the regimes in the 175 homes in the study had no more than a marginal effect on changes in the dependency of residents over a period of two years in care, and differences in outcome were unrelated to the characteristics of regimes. The type of regime appears to figure as a constant in whatever formula actually links the inputs and outputs of care in homes for the elderly.

Overall, the evidence shows that regimes which allow residents less freedom and control over their own lives are no more likely to increase their dependency than others. This unexpected finding was investigated in more detail. It is possible that the differences between the three regime clusters, though real, are not big enough to show up as differences in outcome. In other words, that variations in the type of care only begin to have an effect on residents when, like the tension which snaps a rubber band, they surpass some critical point.

To test this possibility, two sub-groups of homes at each end of the range of regime types were identified. At one extreme, from among the 37 homes with positive regimes (cluster 1), 13 were chosen as having exceptionally liberal environments compared to all other homes in the study. At the other extreme, 16 homes were selected from the 46 with restrictive regimes (cluster 3) as sharing a particularly narrow and inflexible approach to the care of residents. In terms of current ideas about what constitutes good and bad residential practice these homes represent the very best and the very worst to be found in the study. The rates of improvement and deterioration among residents in these 'supergood' and 'superbad' homes were compared. Once again the results confound the predictions of the induced dependency hypothesis:

- Levels of improvement in both the 'superbad' and the 'supergood' clusters were below the average for all the homes in the study.
- Levels of deterioration were above average in 'supergood' homes and below average in the 'superbad' ones.
- Overall, the proportion of 'supergood' homes which performed badly was the same as the proportion of 'superbad' homes which performed well.

A further attempt was made to establish a link by

looking at whether the best and the worst outcomes are typically produced by homes with a specific type of regime. To this end, the ten homes with the highest rates of improvement and the ten homes with the highest rates of deterioration were identified and compared. The split of regime types within each group was identical. Among both the 'top ten' for improvement and deterioration there were four homes with mixed regimes (cluster 2), two homes with positive regimes (cluster 1) and four homes with restrictive regimes (cluster 3). In other words, there were as many homes with a positive approach to residents' capabilities in the 'top ten' for deterioration as there were in the 'top ten' for improvement; and there were twice the number of homes with restrictive as opposed to positive regimes among those with the best outcomes in the study. Once again, the results show no connection between the features of the caring routine and what happens to residents, and give no support to the view that more institutionally-oriented regimes tend to foster dependency.

The possibility was explored that the apparent similarity of outcomes in fact concealed interactions between regimes and sub-groups of residents sharing different characteristics. Lawton and Nahemow (1973) have suggested that 'different people respond differently to institutions'; and Moos (1974) also holds that 'different types of patients react differently to varied ward milieus'. In practice, it is generally assumed that residential environments have different effects on people according to:

(a) The severity of their dependency, with residents requiring only a little support benefiting from a different type of care from those requiring a lot.

(b) The nature of the dependency, with people suffering, say, from mental confusion responding to a different type of environment from those who are incontinent.

Accordingly, the effects of different regimes on severely dependent, moderate and independent residents were explored; and the changes in functioning among individual residents on each of the four separate dependency scales (self-care, continence, social integration and mental state) were analysed by type of regime. Again there was no evidence to suggest that what variations in outcome did emerge were consistently related to the caring routines in the homes (Booth, 1985, chapter 9).

Regimes and Mortality

Many more people died in some homes than in others. The actual numbers varied in individual establishments from less than one death among every seven residents at the lowest end of the range to over half of the initial population at the other. Clearly, the structure of the population in each home will play a big part in determining the rate of mortality. Other things being equal, homes with generally older residents would be expected to have more deaths than those with a younger age distribution, as would homes with a disproportionate share of severely dependent residents.

In order to isolate any effects that institutional regimes may have on survival it was necessary to standardise the mortality rates of homes by controlling for these initial differences in the characteristics of their residents. This was done by calculating the actual deaths in each home as a percentage of the expected number of deaths given the age, sex, dependency and length of stay of residents.

Just under half (47 per cent) of the homes had an 'excess' of deaths compared with the number that would have been predicted given the characteristics of their residents in 1980. On the other hand, slightly over half (52 per cent) had fewer deaths than expected. In short, residents seemed to do better in some homes than others. The key question is whether these differences in outcome were related in any way to the types of regimes in the homes.

In the event, what differences there were between homes in the organisation of the daily routine and the press of the social environment had no conclusive effects on the outcome of care in terms of the survival or mortality of residents. If anything, the relationship pointed in the opposite direction to that expected though not enough to seriously entertain the alternative thesis that homes oriented to the protection of residents succeed in prolonging their lives.

Following the approach to the analysis of regimes and dependency, several further attempts were made to uncover a connection between caring routines and rates of mortality. All homes with over 40 per cent more or 40 per cent fewer deaths than expected were identified and their regimes compared:

(a) Among the twelve homes with the best outcomes in the study there were more with restrictive regimes than with positive regimes;

(b) Among the fourteen homes with the worst outcomes in the study, there were more with positive regimes than with restrictive regimes although the majority were of the mixed type.

As before, two extreme subgroups of homes – the most 'resident-orientated' of those with positive regimes (the 'supergoods') and the most 'institutionally-orientated' of those with restrictive regimes (the 'superbads') – were singled out for closer study. It was found that:

(a) A higher proportion of 'superbad' than 'supergood' homes had fewer deaths than expected;

(b) The 'supergood' homes had more excess deaths than the 'superbad' ones;

(c) The percentage of actual to expected deaths in both

groups was very close to the average mortality rate for all homes in the study.

Finally, the possibility that residents' chances of survival may vary between different regimes according to their status and characteristics was explored. Standardised mortality rates among residents in each type of regime were analysed by age, sex, dependency and length of stay. In each case, however, the broad conclusion was the same: differences in residential practice had little effect, if any, on rates of mortality in homes and did not help to explain the variations there were between them. Once again, the assumption that caring routines in homes for the elderly are crucial determinants of the outcome of care is challenged by the evidence.

Conclusions

Real differences were found between homes for the elderly in rates of improvement and deterioration among residents, as well as rates of mortality and survival. In some homes they died sooner and deteriorated faster than in others. However, the performance of homes appears to vary independently of the way they are run. Differences between regimes had no more than a marginal effect on changes in the dependency of residents over a period of two years in care, and on rates of mortality in the homes, and differences in outcome were unrelated to the characteristics of regimes.

The evidence shows that regimes which allow residents less freedom and control over their own lives are no more likely to increase their dependency than others. On the basis of these findings the induced dependency hypothesis must be rejected.

Another interpretation, however, is that caring practices in homes for the elderly tend to be characterised by a similar press towards routinisation and control. From this point of view, the differences between regimes are little more than a veneer on the massive uniformity of institutional life. The common features of residential institutions are so dominant in their effects as to mask or suppress any influence that small differences in the social environment of homes exert (Lieberman, 1969; Tobin and Lieberman, 1976). Accordingly, the fact that regimes and outcomes are not linked as expected demonstrates only that homes are more alike than the induced dependency hypothesis presumes.

At the same time, it may be supposed that the observed differences in rates of improvement, deterioration and mortality between homes were due to factors independent of the way they were run. Four such possible factors, at least, may be identified:

- the personalities and life experience of residents (Goldberg, 1984);

- the physical health of residents (Pincus and Wood, 1970);
- residents' expectations of behaviour (Clough, 1981);
- the skills of staff (Sainsbury, 1980).
It is not hard, therefore, to find extraneous reasons why the performance of homes might vary that owe nothing to the character of their regimes.

These conclusions seriously question the rationale that informs current notions of good practice in residential work. Whatever factors account for the variations in outcome between homes seem to be outside the immediate control of staff.

References

Booth, T., Barritt, A., Berry, S. et al. (1982) 'Levels of Dependency in Local Authority Homes for the Elderly', Journal of Epidemiology and Community Health, Vol.36, pp.53-57.

Booth, T. (1985) Home Truths: Old People's Homes and the Outcome of Care, Gower Publishing Company, Aldershot.

Clough, R. (1981) Old Age Homes, Allen and Unwin, London.

Davies, B. and Knapp, M. (1981) Old People's Homes and the Production of Welfare, Routledge and Kegan Paul, London.

Department of Health and Social Security (1979) Residential Care for the Elderly in London, Social Work Service, London Region.

Goldberg, E.M. (1984) 'Evaluation Studies: Past Experience and a Future Programme', Research, Policy and Planning, Vol.2, No.1, pp.1-6.

Hughes, B. and Wilkin, D. (1980) Residential Care of the Elderly: A Review of the Literature, Research Report No.2, Department of Psychiatry and Community Medicine, University of Manchester.

Institute of Medicine (1977) The Elderly and Functional Dependency: A Policy Statement, National Academy of Sciences, Washington D.C.

Lawton, M.P. and Nahemow, L. (1973) 'Ecology and the Aging Process', in Eisdorfer, C. and Lawton, M.P. (eds.) The Psychology of Adult Development and Aging, American Psychological Association, Washington D.C.

Lieberman, M.A. (1969) 'Institutionalization of the Aged: Effects on Behaviour', Journal of Gerontology, Vol.24, pp.330-340.

Moos, R.H. (1974) Evaluating Treatment Environments: A Social Ecological Approach, John Wiley and Sons, New York.

Personal Social Services Council (1977) Residential Care Reviewed, Personal Social Services Council, London.

Phillips, D. (1985) 'The Cluster Analysis of Regimes', in

Booth, T. (1985), op.cit.

Pincus, A. and Wood, V. (1970) 'Methodological Issues in Measuring the Environment in Institutions for the Aged and its Impact on Residents', Ageing and Human Development, Vol.1, pp.117-126.

Sainsbury, E. (1980) 'A Professional Skills Approach to Specialisation', in Booth, T., Martin, D. and Melotte, C. (eds.) Specialisation: Issues in the Organisation of Social Work, British Association of Social Work/Social Services Research Group, Birmingham.

Sinclair, I. and Clarke, R.V.G. (1981) 'Cross-Institutional Designs', in Goldberg, E.M. and Connelly, N. (eds.) Evaluative Research in Social Care, Heinemann, London.

Tizard, J., Sinclair, I. and Clarke, R.V.G. (1975) Varieties of Residential Experience, Routledge and Kegan Paul, London.

Tobin, S. and Lieberman, M. (1976) Last Home for the Aged, Jossey-Bass, San Francisco.

Chapter Nineteen

CONFUSIONAL STATES IN ELDERLY PERSONS'

HOME RESIDENTS : A PROCESS OF LABEL

ACQUISITION?

Alex Murdock

Introduction

This paper presents the findings of the author's research in
two contrasting local authority elderly persons' homes in 1981.
It is based upon a combination of approaches. First, the
majority of all staff (managerial, care and domestic) were
individually interviewed by the author to obtain their own
personal definitions of and response to, 'confusional states' in
residents. Secondly, the author spent time in both homes
observing their operation and structure. Thirdly, a close
analysis of residents' admission particulars and file data was
made to provide a further basis for comparison. The
research suggests that a number of characteristics of
residents, homes and staff appear to interact in a process of
'label acquisition'. This is offered as a tentative model of the
labelling process and some practical inferences as to how it
may be ameliorated or reversed are offered.

Confusion and Staff in Homes for the Elderly :
Previous Research

There is a paucity of research examining how staff in homes
for the elderly perceive and define confusion amongst
residents. A survey of the literature revealed only two
pieces of research pertaining to this issue. One is so recent
that it was not available to the author until after the project
had been planned and executed (Evans et al., 1981). While
the other was reported in an American journal (Slater and
Lipman, 1977).
    Slater and Lipman's study (1977) examined confusion as
assessed by senior staff only, compared with an assessment
using a standard clinical test and 'symptoms of confusion'
measure adapted from Meacher (1972). They used three
types of rating measures, in addition to a straightforward
categorisation by senior staff. The results showed significant
correlation between the staff assessments and sections of the

rating scales relating to confusion. The most significant correlations were those concerning the spatial orientation of the resident and one of the items concerning speech ('ability to complete sentences logically').

Slater and Lipman (1977) compare these findings with other studies illustrative of spatial segregation within homes, which show that such phenomena foster restricted verbal interaction. Residents, once labelled as confused, are slotted into a physical venue within the home which minimises interaction with residents who are not so labelled. Thus, residents whose spatial/verbal symptoms are possibly not occasioned by chronic brain failure, are treated as if that were indeed the underlying cause. This could exacerbate their symptoms and thereby create a 'self fulfilling prophecy' when staff observe further apparent deterioration.

Evans et al. (1981) examined characteristics of residents and staff of six elderly persons' homes in the Manchester area. Information regarding both the residents' background and situation in the home was gathered, and assessments of the residents made. The assessments used the Crichton Royal Behavioural Rating Scale. Part of the scale was used as a sub-scale to measure confusion. A number of clinical assessments were carried out on residents which showed this sub-scale to be a good predictor of clinically diagnosed senile dementia.

Their study added weight to the spatial labelling hypothesis: they found there was a definite tendency for residents with high scores on the confusion sub-scale to be seated in certain areas, and that these areas tended to be different from the areas where those residents with low scores sat. Furthermore, the study looked at staff attitudes, roles and training and drew attention to the barren history of earlier work in the UK context: 'In the two major British studies of residential care which have been published (Townsend 1962 and Meacher 1972) and in the wealth of American research into institutional care of the elderly, there is little or no reference made to staff perceptions of their role and work study experience' (Evans et al., 1981).

The study found that staff tended to be female, and that care staff tended to be younger than domestic staff. They also found that staff had been in the same job for some time; 73 per cent had left school with no formal qualifications; about half the care and management staff had no relevant training and, for almost half of these, their training had been limited to in-service courses. In terms of occupational role, they found that domestic staff saw their role as being restricted to the tasks explicitly laid out in their job description. The care staff were less clear about their role, and rated variously the importance of their physical care versus their social care role.

What is interesting, however, is the attitude displayed

by the various groups of staff towards the different types of residents. Nearly three quarters of the staff liked working with the confused residents and 41 per cent saw them as the easiest residents to care for. The authors offer four possible explanations for this, which all have considerable implications for staff attitudes to and definitions of 'confusion'. First, they suggest that the staff might see the confused resident as easier in that he/she is less demanding though more dependent. Secondly, the staff might see the confused resident as childlike and thus use a teacher-child model. Thirdly, the authors contrast the role implicit in caring for lucid residents (where the staff member assumes much of the status of 'servant') with the role of nursing/caring in response to the confused resident. Staff are perceived as preferring the latter role. Finally, the staff might see the confused resident as 'a substitute family' to be cared for and responded to as one would respond to a family member.

Research Methods

To explore some of the issues raised above I collected data in two local authority elderly persons' homes. This was carried out in the following ways:
(1) Individual interviews were held with all available staff. The interviews were relatively unstructured and I used no preconceived notion of 'confusion'. Staff were initially simply asked to list those residents in the home that they believed to be confused (a list of residents was available for the staff member to consult). I then asked what particular reasons the staff member had for listing the resident as 'confused'. (It is important to note that no measure or definition of 'confusion' was offered to guide staff despite many staff specifically requesting some kind of guideline. In this respect this research differs from most other research in that it specifically sought to elicit the definitions staff used in labelling residents as 'confused').
(2) I then examined the admission records of all the residents both to obtain basic data (age and length of time in the home, etc.), and to ascertain whether there were any references to the residents' mental well-being prior to admission.
(3) I also spent time in each home as an observer, sitting in the lounges with residents and observing and recording behaviour at meal times and during the day. A research diary was kept and the location of residents in terms of where they ate, sat and slept was carefully recorded. During this time particular attention was paid to the residents mentioned as 'confused'.

Confusional States in EPHs

Description of Homes (in 1981)

1. Greenacres

This is a purpose built 69 bed home dating from the early 1950s. It is arranged on two floors, with more than half the residents sleeping on the first floor. Almost half of the residents are accommodated in twin bedrooms. The home has no day care. It is staffed by an officer-in-charge and three deputy officers. There are fifteen care staff, eight of whom work part-time. There are also six night care staff whose hours are separate from the day staff. Including kitchen and domestic staff the total complement of the home is thirty four staff.
The home shows many of the design features of its time. Though adequately served by lifts, there are access problems to the home itself for frail people. It has long corridors with the dining-room being located at the opposite end of the home to most of the lounges. There are five lounges, all of which are on the ground floor.
Care staff do not have ready access to residents' admission particulars. Management policy is to furnish such information about a resident to care staff as management feel necessary.

2. Masons' Close

This is a purpose built 60 bed home constructed in the 1960s. It is arranged on three floors. There are twin and single rooms, with about half the residents accommodated in each type. The majority of the residents sleep on the ground and first floor.
The home is staffed by an officer-in-charge and three deputy officers. There are fourteen care staff, eight of whom work part-time, and four night care staff. Unlike Greenacres, a number of the care staff who work during the day also sometimes work nights. The staff complement including domestic and kitchen staff is thirty two.
The home's layout is almost circular and it is possible to circumnavigate it internally on the ground floor (via the kitchen). There is an internal courtyard, accessed by several doors. The home has a very modern appearance, and its design makes for far shorter corridors. There are five lounges: three on the ground floor and one on each of the other floors. A group of residents, who are seen as needing particularly close attention, are accommodated in the 'special lounge' during the day and take their meals there. Care staff have access to residents' admission details, and management practice is to share all file information with them.

Research Findings

The contents of the interviews with staff were used to classify the residents into three broad groups in each home: (1) Those residents not mentioned by any staff member as being 'confused'. (Included in this group were residents mentioned by only one member of staff). (2) Those residents mentioned as 'confused' by more than nine members of staff in each home. (3) Those residents mentioned as 'confused' by more than one, but less than ten members of staff.
    The results were analysed under four headings: (1) An examination of the geographical distribution of residents throughout the two homes, following the work of Slater and Lipman (1977) on 'labelling'. (2) Comparison of staff characteristics with the individual propensity of staff to name numbers of residents as 'confused'. (3) Comparison of resident characteristics with the frequency with which they had been named as 'confused'. (4) An analysis of the reasons given by staff for naming residents as 'confused', and a comparison with my observations and previous work on what constitutes 'confusion' in old age.

Geographical Distribution of Residents

In both homes, residents can be identified in terms of where they sleep, eat and sit during the day.
    Sleeping: Each resident is allocated a particular bed in a particular room and that (with occasional exceptions) is where they sleep. Rooms are allocated upon admission, and in both homes there is some internal movement occasioned by residents' requests and managerial decisions.
    In both homes there was evidence that 'confusion' played a role in room allocation. As Table 1 demonstrates, the 'confused' residents tended to be located more in ground floor bedrooms. In Masons' Close, the top floor consisted virtually entirely of residents not mentioned as 'confused'. Staff acknowledged that there was an active policy of accommodating 'confused' residents on the ground floor. Reasons given varied, but hinged predominantly on ease of management (especially where night staff were concerned).
    Eating: Both homes had large dining rooms and meal times represented a major shift of people from various lounges towards the dining area. In Masons' Close some of the residents ate in a separate room, adapted for this purpose. Residents were allocated to the separate dining room not simply on account of 'confusion' but rather, according to the officer-in-charge, because they needed more help at mealtimes. However, staff clearly perceived this group of

241

residents as 'confused'.

Table 1

Bedroom Allocation: By Floor of Home

	Residents mentioned by 10 + staff as 'confused'	Residents mentioned by 2 - 9 staff as 'confused'	Residents not mentioned as 'confused'
Masons' Close			
Second Floor(13)	0	1	12
First Floor(21)	1	3	17
Ground Floor(21)	9	6	6
	10	10	35
Greenacres			
First Floor(40)	5	15	20
Ground Floor(24)	11	9	4
	16	24	24

The dining rooms proper of both homes showed some evidence of 'grouping' of 'confused' residents both in terms of individual tables, and in terms of area of the dining room. Staff offered various reasons for non-random seating. Some said it was easier to seat 'confused' residents near to the serving hatch and, in Greenacres, the concentration of 'confused' residents by the door of the dining room was viewed as a direct consequence of the residents themselves making a choice over where to sit.

Sitting: Each home had a number of lounges. Though initially residents might be guided or encouraged to sit in a particular lounge, in reality this was the aspect of daily life where the residents could be said to have more most discretion. In Masons' Close, some residents were placed in the 'special lounge' and retained there by management decision. However, all the other lounges had evolved by a degree of custom and practice where staff influence played more role than direction.

In practice, the distribution of 'confused' residents was not random across the lounges (see Table 2). In Masons' Close no 'confused' residents are to be found in the 'Quiet Lounge' or the 'Upstairs Lounges'. Rather, they are in the 'Special Lounge' (for reasons previously described), or in the 'Large Lounge' where they share with a greater number of residents not perceived as 'confused'. In Greenacres the 'confused' residents are in the 'East Lounge'. This was to a large extent a management policy, and the officer-in-charge

was quite open in this regard. However, 'confused' residents
are also found in other lounges which, to some extent, is a
consequence of the higher proportion of residents in
Greenacres perceived as 'confused'.

Table 2

Seating Allocation : By Lounge Area of Home

	Residents mentioned by 10 + staff as 'confused'	Residents mentioned by 2 - 9 staff 'confused'	Residents not mentioned as 'confused'
Masons' Close			
Quiet Lounge (8)	0	0	8
Large Lounge(13)	1	3	9
Upstairs Lounge(7)	0	0	7
Special Lounge(8)	6	2	0
In Corridor (12)	3	3	6
No specific place(5)	0	2	3
	10	10	33
Greenacres			
East Lounge (16)	10	5	1
Front Lounge(13)	4	4	5
Small Lounge(10)	2	5	3
Women's Lounge(13)	0	5	8
Men's Lounge (7)	0	4	3
No specific place(5)	0	1	4
	16	24	24

A number of residents could not be placed within any
lounge by the author's observations. Some were in hospital,
several were ill and virtually bed bound, but a number sat in
or wandered the corridors. This was more evident in Masons'
Close and, in part, this could be due to the existence of
carpeted corridors with seating alcoves as opposed to the
rather more spartan corridors of Greenacres. Of additional
significance was the way in which the circular design of
Masons' Close permitted 'confused' residents to wander around
the home, enabling them to 'opt out' of a seat in one of the
lounges without incurring staff pressure.

Staff Characteristics and the Propensity to Name Residents as 'Confused'

A number of characteristics were selected and examined to
ascertain if they were associated with the propensity to

identify residents as 'confused'. These characteristics included age, position held, length of service in home and previous experience/training.

Age alone showed no clear association. In Greenacres there was a longer served staff group and this accentuated the effect of age. However, even in Greenacres the tendency for older staff to perceive more residents as 'confused' was not strong. In both homes there was a relatively small number of younger care staff who saw more than the average number of residents as 'confused'.

Position held had a very strong association with the numbers of residents perceived as 'confused': care staff tending to name about twice as many residents as 'confused' as the domestic staff. This was most pronounced in Greenacres, due possibly to a policy of job demarcation, giving domestic staff less contact with residents. In turn, management staff tended to name more residents as 'confused' than did care staff which may be a factor of the overview afforded by their position. Night care staff (who did not work at all during the day) named an average of 14-15 residents as 'confused', suggesting that they have a good idea of who the 'confused' residents are.

Length of service in the home ties in closely with age, especially in the case of Greenacres. In both homes there is a small group of younger, more recently appointed care staff, who tend to see more than the average number of residents as 'confused'. There is a considerable difference in staff longevity between the two homes, with Masons' Close staff having served an average of three years and Greenacres staff about twice this. Overall there is not, however, a strong relationship between time served and tendency to perceive residents as 'confused'.

Previous experience/training Care staff who had previous experience and/or training tended to perceive more residents as 'confused'.

Residents' Characteristics and 'Confusion'

Three variables were selected and examined: average length of stay; age of resident; and mental health state prior to admission.

Length of time resident has been in home The figures for average length of stay show an interesting variation between the two homes:

	Masons' Close(N)	Greenacres(N)
Residents not mentioned as 'confused'	4.33years(35)	2.25years(24)
Residents seen as 'confused' by >1 staff	4.05years(2)	2.26years(40)
Residents seen as 'confused by >9 staff	2.56years(1)	2.44years(16)

There are probably two discrete processes at work here. In both homes staff reported that more recently admitted residents were more 'confused'. However, in Greenacres there has been a deliberate policy to admit physically rather than mentally frail residents over the past year or so. It could be argued that were it not for this, then the Greenacres figures would more closely resemble those of Masons' Close.

Age of resident The average age of residents mentioned as confused is only slightly above the average age of homes' residents:

	Masons' Close(N)	Greenacres(N)
Average age - all residents	84.50years(55)	83.75years(63)
Residents seen as 'confused' by >9 staff	84.66years(10)	84.06years(16)

The increasing predominance of very old people in local authority homes may make the relationship between age and 'confusion' less clear and hence, staff no longer equate extreme old age with 'confusion'.

Residents state of mental health reported pre-admission
As might be expected there was a clear relationship between mention of mental frailty on admission forms, and being seen by staff as 'confused'. Eighty per cent of the residents mentioned as confused by nine or more staff were described as mentally frail or confused on their admission forms.

However, a surprising finding was that in both homes a substantial minority of residents not seen as confused were in fact described as mentally frail or confused on their admission forms. In Masons' Close this minority was 30 per cent. There is an implication that the effect of application forms upon staff perceptions of residents' mental health is by no means certain.

Reasons Given by Staff for Naming Residents as 'Confused'

The reasons are best listed under a number of headings:

(1) **Forgetfulness** This was the most commonly given reason. It was not simply absent mindedness but rather forgetting of the fundamental 'where', 'when', 'how' and 'who' knowledge of everyday living. Failure to recall which room the resident lived in, or how to wash, dress or go to the toilet were typical examples.

(2) **Lost Time** This was found particularly in comments about the residents seen as 'confused' by nine or more staff. Residents would be described as talking of long dead people as if they were alive. Residents were seen as fixated in time past, and believing themselves to be children or young adults.

(3) **Delusions** Residents were reported to assert things which never happened. These often took the form of 'false beliefs' about other residents or staff (viz.that things had been stolen or other people's things belonged to them).

(4) **Fantasies** Some residents were reported as 'seeing' imaginary visions or happenings which were unrelated to any part of the home environment or any conceivable part of the resident's past life. One resident had described a spaceship landing outside the home in such a vivid and realistic fashion that staff had rushed out to look!

(5) **Communication/Speech Problems** This was reported by staff in 'confused' residents in a similar fashion to the way Meacher (1972) described it. It broadly took three forms: repetitive speech, abnormal or incomprehensive speech, and the general inability to engage in two way conversation.

(6) **Wandering** All residents who were seen as wandering were identified by staff as 'confused'. However, wandering was seen in two relatively discrete forms. First, there was wandering which was directed with some, albeit unrealistic, destination in mind. Often the resident wished to return to some previous address and quite frequently such residents would leave the home precipitating staff pursuit. Secondly, there was aimless wandering within the home, often without any professed destination or purpose. This sort of wandering was accepted and, in one home, actually facilitated by staff. Often, it seemed to involve more than one resident, and pairs of residents would wander together. When one resident of a pair died, the survivor found a replacement companion to wander with.

The Process of Label Acquisition

The research indicated that a number of characteristics of resident, home and staff seem to combine to identify and delineate a process by which residents are 'labelled' as 'confused'. This begins before the resident even enters the home. Admission particulars understandably influence how staff view the resident. Certainly they might affect the choice of room in which the resident is accommodated and, in some cases, room choice is associated with being labelled as 'confused'.

The internal design and layout of the home is also important. If a group of residents seen as requiring special attention at meal times is separated, then staff will be likely to label them as 'confused' even though this may not be the case. If particular residents are encouraged to use certain lounges, then internal segregation of the home is a likely consequence and staff will be inclined to perceive these residents as 'confused' by association.

The management policy of the home is a further crucial factor. Officers-in-charge can implement a segregationist policy which offers strong cues to staff to view particular residents as 'confused' by locational criteria. Alternatives to explicit or implicit segregation do exist, and reference is made below to what I describe as 'pairing'.

There are some characteristics of the staff themselves which seem to affect labelling. Officers tend to view more residents as 'confused' than do care staff, and domestic staff see the fewest residents as 'confused'. Staff experience/training tends to have an overall effect of increasing the number of residents seen as 'confused'. Then there are the characteristics of the resident him/herself. Shorter duration in the home seems to be associated with being seen as 'confused', but age itself seems less important. However, the actual behaviour or phenomena which go into the definition of 'confusion' used by staff are crucial. Certain reasons stand out, and it is easy to understand why. Wandering and forgetfulness of everyday fundamentals require staff attention to the resident. Communication problems and lost time make it hard for staff to relate to residents over everyday matters.

Another point of interest was the fact that staff did not automatically equate certain characteristics with 'confusion'. Incontinence, blindness, deafness and even awkwardness and abusiveness did not in themselves attract the label 'confused'. However, they could form part of a secondary label if one or more of the earlier identified behaviours or phenomena were present.

Non Segregationist Strategies: Conclusion

Pairing

The research indicated the use of one interesting strategy which could be said to reduce the labelling phenomenon.

This was the existence of what I describe as 'pairing'. It occurs when a 'confused' resident becomes linked to a 'non-confused' resident.

In both homes pairs were to be found and, in Greenacres, there were no less than three 'pairs'. One was a natural evolution and the other two had been encouraged in their development by the officer-in-charge. Only one pair identified with the conventional locations of the 'confused' member, and the willingness of the 'lucid' partner to sit in the 'confused lounge' was a source of some bewilderment to staff (who had tried to discourage it).

Subsequent discussions with staff in other elderly persons' homes indicate that 'pairing' is quite a common phenomenon. I have found no instances of the phenomenon being made a part of a conscious strategy of a social services department, but there are indications that its use is generally beneficial both from the point of view of residents and care staff. Successful 'pairing' is a symbiotic relationship in which the needs of two residents are matched. Often, the 'confused' resident is mobile and the alert resident is of limited mobility. Sometimes the alert resident is in need of 'passive companionship' and the 'confused' partner can be seen as meeting this need.

In terms of the staff of the home, 'pairing' offers obvious advantages. It frees staff time from one (sometimes two) residents. 'Paired' residents can wander without risk, since one of the 'pair' is alert. If the 'confused' resident does get into a risk situation then the alert resident can call this to the attention of staff. Many experienced social workers would in fact recognise that 'pairing', whether of sisters or of spouses, serves to prevent admissions to residential care in the first place. What is efficacious in the community can also be applied in elderly persons' homes.

Perhaps the chief value of 'pairing' is its ease of application. However, sensitivity and diplomacy is of the essence and successful 'pairings' have come about either naturally, or through the skilled assessments of residents' needs, followed by the gentle encouragement of the potential relationship. Care and compassion as opposed to cost must be the order of the day.

Wandering

The apparent dual aspect of 'wandering' suggests that it may be possible to evolve more sophisticated responses to the problem. In one home 'aimless' wandering had been quite successfully contained by enabling residents so minded to wander a circular route. This had required some thought and care in that the route included a tramp through the kitchen (a venue often denied to mentally infirm residents on health and safety grounds). This approach had been successful in containing wandering in the home, without any apparent diminution to the wanderers' pleasures.

There will still be the wanderers who will leave the home with some apparent objective. One strategy which seemed to be effective (though more costly in staff time) was to send a member of staff to 'shadow' the wandering resident. The home found that almost invariably the resident would hesitate after a while and then the care staff would offer their assistance. This enabled the resident to make a choice to return, as opposed to being tacitly restrained from leaving.

One interesting aspect of wandering was that it often occurred in pairs or, in one case, in a threesome. Frequently one of the pair, though 'confused', would have no previous history of wandering. What was even more interesting is what often occurred when one of a pair of wanderers died or went into hospital. Both homes reported that the survivor would usually find another resident and 'train' them to wander. One member of care staff likened wandering to a virus which was communicated from one resident to another. Since my research I have observed that once wandering becomes established in a home it does indeed often endure after the original wanderers have passed on.

References

Evans, G., Hughes, B., Wilkin, D. and Jolley, D. (1981) The Management of Mental and Physical Impairment in Non-Specialist Homes for the Elderly, University Hospital of South Manchester, Psychogeriatric Unit, Research Report No.4.

Meacher, M. (1972) Taken for a Ride, Longman, London.

Slater, R. and Lipman, A. (1977) 'Staff assessments of confusion and the situation of confused residents in homes for old people', The Gerontologist, Vol.17(6), pp.523-530.

Chapter Twenty

AWAY FROM INSTITUTIONAL DEPENDENCE :

TOWARDS A MORE RESIDENT-ORIENTED

INSTITUTIONAL ENVIRONMENT

Stella Dixon

Introduction

A range of studies, from Townsend (1962) and Goffman (1961)
to more recent research, have documented the
disadvantageous effects of admission to residential care on
elderly people's autonomy and the widespread incidence of
institutional dependence. There have also been numerous
suggestions about how to improve residential life. However,
research evidence, together with personal experience of
working with CSS students, suggests that institutional
dependence is not easily eradicated.
The research discussed below, represents an attempt to
discover why it is so difficult to change residential
establishments from places which engender institutional
dependence into more resident oriented environments. Evans
et al. (1981) maintain that a resident oriented environment is
one which first, facilitates resident freedom; secondly, puts
residents' needs before administrative efficiency; thirdly, does
not regiment residents or subject them to block treatment;
fourthly, enhances the individuality of each resident; and
finally, gives the power to make decisions to residents and
seeks to minimise the social distance between staff and
residents. Running throughout these characteristics, and
perhaps at their heart, is the notion of resident power to
determine daily life.

The Experience of Dependency

A review of the literature, both American and British, over
the last 25 years suggests the following causes of institutional
dependence:
(1) Poor admissions: badly planned, resident not involved in
    the decision, no links maintained with the past,
    unrealistic expectations.
(2) Attitudes of staff towards elderly people, particularly
    infantilising attitudes.

(3) Routine over-provision and lack of individuality.
(4) No permission to maintain existing skills.
(5) Loss of role.
(6) A different way of life within the home.
(7) Authoritarian management styles.
(8) Lack of self determination.
All of these institutional features can be seen to involve a loss of power on behalf of the residents.

Suggested methods of improving the residential environment can also be found in the literature, although there is very little on how to achieve them. They include:
(1) Improved procedures.
(2) Recognition of the individuality of each resident.
(3) Acceptance of basic human rights in relation to elderly people in residential homes.
(4) Self determination.
(5) A normal lifestyle.
(6) The attitudes, values and beliefs of senior staff.
(7) Skills to translate a commitment to resident oriented values into practice.
(8) Individual assessments, records, reports and care plans.
(9) Social communication between staff and residents.
(10) Consultation and communication between staff.
(11) A physical design which reflects ideology.
(12) Opportunities for activities.
(13) Participation in decision making.
(14) Contact with the outside world.
(15) Flexible management practices.

Just as the causes of institutional dependence can be seen to involve the loss of power, these suggestions for better practice can be viewed as ways of empowering residents.

Confronting Dependency

In order to investigate why it was proving so difficult to put these ideas into practice, I undertook a piece of action research with the care staff of one elderly persons' home, with the explicit aim of trying to change practices which were seen by the group as likely to result in institutional dependence. The home was a fairly typical, traditional establishment, purpose-built some twenty years ago for 53 elderly people by the local authority.

After a lengthy period of negotiation and preparation, I administered the Analysis of Daily Practices Schedule (Evans et al., 1981) in an attempt to monitor any changes that might occur as a result of the intervention. The responses to the questions are coded and a maximum score of 78 would denote an extremely institution oriented environment, whilst the minimum score of 0 would suggest a very resident-oriented establishment. The home, before the work with the staff was carried out, achieved a score of 34.

The action research itself comprised 15 weekly sessions with the care staff, each session lasting approximately one and a quarter hours. We began by trying to identify the purpose of residential care and later the values and principles which the group considered should guide and inform practice. The following list was eventually decided upon:

The purpose of residential care
Is to provide settings in which people's needs (physical, emotional, social, intellectual and spiritual) are most likely to be met.

Values to guide practice
Dignity
Understanding/patience
Respect for residents and colleagues
Availability of choice
Opportunity for privacy
Time to listen
Recognition of individuality
Communication
Encouragement towards independence (but not officiously)
Opportunities for stimulation (but not enforced)
Participation
Autonomy
As normal a lifestyle as possible.

This purpose and these values were copied onto a large poster which was brought to each meeting of the group; between group sessions it was displayed in the care office where it attracted much comment.

The group then examined areas of practice in relation to the values identified above, and decided to change their practices when they were seen not to reflect these agreed values. The changes agreed upon covered the following areas: first, early morning practice; secondly, the development of the key worker system within the home; thirdly, admission work.

After changes had been agreed upon they were implemented by the staff and later brought back to the group in order to evaluate their success. The process of change thus described sounds eminently reasonable and comparatively painless: in reality of course it was not. However the use of participative exercises in which members were encouraged to share their feelings helped the process considerably and enabled a consensus view to emerge.

Three months after the completion of the sessions with the staff the Analysis of Daily Practices Schedule was administered again: the score had gone down from 34 to 22. In addition, in their evaluation of the group sessions, the staff said that the experience had enhanced their self confidence, their feeling of working as a team and their recognition of the importance of the individuality of each resident. It had also provided them with a model of how to work together to achieve change.

However, despite this generally agreed improvement in the residential environment, change had not proven easy to achieve. Many of the changes that were implemented were very small (for example waking people at 7 a.m. rather than 6.30 a.m.) and almost all involved a great deal of hard work. Partly this difficulty may be attributable to the threat inherent in any action research and people's general resistance to change, but other issues were revealed. In particular, professed values and actual values in practice sometimes appeared very different and this found expression in the group via the notion of 'gentle force' which was how staff dealt with residents who would not do what staff wanted them to. When it was pointed out that 'gentle force' was incompatible with the professed values of autonomy and choice, it was clear that 'gentle force' would win and that underlying its use was the belief that 'we know best'.

Dartington, Miller and Gwynne's work (1981) on attitudinal constructs which regulate relationships between staff and residents, was useful in helping to explain what was occurring. They maintain that one of the most pervasive approaches to residents is illustrated in the Less Than Whole Person attitudinal construct (LTWP), in which the resident is seen as entirely less-than-whole, rather than as having emotional independency needs at the same time as having some physical dependency needs. The key to this attitudinal position is, they say, the 'defensive dynamic of the carer'. In order to cope with their own feelings of inadequacy and lack of self worth, staff project these attributes onto impaired or elderly residents, thus enabling them to perceive themselves as strong whole people who are taking care of the unfortunate residents. Residents are treated in routinised ways since staff are seen to know what is best for them; this renders them dependent on the institution, providing further 'proof' of their less-than-wholeness.

Thus it would seem that a pervasive LTWP attitudinal construct may lie at the heart of the difficulty in putting resident oriented policies into practice, since such practice would require giving at least some of the power to determine daily life to the residents themselves, which is clearly incompatible with the 'we know best' of the LTWP construct.

However, currently resident - oriented values and practices are generally being extolled in policy documents, training courses and the social work press. Thus in some way the incompatibility between such values and the LTWP attitudinal construct has to be resolved. My experience leads me to suggest that this is achieved by paying lip service to resident oriented values such as independence and choice at the same time as redefining them to make them compatible with LTWP. Thus, for example, 'independence' changes in meaning from a 'state of self reliance' (Davis and Knapp, 1981) to a kind of enforced physical independence, in which elderly people are kept going physically, often in quite officious ways, and irrespective of what people themselves want, since the staff know what is best for them. Paradoxically this change in emphasis meant that independence came to mean its opposite, since enforced physical 'independence' could only be achieved by residents becoming dependent on staff making decisions for them. Such redefined, almost bastardised, independence reinforces the defensive dynamic, since it confirms that residents are less than whole and that staff know what is best for them. At the time however lip service can be paid to progressive notions such as independence.

This, it is being suggested, is why there is such a gap 'between the intentions of those who formulate policy, and the day to day experiences of the residential consumer' (Willcocks, Peace and Kellaher, 1982). It is also perhaps the reason why Booth (1982) maintained that 'over 20 years of research-based criticism has done little to change important aspects of institutions'.

Insofar as the action research was successful, it was so because unlike 'research-based criticism' it did begin to address some of the real issues of staff values and attitudes. However, its success was limited by the intransigence of some of these same attitudes particularly in relation to the devolving of power from staff to residents. Interestingly, the change in score in the Analysis of Daily Practices Schedule (Evans et al., 1981) was lowest in the section relating to resident autonomy and much higher in the resident care and organisational practices sections.

Clearly then, policy documents extolling the virtues of resident oriented regimes are not sufficient to get them translated into practice, neither are physical designs which reflect a resident oriented ideology, although both may prove extremely helpful. What is required in addition is a radical renegotiation of resident/staff roles so that people's autonomy needs can be maintained even if they also have physical dependency needs.

Such a 'reorientation of practice', as Willcocks et al. (1982) call it, may well be facilitated by a new design which symbolises individuality and so on, but it can also, in my experience, be achieved, at least to some extent, in a traditional home with staff used to more routinised ways of caring. Such change is not easy, nor is it quickly achieved. It requires commitment and above all the ability to start with and accept people as they are. But it is possible.

Conclusion
The following conclusions, regarding helping people to change were reached as a result of my work with the staff team:
(1) Change is not easy to achieve; the status quo is known and comfortable.
(2) Change can be painful for staff and residents.
(3) Preparation for change is crucial.
(4) Problems following the implementation of change are inevitable - plan for communication.
(5) Some people are more ready to change than others, this must be accepted.
(6) People cannot be forced to change, sabotage is easy.
(7) Involvement in decision to change leads to greater commitment than imposed change.
(8) Start where people are.
(9) If constraints are emphasised, acknowledge their validity rather than minimising them, at the same time encouraging creative ways round constraints.
(10) A shared and explicit value base acts as a reference point to guide the direction of change.
In addition, if a real departure from LTWP is to be achieved staff would have to renegotiate their roles away from doing things to people towards helping people live the life they want to lead. It would also seem that they would need to find sufficient self esteem and job satisfaction from enabling, for the defensive dynamic of the LTWP construct not to come into play. Only then would we move from what Willcocks et al. (1982) call resident care to residential living, or as Clough (1981) states: 'the complex and skilful task of encouraging the individual to decide how she wants to live'.

References

Booth, T. (1982) 'A Confused Mixture', Community Care, 2 December.
Clough, R. (1981) Old Age Homes, George Allen and Unwin, London.
Dartington, T., Miller, E. and Gwynne, G. (1981) A Life Together, Tavistock Publications, London.
Davies, B. and Knapp, M. (1981) Old People's Homes and the Production of Welfare, Routledge and Kegan Paul, London.
Evans, G., Hughes, B., Williams, D. and Jolley, D. (1981) The Management of Mental and Physical Impairment in Non-Specialist Homes for the Elderly: Research Report No.4, University Hospital of South Manchester Psychogeriatric Unit, Research Section.
Goffman, E. (1961) Asylums: Essays on the Social Situations

of Mental Patients and other In-Mates, Doubleday, New York.
Townsend, P. (1962) The Last Refuge, Routledge and Kegan Paul, London.
Willcocks, D., Peace, S. and Kellaher, L. (1982) The Residential Life of Old People, Research Report No.12, Survey Research Unit, Polytechnic of North London.

Chapter Twenty-One

THE DEPENDENCY CHARACTERISTICS OF OLDER

PEOPLE IN LONG-TERM INSTITUTIONAL CARE

D. Ann Atkinson, John Bond and Barbara A. Gregson

Introduction

As part of a DHSS funded study evaluating long-stay
accommodation for elderly people (Bond, 1984), a survey of
the services that already exist for the continuing care of
elderly people has been undertaken. This survey includes a
description of the dependency characteristics of elderly
residents and patients in institutional care. The objectives
were:
(1) To describe the dependency characteristics of elderly
    occupants in long term care in the catchment area of
    three National Health Service experimental nursing homes
    and in three control areas in neighbouring health
    authorities.
(2) To describe the residential accommodation and facilities
    available to residents and patients.
    The six study areas each covered about fifteen to twenty
square miles and as a substantial number of residents in two
of the NHS nursing homes had previously been resident in
hospitals outside the catchment areas, these hospitals were
included in the study.

Method
Selection of Control Districts

Potential control districts with characteristics similar to the
experimental districts were identified from the socio-economic
classification of local authority areas (Webber and Craig,
1978). The control districts were selected after 1981 census
profiles had been obtained for the experimental and potential
control districts and crude measures of the over-65s in
geriatric and psychiatric hospitals and in residential homes
had been obtained for the experimental and the three most
likely control districts. An important consideration was that
control districts were selected within easy reach of the
experimental districts.

Population

The population studied included elderly people in hospitals, residential homes and private homes who were aged 65 years or over and who had been resident 28 days or more at a census date.

Data Collection

Data collection was by means of two questionnaires. The Institutional Environment Questionnaire provided us with information on the quality of the environment in which residents and patients lived, by giving details of the physical and social environment of the homes and wards. The Resident Dependency Questionnaire was based on the modified Crichton Royal Behavioural Rating Scale (CRBRS) (Wilkin and Jolley, 1979). This provided a measure of the physical dependence and mental state of the elderly person. The large amount of time which would be involved for an interviewer to collect data on the levels of dependency of elderly people in institutional care prompted us to develop a self-completing questionnaire to be completed by qualified nursing staff on wards, heads of residential homes and proprietors of voluntary and private homes. In order to reduce the workload of ward sisters and heads of homes, an approximate 50 per cent sample of patients and residents was obtained. However, data were collected for all patients and residents in wards or homes with less than ten eligible subjects.

The results presented here are from the dependency questionnaire only and include patients and residents in geriatric and acute hospital wards, local authority residential homes, private and voluntary homes and NHS nursing homes.

Results
Response

There was a high response from the hospital wards and local authority homes with 97 per cent of wards and 93 per cent of homes completing the questionnaires. This was largely as a result of good preparation and liaison with health and social services.

In the case of private rest and nursing homes, a letter was sent explaining the study, followed by the questionnaires. A telephone call was made to the homes not responding and, subsequently, a visit was made to those proprietors who were willing to complete the forms, from whom we had not heard. This action did result in the completion of more questionnaires but the overall response was poor with only 46 per cent of homes returning completed questionnaires.

Questionnaires were sent to all acute wards that may have had elderly patients resident 28 days or more. All wards were checked, if we had not received any questionnaire, to ensure we had a complete sample. The number of patients resident 28 days or more in acute wards ranged from four in one area to 38 in another. Data were not collected for all psychiatric and psychogeriatric wards in the six areas, so have not been included in this preliminary analysis.

Last Residence

The majority of elderly people entering care were previously resident in their own home, the only exception being those entering NHS nursing homes, who had all been previously resident in hospital. The reason for this is that for an experimental period all potential residents for the experimental NHS nursing homes are referred by the consulting geriatricians.

When the six areas were examined individually there were some differences in the last residence of patients and residents. Of those in private nursing and rest homes, 32 per cent in one area had previously been resident in residential homes. This may partly be due to the large increase in the provision of private homes in this area over the past few years, which also may explain the substantial proportion (24 per cent) entering private homes from hospital in a second area.

A lot of the patients on geriatric wards in one area (27 per cent) had previously been resident in another hospital which implies a fairly regular movement of patients from one hospital to another. Whilst in another, 90 per cent entered geriatric hospital from their own home. This high percentage may be due to the policy of regular intermittent stays at hospital followed by periods at home (e.g. two months in hospital, one month at home) which operates in this area. This illustrates individual differences between areas although in all but one institutional setting, the main last residence of those entering institutional care was from their own home.

Age

Over 74 per cent of residents and patients in all but the acute wards were aged over 75, whereas in acute wards 61 per cent were over 75. For all areas the residential homes and private homes had a slightly higher proportion of elderly residents aged over 75 compared with the geriatric wards. The slightly higher percentage of residents aged under 75 in NHS nursing homes, compared with the other long stay institutions, may be because consultant geriatricians are only

259

referring elderly people who have been in institutional care less than two years and this will probably include a high proportion of people only recently designated as 'long stay'.

Gender

Females predominated in all institutional settings - 4:1 in private nursing and rest homes, 7:2 in residential and NHS nursing homes and slightly less in the geriatric wards. Only in the acute wards were males more heavily represented (2:3).

Length of Stay

The length of stay of residents and patients is perhaps what one might have expected. The residential homes had the majority resident over a year and as many as 25 per cent over four years. The length of stay of the majority of patients in geriatric wards was much less, more than 50 per cent resident less than a year and on acute wards 75 per cent less than four months. Two of the NHS nursing homes had just opened and the other had been open nearly a year, hence the majority of residents had been in the homes less than three months.

In the residential homes in two areas about a third had been resident less than a year whereas in the other areas it was nearer a fifth. Also in one of these areas 40 per cent on geriatric wards had been resident less than three months compared with 18 - 25 per cent in other areas. This may partly be due to the discharge of long stay patients to private homes; 45 per cent in private homes had been resident one year or less.

The length of stay of residents in private homes did vary from one area to another and the data possibly reflect the differing rates of increase in provision in private homes in the last few years in these areas.

Reasons for Admission

Admission to residential care, as perceived by staff, was seen as largely due to the inability of the elderly person to continue caring on his/her own or of the relatives to care for him/her. In the geriatric wards, acute wards and NHS nursing homes, neurological complaints such as hemiplegia, cerebro-vascular disorders and Parkinsons disease figured prominently. It is perhaps interesting to note that four institutional types, residential homes, geriatric wards, NHS nursing homes and private homes, stated confusion as an important reason for admission in over ten per cent of cases, thus confirming that this is a problem in all long-term care institutions. The private homes when looked at individually had residents admitted for similar reasons to the local authority homes: social problems being the main factor causing admission.

Total Behaviour Ratings

The modified Crichton Royal Behavioural Rating Scale was used to measure the dependency characteristics of residents and patients. The total scores on the ten-item scale range between 0 and 38, 0 representing the most able residents and patients, and 38, the most disabled.

Figure 1 is drawn as a box plot and shows the total behaviour rating for residents and patients in the five settings. The upper and lower quartiles of the data are portrayed by the top and bottom of the rectangle and the median is the horizontal line within the rectangle. The area of each box is proportional to the number of residents or patients and the lines extend from the ends of the box to the upper and lower values.

The pattern of dependency in the five settings is perhaps what one might expect, the geriatric wards and NHS nursing homes caring for the most dependent group of elderly people, with more than 50 per cent severely dependent (having a total CRBRS score of over 21). Whereas in the residential homes and private homes less than 25 per cent were severely dependent. The acute wards had a considerable percentage severely dependent (38 per cent), but in all settings there was considerable overlap. These figures do however hide individual differences from area to area, when comparing institutional settings.

Figure 2 shows the number of residents and patients in each area in three institutional settings who were severely dependent. We report no data on private homes in areas 1 and 2 because at the time of data collection there were only four homes in total in the two areas. Of these, two had recently registered and had only just begun to admit residents and there was no response from another home.

In areas 4 and 6, the percentage of residents in private homes who were severely dependent was substantially more than in the other two areas, 23 per cent and 25 per cent respectively compared with approximately five per cent in the other two areas. The private homes in area 6 were in fact catering for a more dependent group of elderly than the residential homes. It appears that in area 3 the private homes were catering for a much more able group of elderly people as 84 per cent of residents were rated under 11 on the scale.

In the residential homes severe dependency ranged from 19 per cent to 29 per cent but of greater significance is the

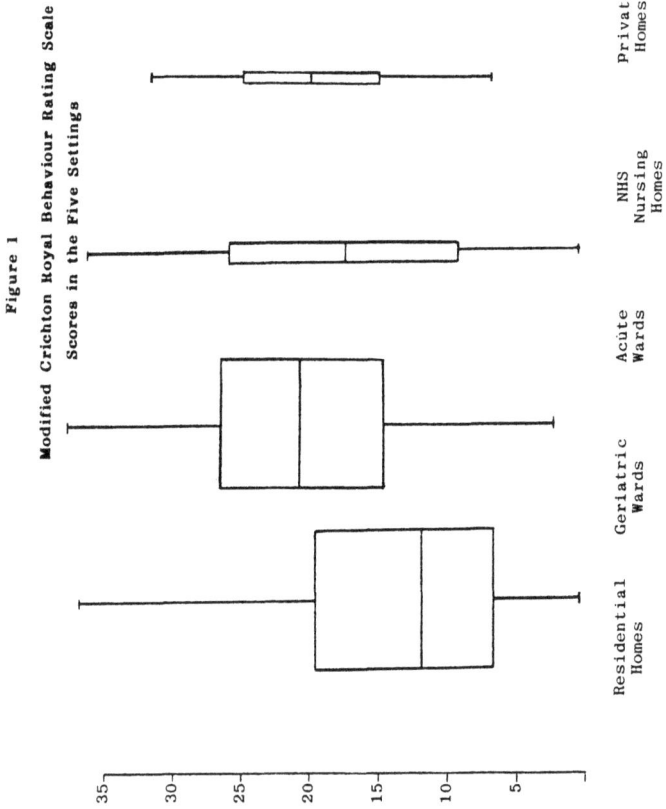

Figure 1

Modified Crichton Royal Behaviour Rating Scale Scores in the Five Settings

Figure 2

Bar Chart to Show the Percentage of Patients/Residents
Severely Dependent in Three Settings in Six Areas

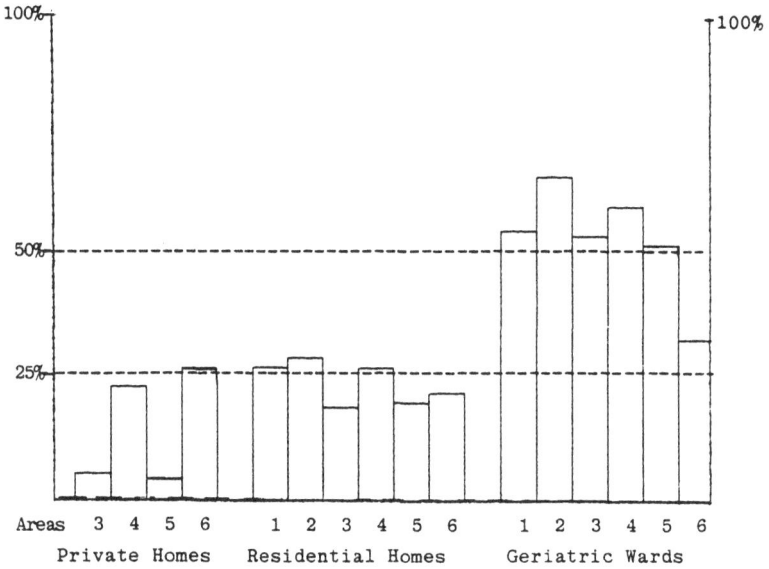

difference between geriatric wards from area to area where severe dependency ranges from 33 per cent in area 6 to 66 per cent in area 2. In area 2 both geriatric wards and residential homes had a higher percentage severely dependent when compared with the other five areas.

Area 4 had a substantial proportion of severely dependent elderly in all three institutional settings, residential, private and geriatric wards, whereas in area 6 the high dependency in the private homes seemed to compensate for the geriatric wards which had the smallest percentage of severely dependent compared with geriatric wards in other areas.

Mental Disturbance

A measure of confusion, (ranging from 0 to 11) can be obtained by grouping the scores on three items of the CRBRS (memory, orientation, communication), (see Figure 3). Moderate or severe confusion (a score of 4 or more) was high in the geriatric wards and NHS nursing homes, over 50 per cent and 70 per cent respectively. In the acute wards the percentage was 48 per cent which was similar to the residential homes at 47 per cent. A third of patients in private homes were moderately or severely confused. However all institutions had the full range, with lucid to severely confused residents and patients.

There are however differences from area to area, reflecting the total CRBRS scores (see Figure 4). In the private homes moderate or severe confusion ranged from 13 per cent in area 3 to 43 per cent in area 6. In the geriatric wards the range was 47 per cent in area 6 to 71 per cent in area 4. In all three NHS nursing homes over 70 per cent were moderately or severely confused.

Incontinence

Incontinence and immobility are two important criteria with regard to admission to a particular type of care. Regular incontinence was prevalent in all four settings. In private homes 34 per cent were regularly incontinent in area 6 compared with seven per cent in area 3. The other two areas had 19 per cent and eleven per cent regularly incontinent. The variation between residential homes was also quite marked with between 17 per cent and 37 per cent regularly incontinent. However the geriatric wards had the highest percentage regularly incontinent, 61 per cent overall.

Mobility

In terms of mobility the residential homes had the smallest percentage overall bedfast and chairfast (ten per cent),

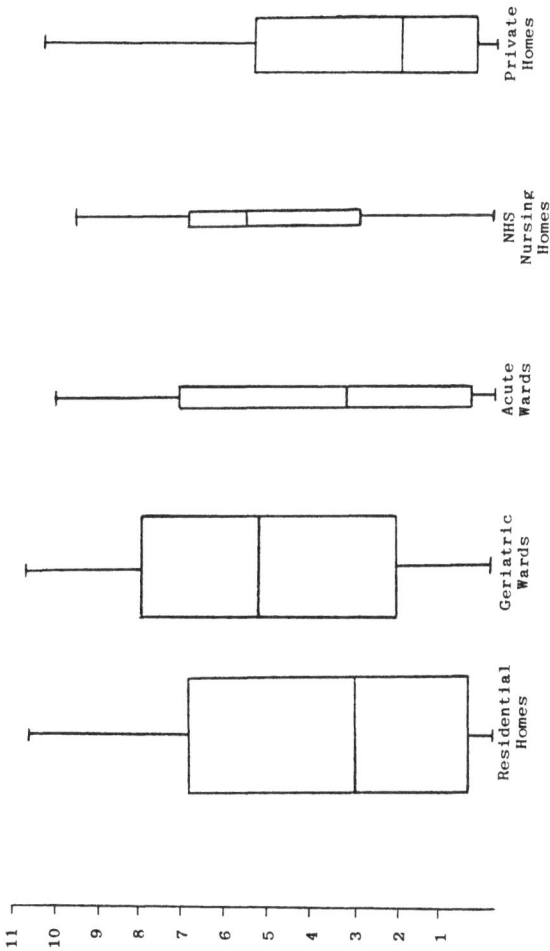

Figure 3

Confusion Subscale Scores in the Five Settings

Figure 4

**Bar Chart to Show the Percentage of Patients/Residents
Moderately/Severely Confused in Three Settings
in Six Settings**

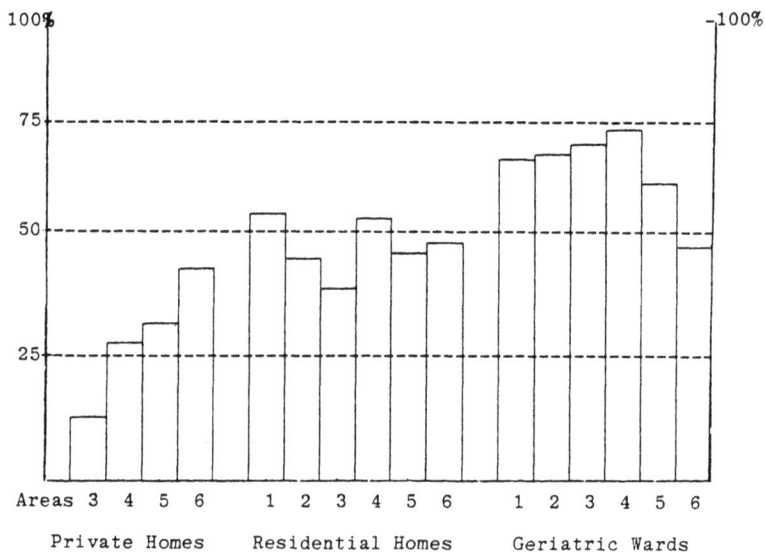

whereas in the private homes it was 17 per cent. There was however variation in the private homes from area to area, ranging from seven per cent to 20 per cent. The variation between local authority homes was between six per cent and 13 per cent bedfast or chairfast. The hospital wards and NHS nursing homes had the largest percentage bedfast or chairfast, over 60 per cent overall, but in area 5 as many as 82 per cent were chairfast or bedfast on geriatric wards.

Discussion

The combined data for each institutional setting on the dependency characteristics of elderly residents confirms existing knowledge about this area. Whilst there were differences between residents of local authority, private, NHS nursing homes and patients in geriatric wards, there were many important similarities, not only in terms of social and demographic characteristics, but also in terms of physical and mental functioning. Geriatric wards and NHS nursing homes contained heavy concentrations of severely disabled people, but there were many in residential homes and in some private homes whose needs for care were the same as those of hospital patients. This observation has also been made in other surveys (Townsend and Wedderburn, 1965; Wilkin et al., 1978; Bond and Carstairs, 1982; Wade et al., 1983). When the institutions were looked at individually from area to area differences did arise, particularly in terms of the kind of residents in private homes. In one of the areas there was a tendency for the heavily dependent to be spread between institutions, the private homes in area 6 sharing the burden with the geriatric wards. Whereas in area 3 there were greater extremes. The very dependent elderly were prominent in the hospital wards whilst the private homes cared for much more able residents where only five per cent were severely dependent.

The levels of dependency that exist in each institutional setting in each area will be influenced largely by the operational policy in each area and the demands on the service. However, these data do not provide any insight into the care of older people at home or experiencing respite or shared care which we think might explain much of the variability between areas.

It is obvious from our comparisons of elderly people in residential and hospital care that the same needs are being met in a variety of different settings. It is also clear that despite increasing numbers of very old people in the population, the broad pattern has changed very little. However it is very difficult to generalise, particularly with regard to the private sector, as to the levels of dependency of elderly residents in different areas. At a time when private homes are expanding and are being used by the NHS, it is perhaps important to look more thoroughly at the service they provide. Do they bridge some of the gaps in the service that is needed for the increasing number of elderly who need continual care, or are they providing care for the fitter elderly person, who only needs partial attendance from staff? It is therefore important to regularly monitor dependency levels in long-term care institutions.

It is essential that, whatever provision is made for long-term care in the future, careful monitoring and evaluation should be carried out. The costs of these exercises are small when compared to the costs of providing care, but the potential benefits to the service providers and to the elderly people are considerable in assisting planning and ensuring that the needs of elderly people are adequately met in the future.

References

Bond, J. (1984) 'Evaluation of Long-Stay Accommodation for Elderly People', in Bromley, D.B. (ed.) Gerontology: Social and Behavioural Perspectives, Croom Helm, London.

Bond, J. and Carstairs, V. (1982) Services for the Elderly. A Survey of Characteristics and Needs of a Population of 5000 Old People, Scottish Health Service Studies No.42, Scottish Home and Health Department, Edinburgh.

Office of Population Census and Surveys (1981) County Reports Part 1, South Yorkshire. Lancashire, Hampshire, HMSO, London.

Townsend, P. and Wedderburn, D. (1965) The Aged in the Welfare State, Bell and Sons, London.

Wade, B., Sawyer, L. and Bell, J. (1983) Dependency with Dignity, Bedford Square Press, London.

Webber, R. and Craig, J. (1978) Socio-Economic Classification of Local Authority Areas, Studies of Medical and Population Studies No.35, OPCS, HMSO, London.

Wilkin, D. and Jolley, D.J. (1979) Behavioural Problems Among Old People in Geriatric Wards 1976-1978, Research Report No.1, Department of Psychiatry and Community Medicine, University of Manchester.

Wilkin, D., Mashia, T. and Jolley, D.J. (1978) 'Changes in Behavioural Characteristics of Elderly Populations of Local Authority Homes and Long Stay Hospital Wards, 1976', British Medical Journal, Vol.2, pp.1274-1276.

Acknowledgement

We are grateful for financial support from DHSS and to colleagues in the Health Care Research Unit, particularly members of the project team: Eva Brown, Senga Bond, Joyce Crawley, Gillian Donkin, Cameron Donaldson, Margaret Hally, Jan James, David Newell, Lesley Speakman, Judy Thompson and Lorna Wake for their help in the preparation of this paper.

Chapter Twenty-Two

THE PAYING PATIENT : CUSTOMER OR COMMODITY

SURVEYING PRIVATE NURSING HOMES

FOR THE ELDERLY

Linda Challis and Helen Bartlett

Introduction

One of the arguments advanced by the proponents of private
care is that by purchasing care, consumers gain more control
over the service they receive than their counterparts in the
NHS and that furthermore, unlike NHS patients, they have
the ultimate sanction of the withdrawal of their custom if the
care being delivered is not up to the required standard.
Against this argument is the view that in the case of nursing
home care for the elderly, the clientele are likely to be so
frail and demand for places is so substantial, that the
supposed merits of private provision - control and choice -
simply do not exist (Harris and Seldon, 1979; Knapp, 1984;
Grant, 1985). Research into private nursing home care being
conducted at the University of Bath is beginning to shed
some light on this debate. It seems that both sides are to
some degree correct but that the environment of care is very
much more complicated than has hitherto been recognised.

The Debate

It is of course the case, in theory at any rate, that someone
able to command sufficient money to pay for private home care
can enter a nursing home at a time which the customer
decides is appropriate. This capacity gives such a person a
considerable amount of control over their own care. They
can choose which home they wish to enter, whether to occupy
a single or shared room, whether to enter a home near where
they have lived or to move to another area either to be
nearer to relatives or simply to enjoy new territory. Ideas of
good practice in the care of the elderly have emphasised the
importance of the individual entering care with a positive
rather than negative attitude (PSSC, 1977; Brody, 1977;
Goldberg and Connelly, 1982). It seems reasonable to
suppose that positive attitudes are more likely to be fostered
in someone making the decision to enter care whilst they are

still fully able to make such decisions themselves and not because there are absolutely no other options open to them. If people can enter care before they absolutely must, they have more time with their physical and mental faculties at least partially intact in which to adjust to their new environment.

It is also true of course that the customer has the ultimate weapon at their disposal - they can leave a particular home and find care elsewhere. Although this 'threat' may not often be realised, it may be thought of as a fairly powerful weapon in arguing for better/different care within a home. This is so because not only the home proprietors lose a customer if the patient remains dissatisfied but also because it may lead to bad publicity for the home which in turn may affect the willingness of other patients to stay in the home and of new ones to enter it. Even proponents of private care who recognise that in reality patients may be so frail as to be unable to exercise either choice or control on their own behalf may still argue, with some justification, that many elderly people do have relatives or other agents, like solicitors for example, to exercise choice and control on the patient's behalf. Furthermore, the registering authorities, the district health authorities (DHAs), may ask some penetrating questions if the home is seen to be having a high drop-out rate.

The research at Bath suggests that for some patients in private care this view of the customer's ability to choose and control is a fairly accurate one, but the research also suggests that given the constraints on both patients and providers and given the background of providers, it is rather surprising that there should be any truth at all in these claims. For some patients and for some providers there is very little room for either choice or control. In this respect, private care may be no better or worse than the NHS.

Entering Care

The numbers of elderly people in the Bath study who arranged their own admission was quite small (5 per cent); relatives or friends were responsible for arranging 49.5 per cent of admissions, and professionals, i.e. doctors, social workers, etc., had placed 40 per cent. Even allowing for the necessarily tentative nature of this data, provided as it was by home proprietors who might not know the full extent of a patient's participation in the decision making, it seems likely that it is a minority of patients who themselves decided and arranged for admission. Furthermore, it does not seem to be the case that patients were choosing to enter care before they had reached a critical physical or mental state or whilst there were still other care options open to them. Often admissions had been hurriedly arranged by relatives when a situation had reached a crisis point and an immediate solution was being sought. In very few of the nursing homes visited was it common for patients to have made plans some years previously to enter that particular establishment. One of these was Brendon Care at Winchester - a voluntary nursing and residential home catering mainly for local elderly residents - where they kept a long waiting list of people who had decided much earlier that at some time they would move into the home. Another home with a similar policy was run by the Licensed Victuallers Association, where care was provided in a village setting in either sheltered housing, a residential care wing or a nursing home. Such homes were, however, the exception.

The majority of patients (85 per cent) were said to be suffering from both physical and mental conditions and only 10 per cent were described by the proprietors as being primarily fit upon admission. Most patients were admitted from hospital or from their own homes and the reason for admission most often given was that the relatives were unable to cope for one reason or another, or that there was no-one to care.

Whatever the circumstances of a person's admission to a home, there is little information available to patient or relatives to help them make an informed choice. Only about half (49 per cent) of the homes had produced brochures and these differed considerably in their usefulness. This lack of information is made more serious by virtue of homes being so completely individual, offering different facilities, and having different regimes. The fees ranged from £55 to £335 per week for a single room and it was often not apparent what people could expect for their money.

There are important 'official' reasons why the majority of patients in nursing homes are so dependent. The 1984 Registered Homes Act and accompanying guidance makes it clear that DHAs should advise nursing homes who have four or more people who do not need nursing care to register with the Local Social Services Authority (LSSA) as well as with the DHA (NAHA, 1985, HC (84) 21). The unwillingness of some proprietors of nursing homes to do this seems to stem from several factors. First, they fear that becoming 'dually registered' will diminish their status and so have an effect on their attractiveness to customers and referrers. Secondly, they fear they might not be able to continue to charge the higher rates charged by nursing homes. Thirdly, they may be unwilling to submit to another round of investigation, especially by people they feel to be less qualified than themselves. These factors militate against the use of private nursing homes as receivers of pre-dependent people and consequently the Act may be said to have put an obstacle in the way of the realisation of good practice by consumers and referrers alike.

Financing Care

An appreciation that many elderly people are entering care because someone else has made the decision for them seems to challenge the belief that the existence of a private sector gives people choice. However, an even greater constraint on patients is that of money. It is now well-known that elderly people can be supported in private nursing home care by Supplementary Benefits (SB) through the board and lodging scheme. It is also well-known that this system has recently been reviewed and that further reviews seem likely. We do not propose to discuss the changes in detail here (see, for example, Challis and Bartlett, 1985), but the important point to note in this context is that a sizeable number of elderly people in nursing homes are paid for by the state. Data from 50 interviews conducted with proprietors suggests that 39 per cent of patients in these homes are SB supported. Most proprietors consider that the April SB limits and even the new November increases have been pitched too low. Homes that are continuing to take patients supported by SB are faced with three options: first, they can limit the choice of rooms available for SB patients to those which are either cheaper or shared; secondly, they can increase the fees of the privately paying residents so that they subsidise the SB residents; or thirdly, they may simply reduce the quality of care being offered. Those already in homes and supported by SB are at risk because they may not, despite the transitional arrangements whereby SB will continue to pay their fees at pre-April, 1985 levels, be able to meet increasing home charges. Such a situation not only undermines the view that customers of private care have a choice of all the homes available but also undermines the view that such patients can withdraw their custom if care is not up to scratch. Patients with transitional arrangements are locked into their present homes and new SB patients may have great difficulty in finding homes at a level of charge which the DHSS is prepared to pay. Our survey has shown that the fees for single rooms were above the national limits set in April in 80 per cent of homes. Indeed, two-thirds of local DHSS offices in England and Wales had set, before the freeze on local discretion, a local level in excess of the new national rate introduced in April 1985.

One of the reasons for saying that the Bath research is showing the picture to be more complicated than the rhetoric is that if proprietors do increasingly seek to attract more 'private' patients then the reality of the sanction of withdrawal of custom for some patients may become more powerful. Fewer people are able to afford higher rates and consequently proprietors catering for this 'up market' end of consumers may well become especially sensitive to consumer wishes and preferences. The homes we have visited which are already catering for this group show every sign of being particularly attuned to their residents' desire for, for example, privacy. Anyone who has visited Part III homes or private nursing homes will know that it is not uncommon for visitors to be ushered into patients' rooms with only cursory attention paid to the patients' wishes in the matter. In one deluxe home we visited the proprietor was not prepared even to knock and ask the resident's permission to show us the room on the grounds that it would constitute an invasion of their privacy.

Supply and Demand

It is apparent from the discussion so far that the relationship between supply and demand for homes is important in determining how much choice and control a customer of care has. Establishing what the relationship is between supply and demand is not a simple matter. First, it is not just a case of whether there are in total enough nursing home beds to meet demand/need but rather a case of whether there are enough beds at the right charge, of the right kind in the right place, at the right time. Our study is showing that homes quite close to each other may have quite different demand experiences, i.e. that cheaper homes may be full whereas some more expensive ones are not, or vice versa. Secondly, the nursing homes are not necessarily competing with other nursing homes but with residential homes and with domiciliary services which enable people to stay in their own homes. In other words, the demand for places is not a constant and may change according to the perceived merits and demerits of the local establishments. Much of this is at present fairly academic because the demand is so great that its effect swamps the subtleties of customer preferences. Seventy per cent of the homes surveyed had waiting lists, only 21 per cent had vacancies and this is likely, on the evidence of the interviews, to be an overestimate since many vacancies are only for very short periods whilst waiting for a known person to be admitted to the home. This overwhelming demand for places, militates against customer control. The proprietor knows that if someone leaves he or she can fill that place very quickly and easily. Since homes usually insist upon four weeks notice the financial consequences of people leaving because dissatisfied are minimised. Not that it happens very often. Most patients leave homes to enter hospital or die and anyone who wished to leave because they were dissatisfied would face all the problems (and more) that any entrant to the care world faces, namely finding somewhere else (better) to go.

Care, Regulations and Complaints

There are three other major sources of constraint on private patients and proprietors which are worth considering in the context of patients as customers or commodities. The first of these is staff. Nursing homes have to be run by a qualified 1st level nurse (RGN) and although some of the proprietors/matrons we have interviewed had had previous experience of private nursing, all of them had had considerable NHS experience. Although the motives of trained nurses entering the nursing home business are many and varied, frustration with the NHS way of doing things played a part, in a majority of cases, in the decision to set up in business on their own. These people seemed to be very involved in patient care and some at least were finding the business aspects of the home a chore. It is also true that one does not spend a large part of one's professional life in the NHS without being imbued with the values of nursing and medical practice in the NHS. It would be dangerous and foolish to assert that all nurses have the same view of nursing in general or indeed of nursing older people in particular. Nevertheless, the nurses we have interviewed by and large apply the medical model to their task of caring for older people. Although they place importance on providing a 'homely' environment, their approach seems mainly to deal with physical needs, and gives relatively little attention to patients' social needs (such as the need for self-fulfilment, independence and privacy) and certainly does not view the individual as a whole person. In some ways this is a strength because it does not prompt nurses to embark upon the wilder ambition of some non-nursing staff working with the elderly, who seem to feel that every need must be catered for even if privacy and independence are sacrificed in the process.

Our data is not of the kind which would allow us to compare the approach of nurses who have no previous professional experience with the elderly with those that have, but it is of note that a sizeable minority of those we have interviewed had no post-qualifying experience of working in geriatric care. It is not obvious that having worked in NHS geriatric care is an advantage, since it is not at all clear that the NHS has fully incorporated a more individualised approach into its care of the elderly (Wells, 1980; Denham, 1983). Indeed, some nurse proprietors complained to us that qualified staff recruited straight from the NHS had to be virtually retrained. Others have argued that this approach - the nursing process - is not appropriate in a nursing home, either because the patients' needs and requirements do not change significantly and because the patients are too confused, or because homes do not have the staffing levels to make this system work. A few have seemed unaware even of

the debate and consequently the risk of treating people
simply as bundles of physical needs (i.e. commodities) is
increased. It is worth adding here, however, that the NHS
has much to learn about long-term care of the elderly from
many of the homes we have visited. Two in particular,
owned by ex-hoteliers with obvious business motives, were
offering a completely individual and customer oriented service
to their patients.

Regulation of private nursing homes constrains, as it is
intended to do, the operation of homes. The Registered
Homes Act 1984 and the accompanying code of practice
prepared by NAHA are concerned primarily with quality of
care through the setting of minimum standards (NAHA, 1985).
Insofar as these standards are applied they constrain the
proprietor in the kind of care and the environment which can
be offered to the customer. On the whole this may be
considered a good thing in that it may protect the consumer
from ill-treatment and abuse but it is worth noting several
ways in which the enforcement of standards may encourage
the treatment of patients as commodities rather that
customers. Fire regulations is one area where strict
adherence to the guidelines can undermine those aspects of a
home which may be particularly attractive to a consumer. Let
us give an example from the Bath study.

One home in the heart of the countryside had been set
up in the proprietor's family house. It is a small
establishment catering for about eight patients even though it
is registered to take twelve. The building itself is very
distinctive in that the original builder fitted it with very
intricately carved wood panelling. This panelling gives the
home a very distinctive character and one which prospective
customers might find very attractive or very unattractive.
Presumably those people already in the house found the
ambience given to the home by this carving attractive. Just
before we visited the home the regulation authorities had
started discussions with the proprietor about the need to
remove the panelling in the interests of fire prevention. It
seems unlikely that they will insist upon this because the
proprietor has made it quite clear that she will not 'destroy'
her home but it is by no means certain that the panelling is
safe from the regulation authorities. If it is removed there is
little doubt that the character of the home will have been
changed and little doubt that the potential fire hazard will not
have been reduced. At no time had it been suggested by the
regulatory body that the patients should be asked what they
thought about the panelling.

Another and less idiosyncratic example of the impact that
regulations can have on homes and their patients is that of
the keeping of pets. One home which we visited was keeping
pets in direct opposition to the wishes of the regulation
authority. The patients had decided that these pets - three

cats and a dog - should remain in the home, and they were obviously an important aspect of the life of the home.

Planning departments too are attempting to place constraints on the operation and development of homes. In Bournemouth, for example, proprietors of existing homes who apply to extend their premises and proprietors of new homes have to sign an undertaking that they will not accept patients who have not been resident in the Bournemouth area for two years. Planning permission is not granted unless such an undertaking is obtained. This procedure has been introduced because of fears that the nursing homes were causing an influx of elderly people, with a consequent drain on the area's health resources. This restricts consumer choice for a minority of consumers; our survey has shown that only 8 per cent of patients moved from another area directly into a nursing home.

The third constraint to be discussed in relation to the customer/commodity debate is that of representation. Consumers of private nursing home care do not have adequate channels of complaint. The DHA may not be able or willing to become involved in individual complaints; the Community Health Councils were set up for NHS patients and have no jurisdiction in the private sector. Apart from relatives or solicitors patients in private homes do not have an effective, independent channel through which to voice complaints. It is often unclear what would constitute a reasonable complaint because few homes (40 per cent) have any form of written contract with their residents. Those that do seem mainly for the benefit of the proprietor and not the patient, and are concerned typically with payment of fees or idiosyncratically with details about clothing to be brought in, such as boilable knickers.

Conclusion

We indicated at the beginning that some people would argue that, in theory at any rate, elderly people have control and choice in entering private nursing home care. This discussion has identified some of the constraints on elderly people which limit the extent of control and choice that they can exert. Not all of these constraints are imposed by nursing homes themselves; rigidities in the stock of premises and limited availability of qualified nursing staff are two examples outside the home's control, which both have an effect on the development of nursing homes. In some ways it is surprising that any private patients have any control or choice at all so great are the constraints on customers and providers. Nevertheless, some people do have it and if we are serious about fostering good practice, as legislation like the 1984 Registered Homes Act suggest we are, then we should take care that we do enough to preserve and develop

The Paying Patient

what is there already, but not so much as to destroy what is undoubtedly a very delicate balance between private control and public concern.

References

Brody, E.M. (1977) Long Term Care of Older People, Human Sciences Press, New York.
Challis, L. and Bartlett, H. (1985) 'Upsetting the Elderly', New Society, 4 October, 1985.
Denham, M.J. (ed.) (1983) Care of the Long Stay Elderly Patient, Croom Helm, London and Canberra.
Goldberg, M. and Connelly, N. (1982) The Effectiveness of Social Care for the Elderly, HEB, London.
Grant, C. (1985) Private Health Care in the UK: A Review, Economist Intelligence Unit.
Harris, R. and Seldon, A. (1979) Over-Ruled on Welfare, Institute of Economic Affairs, London.
Knapp, M. (1984) The Economics of Social Care, Macmillan, Basingstoke and London.
National Association of Health Authorities (NAHA) (1985) Registration and Inspection of Nursing Homes: A Handbook for Health Authorities, NAHA, Birmingham.
Personal Social Services Council (PSSC) (1977) Residential Care Reviewed, PSSC, London.
Wells, T.J. (1980) Problems in Geriatric Care: A Study of Nurses' Problems in Care of Old People in Hospitals, Churchill Livingstone, Edinburgh.

Acknowledgement

The research is being funded by the King Edward's Hospital Fund.

Chapter Twenty-Three

THE ASSESSMENT OF DEPRESSION IN ELDERLY PEOPLE

BY NON-CLINICIANS

Catherine Thompson

Introduction

I became interested in the assessment of depression in elderly people through my work as a researcher on a project whose aim is to determine whether the provision of supplementary home support makes it possible, cost-effectively and satisfactorily, to maintain elderly people with dementia in their own homes for longer than is normally possible with support only from existing services. The project is being carried out in two contrasting areas: a county town (Ipswich) and an inner-city area (the London Borough of Newham). For this research project it was deemed important to assess how many of the elderly demented people in our study were also suffering from depression and to monitor any changes in this state as the project progresses. My interest in depression has also been furthered by being involved in the planning and pilot work for a new project looking at the prevalence of mental disorder amongst elderly people in an inner-city area.[1]

For both these research projects resource constraints have meant that it has been impossible to employ psychiatrists to interview all the subjects and assess their mental state. It has, therefore, been necessary to employ some method of assessing depression which can be undertaken by non-clinicians. There are enormous advantages to the researcher in using an established schedule where some work has already been done on assessing its validity and reliability rather than constructing a completely new one. After considering a number of existing schedules, two scales from the Comprehensive Assessment and Referral Evaluation (CARE) Schedule (Gurland and Wilder, 1984), namely the Organic Brain Syndrome (OBS) scale and the depression scale, were selected for use. However, in this paper I shall only be focussing on the latter scale. For both research projects the scale items were incorporated into interview schedules which also included a number of social and

Assessment of Depression

demographic items.
The CARE is a semi-structured interview schedule which
was developed during a series of studies of elderly people in
London and New York (Gurland et al., 1983). Our research
team was trained in the use of the CARE OBS and depression
scales by a psychiatrist who had been involved in these
cross-Atlantic studies. It was decided only to use two scales
from the CARE schedule and develop our own additional items
of a social and demographic nature, since the whole schedule
contains some 1,500 items and can take up to three hours to
administer.

The CARE Depression Scale

The CARE depression scale consists of 25 main items relating
to symptoms which are either present at the time of interview
or which have occurred during the past month. Several
questions may be needed to elicit the information required for
one item. The interviewer asks the respondent the questions
directly, exactly as they are written, and the item is rated
by the interviewer in accordance with the subject's verbal
response. If the subject's response to a particular question
indicates that a symptom may be present then the interviewer
follows this up with a series of probe questions. A negative
response, then, to an initial question about a depressive
symptom acts as a cut-off point and the interviewer goes on
to the next item. Thus, for example, with the question
relating to loneliness:

Have you felt lonely in the past month?

If the respondent answers negatively then the interviewer
passes on to the next item; on the other hand a positive
response would be followed by a number of probing
questions:

How often have you felt lonely?
Can you turn away from it?
Does it bother you very much?
Does it make you feel depressed?

The majority of the CARE depression questions are
open-ended in this manner and as such they can often become
part of a conversation, with the respondent answering in
his/her own words and the interviewer following up with more
detailed questions. For sensitive items relating to people's
feelings this seems preferable to asking closed questions such
as:

Have you felt lonely in the past month?   - all the time

                                            - often

                                            - sometimes

                                            - seldom; or

                                            - never.

For the majority of depression items the respondent scores 1 if the symptom is said to be present and 0 if absent. Several of the items are graded according to the severity of the symptoms and respondents can receive slightly higher scores on these. The individual item scores are then summed to produce an overall depression score which can range from 0 to a possible maximum of 30.

The CARE depression scale appears to have been extensively tested for reliability and validity and the results are reported in a series of articles by Gurland and his colleagues (Golden et al., 1984; Gurland et al., 1984; Teresi et al., 1984a, 1984b).

The Use of the CARE Depression Scale

The CARE depression scale then appears to represent a reasonable method by which non-clinicians can assess depression: it has been developed with elderly people and it has been tested for validity and reliability. It forms part of a semi-structured interview which means that respondents can answer in their own words whilst ensuring that important items are not forgotten by the interviewer. All in all, the CARE scale seems to be one of the better depression scales which are available for use by non-clinicians.

As far as I am aware there are no published comments about the difficulties of administering depression scales, such as the CARE, to elderly people. However, in practice, I and several of my colleagues found that the scale was over-lengthy and clumsy in parts, with many questions being badly worded and difficult for people to answer. Furthermore, I have grave doubts as to whether it is possible to identify depressed elderly people in the community using such a scale.

Firstly, I would like to consider the issue of poor question wording by the use of a few illustrative examples. One of the questions asks:

Do you get out as often as you need to get out (e.g. to get pension, cash cheques, go to the doctor's)?

If the respondent answers negatively the interviewer follows it up with:

How do you feel about that?

It is difficult for people to know what 'need to get out' means, particularly for those people who have a home help who performs chores or for husbands where their wife has always done the shopping etc. They might want to go out but is that the same as needing to go out?
Another question asks:

When did you last feel happy?
And in the past month?

I am sure many people would have difficulty in answering that. A common reply was 'I don't know - I'm not unhappy but I wouldn't say I was happy.' The word 'happy' seems to imply a very positive elated feeling whereas perhaps 'content' or 'not unhappy' is a better description of the way many ('non-depressed') old people feel.
Another problem with the scale is that it does not consider the duration of symptoms, but merely ascertains whether they have been present or absent during the past month. Thus it cannot distinguish a transient depressive episode from a sustained depressive illness. During one of my interviews I asked an elderly woman:

During the past month have you ever felt that life wasn't worth living?

and she answered 'Yes', then paused and added 'Yes - last week when I had the runs, I have!' This seems to me very different from someone who often has the feeling that life is not worth living.
The scale does not identify those people who are suffering from depressive symptoms which seem to be a reasonable response, perhaps to some loss or event, and which they may get over in several days. This lack of attention to the severity and duration of symptoms seems to be a very common problem with depression scales and it is one which is particularly worrying since some clinicians and researchers have observed that elderly people suffer from a higher incidence of transient depressive episodes (Raskin, 1979). The issue is not clarified in any way by the controversy amongst psychiatrists and other mental health professionals as to whether transient attacks should be classified as true depressive episodes.
According to Klaus Bergman (1978), from a clinical point of view when assessing depression in the elderly the '.... most important question is, is this depression a recurrence of similar attacks in earlier life or is this a depression starting in old age?' (Bergmann, 1978, p.275). The response to this question has implications for outcome and consequently for

service provision. Those people whose first depressive attack occurs in later life are more likely to suffer relapses. However depression scales tend to consider only symptoms which have occurred over a fairly short time period and do not take account of the respondent's case history.

A major difficulty in using depression scales with elderly people lies in the meaning assigned to somatic complaints, such as lack of energy, headaches, loss of appetite and sleeplessness, which are usually regarded as depressive symptoms. There seem to be three main problems here: firstly, some somatic complaints may be associated with so-called 'normal' ageing - in other words they may be physiological changes which occur in non-depressed elderly people. For example, there is some evidence to suggest that in general older people sleep less and that they waken more frequently and for longer periods (Prinz, 1977).

Secondly, such symptoms may result from physical illness, for example, cardiovascular problems may cause sleep disturbance and loss of energy. Blumenthal (1975) argues that somatic complaints in older individuals are more likely to reflect 'true' physical problems than depression. She suggests that the inclusion of such symptoms on a depression scale for use with elderly people may result in spuriously high ratings. Obviously, in practice it is very difficult to distinguish 'true' physical complaints from those which indicate depression, particularly when using a standardised questionnaire.

The meaning attached to somatic complaints may well go some way towards explaining the discrepancy, noted by Gurland (1976), between studies based on clinical interviews, where the highest rates of depression have been reported for people aged 25 - 64, and studies based on assessment of symptoms, where the highest rates were found for those aged 65 and over.

Thirdly, many drugs used to treat a wide variety of medical conditions in the elderly are capable of producing depressive symptoms. For example, diuretics, which are commonly prescribed to treat hypertension and other cardiovascular problems, may produce lethargy and weakness.

The way the CARE depression scale handles somatic complaints seems to be somewhat inconsistent. It does use detailed probes for some somatic items, such as sleeplessness and loss of appetite, to try and establish whether or not the complaint can be attributed to psychological causes. In the case of sleep disturbance the procedure for attempting to establish whether it is due to 'mood change, tension, or depressed or anxious thoughts' is fairly clumsy and difficult to carry out in practice, and with many old people the regular and prolonged use of sleeping tablets further complicates the issue. The two opening questions are:

Have you had any trouble sleeping over the past month
- I mean regularly?
Have you been taking anything to help you sleep?

If a person answers 'yes' to either question the
interviewer has to ask a series of detailed probe questions.
(If they answer 'no' the interviewer breathes a sigh of relief
and rapidly goes on to the next item). For people who do
not have trouble sleeping but who do take sleeping tablets
you have to preface the probe questions with 'if you were not
taking these tablets....' For example:

If you were not taking these tablets, would your sleep
be interrupted during the night?

If you were not taking these tablets, would you wake
very early in the morning?

For some people who have been taking sleeping tablets
for perhaps twenty years this is a highly dubious exercise.
On the other hand, with somatic complaints such as headaches
and loss of energy the interviewer is only required to
establish whether the symptoms have been present during the
past month.

A further complicating factor, acting in the opposite
direction, is that many old people seem reluctant to admit to
psychological problems. This could possibly be something of
a cohort effect in that they belong to a generation which
tended to express malaise mainly in terms of bodily complaints
and, for example, did not bother the doctor with
psychological problems. In my experience older people do
seem more willing to admit to physical problems and problems
which may be socially accepted as associated with ageing,
such as loneliness.

Their reluctance to acknowledge the presence of certain
psychological symptoms is not eased, I feel, by the use of a
standardised questionnaire. It is quite understandable that
after only five minutes' conversation with a virtual stranger
you may not want to admit that you often wish you were
dead. It is not the kind of topic that normally crops up in
everyday conversation.

Standardised questionnaires are based on the
self-reported symptoms of the respondent and in general little
account is taken of the interviewer's observations and the
views of people who are in close contact with the respondent.
For example, I can clearly recall one interview with an elderly
woman who would not admit to any depressive symptoms - she
just seemed to want to get through the interview as quickly
as possible. Her husband looked on in amazement and
afterwards, when we were alone, disagreed with much of what
she had said. Throughout the interview she looked clearly

distressed - there were tears welling up in her eyes and she kept biting her lip - but she said 'yes, she was happy all the time'. She was diagnosed by a psychiatrist as suffering from depression, but according to the scale she was not depressed. Again, there are many instances where I have asked the respondent:

Have you felt like crying in the past month? and they have said 'no', but a relative has looked on in total disbelief and said 'But he/she cries all the time'.

Problems such as these, encountered when administering the scale, mean that it is difficult for the researcher to interpret the meaning of an individual's depression score. It is quite possible that some depressed people will score very low on the scale whilst other non-depressed people may achieve higher scores. This must raise doubts as to the appropriateness of summing individual items to produce total depression scores. Arising from these points is a more general question concerning the validity of the CARE depression scale.

As mentioned earlier, there has been a series of studies conducted on the validity of this scale. A detailed examination of the results and implications of these studies is outside the scope of the present paper. However, such a discussion will form the basis of a further paper which is currently in preparation.

Whilst this paper has focussed primarily on the CARE depression scale, it is likely that many of the arguments and criticisms put forward could be applied to other standardised depression scales.

Conclusion

Overall then, I feel that using standardised questionnaires is a less than ideal method of assessing depression in elderly people. Ideally one would need to take into account many other factors, in addition to a respondent's self-reported symptoms, when assessing depression. We can gain some insight into the process of assessment by studying the way in which a good clinician arrives at a diagnosis of depression. The literature suggests that a clinician would make use of data from a variety of sources and in addition to self-reported symptoms would consider factors such as:
  - the presence of other mental conditions, e.g. dementia;
  - the presence of any physical illness(es);
  - psychiatric case history;
  - the use of medication - prescribed and over the counter;
  - non-verbal communication;

- observations and comments of people close to the respondent; and
- the respondent's living environment.

It would seem that a good qualitative in-depth interview using highly trained and skilled researchers who are able to recognise and sensitively probe beyond surface denials and are able to utilise information from many sources, would be better than a standardised questionnaire for approaching this complex task of assessment. Clearly this would be a very expensive option and in the majority of cases researchers will no doubt continue to use standardised instruments if they want to assess large numbers of people. Given that this is the case there is much that could be done to ensure that standardised questionnaires become more useful indicators of depression then they are at present. For example, it is necessary to tackle the issue of the duration and severity of symptoms. In addition, there would appear to be considerable room for improvement in question wording and design.

Whilst recognising that depression scales are not intended for use as diagnostic instruments, it would be helpful if the relationship between a psychiatric diagnosis of depression and an assessment of depressive symptoms were to be clarified.

However, the process of development and refinement of existing scales is made extremely difficult in view of the absence of a large body of data on depressive symptomatology from a representative sample of people of all ages who cover the range of mental states from 'normal' to 'severely depressed'. As Raskin points out, at present there is a lack of normative data:

> .... we do not know, for example, which signs and symptoms of depression are unique to elderly depressed patients, which signs characteristic of depression in general, and which signs are found in all elderly persons, normal as well as depressed.
> (Raskin, 1979, p.15)

Notes

(1) These two studies are being conducted by members of the Age Concern Institute of Gerontology in collaboration with the Psychogeriatric Unit at the United Medical and Dental Schools, Guy's Hospital, London, under grants from the Guy's Hospital Special Trustees and the Sainsbury Family Charitable Trusts.

References

Bergmann, K. (1978) 'Psychogeriatrics' in Carver, V. and Liddiard, P. (eds.) An Ageing Population, Hodder and Stoughton in association with the Oxford University Press.

Blumenthal, M.D. (1975) 'Measuring Depressive Symptomatology in a General Population', Archives of General Psychiatry, Vol.32, pp.971-978.

Golden, R.R. et al. (1984) 'Development of Indicator Scales for the Comprehensive Assessment of Referral Evaluation (CARE) Interview Schedule', Journal of Gerontology, Vol.39, No.2, pp.138-146.

Gurland, B.J. (1976) 'The Comparative Frequency of Depression in Various Adult Age Groups', Journal of Gerontology, Vol.31, No.3, pp.283-292.

Gurland, B.J. and Wilder, W.D. (1984) 'The CARE Interview Revisited: Development of an Efficient, Systematic Clinical Assessment', Journal of Gerontology, Vol.39, No.2, pp.129-137.

Gurland, B.J. et al. (1983) The Mind and Mood of Ageing: The Mental Health Problems of the Community Elderly in New York and London, Croom Helm, London.

Gurland, B.J. et al. (1984) 'The SHORT-CARE: An Efficient Instrument for the Assessment of Depression, Dementia and Disability', Journal of Gerontology, Vol.39, No.2, pp.166-169.

Prinz, P.N. (1977) 'Sleep Patterns in the Healthy Aged: Relationship with Intellectual Function', Journal of Gerontology, Vol.32, No.2, pp.179-186.

Raskin, A. (1979) 'Signs and Symptoms of Psychopathology in the Elderly' in Raskin, A. and Jarvik, L.F. (eds.) Psychiatric Symptoms and Cognitive Loss in the Elderly, Hemisphere, Washington.

Teresi, J.A. et al. (1984a) 'Construct Validity of Indicator-Scales Developed from the Comprehensive Assessment and Referral Evaluation Interview Schedule', Journal of Gerontology, Vol.39, No.2, pp.147-157.

Teresi, J.A. et al (1984b) 'Concurrent and Predictive Validity of Indicator Scales Developed for the Comprehensive Assessment and Referral Evaluation Interview Schedule', Journal of Gerontology, Vol.39, No.2, pp.158-165.

Chapter Twenty-Four

PEER HEALTH COUNSELLING :

A WAY OF COUNTERING DEPENDENCY?

Miriam Bernard and Vera Ivers

Introduction

This paper discusses the development of a pilot project which
was designed to train older people to become 'peer health
counsellors'. The initial course, is an integral part of a much
wider self-help health initiative by the Beth Johnson
Foundation which aims to encourage and foster positive images
of old age and ageing amongst professionals and lay people
alike, as well as developing preventive health measures
amongst older people themselves.

Background to the Project

Although peer health counselling and peer support are not
new concepts and have been used in various settings
including careers advice (France and McDowell, 1982) and
education (Hamburg and Varenhorst, 1972; Wheldall and
Mettem, 1985), peer health counselling has not, to our
knowledge, been applied to older people in this country.
Only in North America has it been employed as part of a
growing movement towards comprehensive self-health
programmes (Warner-Reitz, 1981; Fallcreek and Stam, 1982;
Savo, 1984). Contrary to these progressive developments,
similar preventive work with older people in this country is
very poorly advanced.
    This view was confirmed in 1981 when the Foundation's
Development Officer visited the United States on a Winston
Churchill Memorial Fellowship. While there, her interest and
enthusiasm for self-health care was fired by a number of
visits, not least one made to the Centre for Geriatric Medicine
in Santa Monica, Los Angeles. At this centre, those aged 55
and over were offered free health screening, and advice and
guidance on matters relating to stress, diet and exercise.
Unfortunately, the professional workers at the clinic were
unable to offer follow-up appointments which, particularly in
the case of stress management, gave them serious cause for

concern. As a result, they decided to develop a peer support system for clients. Older workers were recruited and offered training in counselling and self-health care. They then went on to help clients referred by the clinic's professional staff and, in turn, held regular meetings with the doctors and nurses to discuss particular clients and any problems they might have encountered.

This first-hand experience of peer health counselling in action, was reinforced by discovering a small, but growing, interest in the elderly and self-health care around the world (U.S. Department of Health, 1979; Amann, 1980; WHO, 1981; Hatch and Kickbusch, 1983; Coppard et al., 1984). In addition, in the early 1980s, the Foundation had itself begun to develop innovative and preventive health and social developments with, and for, older people. In 1982, for example, the Beth Johnson Leisure Association was established. This self-help organisation was concerned with opening up local opportunities for older people to engage in sporting and other recreational activities. At around the same time, plans were made to open a Senior Centre where retired people could be encouraged to experiment with new interests and activities. The Centre opened in a city-centre church in 1983 and offered various kinds of advice; opportunities to make social contacts; and to learn new skills. It also became a venue for activities such as yoga, dancing, popagility and indoor bowls, as well as providing courses and classes.

One of the most striking features arising out of these developments, was the keen interest that many older people had in maintaining their own health. Indeed, a course on 'First Aid in the Home', held at the Centre in early 1984, proved to be particularly popular. At this time too, Allin Coleman, who was undertaking a Health Education Council funded research project looking at Pre-Retirement Health Education, became interested in the Foundation's work. As a result, we began a mutually fruitful co-operation with this project by, initially, setting up three 'health issues discussion groups'. These groups were designed to facilitate exploration of a wide range of issues related to health in retirement, and to try out some experimental materials being developed for potential use on pre-retirement courses.

Our first discussion group was drawn from people who had attended the 'First Aid in the Home' course. In common with many other people, this group's worst fears centred around being unable to look after themselves and becoming dependent upon others. This was countered by an equally strong desire and resolve to stay as fit and active as possible, and to learn more about how to remain healthy. Participants, like those in the two subsequent groups, also valued the sessions for the opportunity they gave them to share their (good and bad) experiences of preparing for retirement; to talk about their dealings with GPs, dentists and other health professionals; and to air their views about what was needed for older people in relation to health. Particularly pertinent, was the comment that 'what we need is somewhere to go when we're well - somewhere to ask about anything that is worrying you - where you can chat over the little things'.

Many of this first group went on to participate in a 'Staying Healthy in Retirement' course, led by a local Health Education Officer. This course began by offering ten weekly discussion and participation sessions. However, the input from participants was such that further sessions were organised, resulting in the course lasting for five months! (details of this course can be found in Glendenning, 1985).

The second health issues discussion group comprised active 'swimmers and ramblers', while the third group was made up predominantly of older 'unemployed' people. The swimmers and ramblers all belonged to the Leisure Association and, not surprisingly, were very health conscious. They were strongly of the opinion that people should be encouraged to be active much later in life; they wanted professionals to stop labelling them as old; GPs to stop talking down to them; and teachers and providers to break away from the traditional view that education is just for the young, and to appreciate that they too have much to offer. Moreover, they were also very aware of the need for mutual support and realised that 'we ourselves have to encourage other people to come and join us.'

Lastly, the 'unemployed' group were the most acutely conscious of the close link between their feelings and their health and well-being. They were particularly concerned about personal status, relationships and mental illness, and strongly demonstrated the value and importance of being able to 'talk things through' in the supportive company of their peers.

Emerging from these groups, and the increasing involvement of older people in the Leisure Association and Senior Centre, a core of people began to express an interest in becoming group facilitators or leaders themselves. Thus, the potential for 'peer health counselling' was in fact arising naturally out of the Foundation's current work. Consequently, plans were set in motion to initiate an experimental programme of training in response to this interest. Furthermore, late in 1984, the Foundation made a positive commitment in its long-term thinking and planning, to developing a more comprehensive programme of self-health care for older people, in which peer health counselling would play an integral part.

Research Methods

Although we have evidence from work in the United States about the development and benefits of self-care programmes for older adults (Savo, 1984), there is a paucity of comparable work in this country. Thus, an early decision was made to closely monitor the actual process of development of our own initiatives in this field. Indeed, it has been argued by Barker (1983) that basic descriptive monitoring:

> will often.... result in helpful guidelines to other service planners who need to know about the 'nitty-gritty' details of how a scheme was set up, how goals changed and what obstacles were encountered and how they were dealt with.

As a result, the Foundation's Research Officer has been following this development process by, for example, attending and making notes at meetings; recording and transcribing the early health issues discussion groups; and getting to know participants. Furthermore, participant observation of the whole pilot training project was carried out; participants were asked to complete pre- and post-weekend questionnaires; tape-recordings were made of the weekend sessions; a photographic record kept; and written perceptions and comments from course leaders elicited. Since the ongoing monitoring obviously links very closely with the development process, it has also been used in feedback sessions to contribute to the continual learning and evaluation within the overall project.

The Pilot Peer Health Counselling Project

Drawing on the points which had been learnt from the developments discussed above, and from the expressed concerns and interest of participants, the pilot course aimed to help older people who had already retired, acquire some of the basic skills needed to enable them to go on and lead groups of their peers in health-related discussions/explorations/activities, or to engage in one-to-one counselling and support work.

The ten-session training course was held between January and June, 1985. It comprised two introductory sessions (in January and February) a six-session residential weekend (in March); and two follow-up sessions (in May and June). It was led jointly by two course tutors: the Foundation's Development Officer, and a member of the Health Education Council's Pre-Retirement Health Education Project; and monitored by the Foundation's Research Officer.

Following the two introductory meetings at which the aims of the course were discussed, a draft programme drawn up, and an indication given of what might reasonably be expected of participants after the initial training; eleven people decided to come on the residential weekend. Eight of the participants were women, and three men, and their ages ranged from 52 to 70. All the women had been at work, which is in keeping with the Potteries' tradition of female employment, and only one had retired from personal choice. Two of the men had retired through personal choice, and the third for health reasons. The majority of the group were already taking part in sporting or fitness activities, and many were engaged in voluntary work. Interestingly, although they did not have difficulties as regards personal mobility, a majority of them did experience problems with arthritis and rheumatism, and with indigestion and sleeping.

The six-session course began on Friday afternoon and ran through until Sunday tea-time. It contained three main elements:

(1) Programmed Sessions - these were run along various lines and ranged from lectures to small group discussions, role playing sessions and open discussions.

(2) Programmed 'Optional' Sessions - which included an ice-breaking visit to a 'Medicine Through the Ages' exhibition; swimming and badminton at a nearby leisure centre; a showing of the film 'On Golden Pond'; and a period of worship.

(3) Unprogrammed 'Optional Extras' - since the basis of the weekend was to be a mutual learning and sharing of experiences, participants were encouraged to bring along and share with others, any special interest they had. During the weekend, ten of these 'optional extras' found their way into the programme, including demonstrations of different massage techniques; meditation; fencing; deep relaxation; early morning jogging; music appreciation and yoga.

Before we turn our attention to what has happened since the weekend, what we might ask, did participants feel were the most important things they had gained? First, they particularly welcomed the balance between formal learning/information giving sessions, and the opportunities for physical exercise, relaxation and personal reflection, and felt that the 'optional extras' were valuable and worth repeating at any similar future training sessions. Secondly, many of them felt they had acquired some knowledge; either generally, or in specific areas such as how to work in groups; how to approach people; how to present a subject or activity to others. Thirdly, on a personal level and in terms of their interaction with others, they felt that the weekend had encouraged them to think more deeply about things; that it had helped to build up self-confidence and given them companionship and a sense of sharing and bonding with their peers. The following responses are illustrative of these feelings:

> Before I came here I thought, 'You're not going to get me on this lark', and yet now I feel at home and think, 'Yes, I could do this'.

> We had an insight into the subject but it was superficial. We've gone deeper and, having tasted it, you want more.

> I've gained a deeper insight into things which had never crossed my mind.

> Even though some of us might not emerge as Counsellors, it's been invaluable in terms of contact.

In sum, their responses were generally positive, with participants feeling they had gained a deeper insight into what they might do, and more confidence in actually doing it.

Developments in Peer Health Counselling Since the Weekend

The first follow-up session was held in May. At this meeting we recapped on the weekend and the two preceding sessions, discussed the findings from the pre- and post-weekend questionnaires, and showed slides of the weekend. Since some participants had expressed concerns over what exactly was meant by peer health counselling and what they might be required to do, we also discussed further what it might entail and what participants felt they could offer. After considerable discussion, it was concluded that in fact it was difficult to say precisely what peer health counselling is, because in essence it is so simple. A working definition of peer health counselling emerged as being:

> Partly what you can tell people – partly able to share things and interests – and partly what the peer health counsellor is him or herself, i.e. someone who has got themselves involved and is an example to others.

In addition, a peer health counsellor is:

> Someone who cares enough to be there; who has the time to listen; to share and to care.

This definition, interestingly, echoes the work of Canadian writers on peer health counselling who have described a peer health counsellor as being a person who is willing to talk to others, and who genuinely cares about them (Carr and Saunders, 1980).

In effect then, we were not asking participants to do

much more than many of them were already doing though, to date, this was happening in a fairly unstructured way. However, many of them felt they also needed more in the way of confidence building, if they were to be able to go on and eventually lead groups of their peers.

At this May meeting too, a proposed week long Health Fair, organised as part of the Health Education Council's National Fun Run, was discussed. The Beth Johnson Foundation had been asked to organise a 'Fifty Plus Day' within the week, and it seemed to be a suitable opportunity for the fledgling peer health counsellors to try their wings. Most participants were excited at the prospect and a rota for the day was organised in which the counsellors would work in pairs. The day, on June 11th 1985, attracted over 2,000 visitors, and peer health counsellors were on hand to offer advice about available resources, to talk to people about health issues in retirement, and about how to get started and keep involved in activities.

At the last session of the pilot training course in mid-June, a post-mortem was held on the Health Fair, together with further discussion about which directions peer health counselling was going in. Though happy with the event, the peer health counsellors unanimously decided that it was virtually impossible to give much help at such large functions. However, during the course of the day, many contacts were made, four of which were considered to warrant follow-up:

(1) A married couple felt that having time for more holidays had proved to be less exciting than they had anticipated. They really wanted something different but not expensive. This was followed up by introducing them to a rambling group who organise frequent walking weekends and weeks at low cost. The couple were encouraged to keep up their walking between holidays and subsequently joined the regular rambling group.

(2) Two women enquired about an activity that they could undertake with no previous experience. In discussion, they were encouraged to try swimming. Their names were passed on to the organiser of a swimming group who contacted them, and they began to take lessons.

(3) A recently retired man, though married, was lonely and depressed, and felt that his physical and mental health might deteriorate through lack of activity. He was interested in painting and has been encouraged to join an art group, and to go rambling - supported each step of the way by the peer health counsellor.

(4) Two residents of a sheltered housing complex expressed an interest in developing some activities related to health and exercise, and felt that the common room could be used for such activity. Four peer health counsellors visited the flats and spoke with the warden and some of

the residents. They then began to work weekly, with a group of frail residents, on a gentle programme of chair-based exercises and relaxation.

During the rest of 1985, peer health counsellors were asked to be present at other functions of the Health Fair type. This included a 'Retire into Activity Festival', and a 'White Cane Day' for blind and partially sighted people. In addition, a further request came for a group to work within a residential home. A new principal officer was in post and there was a feeling amongst staff that they would like to involve residents in fresh activities. However, it had been difficult to engage the residents' interest, and the appeal to peer health counsellors was an attempt to see if an outside group might prove more successful.

The first visit of five counsellors was a considerable success, with 27 (out of 60) residents and a number of staff, taking part in half an hour of gentle exercise and discussion. Although the initial group was too large for intimate work, subsequent meetings have involved small group sessions according to ability, and larger meetings now take place as special events.

Through this work it is evident that a number of avenues or areas of involvement are emerging. These are:

(1) One-off days, fairs, exhibitions, workshops, visits to clubs etc. - where peer health counsellors are on hand to talk about what they are doing, to pass on information and to discuss health issues.

(2) One-to-one counselling/work with individuals - to help people establish their own self-health care programme through, for example, diet, exercise and stress management strategies.

(3) 'Long-term' group work - in, for example, residential homes, sheltered housing, day centres etc., with groups of frail elderly people, teaching them gentle exercise routines and relaxation, and encouraging discussion on health issues.

(4) 'Short-term' group work - similar to (3), but for an agreed short term, in order to establish a programme which staff might then take over.

Moreover, it was evident that some peer health counsellors gravitated naturally towards one preferred method of working. Sometimes though, this has surprised us. For example, one very active lady regularly helped at a swimming class and seemed a 'natural' to lead activity groups. However, she emerged as a sensitive personal counsellor who, at one meeting, described her involvement with a newly bereaved woman. She patiently encouraged this lady to accompany her to various activities, until she was able to build new relationships and new interests, including a personal fitness programme.

Ongoing Support and Training

In addition to the actual work, it was also evident that there was a need for ongoing support and for occasional training in specific areas. The support/training group meets monthly and peer health counsellors report back on their work and discuss any difficulties which may have arisen. In order to assist this process, they keep work sheets on which are entered details of various contacts/involvements they have had during the preceding month. Furthermore, these sessions have included learning about suitable exercises for frail, chairbound older people; social service provision; counselling and diet. Subjects to be included come from the peer health counsellors themselves.

The scheme is also now beginning to be more widely publicised locally, and there is already sufficient interest for a further induction training course to be run in 1986. At this second residential course, it is envisaged that the existing group of peer health counsellors will join in for at least one whole day, to help pass on their experiences to the 'new' potential counsellors.

Further Developments

As indicated in the introductory section, peer health counselling is an integral part of a much wider self-health initiative which the Foundation has undertaken. Towards the end of 1985, we were fortunate in securing a three-year grant under the European Economic Commission's second special programme to combat poverty. Sixty-one projects are being funded across the, then, ten member states, though we are only one of two organisations in England to be funded for work specifically aimed at older people. All the projects are termed 'Action Research Projects' and, in addition to the monitoring which will continue to be carried out by the Foundation's Research Officer, a large-scale evaluation is to be undertaken by a team based at the University of Bath.

The principle objective of our own 'Self Health Care in Old Age Project' (as set out in our contract with the EEC), is:

> to increase older people's ability to maintain or increase their health through involvement in health care projects. It is hoped to attain these objectives by developing self-care programmes and courses; in addition to developing an innovatory health counselling scheme for older people; at the same time as the establishment of a health advice centre for the same age group.

Peer health counselling, as we have seen, is already well under way. Thus, our intention from 1986 onwards, is to focus further development on the opening of a city-centre Senior Health Shop. The shop will provide a base for peer health counsellors; it will house a wide range of literature on health related issues; professional staff and volunteers will be on hand to offer appropriate information and advice; individual and small group exercise/fitness programmes will be available; there will be a 'Healthy Eating' cafeteria; and a telephone link scheme for the housebound elderly. In this way, it is hoped that the shop and its related activities will provide an accessible, attractive and popular means of furthering health education and promotion amongst older people, in a similar way to an experimental women's health shop in Edinburgh (Robinson and Roberts, 1985).

Conclusion - A Way of Countering Dependency?

We hear increasingly these days about the strains within our existing health care system, and about how older people make greater use of formal health services than other sectors of the population. For these reasons, and because of a growing awareness of the importance of an individual's right to and responsibility for, control of his/her own personal health, a number of individuals and organisations are looking towards the promotion of self-health care as a way of countering dependency in later life. For older people, these concepts of self-care and self-health are nothing new, since most of them have been dealing with health-related issues throughout their lives. What it does imply though, is that people have the necessary knowledge, freedom of choice and ability to take charge of their own health, and it is here in particular that peer health counselling has a crucial role to play.

By passing on their knowledge, and by offering support and encouragement we can hypothesise that the people involved with peer health counsellors in, for example, the sheltered housing scheme, will not only be helped to retain their independence but also perhaps to become less passive and dependent than they currently are. Moreover, since many of the peer health counsellors are themselves the 'young-old' (Neugarten, 1975), we can further hypothesise that their continued interest and involvement in health-related activities will render them less dependent as they grow older.

In addition, there is a growing, if somewhat belated, awareness that older people themselves have much to offer to both lay people and professionals alike. For such a project to be successful, there needs to be a non-threatening and mutual exchange of ideas and experience between professional workers and older people: in effect, a recognition that we can all, in varying ways, be 'health educators' in the broadest sense of the term. In essence, this is what our wider Self Health Care Project will be attempting to put into practice. In order to tap the undoubted potential of older people, there

may also be a need, as the pilot peer health counselling
course revealed, to first build up their confidence and self
assurance; to reinforce the skills and abilities they have
acquired over a lifetime; and to establish a supportive and
secure foundation from which they then feel able to pass on
their knowledge, skills and enthusiasm to their peers. On
the part of the professionals, this also implies a willingness to
come out from behind professional barriers and to accept that
ultimately we are all working to the same ends. In this way,
it should be possible to foster more positive attitudes towards
growing old, and to counter the negative stereotypes and
problem-oriented notions of old age which lie at the root of
dependency in later life.

Finally, any new and innovative project of this type is,
to a certain extent, a leap of faith, although as we noted
earlier, there is some evidence from North America to support
the value of the peer health counselling model and the
development of self-care programmes. Obviously, the quality
of the counsellors and the effectiveness of their work, will
reflect the quality of recruitment and the nature of the
training and support they receive. We ourselves are in the
early and experimental stages of this process, but we hope
through close monitoring and dissemination of our work, to
encourage further discussion and other applications of a model
and a strategy which, we believe, has a potential part to play
in helping to counter dependency in later life.

References

Amman, A. (ed.) (1980) Open Care for the Elderly in Seven
    European Countries, Pergamon Press, Oxford.
Barker, J. (1983) 'Evaluating Provision for the Elderly',
    Journal of the Market Research Society, Vol.25, No.3,
    pp.275-286.
Carr, R. and Saunders, G. (1980) Peer Counselling Starter
    Kit, Peer Counselling Project, Victoria, British Columbia.
Coppard, L.C., White-Ridley, M., Macfadyen, D.M. and
    Dean, K. (eds.) (1984) Self Health Care and Older
    People - a Manual for Public Policy and Programme
    Development, WHO, Copenhagen.
Fallcreek, S. and Stam, S.B. (eds.) (1982) The Wallingford
    Wellness Project: An Innovative Health Promotion
    Programme with Older Adults, University of Washington,
    Seattle.
France, M.H. and McDowell, C. (1982) 'A Peer Counselling
    Model for Computer Assisted Career Counselling',
    Canadian Counsellor, Vol.16, No.3, pp.230-237.
Glendenning, F.J. (ed.) (1985) New Initiatives in Self-Health
    Care for Older People, The Beth Johnson Foundation,

Stoke-on-Trent, in association with the Department of Adult Education, University of Keele, and the Health Education Council.

Hamburg, B. and Varenhorst, B. (1972) 'Peer Counselling in the Secondary Schools: a Community Mental Health Project for Youth', American Journal of Orthopsychiatry, Vol.42, No.4, pp.566-581.

Hatch, S. and Kickbusch, I. (eds.) (1983) Self-Help and Health in Europe - New Approaches in Health Care, WHO, Copenhagen.

Levin, L.S. (1982) Yale Self-Care Education Project - Final Report, Connecticut.

Neugarten, B.L. (1975) 'The Future of the Young Old', The Gerontologist, Vol.15, No.1, pp.4-9.

Robinson, S.E. and Roberts, M.M. (1985) 'A Women's Health Shop: A Unique Experiment', British Medical Journal, Vol.291, 27 July, pp.255-256.

Savo, C. (1984) Self-Care and Self-Help Programmes for Older Adults in the United States, Working Papers on the Health of Older People No.1, Health Education Council in association with the Department of Adult Education, University of Keele.

U.S. Department of Health Education and Welfare (1979) A Guide to Medical Self-Care and Self-Help Groups for the Elderly, Government Office, Washington, DC.

Warner-Reitz, A. (1981) Healthy Lifestyle for Seniors: An Interdisciplinary Approach to Healthy Aging, Meals for Millions/Freedom from Hunger Foundation, New York.

Wheldall, K. and Mettem, P. (1985) 'Behavioural Peer Tutoring: Training 16-year-old Tutors to Employ the 'pause, prompt and praise' Methods with 12-year-old Remedial Readers', Educational Psychology, Vol.5, No.1, pp.27-44.

WHO (1981) Self-Help and Health, Report on a WHO Consultation, Copenhagen, 3-6 December 1980, WHO Regional Office for Europe.

PART THREE : EXPERIENCES OF GROWING OLD

PART THREE : Experiences of Growing Old

Chapter Twenty-Five

MISSING OUT : LABOUR MARKET AND LATE WORKING

LIFE EXPERIENCES AS FACTORS IN

OLD AGE DEPENDENCY

Phil Lyon

Introduction

Analysis of retirement life-styles obviously transcends
consideration of where retired people used to work.
However, former employment or rather, labour market
history, undoubtedly has a bearing on life in retirement
(Lehr and Dreher, 1969).
    Equally, looking at jobs and labour markets and their
effects on the subsequent retirement poses a greater range of
questions than it is possible to address in this chapter. The
following discussion is limited to comments on labour market
experience and late working life circumstances as they relate
to relative disadvantage under the terms of occupational
pension schemes, and access to pre-retirement courses.
    The data referred to are extracted from interviews with
33 current and 77 retired male manual employees of two
organisations - a paper mill and a local authority direct works
department.[1] These interviews, focusing on perceptions of
late working life and either the prospect, or the actuality of,
retirement were conducted in the period October 1981 to
October 1983. The two organisations proved to be very
different contexts for the late working life of manual
employees and both, as a result of the difficult economic
circumstances of the last few years, were undergoing changes
that altered prospects for older workers and had implications
for their retirement.

Factors Affecting Reckonable Service

Among the retired there is polarisation between those whose
life styles become increasingly dependent on the level of state
benefits, and those who can adequately, and progressively,
finance their later lives (Townsend, 1979).
    The financial prospects for retirement are enhanced if
older people are in receipt of occupational pensions. We know
that inclusion in such schemes is notoriously uneven

(Fogarty, 1981; McGoldrick, 1984), but it would be oversimplifying matters to equate inclusion in occupational pension schemes with the elimination of financial problems. For example, workers who change employers can find that service in previous schemes is not recognised and the value of their pension under former schemes is not preserved.[2] The net result could be life-long inclusion in pension schemes with minimal benefits on retirement. Furthermore, men and women are unlikely to benefit equally from occupational pension schemes. As McGoldrick's (1984) research has revealed, broken service and an earlier 'standard' age of retirement mean that women's occupational pensions are likely to be relatively small.

As if this is not difficult enough, it is intended here to add one further factor to the list of complications. Even when an employer operates an occupational pension scheme, the benefit derived by workers in a given pay grade is largely dependent on their reckonable service, i.e. the number of years of scheme membership plus years allowed for recognised service with former employers. Reckonable service is, however, a product of the vicissitudes of organisational careers.

The two organisations - the paper mill and the building and works department - on which the accounts of late working life were based, differed considerably in their patterns of recruitment and retention of manual employees. Reckonable service could be seen as a product of differences in labour market experience, and the kind of vulnerability that age brings in contrasting work situations.

When the paper workers were young, the mill had dominated the local labour market, and had employed successive generations of men and women from a relatively small catchment area since the early nineteenth century. A lack of real alternatives and family traditions gave substance to the idea that a job at the mill was a job for life.

I had a couple of years on a butcher's bike, you see. I was looking for a job all the time I was working at the other job.... So, every week I was down to see if I could get a job at the mill, and once I did get the job, I was in there and that was that....the same as my father and them before me, you see. They just said, 'Well, go down the mill and it's a job for life.
(Worker, aged 61 years).

It's a long story....No, it's not a long story really. It's a bit like the miners....My family worked there. Both grandfathers worked there, and my grandmothers. My father worked there and he was in the same department that I supervised.... You had to be family in them days. You didn't get through the gate unless you

qualified with twelve relations....(laughs)....I think I
had four uncles who all did 51 years. My oldest brother
- he died three years ago - he did 46....I did 41
years....Up until ten or fifteen years ago, you daren't
speak about somebody because he was a cousin, or an
uncle, or something like that to the person you were
talking about. You had to tread warily. It was a great
family feeling though.
(Retired employee).

Although local employment opportunities expanded in the
1970s, they came too late for the older workers and retired
employees considered here. Just over 40 per cent of the
retired men and just under 30 per cent of those still employed
had started work in the mill at, or before, the age of twenty.
Furthermore, approximately 60 per cent in both categories
had been working there by the age of thirty. By the 1970s,
then, they were entrenched in the esoteric occupational
culture of papermaking and had made their organisational 'side
bets'[3] with that employer.

By late working life, the mill was a known environment
with, importantly, a reputation - as part of the complex
reciprocity of paternalistic capitalism - of valuing long service
employees. Years of service were formally recognised by mill
management in award ceremonies at the fifteen and thirty-five
year point, which not only marked workers out 'at the time'
as members of an elite group, but determined the lavishness
of the 'leaving do' when the worker eventually retired.

It was apparent that service levels meant something to
workers for it was not uncommon to find health retirees
cursing their medical problems as much for what it had done
to their chances of achieving long service status as for what
it had done to their strength, mobility and physical
well-being. One man, in spite of a history of serious
ill-health, had baulked at the idea of retirement at 63.
Asked whether he had wanted to retire, he said:

No, I'll be honest....The wife'll tell you....I took a long
time to make up my mind. I was wanting to do the fifty
years. I was going to be proud of my fifty years.

High levels of reckonable service at the point of
retirement were not just the result of employer domination of
a local labour market. Careers that stretched back several
decades could be foreshortened by poor health (as in the case
above), by 'industrial senescence'[4], or by the changed labour
requirements normally attendant on process innovation.

In this organisation, such problems were handled with
due regard to a paternalistic frame of reference. However,
mill management's manpower strategies were not just
dependent on an historically conditioned willingness to

redeploy older men in the face of changing personal and organisational circumstances. The complex technical division of labour within the mill gave management and supervisory staff the capacity to move workers within, or between, process, ancillary and trade roles.

Impaired health, short of total incapacity, and industrial senescence had traditionally been dealt with by formal and informal redeployment to less arduous work. One retired man talking about his brother commented:

> His job was in the Sanitorium....The Dispatch Department. They used to speak about it being the Sanitorium....with.... all the old people, ill people.

Light work posts for ailing or ageing manual workers were not in unlimited supply. They became even scarcer as a changing market for paper products and reactive process innovation heralded labour force contraction and redistribution. From the retired workers' accounts it was clear that management had continued redeploying older men to a shrinking pool of light work posts.

> ...they're just not so keen now to give you light duties as they used to be because there's not the jobs for them....'How long did it take to get a light job for me?' (to wife)....It took months and months.
> (Retired employee).

Among the retired employees, being moved to lighter work posts facilitated industrial survival. Of those who retired at 65, 70 per cent had changed their jobs within the mill in the last eleven years of work and in the vast majority of cases, final jobs were rated as 'less demanding' in terms of functional role, shift patterns, job pacing, physical effort and interactional context.

Constrained by low levels of staff turnover, especially in the middle and upper range, the strategies that had prolonged working life became secondary to the promotion of early retirement. In the Personnel Manager's words:

> I am going to stick my neck out here and say that, in the next two or three years, I doubt there will be anyone in this place over sixty years of age.

Going by the experiences of the retired men, reckonable service was not only long as a result of labour market factors operative earlier in their careers, but was enhanced by organisational factors in late working life.

In comparison, men who had retired from the building and works department did not achieve anything like the levels of service that had been characteristic of the mill retirees.

The building trade workers and retirees had had careers that centred more on occupation than on a specific employing organisation. None had started their working lives with the council.

A relatively small proportion of these men had started working with the department at, or before, the age of thirty. Nearly 40 per cent of the retirees and just over 40 per cent of the current workers had been in their forties and fifties when they came to this employer. The council, because of its low wages relative to private sector building firms had been seen as something of a distress employer, when nothing else was available or attainable. They stayed because by middle age, or late working life, a regular wage was thought to compensate for the size of the wage packet.

> With the council you knew your pay was coming in every week irrespective of the weather or such as that. The wage was maybe not as big as you were making outside, but you knew you were going to get a specific wage for fifty-two weeks a year. That made a big difference.
> (Worker, aged 56 years).

> There was more security there than doing jobs where maybe, when you were finished you were laid off....In the painting trade there was a lot of unemployment in the wintertime. They'd try and keep you working in the council, you see.
> (Retired employee).

Although in many areas there has been a recession in the building industry, there was a steady local demand for building trade workers. Younger men could command better wages in the private sector and, presumably, saw security in being able to get sequential employment. In these circumstances, the management was inclined to look favourably on applications from older men.[5]

Once employed by this particular local authority, the work was arguably quite well suited to older experienced men as it was virtually all repair and maintenance. However, the jobs offered by the department were not, in comparison with some employment, light and easy in nature. Awkward and heavy tasks were involved and many trades had to contend with wet and cold conditions.

> Our job, we're invariably on our knees or lying on our back under basins.... You seemed to be folded up and lying on your back, and you're in the most awful positions. That's what's the trouble with my neck, you see. I felt the strain.
> (Retired employee).

It was a cold job in the winter, mind, whatever age you were, and as you were getting older you felt the cold more than you did normally, you know. The younger you were in this job, the better. Well, I think you were anyway. It was a really good job in the summer as long as you were fit, like. But as I say, the winters....and as you grow older it was a killer right enough. I mean, when I first went there nothing was any trouble to you, but as I said, when I was getting older you could feel it, you know.
(Retired employee).

There was no technological change to invalidate their experience but older men were vulnerable if their health was impaired or they became industrially senescent. In the past, such problems were handled, in the first instance, by trade foremen's discretionary redeployment to easier tasks within the normal range of work. If this did not happen, or proved to be an inadequate solution, early retirement was the only option as stores and preparatory workshop posts were scarce.
  The limited amount of accommodation that had been possible was jeopardised by a series of organisational changes. The Local Government Planning and Land Act (1980) demanded a closer approximation to private sector business practice. This demand for notional competitiveness found expression at worker level in the closer monitoring of work, and the tighter association of pay and performance. These changes allied to the replacement of trade foremen with multi-trade supervisors changed the tenor of late working life. Informal redeployment within the normal workload became more problematic, and performance monitoring meant that older workers' control over pacing was much reduced.

I've heard it said on a few occasions....'If you're not fit for the job, get out'....more or less, you know what I mean. That's the attitude. You're required to do a job and that's it. It might have been....a year or two back when the foremen and all the rest were there, you know, but not now. I mean, we have no foremen....
(Worker, aged 61 years).

Among the department's retired employees, less than 42 per cent changed jobs between 54 and retirement. This figure was, moreover, distorted by the level of late entry, i.e. men joining the department at, or after, the age of 54. Of all the retired men, only 25 per cent had changed jobs within the department.
  It was not just that internal redeployment was a rarer phenomenon in the department than it had been at the paper

mill, there was relatively little easement of working conditions even if jobs were changed.

The two organisations differed, therefore, not only in their recruitment patterns but in the extent to which they were able to accommodate older workers with lighter jobs to prolong their working lives. Although the two organisations had comparable pension schemes, reckonable service levels varied considerably. At the mill, 68 per cent of the retirees had accrued more than 31 years service. At the building and works department, only 19 per cent achieved this level of service, and 42 per cent had retired with up to 20 years.

Access to Pre-Retirement Courses

Discussion of pre-retirement education tends to focus on the general extent of provision, and the type of course being offered (Coleman, 1983; Phillipson and Strang, 1983). These major concerns have tended to overshadow another problem - access to courses that are part of the current level of provision.

Even though it is fairly safe to say that few pre-retirement courses are events that change lives they are, as Parker (1980) wryly commented: 'one way of obtaining information' relevant to one's retirement. Late working life circumstances in the paper mill and the building and works department operated in such a way that those who would arguably benefit most were, paradoxically, least likely to gain access.

The mill had a well established pre-retirement course which took the form of a one-day seminar.[6] Although it was organised by the Personnel Department, there was a heavy reliance on 'outside' speakers. Their availability was cited as a major reason for biannual staging. To increase the frequency without these contributions, it was argued, would lower the standard of the course. Given the practice of using particular individuals rather than a pool of speakers, this may well have been valid comment although administrative and financial factors were equally relevant.

Biannual staging brought problems even with retirements at state pensionable age as there could be no standardised timing in relation to sixty-fifth birthdays. Set against a much less predictable and increasing flow of early retirees, this staging had created even greater problems.

Of the retired mill workers interviewed, only 54 per cent had been on a pre-retirement course. This was a surprisingly low proportion given that the course had been theoretically available to all retiring workers for a considerable number of years.

This pattern could have arisen because they had been invited but chosen not to attend. This explanation did not, however, fit retirees' accounts and while they were often quite critical of the firm's handling of their retirement, none spoke against pre-retirement seminars in principle, or in terms of relevance to them as individuals. It was usually the case that they had been off sick at the time of the seminar, or there were difficulties with cover while working shifts, or because they made the decision to take early retirement and left between courses. Overall, a substantial proportion of the retirees slipped through the net of company provision. They were largely victims of management's unwillingness to cope with the disparity between its policies on demanning, and the staging of the pre-retirement courses. While 75 per cent of those who retired at 65 had attended, 67 per cent of those who retired early, did not attend.

Management recognised the difficulty, and invited those who had not been able to attend to join a seminar after they had actually retired.

> We often sort of catch up on those we've missed the previous year, but they're normally within either a year of retirement or have retired a few months....maybe up to six months.
> (Personnel Manager).

Of the 54 per cent of retired men who had attended, 20 per cent had gone along after their retirement. The irony of this situation was not lost on the retirees:

> I maintain that the seminar we got was at the wrong time. If it's 'pre-', it should be before you actually retire. I would give it at least two months to sink into everybody's mind the fact that he's leaving.'
> (Retired employee).

Management's efforts to remedy the situation were genuine enough, but they were only partially successful. The 'post-' retirement opportunity meant that instead of 34 per cent, 54 per cent eventually attended but this still left 46 per cent without benefit of a pre-retirement course. Not all men received invitations they could accept, and the gap between retirement and the course reduced salience.

> The seminar is more useful to people before they retire rather than after it. I've been retired about three months now, and I've made my own adjustments.
> (Retired employee).

In the context of active demanning, it was early retirees who were most disadvantaged. Access to the retirement seminar was significantly related to the predicability of the actual time of retirement. To retire at the state pensionable age meant that a man could be more easily 'placed' on a course. Early retirees - leaving in the wake of a quick early retirement deal with management, or because their health was bad, or because there were no light work jobs for management to offer those with lesser health problems - were very lucky if their leaving coincided with course opportunities.

Turning to the local authority retirees, it was found that there was also a problem of access, and although there were differences of detail it was still early retirees who were most disadvantaged.

Until 1979, the council did not offer pre-retirement courses to any of its employees. In the first years the course had been organised by the Workers' Educational Association but latterly, design and administration had been undertaken by the council's own training section. Carried over from the early days, however, was the arrangement of the course (five successive Wednesday afternoons), a large number of participants drawn from all council departments, and a heavy reliance on outside speakers. These features were cited as major reasons for provision being limited to one course per year.

As far as these retired men were concerned, the inflexibility of the staging proved to be a greater problem for access than the late start of provision. Less than 20 per cent of retired men left before the introduction of the course but of the remainder, over 80 per cent had not attended even though courses had, technically, been available.

When the course first started it was addressed to a population of employees for whom retirement was imminent. Thereafter, a 'younger' cohort was encompassed in the routine offer of a place. Having caught up with what were seen as the immediate demands, the extension of opportunity to men of 62 and 63 should have meant that very few could slip through the net.

However, of the 36 retired employees interviewed, twelve had been 61 or younger at the time they left, and a further six had been marginal in terms of current course thresholds as they had retired at 62. So, in spite of the increased coverage of older workers - up to three years before state pensionable age - the courses still failed to net a substantial proportion of the early retirees.

> ...we ask, in our letter we send around departments, for people who will be retiring in the next two or three years. So, we're catching them quite early and that's the only way we can do it at the moment. We're not catching the people who, say, take early retirement and, you know, they're gone before we can offer them a place on the course.
>
> (Official, Training Section, District Council).

Late Working Life Experience

Of those early retirees who had left since 1979 (n=24), less than ten per cent had been able to attend a pre-retirement course. The reasons for this exceptionally low figure were threefold. First, three-quarters of the early retirements had been health related, there being no attempt to use early retirement for reducing manpower. Health problems could be quite sudden, certainly in comparison with the annual staging of the pre-retirement course. With health problems as a prelude to retirement, it was particularly disappointing that so many missed out on information that might have made the tangle of benefits and services less awesome.

Secondly, the early retirees had been relatively young, certainly by the standards of mill retirees where opportunity for less arduous working conditions had helped to prolong working life.

Thirdly, if a council retiree missed a pre-retirement course before he finished work, he missed it completely. There was no system of recall as there had been at the mill.

Summary

Occupational pension schemes and pre-retirement courses are important employer provisions that can enhance retirement. While our attention has rightly been drawn to questions of provision and non-provision the foregoing, using data from two particular employment contexts, has underlined the fact that problems exist in spite of employer provision. Problems related to reckonable service are largely intractable until there is the political will to adequately finance old age irrespective of labour market history. Problems related to pre-retirement course access, on the other hand, would appear more easily avoidable.

Although this small research project focussed on male manual workers and retirees, I would be surprised if the problems were unique to these interviewees.

Notes

(1) Current workers were aged between 54 and 64 years. Retired men were 54 to 70 years at the time of the interview.

(2) See, for example, Hunt and Palmer (1982) where the pensions of two hypothetical retirees are contrasted. One, who changed employers every ten years, and derived an 'unpreserved' pension from each, ended up with just over half the pension obtained by the other who worked 40 years with

a single employer.

(3) Becker, H. (1977, pp.261-273) uses the 'side bet' analogy in a discussion of commitment. Individuals may wish to leave a particular work organisation but find their freedom of action limited by factors such as their stake in non-transferable pension schemes, or where their involvement in one organisation has made them unsuitable for others.

(4) 'Industrial senescence' is to be distinguished from poor health. The former refers to a mismatch between the effects of ageing and the demands of one's work. See Clark (1954).

(5) There is some evidence to suggest bias against older job applicants if there are younger alternatives. See Jolly (1980)

(6) Section on mill pre-retirement course experience relies heavily on a discussion previously developed for an incomplete sample. See Lyon (1983).

References

Becker, H. (1977) Sociological Work, Transaction, New Brunswick.

Clark, Le Gros, F. (1954) The Working Fitness of Older Men: A Study of Men over Sixty in the Building Industry, Nuffield Foundation, London.

Coleman, A. (Edited by Groombridge J.) (1982) Preparation for Retirement in England and Wales, National Institute of Adult Education, Leicester.

Havighurst, R. et al. (1969) Adjustment to Retirement, van Gorcum, Assen.

Hunt, P. and Palmer, S. (1982) 'Preserving the Pension of Job Changers', Personnel Management, Vol.14, No.7, July, pp.39-41.

Jolly, J., Creigh, S. and Mingay, A. (1980) Age as a Factor in Employment, Unit for Manpower Studies, Research Paper No.11, Department of Employment, HMSO, London.

Kinnaird, J., Brotherston, J. and Williamson, J. (1981) The Provision of Care for the Elderly, Churchill Livingstone, Edinburgh.

Local Government Planning and Land Act (1980), HMSO, London.

Lyon, P. (1983) 'The Paradox of Access: Pre-Retirement Courses in an Industrial Recession', Scottish Journal of Adult Education, Vol.6, No.2, pp.28-34.

McGoldrick, A. (1984) Equal Treatment in Occupational Pension Schemes, Equal Opportunities Commission,

Manchester.

Parker, S. (1980) Older Workers and Retirement, HMSO, London.

Phillipson, C. (1980) 'The Sociology of Transition', in Johnson, M.L. (ed.) Transitions in Middle and Later Life, British Society of Gerontology / Policy Studies Institute, London.

Phillipson, C. (ed.) (1983) New Directions in Pre-Retirement Education, Beth Johnson Foundation, Stoke-on-Trent.

Phillipson, C. and Strang, P. (1983) The Impact of Pre-Retirement Education: A Longitudinal Evaluation, University of Keele, Keele.

Townsend, P. (1979) Poverty in the United Kingdom, Penguin Books, Harmondsworth.

Chapter Twenty-Six

MAKING WAY : THE DISENGAGEMENT

OF OLDER WORKERS

Bill Bytheway

Introduction

Given present levels of unemployment and the popular concern
with the futures of unemployed young people, it is hardly
surprising that the view is widely expressed that in the
labour market the older generation should make way for the
young (Casey and Bruche, 1983; Jackson, 1984).
    This idea has been considered in the 1983 report of the
House of Commons Social Services Committee on 'The Age of
Retirement'. It is useful to examine this report in some detail
because it illustrates how the idea of 'making way' has come to
be conceptualised at the broad policy making level.   Ray
Buckton, presenting the submission of the Trades Union
Congress, comments:

> I think there is a very strong moral view by workers to
> say 'Perhaps we'd better go out, to make way for the
> over one million young people who are without jobs
> today.' That is the talk amongst masses of people today.

In an answer to a question about the cost of policy changes,
he makes the connection between making way and shifting the
burden of unemployment more explicit:

> Now we have millions of people who are not working and
> we have to pay them to sit at home doing nothing at the
> present time.   Perhaps we could shift that to people
> over 60 and let them retire gracefully with an adequate
> pension, thereby letting these younger people come into
> industry and start producing the wealth we are looking
> for.

Apart from the unfortunate implicit equation of graceful
retirement with sitting at home doing nothing, the significance
of these comments is in the personalisation and associated
morality of national policies.   On the one hand, 'we' who are

engaged in policy making can shift people around in this way,
and on the other hand, 'we' the older workers had better
make way for one million younger people.

McGoldrick and Cooper submitted to the Committee some
results from their research: they reported that 70 per cent of
the early retired believed that 'men should accept early
retirement if they are financially able to do so, in order to
free jobs for younger workers.' This kind of statistic lends
substance to the evidence presented by Buckton.

The moral view, represented by Buckton's comment, can
generate considerable pressure among those most closely
involved. Buckton was asked: 'Do you agree that there are
signs of employers and unions joining forces - ganging up, if
you like, against older workers - in order to make room for
younger people to come in?' The fact that such a question is
worded in this way and asked at all is of considerable
significance. Not surprisingly perhaps, Buckton denied that
this has happened. McGoldrick and Cooper, however,
provide conflicting evidence. In response to a question about
accepting early retirement, about half of their sample
'believed that younger workers expected them to do so.' This
might not amount to 'ganging up', but there can be no doubt
that expectations of this kind do exist and do create
pressure. Cribier (1981), for example, has reported that in
France people over 65 years of age in full-time employment
are sometimes called 'job-stealers'.

The Committee heard only one voice against those under
pensionable age making way. Alan Walker challenged the
prevailing view:

I am opposed to a policy of early retirement on the
grounds of making way for younger workers, because I
think that unemployment should be shared equally
amongst people. I think the last submission (McGoldrick
and Cooper) was very important in indicating that a
large number of older workers felt that they should make
way for younger workers and in many ways that attitude
has been encouraged over the last few years by some
government policies.

The Committee itself commented:

'The strongest pressure comes from the high rate of
youth unemployment, leading to individual and collective
belief that older workers should retire to make way for
younger ones - a belief encouraged by the media and
fostered to some degree by employers, unions and
Government. Most of the bodies prefer, however painful
the choice, the prospect of earlier mandatory retirement
of older workers to continued unemployment among the
young.

Whilst Walker and the Committee are undoubtedly right that this view has been fostered by the Government, it would be a mistake to think of making way simply as a compliant response to the political belief that there are insufficient jobs to go round. It is a much more complex act which reflects features of both the (macro) political economy of age and the (micro) interpersonal economy of age and generational differences.

Although the term 'make way' is used repeatedly in the proceedings of the Committee, it is an action that has rarely been studied in detail in recent gerontological studies of work and retirement (Kohli et al., 1983; Parker, 1982; Makeham and Morgan, 1980; Walker, 1984; McGoldrick and Cooper, 1980).

Redundancy in Port Talbot

This paper draws upon some empirical research that examined the effects of redundancy upon the lives of male steelworkers in Port Talbot, who were aged 55 years or over (Bytheway, 1985). A redundancy programme called Slimline was put to the workforce at the Abbey works in Port Talbot early in 1980. The object of Slimline was to reduce the workforce by about 5,000. This was achieved through a policy of closing selected departments (in some instances putting work out to contractors), and by the unions calling for an agreed number of volunteers in other departments. There were supplementary funds to help the process of the 'readaptation' of redundant steelworkers. This, the Iron and Steel Employees Readaptation Benefits Scheme, draws upon funds from the European Coal and Steel Community. The scheme provides aid to steelworkers:

> ...who are redundant or redeployed to new jobs at lower rates of pay providing this results from a 'relevant event'. This is defined as a permanent reduction or change in the activities of a steelmaking company caused by fundamental changes in market conditions for the steel industry.

The concern to assist the steelworker to readapt reflects the fact that the steel industry is a mass employer in certain localised labour markets. Any event which leads to large scale redundancies is a serious threat to the local community. The Scheme is intended to smooth the process and attempts to achieve this in two ways. One is to assist certain redundant workers find work in the wider labour market - retraining, travelling, resettlement and wage supplements. The other is to encourage others, notably older and disabled workers to withdraw from the labour market.

Older workers (those aged 55/50 or over[1] were seen in two entirely consistent ways: first to be vulnerable to long term unemployment, and, secondly, as a threat to the employment prospects of younger redundant workers. As a vulnerable group they needed financial aid to offset the effects of long-term unemployment, and encouragement to accept the status of early retirement. As a threat they were perceived to be a nuisance to those attempting to manage the local labour market and, in the case of those with marketable skills and experience, serious competition for the younger generation. The answer on both counts was a redundancy package for those aged 55/50 or over which offered a certain degree of financial security and which was a positive disincentive against further participation in the labour market.

Briefly, there were three main elements in this package for those aged 55/50 or over:

(1) an immediate single payment - averaging £10,000

(2) make-up money - in effect a wage/benefit substitute or supplement, bringing income up to 90 per cent and then 80 per cent of previous earnings (excluding overtime) and available for a limited period of time (up to two and a half years).

(3) the British Steel Corporation pension - averaging £20 to £30 per week.

There are two important differences between those age 55/50 or over and those under that age. The first is that those 55/50 or over at the time of redundancy received their pension immediately. To those made redundant under this age, the pension is paid only upon reaching state pensionable age or upon becoming registered as disabled. Secondly, if aged 55/50 or over, make-up money is paid automatically, irrespective of employment status. Under 55/50 it is paid only if the worker is employed and only during the course of the eighteen months following redundancy.

Make-up money is in effect a policy which is intended to provide a personal income that declines according to a controlled schedule whilst readaptations are being made. Those under 55/50 are expected to readapt through active involvement in the labour market. Given any kind of paid work, they will receive an income that is close to what they received from the steel company - irrespective of the pay actually paid by the new employer. In effect they (and their new employers) are rewarded with make-up money for cooperating in the readaptation process. Conversely those aged 55/50 or over are expected to stay out of the labour market, readapting to a life without paid employment but with a variety of reduced income options. They are of course free to take paid employment in much the same way as are those over state pensionable age. The problem is that they gain little financially in the first two years, are subject to demoralising problems in managing their income tax and, most significantly, are not expected to seek employment and are discriminated against as a consequence: in the queue for jobs they are expected to make way for younger people.

Thus the scheme appears to be designed to mutually and voluntarily disengage older redundant workers from the labour market. What was the response of those who accepted the invitation?

The Experience of Redundancy

The following is based upon interviews in 1984, with 108 of those men who were 55 years or over when made redundant in 1980. Each had already been interviewed three times as part of a broader enquiry into the effects of Slimline upon Port Talbot. This fourth interview was open-ended and only loosely structured. Towards the end I asked them to draw comparisons between their generation and those of their fathers and their sons. This usually led to a question about their making way for the younger generation and this analysis is based largely upon their response to this question. Of the 108, 57 (over half) expressed agreement with making way, eleven disagreed (10 per cent) and the remaining 40 offered no view. These figures are compatible with those of McGoldrick and Cooper.

Beginning with those who disagreed, there were only two who said they had argued in 1980 against older workers taking redundancies. Another five or six disagreed in the sense that they said Slimline was about cutting jobs rather than making way. The following are the words of one:

> When you finished, did you actually make way for a younger man?

> No, they just cut down, didn't they. They cut down staff by practically a half in Port Talbot.

> So it wasn't a question of your job being handed over to somebody else?

> Oh, no.

> And you didn't feel by your going that some younger man would stay?

> Well, I knew it wasn't happening.... If it had have happened, it would have helped me to go out really....

Rather more common than explicit hostility to the idea were other comments that were unsympathetic with the idea of making way. One concerned the right of older unemployed workers to seek work. A total of 25 obtained work in the four years following redundancy despite the substantial disincentives, and there were about as many again who looked but failed to find any. Several of these men asserted the right of the older men to seek work and others offered accounts of discrimination against them. One, for example, working for a contractor on the Abbey site was told by a steel company shop steward:

You took redundancy and that should be the end of it.

Another kind of hostile expression was focused upon the effectiveness of younger workers. Eighteen made some such comment. It was frequently directly relevant to the idea of making way in that it was comparative: older workers were better than younger ones. The following is the comment of a fitter:

I was wondering if you felt you were being asked to make way for younger men in 1980?

Well, I don't know because.... depends on what level. Maybe higher levels, they were making way for younger, but at the departmental level, the engineers didn't like to see us go, because we were more reliable and experienced than the younger men, because some of the young ones were bloody hopeless.... some of them were terrible. You know by our standards, you know what I mean.... The way they looked at it, these engineers: if there was something to do, they knew that.... you didn't have to bother supervising if we did it. We did it on our own. We knew what we were doing and it'll be all right in the end. While these younger ones, standing over them all the time and making sure they did it properly.

One interviewee did report direct pressure from younger men. He claimed that they were pushing the older generation out. Another said the younger boys were worried. By and large, however, pressure came from within the older workers themselves. One said that they had a motto: give the youngster a chance.

There were 23 who volunteered critical comment about the role of management or the unions in respect of making way. Workers were being bought off or pushed out. Management were not creating work for younger people, and they were placing the future of the Abbey in the hands of a workforce that was too small and too inexperienced. This is one commentary:

Do you feel the Slimline programme in general was encouraging older workers to make way for younger workers?

Oh, yes.

And did you approve of that?

You see.... I can answer this in a selfish way.... I can say, yes. It benefited me, but look at it, the overall picture, no definitely not. Because let us assume it was adequate for those finishing at the time, but what you must remember is this, you were closing doors.... for people coming in, you've got to remember the younger generation.

What, fewer jobs?

Fewer jobs.

Do you feel it was bad for the steel company anyway because experience was being lost?

Oh, definitely. Oh, yes. No question about that. Younger men who didn't have the proper.... were shoved in at the deep end and they were having problems. 'Course, they don't tell you this.... definitely having problems.

There was also some discrete criticism of methods of creating pressure. Consider this example:

Do you feel though that by taking redundancy you made a job for a younger man?

I would like to think so, yes.

But you're not sure.

Well, I mean, the person that took my place was a younger man than me, but when the job got altered, so I understand, the people weren't keen to have it. So what they do now is when a fellow gets to about 55, they move him into it hoping he'll go. This is actually what's happening, see?

In total, 48 of the 108 who were interviewed offered some kind of critical comment. In general, there is a certain cautious acceptance of the principle of making way, but one that is subject to a number of serious reservations.

If we turn to those who offered some positive comment,

we again find a variety of views and circumstances. Enthusiasm for the principle is best illustrated by the fifteen or so who reported that one particular younger man did in fact take over their job. These are two examples:

(A) But they wanted you to stay?

> Well, they were loathe to let us go. Let's put it that way. But, you know, I mean at the time you could understand the situation. They were going to lose all their old hands, most of them anyway, and we got some young foremen. As a matter of fact, one of the reasons I went was that there were about three foremen who I had recommended that had been on my shift and taken foremen's jobs as other plant opened up, and one of those - he still comes here as a matter of fact - was one of the ones due to go. Well, I don't see, you know, that I could stay there when I could come out on a pension, live pretty well as I'd normally lived, and a young fellow go out when he could take my place.... he's still doing my job as a matter of fact.

(B) Did you feel you were making way for a younger man?

> Well, I did. My job was open. The man who took my job now, I see him now and again. Jim. Well, he was 38 and he had asthma....

> Do you feel better about it, knowing that he's got that job?

> Oh, yes.

> Would he have got one if you hadn't, do you think, or....

> Well, put it this way, he wouldn't have gone out but they would have put him in part of the mill where the poor chap would be (panting) and then what would have happened? He'd have had a medical and they'd say: 'Well, I'm awfully sorry....' It could have been.

Knowing the actual demands of Slimline, these men believed and some claimed to know that had they not gone the younger men would have been out. There was a definite sense among these interviewees of having saved these younger men.

In addition to this group there were another two dozen who felt (or who suggested) that the older generation had fairly directly made way for younger men. They each believed that a younger man's job had been saved by their action, but were not in a position to identify one particular person. This example illustrates how cross-posting operated to keep some unknown person in employment:

> I was wondering about the younger generation. Did you feel that you were making way for them?

> Well, that was the idea: with me going that somebody else would take my job like. 'Cause it was Slimline. 'Cause somebody could come and take my job, from another department, as long as I.... a man went out, see?

> And you were happy with that?

> Oh, I was happy with that.

This response overlapped substantially with the idea that Slimline, and therein the sacrifice of those who had taken redundancy (largely older workers), had saved not just the jobs of young men but the entire steelworks. For some the answer was obvious and the question hardly needed asking.

There were others again who took redundancy in different circumstances or for other reasons but who nevertheless approved the principle of making way. For instance two did so implicitly by criticising those older workers who had stayed on. Many, of course, knew that the redundancy package favoured the older worker. Many believed that the terms offered to the older worker were preferable to the alternative of remaining in work, despite the overall fall in income. To use Buckton's words, most genuinely saw it as an opportunity to retire (or at least withdraw) gracefully with an adequate pension.

Those in two minds were perhaps persuaded to take the redundancy offer not only by the reasoning of those who had decided to volunteer, but also by the prospect of their absence: of having to work with a smaller group of men who were noticeably younger than themselves. Many of the working practices and routines were due to change with less emphasis being placed on the established maxim of each man to his trade, and more upon increasing productivity figures.

Following the unprecedented break of the twelve week strike, many returned feeling physically unfit for work. They did not look forward to the prospect of arduous labour through the winter of 1980/81.

Discussion

The evidence from this study suggests that some older workers are happy to make way for the younger generation in certain circumstances and subject to there being satisfactory compensation. It is significant that few of those I interviewed complained about the compensation, and most acknowledged the contribution of the European Benefits. One or two felt that it was not as generous as they had first thought and others were envious of the deal that they understood others had been offered, but rather more in number counted themselves fortunate as a result of Slimline.

What they were not so happy about was the loss of jobs and the attitudes of the younger generation. It is important that we should be suitably sceptical of what is said retrospectively about something that many claimed to have been a traumatic experience for others. In criticising management and their juniors there may be a touch of guilt in having been bought off. It might be said that rather than defending jobs on behalf of the next generation, they had been tempted by the prospect of ready money. On the other hand it may be true that their sacrifice had indeed saved the Abbey. It is of course difficult to know the truth, but some certainly felt aggrieved that more jobs have not been created subsequent to the grand shake-out. Some of them know of men still at the Abbey who are involuntarily working substantial amounts of overtime, and who are being required to do many different jobs instead of the one that is their trade. They deplore these trends.

What is significant is that this data accords with the ideas expressed in the House of Commons Committee report: people are indeed talking about 'making way' and are readily casting themselves in the role. It may be, as Walker has argued before the House of Commons Committee, that some have been persuaded to think in these terms by the Government and the national media, but it is more probable in this instance that it was in the discussion of the hard decisions that the Corporation was asking them to make that it became clear that it was 'me or him', the older man or the lad. They knew the score and they knew it would be easier for them, the older men.

Finally, some important theoretical issues are raised by this study. Disengagement is a concept that has been stigmatised by the debate about structural-functionalism that followed the formulation of disengagement theory (Cumming and Henry, 1961). So many have disputed the idea that 'society' and 'the elderly person' mutually, naturally and inevitably disengage, that now one has to be very careful before choosing to use the term.

Engagement implies a relationship in which two parties have agreed, with a certain degree of formality, upon certain courses of joint or collaborative action. It implies a certain mutuality of interest and shared expectations about the consequences, but it implies neither symmetry nor the absence of conflicting interests. The prefix 'dis-' implies both the opposite and the discharge from engagement. Disengagement is the state of not being engaged which follows rather than precedes the state of being engaged. Some gerontologists might prefer the term 'exclusion', and certainly forced expulsion followed by exclusion is one particularly harsh example for which disengagement sounds positively euphemistic. What is more debatable is whether or not highly effective disincentives constitute exclusion: in the interests of good analysis it seems sensible to distinguish between transitions that are involuntary and enforced and those that are induced and voluntary.

The 108 steelworkers whom I interviewed are in many ways a distinctive and peculiar group. Nevertheless, they have been through an ageing experience which may characterise many other groups that are differently distinctive and peculiar. They were invited by their employer to disengage. Under some pressure, not least from amongst themselves, they chose to accept. An important reason or rationalisation for doing so was the belief that acceptance would save the job of a younger man. Four years later when interviewed by an enquiring stranger, they expressed a wide range of concerns for the future of younger people. They have abandoned any hopes of regaining full-time paid employment. This ageing experience was the result of an act of disengagement. There was nothing natural, inevitable or symmetrically mutual about it. To that extent, the maxims of disengagement theory are irrelevant. I would like to suggest, however, that theoretical initiatives in social gerontology should repossess the extremely pertinent concept of disengagement.

Notes

(1) The critical age was 55 years for men and 50 years for women. My interviewing was limited to 108 men aged 55 years or over.

References

Bytheway, W.R. (1986) 'Redundancy and the Older Worker' in: Redundancy, Lay-Offs, and Plant Closure: The Social Impact, (Editor, R.M. Lee), Croom Helm, London, (forthcoming).

Casey, B. and Bruche, G. (1983) Work or Retirement?, Gower Press, London.

Cribier, F. (1981) 'Changing Retirement Patterns of the Seventies: The Example of a Generation of Parisian

Salaried Workers', Ageing and Society, Vol.1, No.1, pp.51-76.

Cumming, E. and Henry, W.E. (1961) Growing Old, Basic Books, New York.

House of Commons Social Services Committee (1982) Age of Retirement, HMSO, London.

Jackson, M. (1984) 'Early Retirement: Recent Trends and Implications', Industrial Relations Journal, Vol.15, No.3, pp.21-28.

Kohli, M., Rosenow, J. and Wolf, J. (1983) 'The Social Construction of Ageing Through Work: Economic Structure and Life-World, Ageing and Society, Vol.3, No.1, pp.23-42.

Makeham, P. and Morgan, P. (1980) Evaluation of the Job Release Scheme, Research Paper 13, Department of Employment, London.

McGoldrick, A. and Cooper, C.L. (1980) 'Voluntary Early Retirement and Taking the Decision', Employment Gazette, pp.859-864.

Parker, S. (1982) Work and Retirement, George Allen and Unwin, London.

Walker, A. (1984) Older Workers and Early Retirement in the Sheffield Steel Industry, Report to the Economic and Social Research Council, London.

Acknowledgement

(1) This research was funded by a grant from the Economic and Social Research Council, 1983-1984.

Chapter Twenty-Seven

UNDERSTANDING THE 'MANAGEMENT' OF

EVERYDAY-LIVING

A Study Based on the Life-Histories of a Group of Older
People in Leeds

Silvana di Gregario

Introduction

Later life, particularly the period after the age of 75, has
been identified by policy-makers as a particularly difficult
time 'to manage'. The individual has been excluded from the
labour market for many years, health starts to decline if it
has not been in decline already, family and friends are dying
off, and the individual may find her/himself more and more
isolated and possibly less capable of 'managing' on her/his
own. The over 75s have received particular policy attraction
because they are expected to comprise 47 per cent of the
over 65s by the turn of the century (CSO, 1985). Hence, a
larger proportion of the population will need 'managing' help.
But unfortunately, the 'management' problems of this group
are usually seen solely in terms of their extreme age.
Previous management problems are often ignored, as are
previous experiences of 'managing'. 'Managing' is usually
thought of as something done to this group of people rather
than done by them. Hence, 'managing' in old age is usually
perceived in terms of the notion of 'dependency'. Yet
'dependency' is really just one form of 'managing'. Most
people experience 'management' problems throughout their
lives and have constructed strategies for dealing with them.
In trying to help older people 'to manage', it is important to
understand the individual's own perception and attitudes
towards such an experience.

Research Methods

In order to examine such perceptions and attitudes I have
adopted a life history approach. To some people, the life
history might appear to be a curious method to adopt. It is
hard to believe that during the formative years of American
sociology (particularly at the University of Chicago in the
1920s and 1930s), the pursuit of life histories and so-called

327

'soft' methods of analysis were equal competitors with the
'hard' quantitative school which was concerned with
constructing reliable indices or measures of behaviour.[1]
There is no doubt now that the 'hard' school of sociology won
hands down. As Faraday and Plummer have found:

> ... the life history technique is viewed with scepticism
> because it is held to provide no wider link to theoretical
> understanding, have little power of generalizability, and
> to be an extremely time-consuming method. (Faraday
> and Plummer, 1979, p.774).

But this can hardly be called a fair criticism. It is
using the criteria of one type of methodology to judge a
totally different type. In fact, the life history technique
highlights areas which are often neglected in conventional
social science research. In the field of ageing, the social
problem approach has encouraged researchers to look at the
elderly as a group set apart from society and social
processes. Older people have all too often been treated as an
homogeneous group - despite differences regarding gender,
ethnicity, class, regionality, and even age. This tendency is
easily encouraged by a survey approach which aims to
generalise about the characteristics of a target population.
Instead, the life history approach focuses on the subjective
reality of the individual. It strips away assumptions
observers make about people's lives by concentrating on the
individual's interpretation of events she/he has experienced.
    In addition, conventional approaches tend to segment
life, emphasising the constitutive elements of life rather than
focusing on the whole. In terms of understanding old age,
life histories help the researcher to see not only an old
person but the same person as, for example, a child,
adolescent, young worker, all of whose experiences contribute
to that of the person in old age. It contextualises the older
person's life today with the life and circumstances which came
before it. It also interweaves the various elements of an
individual's biography - such as the relation between home
and work - to give a fuller picture of the interconnections at
play in an individual's life. Above all, it conveys the
richness and depth of a life - it adds flesh to a study while
the aims of more conventional sociology necessitate laying bare
the bones for analysis.
    Not only do the strengths of the life history approach
make up for the weaknesses of more conventional quantitative
styles of analysis, it is particularly suited for study in ' ...
areas in which the conceptualisation of problems has been ill
worked out' (Faraday and Plummer, 1979, p.774). The social
scientific study of age has become intertwined with social
policy concerns 'of the moment'. By following the lead of
social policy concerns, social scientists have often reinforced

and legitimised conceptualising the problems of the old as the problems of the 'individual' and of 'age' - both at the expense of wider social events which may have affected lives, and the cumulative effects of personal experiences earlier in life. This narrow focus of perception is part and parcel of approaches looking only at the present-day circumstances of older people. The emphasis has been on the collection of the aggregate 'facts' and their verification at the expense of the development of appropriate theoretical frameworks on which to base analysis of older people's lives. The life history approach lends itself to the production of relevant concepts.

I have followed the trajectories of older people's lives in the hope that the structural constraints during their lives and their effects will become more clearly delineated. The over-75s who are the subject of my study have actually lived through enormous changes in British society. They grew up during the Victorian and Edwardian periods when Britain was an imperial power. They experienced the effects of the two world wars, the economic decline between the wars, and the development of the Welfare State after the Second World War. I am not so much interested in looking at these people as 'old people' but as 'whole people' - people with a personal history of 'managing' their lives. I am also interested in their own perceptions of their lives - their view of their own history. Rather than impose prior conceptualisations on their lives, I have allowed perspectives on their personal histories to evolve from their accounts.

Analysing Life Histories

I analysed in depth 66 of the 335 life histories which were collected in the Leeds Metropolitan area during 1979-1980.[2] The respondents were born between 1884 and 1905 and were 75 or over at the time of the interview. I found that the life histories contained four main sub-histories. These were: first, a personal economic history; secondly, a family history; thirdly, a health and debilities history; fourthly, a formal social support history. Of course, these sub-histories were interwoven and inter-related in the accounts given by the older people. But by separating out these sub-histories for analysis, I was able to compare work history with work history; family history with family history and so on, as well as compare items found in one sub-history with others in a different sub-history within the same life story.

Since I was interested in how people 'managed' during their lives, I began by concentrating on comparing work histories. I looked at how the families to which these individuals belonged 'managed' as a whole and identified the major income provider(s) during the respondents' lives. From this information I was able to construct a typology of what I call 'economic units'. Five types of 'economic units' emerged.

These were:
(a) where the man or husband was the sole earner
(b) where the women or wife was the sole earner
(c) where the woman or wife was a joint earner and a major contributor
(d) where the woman or wife was a supplementary earner and a minor contributor
(e) an inconsistent economic unit where different individuals were income providers during different periods of an individual's economic history.

This last type - an inconsistent economic unit - proved to be the most illuminating. It characterised nearly one-third of the women I studied but none of the men. Obviously, this situation caused dramatic upheavals for these women's financial security, and I decided to document the experiences of these women.
Despite this very important finding, I discovered that 'economic units' alone did not sufficiently analyse how individuals 'managed' during their lives. I needed a more temporal framework. That is when I realised I needed a 'Work Shape' typology. I needed to understand the consistencies and/or inconsistencies of an individual's relation to the labour market; whether there was a set career structure or not; how personal misfortune or ill-health affected an individual's ability to participate in the labour market and how she/he coped and so on. By comparing the work histories again I discovered four basic types of 'work shape'. These were:
(a) a continuous career with trade and/or employer and no disruptions
(b) a continuous career with trade and/or employer but with disruptions due to:
    (1) short-time
    (2) frequent redundancies
    (3) drink
    (4) illness
(c) occupation change through
    (1) choice
    (2) health
    (3) bankruptcy
    (4) unemployment
(d) multiple job change came through
    (1) drink
    (2) illness
    (3) unemployment.
I decided that by presenting the life histories according to the type of 'work shape' which characterised an individual and family, the various 'management' issues which people experienced during their lives would unfold naturally.

I will discuss two of the major themes from the analysis of the 'work shapes'. They reflect expectations about women's and men's respective relations to the labour market. For women, there were inconsistent expectations about their relation to the labour market which were bound up with their roles as carers. These expectations can be summarised as follows:

(a) If a woman had no caring commitments, she was expected to pay her own way.

(b) If a woman had caring commitments, she was expected to assume a caring role at the expense of an economic role.

(c) If the major income provider became ill or deceased, a woman was expected to take over the economic role as well as to continue with her caring role. As a consequence, she could only take up work which could be 'fitted round' her caring responsibilities. Such jobs tended to be poorly paid part-time work.

(d) As a general principle, it appears that whether or not a woman works, and the type of work she does is related to the security or insecurity of her father's/husband's job.

In industrial Leeds where these women grew up, women's work was an accepted part of life. The mills and tailoring industry, in particular, depended mainly on female labour. Yet a flexible attitude towards women and work persisted. All the women studied went out to work after they finished their schooling - usually around the age of thirteen. However, if the need for care developed in a woman's family, she was expected to assume the caring role and drop her work role. For example, one of my respondents, Ellen Dixon, worked in a shop after she left school. As she says: 'It was necessary for the money to keep things going ... '

But when her mother died, Ellen (who was the oldest daughter but not the oldest child) had to give up her job and take care of her father and nine brothers and sisters. She was eighteen at the time. When Ellen finally married and left, the next oldest female in the family left her job and took over Ellen's household and caring roles.

This seems to be a common pattern. It is important to remember that most of the people interviewed came from very large families - where a 'division of labour' between caring and work roles made sense and where younger members of the family could take over from their older brothers and sisters when they left home. But most of the families were very poor and needed all the children - girls as well as boys - in work to make ends meet. And it was the females who experienced the pressures of being expected to switch from work to caring roles and back.

There were a few women in this study who were fortunate enough to marry men who had secure jobs with an adequate income. These women did not need to work. But even when they had to prepare for marriage. For example, the Addisons and the Wilbeys both had long courtships (of about ten years) where both parties were working in order to save enough money to get married. The Coopers got married because it was 'convenient' as he got a house when he became manager of a grocery.

However, the majority of women in my study had to work at some time if not during all of their adult lives. This is related to the second major theme which emerged from the 'work shapes' - the expectations about a man's relation to the labour market. These were:

(a) A man was expected to be the provider.

(b) If a man's job was threatened by short-time, illness or redundancies, his wife was expected to work to make ends meet.

(c) A man was not expected to assume any caring roles. He could rely on mothers, sisters or daughters to fulfil these responsibilities.

Although there were consistent expectations about a man's relation to the labour market, there were not consistent opportunities for men to work during this period. It was a time of industrial decline in the Leeds area. Particularly hard hit were those who worked in the engineering trade. There were frequent redundancies, and short-time became a commonplace feature of the work. These were long-term disruptions which meant that these men were unable to fulfil their role as the main income provider during their working lives. They had, instead, to depend on their wives working to make up a decent income.

There seems to have been a contradiction between how men were expected to operate in the labour market and how a lot of them had to 'manage'. There were few direct comments about men's or women's attitudes towards working wives. But evidence of attitudes towards working wives is indicated by the fact that when circumstances permit, by and large the wives do not work. These circumstances are generally that the man is in a secure job with a guaranteed income. But when the job is not secure, and the income coming in is very low, then wives are working. There were a few exceptions among my female respondents who enjoyed their own working careers. But for the vast majority of women, work was not a career but a way of supplementing their husband's income or a way of just 'managing'. It is clear that for many men the opportunity to fully provide for their families did not exist. And there were no other roles for men to fill. They did not take on caring roles - that was left to women. One could speculate that taking on a caring role would be for a man tantamount to admitting to being a failure in the income-providing role.

In addition, the expectation that husbands should be financially responsible for the whole family placed women in a very vulnerable position. As I mentioned earlier, nearly one-third of the women interviewed were classified as having an inconsistent 'economic unit'. That is, they depended on a variety of people for support during their lives - many of them suddenly finding that they had to support themselves and a family on their own. They 'managed' by taking poorly paid part-time work and never expecting very much. These women lived very modest lives with very low expectations. It was the only way to 'manage' if caring and working roles had to be confined in a woman. And it is the way most of them have continued to 'manage' in later life.

The two major themes just discussed provide a background to understand the context within which this particular generation of older people had to 'manage'. Both women's and men's relation to the labour market as well as their scope for choice or self-determination in their lives, and relative expectations about a secure or insecure future, all influence an individual's capacity and willingness 'to manage'. I must stress that the object of this study has not been to provide means for predicting the ways groups of individuals will be able to 'manage' their lives in later life. Instead, the object has been to uncover the various ways people have 'managed' and to contextualise the various ways of 'managing'. The focus has been in understanding the influences in the individual's past which have 'moulded' a certain way of 'managing'. It is important to view 'managing' as a continuous, life-long process.

Experiences in Old Age

I have looked at my respondents' circumstances in later life and have compared them with their experiences earlier in life. It is interesting to note that previous 'work shape' does not seem to affect the range of disability experienced by each group. (Of course, one must remember that my sample represents only the survivors of a generation). But there were differences in how previous 'work shapes' affected attitudes to help. Those who experienced a continuous work career found it difficult to accept help when struck down by restricting illnesses. They had always been self-reliant and were proud to maintain their own independence. For example, Frank Sykes worked all his life for Rotherham Corporation Transport. He began as a bus driver, was promoted to inspector, then became a bus driving instructor, then later an examiner. He was also very active in the local community - particularly the parish council. When his wife died, Frank's health deteriorated rapidly.. He became housebound and decided to move in with his oldest daughter and her husband. But he feels guilty that he has to rely so heavily on his daughter. He tries to reciprocate by paying his daughter for his keep and by buying presents for the family from time to time. However, he does not feel comfortable being dependent:

> It bothers me now that I can't do things for other people.
> I feel guilty that people have to look after me. I don't
> expect to be waited on. I've heard pensioners talk of
> what they can get for nothing or cheap and I think that's
> wrong. My pleasure is what I can buy my family. I pay
> my daughter well for my keep and I enjoy doing that.

However, a 'practical' attitude to help was the most
common response from the other 'work shape' types. If they
need help, they are happy to accept it.

May Steed is unsteady and housebound and depends
heavily on her widowed daughter with whom she lives. She
does not seem to feel at all guilty about this dependence –
but then she spent most of her life caring for others. First,
an ill husband who died leaving her with a young daughter to
bring up. Then, for twelve years she had to care for her
own mother while working to support the family. On her
present life, she simply comments: 'Everybody seems to be
kind to me.'

A minority of the group had either given up on wanting
or expecting any help or had adopted what I call a 'realist'
view of what they could or could not expect as help. The
first group had 'given up' on life in general as well as on
their expectation of receiving any help. The second group
are also pessimistic although they have not entirely given up
on life. Instead, they have a 'wordly-wise' attitude to life.

Martha Salt knows the limits of the kind of help she can
expect from the social services. Her home help was stopped
a month before the interview.

> I have had a home help until a month ago. They asked if
> I wanted meals-on-wheels but I cook for Ronnie [her son]
> each day. I don't suppose I'd bother for myself ... I
> think there is a lot of 'putting on' by people who don't
> need it [help] and others who don't get what they
> should. People are too independent sometimes. Nurses
> are in short supply like home helps.

Finally, there is a small group of people who thought the
way help is given to older people is unfair.

James Simpson who had two successful careers in the
Army and in the Civil Service is feeling the pinch in his later
life. He almost feels punished for having done so well.

> I think the services are good but they are abused by all
> ages of people.... I think it's bad that we have to pay
> income tax on our pension when we've been careful all our
> lives and worked hard for so little. We can't get rate
> rebates or help with the electricity bills and I had to

work after retirement to pay for this house.

Conclusion

The above analysis suggests that it is important to link present-day attitudes to help and ways of 'managing', to the context of an individual's past and present life. Those who seemed to have the most difficulty in accepting help are those who have always been independent and have been struck down by ill health. The majority of people, though, have a practical attitude towards help, accepting what is available if they need it. However, many are not aware of the range of services available. A few who have tried to get services but found it difficult, adopt a 'realist' approach i.e. there are too many old people for services to go round. Others who have been adversely affected by having a bit more than others, complain bitterly about the unfairness of policies for helping older people. They see that some peple get more while others are actually penalised for doing well in the past. It seems people try to 'manage' the way they have always tried in the past - some more successfully than others. It is important to remember that this generation of older people put up with a lot of disruptions in their lives and coped with making do with what they had. At the same time, the virtues of the male breadwinner, frugality, and a temperate life were preached at them. Most have very low expectations (compared to the rest of the population) and hence make few demands. Perhaps this may explain the majority's 'practical' attitude to help. They have had to be practical for most of their lives.

I hope that this life history approach has given back to older people their 'individuality'. By focusing on a group of over 75 year olds - an age group which has been unambiguously labelled as a 'problem' group due to their age - it has been possible to disentangle these people's present difficulties from the difficulties they have encountered during the whole of their lives. And of course each generation of older people will have their own unique attitude to 'managing' based on the circumstances of their earlier lives.

For the practitioner, the life history method can help one to understand the wider problems behind an illness or breakdown. It can also indicate what kind of treatment to which an older person will respond. Most importantly, it restores the dignity of the older person. She/he is seen as a 'whole' person - not as a 'burden' or a 'problem' which must be solved. For the social scientist, the life history method offers a dynamic view of ageing. It also helps make research a collaboration between the investigator and the respondents. During the course of this work I came to the conclusion that there cannot be a sociology of old age or a social gerontology without a sociology of ageing. It seemed artificial to try to

separate one period of life from the context of the rest of
that life. Individuals' perceptions of themselves are rooted in
their personal history - their accumulated experiences. Some
may query whether it is wise to take on face value people's
word on events in their lives. But it does not matter if some
statements from the respondent are not factually true. It is
the way people interpret events which provides the clue to
how they view themselves. The social investigator must
strive to understand the self-images people have of
themselves regardless of the objective reality. Only by
understanding how people interpret what has happened in
their lives, can social scientists begin to understand the
effects wider social changes have on their lives.

Notes

(1) 'The 'case study' and the 'statistical method' generally
appear to have been the two major approaches to research
during the 1920s....', Ken Plummer, Documents of Life: An
Introduction to the Problems and Literature of a Humanistic
Method, George Allen and Unwin, London, 1983, p.45; also
see Barry G. Glaser and Anselm L. Strauss, The Discovery
of Grounded Theory: Strategies for Qualitative Research,
Aldine Publishing Co., New York, 1967, pp. 12-18 which
gives an historical account of why the verification of theory
(and statistical methods) rather than the generation of theory
(and qualitative methods) became the dominant orientation in
sociological work.
(2) Between 1977-80 I was employed on a DHSS sponsored
project on meals services for the elderly whose research
director, Malcolm Johnson, was sympathetic to the collection
of life history documents. After negotiation with the DHSS,
it was agreed that the collection of life histories could be
carried out simultaneously with the survey of consumer
responses to meals services. In this way, I was able to
collect a large number of life histories. A full discussion of
the sampling method used can be found in Malcolm Johnson,
Silvana di Gregario and Beverley Harrison, Ageing, Needs
and Nutrition, PSI Research Paper 81/8, Policy Studies
Institute, London, 1981.
    The 66 life histories I subsequently analysed were
randomly selected from the over 75 population of the original
335 documents. The number selected only reflects the
number of life histories possible to analyse manually. As
they were analysed for the generation of theory rather than
the verification of facts, the actual size of the sample is not
crucial as it would have been for a quantitative study. See
Glaser and Strauss, op.cit., pp.62-65, on the difference
between statistical and theoretical sampling.

References

Central Statistical Office (1985) Social Trends, No.15, p.21, HMSO, London.

Farraday, A. and Plummer, K. (1979) 'Doing Life Histories', Sociological Review, Vol.27, No.4, November, pp.774.

Chapter Twenty-Eight

INDEPENDENCE AND HOME IN LATER LIFE

Andrew J. Sixsmith

Introduction

The principle that older people should be able to live in their
own homes as far as possible, is central to most health and
welfare policies for the elderly. The home environment is
seen as playing an important contributory role in the general
'well-being' and the physical and mental health of older
people. However, beyond this assertion, the nature of the
person-home relationship in later life is little understood. Of
the growing literature on the home (Hayward, 1977; Kron,
1983; Sixsmith, 1984; Altman and Werner, 1985), only a few
studies have addressed the issue of old age (Csikszentmihalyi
and Rochberg-Halton, 1981; Peace et al., 1983). There is a
need, it would seem, for systematic research that reaches
below the surface of 'belongingness' to reveal the essential
qualities of home in later life.

This paper presents some of the results of an
interview-based study undertaken by the author into the
meaning and experience of home in later life. A
characteristically complex picture of home and old age
emerged from the interviews. To illustrate, older people are
likely to have lived in their present homes for a long time
and thus have many associated memories. They are
surrounded by their possessions, which contribute to a
feeling of familiarity. They may also feel at home because
their husband or wife is sitting in the chair opposite. These
are perhaps those subjective qualities that make a home.
However, there are also instrumental aspects: the need to
keep warm in winter and the ability to manage the house. All
these factors may affect how an older person feels about their
home.

The point is that the concept of home is not
straightforward. It is an amalgam of subjective feelings and
physical opportunities and constraints. Moreover, as a
person reaches later life, the home may take on a new and
more significant role in the context of the changing physical,

social and personal circumstances that often accompany old age. One of the recurrent themes in interviews was the significance of independence. Independence is an important value for most older people, but has received little formal attention compared with the more specific issue of physical dependency. Another theme to emerge from the interviews was the importance of people's homes, both symbolically and instrumentally, in affording independent life. It is this relationship between home and independence that is the focus of the present paper.

The Study

Two problems are addressed. First, what is the everyday meaning of the word 'independence'? Secondly, how does an older person's home contribute to their independence? These questions were explored in semi-structured interviews with some sixty people in Newcastle-upon-Tyne between October 1984 and May 1985, as part of a wider investigation into the meanings and experiences of home in later life. The only qualifying factors for choosing participants was that they lived in their own home, either rented or owned, and that they were aged over 65 years old. Interviewing was restricted to two districts of Newcastle. Both were primarily working-class areas, but included all housing tenures: owner-occupied, housing association, council rented and private rented.

Interviews lasted between one and four hours and consisted of open-ended questions covering areas such as the significance of the home in a person's total environmental experience, what makes a house into a home, and how home experience is related to ageing. Some participants were visited just once, but most were interviewed two or more times, including a core of half a dozen people who were interviewed on many occasions as the basis of a case study approach to the problem. This latter approach provided the most interesting and essential insights into the meanings and experiences of home in later life, insights into a complex system of personal meanings that are not always accessible through conventional research perspectives (Rowles, 1978; Yin, 1984).

The two issues of the meaning of independence and its relationship with the home were explored using the following questions as a basis for discussion:

* Retired people seem to value their independence a great deal. What does being independent mean to you? Why do you think it is important to you?
* Does your home assist in keeping you independent? In what ways?

Participants were encouraged to expand on their views and to talk freely about their own feelings and experiences.

Independence and Home in Later Life

A great deal of qualitative data was generated from the discussions. Initially, this was reduced to a set of manageable conceptual categories using content analysis (Weber, 1985), where the salient points from each interview were assigned to a set of meaning categories. These categories were not predefined, but were developed from the responses themselves by a continuous process of sorting and grouping. To avoid a subjective category scheme based solely on the researcher's own notions, the responses were assigned to the categories for a second time by an independent person. Disagreements can be negotiated between the raters to define a final set of meaning categories. The rest of this paper presents the results of this analysis.

The Meaning of Independence

What does one mean by the word 'independence'? At one level it is possible to construe independence as the opposite of dependence. It is this construction that is usually of interest to caring authorities. 'Independence' in this sense is the ability to live without relying on external help. At an individual level though, the notion of independence may be personally defined and independence and dependence need not be constructed as opposites. As Munnichs (1976, p.6) points out, for an older person:

> ....dependency is only perceptible when changes in his existence which concern himself present themselves or are introduced: relocation, admission to hospital, removal to a home for the aged, dying of his partner. These are examples of possible emotional dependency. Indeed, he can become instrumentally more dependent, e.g. through only getting a pension instead of wages, or through another system of services, but this need not affect his self-integrity. Therefore the emotional changes are the most drastic.

Clearly, when one is talking about the notion of dependence, one is dealing with a highly symbolic phenomenon. Nevertheless, 'independence' exists as a highly pertinent value amongst older people and should be seen as no less 'real' for all its subjective connotations. Because of this, it is important to examine how older people use the notion of independence. This was done by asking participants what being independent meant to them. The content analysis of responses defined three consistent themes, representing specific modes of being independent. First, independence meant being able to look after yourself, that is not being dependent on other people:

Take away your independence and you are finished. People finish themselves - they get people to do this and that for them. I am the most independent person in the world. I like to be able to do things myself. If you're not independent, you are relying on everybody all the time. You just deteriorate and that's it.

Participants also saw independence as the capacity for self-direction, that is the freedom to choose what they do:

I don't want people to tell me what I can do and what I can't do. You like to do the things that you want to do, how you want and where you want. It's your life isn't it?

Thirdly, the idea of independence was linked to feelings of obligation:

I like to be independent - I don't want to be beholding to any man. We don't owe a penny between us - it is one of our principles. Nobody likes to sort of beg for anything, waiting for handouts all the time.

The value placed on being independent is undeniable and characterised most of the interviewees. The present generation of over 65s is popularly associated with a desire for independence and this must account for the strength of feeling on the part of many of the participants. However, is this desire for independence simply a cultural product or is it also a function of the process of ageing? In some of the interviews a more ambivalent attitude was expressed, which may shed some light on this question. Consider the following statements:

Older people like to be independent. Partly, it's that older people don't want to think they are dependent on anybody else and partly because they are and don't want to admit it. It's a bit of an illusion.

To tell you the truth I was an awful fellow for being independent, but it is a fool's game. As you get on a bit, you are glad of help now and again - it proves to you that you can be too independent. You are looking for a bit of help and company when you are older.

The implication is that some degree of dependence is inevitable in old age. The realisation of this possibility may lead an older person to place a greater value on being independent. At least the realisation of a possible loss of personal capability will serve to bring the issue of 'independence' into consciousness.

Home and Independence

The main interest behind this paper is the role of a person's home in the experience of independence. From speaking to older people about this subject, it became clear that their homes played an important part in their maintaining independence, both symbolically and instrumentally. In the interviews, this assertion was explored more formally by asking participants to express their views on this subject. Overwhelmingly, people felt that their own home helped to keep them independent. Only one person said that it did not, and two said that they did not know. It is difficult to measure objectively the strength of feeling on this issue, but most people were quite insistent on the significance of their homes in maintaining independence. Indeed most felt that the answer was self-evident, which it is, at the level of taken-for-granted experience.

It is important to explore more closely the relationship between home and independence. This was done by asking participants to expand on their views and to explain exactly what they felt on this issue. Content analysis of the answers produced a set of meaning categories for the home-independence relationship (Table 1).

Table 1

Categories of the Home-Independence Relationship

Categories	Number of People Using this Category
1. You do things for yourself	13
2. Home as a symbol of independence	11
3. Contented at home	9
4. Can do what you want here	7
5. Not beholden to anybody	5
6. Stability and protection	5
7. You don't depend on anyone else	4
8. Nobody tells you what to do here	4

The defined categories have distinct parallels with the three modes of independence that were described earlier: not being dependent; self-direction and obligation. For example, the categories of 'doing what you want' and 'nobody tells you what to do' correspond to the idea of self-direction. Two categories are not readily associated with the model of independence. These are 'stability and protection' and 'contentedness'. These would seem to have more in common with Bachelard's (1969) notion of the home as a protective shell, rather than any clear relationship with the experience of independence. However, from the evidence of the other six categories, it seems that people's homes play a significant role in promoting independence in all three modes.

The six categories of the home-independence relationship in Table 1 also point to a further dimension of the experience of independence. In the first instance, three modes of experience were defined, but within this it is possible to identify a distinct and consistent orientation between the self and others. This allows the construction of a more detailed model of the independence-home relationship, which is given in Table 2.

Table 2

Structures of Home-Independence Relationship

Mode of independence	Self/others	Significance of home
Not dependent	Self	Do things for yourself
	Others	Not depending on anybody
else		
Self-direction	Self	Can do what you want
	Others	Nobody tells you what to do
Obligation	Self	Symbolic of independence
	Others	Not beholden to anybody

To understand independence, one must consider not one but two facets of experience: mode and orientation. For example, the mode of self-direction can be defined in two ways. It is being able to do what you want to do; that is the self-orientation. Alternatively, it is being free from anybody telling you what to do; that is the others orientation. The self-others duality is also quite clear in respect to the mode of 'not being dependent'. The operation of the self-others facet is perhaps the least convincing in respect of obligation. The others orientation of the category 'not beholden to anybody' is clear, but the self-orientation of 'symbolic of independence' is not self-explanatory and needs clarification. 'Symbolic of independence' has been used in an all-embracing way to include such issues as the achievement of ambition and the symbolism of owning a house. None of these fall within the others orientation, but are allied to the idea of identity and the preservation of personal integrity. In this sense the home symbolically represents the independent self.

It should be remembered that the focus of attention in

these interviews was on the role of the home rather than independence per se. It is interesting to note that the self-others facet became apparent from questions that specifically involved the home. This suggests that the home is an integral dimension of independence. That is to say, the home is a material part of being independent and that independence in later life cannot be fully understood without reference to the home. The home can possibly be understood most clearly as a mediator between self and others. To illustrate, at an instrumental level, the home is the domain of the person and not of others:

> You can do what you want in your own place. You can come in and lock the door behind you and you know that nobody is going to bother you.

The point is intuitively obvious: the home is the place of the self, outside is the more general place of others. The home provides the physical demarcation between self and others, along with the assurance of authority to exclude others from the home domain. Without the physical barrier, independence in any mode may be difficult to sustain. This broadly coincides with the idea of an existential space (Norberg-Schultz, 1971), where physical and psychic space are congruent, with the home as the locus of the self and independence.

The Role of the Home in Promoting Independence

So far, the issue of independence and the home has been discussed in fairly general terms. At this point, it may be useful to examine how the home might promote independent life. For example, a person's home may contribute directly to the promotion of independence in the sense of 'not being dependent'. Several participants were quite seriously disabled, particularly in respect of mobility. To these people independent living represented a very physically demanding way of life; when you live on your own you have to do things for yourself. To be able to do things for yourself in the face of physical disability brings with it a sense of achievement. To do something for yourself, however small, is to be independent. But apart from this symbolic quality, to live at home may have a direct instrumental value. This is perhaps best illustrated by the case of Robert, a widower living alone, who is semi-paralysed after a stroke ten years ago.

> The stairs are the best thing in the world for me - exercise. It's the finest exercise in the world as far as I'm concerned. I never let the stairs worry me. You never get from where you are if you don't try to get

up. Determination is the finest thing in the world. If you get tired half-way up, just bend down and put your hand on the step and have a rest.

This provides a unique and perhaps idiosyncratic perspective on the problem of coping with stairs. Nevertheless, one can see that physical exercise, the use of impaired faculties, etc., are important in maintaining physical capability. The demands of living at home make this a necessity. Moreover, to do things and to look after yourself also lends to a belief in your physical capabilities. Robert himself used to look after a friend who had been confined to bed. This involved getting up and down stairs with a meal tray and lifting and washing the other person. All these would seem impossible for a man who has little use down one side of his body, due to a severe stroke. Yet for all his desire for independence he was happy to accept help in those areas that he felt he needed it. Living at home showed him what he could not do as well as what he could do. However, at the symbolic level, Robert's knowledge that he was at least able to do some things himself is important in maintaining his self-esteem:

After the stroke I couldn't do much for myself for the first six months, but I was determined I was going to do something. I say you don't get very far sitting around moping or you'll be in the box. If you just sit around relying on everybody you just deteriorate. I'm not trying to boast, but it's the attitude that everybody should take. I can do more for myself than he can do next door. He can do it, but he's got his sister to do it for him. If he'd been on his own like me, he'd definitely have to do it. The place would be a pig sty. You see what I mean. I'm not proud, but I'm particular. I like to keep things nice and tidy - neat.

Robert is a man of exceptional determination and sense of independence, but his attitude and situation was mirrored by many of the participants. However, Robert's case illustrates not only the instrumental value of living at home, but also how this has implications for being independent in all its modes of experience.

Conclusion

Given the importance of independence, from the point of view of both the elderly and policy-makers, it is surprising that its meaning has received little attention. As with all everyday terms, 'independence' is intuitively known and is normally used without reflection. However, this level of understanding is inadequate from a theoretical perspective.

Independence and Home in Later Life

In summary, this paper has shown that the term 'independence' conveys a number of meanings. The research identified three modes of independence: not being dependent, self-direction and obligation. People's understanding of the relationship between home and independence also reflected these modes, but also involves a symbolic and instrumental demarcation between the self and others. The home seems to contribute towards maintaining independence in later life, and thus provides a material context for independence.

Home can be an important part of being independent, and as such, living at home can be construed in a positive way. But there may also be negative aspects to this. For example, the idea of disengagement in old age (Cumming and Henry, 1961) involves a mutual process of separation between individual and society. Whether or not this is a matter of mutual benefit is a controversial issue. However, in the context of this paper, there may only be a fine distinction between being independent and being disengaged. Certainly, the images of independence presented earlier are very individualistic. Moreover, the home is seen as the domain of the self and as a means of excluding others. Thus, the home can be as much a context for disengagement as it is for being independent. This reservation needs to be borne in mind, particularly if disengagement is not always beneficial to the older person.

References

Altman, I. and Werner, C.M. (1985) Home Environments, Plenum Press, New York.
Bachelard, G. (1969) The Poetics of Space, Beacon Press, Boston.
Csikszentmihalyi, M. and Rochberg-Halton, E. (1981) The Meaning of Things: Domestic Symbols and the Self, Cambridge University Press, New York.
Cumming, E. and Henry, W. (1961) Growing Old: the Process of Disengagement, Basic Books, New York.
Hayward, D.G. (1977) Home as an Environmental and Psychological Concept, Landscape, Vol.20, No.1, pp.2-9.
Kron, J. (1983) Home-Psych, Potter, New York.
Munnichs, J.M.A. (1976) 'Dependency, Interdependency and Autonomy; an Introduction', in Dependency or Interdependency in Old Age, J.M.A. Munnichs and J.A. van den Heuval (eds.), pp.3-8.
Norberg-Schultz, C. (1971) Existence, Space and Architecture, Praeger, New York.
Peace, S., Kellaher, L. and Willcocks, D. (1983) The Essence of Home, Seminar Report, Centre on Environment for the Handicapped.

Rowles, G. (1978) 'Reflections on Experiential Field Work', in Humanistic Geography: Prospects and Problems, D. Ley and M.S. Samuels (eds.), pp.173-193.
Sixsmith, J.A. (1984) Phenomenological Perspectives on the Concept of Place. Paper presented at the 8th IAPS conference, Berlin, July.
Weber, J. (1985) Basic Content Analysis, Sage, Beverley Hills.
Yin, R.K. (1984) Case Study Research: Research Design and Methods, Sage, Beverly Hills.

Chapter Twenty-Nine

ME DARBY, YOU JOAN!

Dorothy Jerrome

Introduction

Research on voluntary organisations in retirement has drawn on several theoretical traditions. Earlier work on rates of membership of voluntary organisations, attendance at meetings and other objective, easily measured criteria of involvement, rested on the assumption that social participation was healthy and contributed to successful ageing.[1]   This, a premise of the activity theory of ageing, underlies much research on different types of social involvement, e.g. with kin, friends and wider community.

Other writers have examined voluntary groupings in terms of a different theoretical issue: the importance of age as an organising principle in society.   Studies of age-segregation, age-relations and subjective identification in terms of age, have developed from the earlier theoretical formulations of such sociologists as Linton, Eisenstadt and Mannheim.   They have also grown out of an anthropological concern with age differentiation (the extent to which age is a social boundary) as a cultural phenomenon.   Research in this tradition has used a more qualitative approach than studies in the social integration tradition.   The focus has been on subjective meanings attached to participation in voluntary organisations and groupings, their role in the provision of support and socialisation to old age, and patterns of conflict and cooperation among group members (Myerhoff, 1980; Hazan, 1980; Francis, 1981; Keith, 1982; Breytspraak, 1985). More broadly, they have been concerned with the significance of age boundaries in voluntary association and the conditions in which age provides a basis for community formation.

Several writers have suggested that identification with the peer group is particularly marked at certain times of life, the early years of retirement being one of them (Eisenstadt, 1956; Harris, 1975; 1983; Dono et al., 1979; Fry, 1980).[2] In this view an old people's club might be seen as a response to liminality (the experience of being marginal and between two statuses), the need for solidarity in a state of relative deprivation and low status, and for guidelines for behaviour in socially uncharted waters.[3]

The literature demonstrates both theoretically and empirically the likelihood of people in particular age categories recognising common interests and forming social bonds to promote them. It also offers explanation for such groupings in social, cultural and psychological terms. But relatively little evidence exists of the precise social mechanisms whereby the social and personal ends mentioned above are achieved. There are hints in the literature at the way in which elderly people's perceptions of their shared circumstances encourage them to associate with each other. Of the friendships and other peer relationships through which common interests are articulated, little is known.

American research on community formation and social processes in the elderly peer group offers, by comparison, fascinating insights. The absence of comparable studies in Britain is tantalising. Something is known about the extent of involvement in age-segregated voluntary organisations (Hunt, 1978; Abrams, 1980; Harris, 1983; Wenger, 1984), but British research has so far tended to stop short of a detailed analysis of social processes within age-specific clubs and societies. We do not know whether old people's clubs are a response to a wish to dissociate themselves from younger groups, or a product of necessity in the face of deprivation, although these questions may have been with us for some time (Rosow, 1967; Harris, 1975). Perhaps age-segregated groupings such as this give scope for competitive strivings in retirement which are satisfied through other channels earlier in life (Unruh, 1983). We do not know how far such concentrations of older people, with their potential for friendship and sociability (Karn, 1977), and the known benefits of such bonds in later life (Hess, 1972; Jerrome, 1981) enable club members to make friends.

It is against this background that the research reported in the following pages must be interpreted. In January 1985 I started an anthropological study, funded by the Economic and Social Research Council. The object was to develop and extend my earlier research on the friendship patterns of older women (see Jerrome, 1981; 1983; 1984). The aim of the proposed research was to look at the broader effects of friendship and intimacy on the ageing process. My research population consisted of three age-specific associations in an age-mixed church community in a large south coast conurbation and nine pensioners' clubs in the same area.

In this paper I offer some findings about social processes in the old people's clubs. The following pages consist not of a detailed analysis (that has yet to be made) but a set of initial impressions at a fairly general level. The information was gathered by means of unstructured interviews

Me Darby, You Joan!

and participant observation at club meetings, on club outings and parties, and among small groups of friends in different settings. Over the eight months of fieldwork I attended about forty club meetings and went on three coach trips. I got to know 150 club members and organisers, some intimately; detailed information was collected on over fifty. I also learned a lot about the histories of the clubs in lengthy interviews with club officials and members.

Club-Going in Old Age

At about half-past one on a normal weekday there occurs a shift in the elderly population in Brighton. On foot, by bus or taxi, or car of a kind daughter or friend, the sociable and able-bodied go in search of company and occupation. Their destination is probably a club, or one of their clubs, for people who go to the clubs at all tend to belong to several. Club-going is a way of life, hence the indigenous expression 'in the clubs'; 'she's like, in the clubs'. This describes someone's involvement in a system or circuit. Multiple membership is normal among club-goers. This has implications for the exchange of information and growth of a club culture which I shall mention shortly.
  Although their memberships are substantially overlapping, the clubs themselves are organisationally autonomous. Independent, self-financing and self-supporting, they collaborate only to fill the coach for the annual summer holiday. Some are nominally church-based and others are affiliated to the National Federation of Retirement Pensioners' Associations, but they are run largely as personal projects by leaders with entrepreneurial leanings and a social conscience. Leaders talk about 'my club' and 'my members', and once incumbent hold office for years, their tenure disrupted only by death or disability.
  A typical member is widowed and in her 70s, having joined on the death of her husband or, in some cases, together with him on his retirement. There are some unattached men and married couples, and a disproportionate number of them hold office. But in general the clubs are female-dominated. Indeed, where the 'chairman' is female, as is the case in most clubs, members may be addressed collectively as 'ladies'. The few men are socially invisible.
  Some clubs in Brighton today have been operating for more than thirty years. The majority were founded more recently. They vary in size from nearly 250 members to less than 30, though the majority have perhaps 80 to 100, with a weekly attendance of 50 or 60. Memberships fluctuate with crises or coups. The larger the club, the more attractive it is, for large means wealthy, more and better outings, popular leaders and a buoyant crowd. When a club falls below a certain number it ceases to be viable, for the rental of the

meeting place (normally a church hall) consumes too much of the income, and a sense of sadness pervades meetings. Several clubs have folded recently in this way. But even the larger clubs have suffered losses in membership through ageing and death and in several senses things are not what they were.

In terms of weekly procedure - business, followed by tea and biscuits, then entertainment, a raffle and parting rituals - the pattern has generally remained unchanged for years. But in terms of numbers of people, the quantity of goods at bring-and-buy sales, the quality of effort made in fund-raising events and parties, there has been (in the view of members) a sad falling off in recent years. The clubs seem to age with their members. Rather than belonging to the age grade, with people passing through on their way from the grade below to the grade above, the organisation seems to become the property of the particular cohort which founded it, and moves forward with it. The life cycle of the club matches that of the dominant members. (This is especially so with church-based religious organisations in my study, which will form the subject of another paper). However not all clubs suffer this fate. Decline and death has been more marked in some clubs than others. The successful clubs, those which go on recruiting rising 60s, are relatively young and have relatively young committee members. They also have weekly bingo sessions rather than sing-alongs and monologues. The less successful have leaders who are chronologically older and a programme of entertainment which locates them socially and historically as members of an older generation. It is the culture of these clubs which limits recruitment, as well as the depressed atmosphere induced by frequent deaths.

Concert parties perform popular songs dating from the 1920s and 1930s, offer ageist jokes and sketches, and confirm the members' belief in their cultural and moral superiority over younger generations. A sense of separateness is expressed by the chairman on behalf of everyone and informally among friends. At every turn, warmth gratitude, affection and dependency among the old are coupled with dislike and distrust of the young. Every opportunity is seized to draw invidious comparisons between themselves and younger people (defined as those who reached adulthood after the war). Thus in one club, recollections of V.E. Day celebrations in Trafalgar Square moved swiftly to the behaviour of modern youth on New Year's Eve. The Juventus incident unleashed a torrent of criticism of contemporary education, child-rearing, industrial relations and social policy in general. Members tend to think of a particular piece of behaviour, minor deception, or petty theft known to be practised by, say, a young relative, as belonging to that generation and as practised universally within it. I was occasionally berated as the representative of this errant generation, spoilt by the welfare state, permissive parents and an absence of military service.

These sentiments are supported by readings from books like Francis Gay's 'Friendship Book': the most popular source of material for leaders, visiting performers and members' private use. Moralistic, semi-religious, sentimental even mawkish, selected readings underline the expressive orientation of members. This book can be seen in homes where there are no other books.

To stray for a moment into methodological waters, it is of course difficult to say whether these sentiments, semi-religious morality and ageist attitudes are peculiar to this generation or this period in these old people's lives. Without examining the same group in an age-mixed setting or over a long period it is uncertain whether their morality is age-, generation- or class-based. The same uncertainty prevails over such practices as the touching I observed and experienced. The tendency to hang on to someone, place an arm round their shoulders as a gesture of affection, or the hand on the arm either to detain or to emphasise a verbal utterance, could be age-related or a continuation of life-long styles of communication. This is a methodological problem which must beset any study of behaviour in old age which is not set in the context of the life cycle in general.

In view of the common tendency to regard themselves as apart from and superior to younger people it is worth looking at members' own age categories and terms. In age terms people in the clubs regard themselves as old though not uniformly so. They have in common their status as pensioners and membership of the same generation, pre-welfare state etc. Within that social category broad distinctions are made, but not universally. An 83 year old chairman might refer to 'young people' meaning newly retired. Most talk about the 'really old' meaning old and frail members, 'waiting to be called'. The majority are simply 'old', in their own and others' reckoning.

Expressions such as 'old dears' and 'old girls' on the one hand and 'young ladies' on the other hand can be heard. They refer not so much to chronological age as social age, or age roles. The former - old dears - are passive recipients of a service. The latter - young ladies - (said without irony) describe members engaged in stereotypically youthful behaviour - a slimming competition or entertaining on the piano.

The majority think of themselves as relatively young, fit and active old people, thus distinguishing themselves from the few mentally infirm members who are said to be 'a bit, you know.... funny'. The confused are at best ignored, at worst laughed at. Attitudes are (to me) surprisingly callous.

Veronica, deaf and forgetful, is a source of amusement

to others on her table. She is tolerated for her dry wit and
capacity to laugh at herself.... 'I don't know whose head
this is, they <u>gave</u> it to me!' She irritates by her capacity to
get lost on outings and is treated at times like a Victorian
circus freak whose antics are a legitimate source of
amusement. The others identify with Veronica only as a
mother who could expect more help from a neglectful son.
Beyond that, they distance themselves from the confused,
critical rather than sympathetic. Perhaps it is more
comfortable to regard mental frailty as a product of moral
weakness rather than a condition that might affect anybody,
however 'worthy'.

People like Veronica cannot play bingo but to come to
meetings is better than to stay at home. This applies to
everyone. Some of the benefits of membership are obvious.
The reasons given for participation include: 'somewhere to
go'; 'something to do'; 'someone to see' and so on. Club
members give similarly negative reasons on behalf of their
members (but not generally themselves): loneliness; boredom;
the need to get away from the same environment. For some
people who live alone and have little beyond housework and
solitary leisure activities (knitting, watching television) to
occupy them, attendance at a club does provide an
occupation, a focus, a structure for the day and week, and a
social network. This matches the popular stereotype of the
club member as isolated, friendless and needy. This popular
conception is shared by some Age Concern organisers who
run their clubs accordingly and by some children who
designed and performed a sketch for club members called 'How
can we help old people?' (This sketch was met at first with
polite silence and murmurs of appreciation, then sotto voce
protests and finally ribaldry).

The club provides security, both physical and emotional.
New members are integrated into a fixed and unchanging
structure of predictable routines, recurrent phrases,
comforting rituals and fixed seating. There are slight
variations in practice but most meetings start with a hymn
and a prayer. The latter may be customary practice rather
than a religious ritual, gabbled off in the upstairs room of a
pub as a prelude to the most important part of the meeting:
tea and conversation. Minutes are read, financial statements
given, sick news read out and returning members applauded,
birthdays acknowledged with a song, a card, a kiss and
occasionally a Kit-Kat or a bar of soap.

The formal proceedings are introduced and terminated by
long-established phrases. Every club has its own parting
rituals, typically a club song or hymn, followed by Auld Lang
Syne, hands linked where seating permits. The songs could
be seen to symbolise members' somewhat tenuous hold on life,
with such phrases as 'We hope to meet again....'; 'God be
with you.... till we meet at Jesus feet' (i.e. if not next

Me Darby, You Joan!

Wednesday, then in Heaven).
Another feature of permanence worth mentioning is the
seating. The arrangement of chairs, as every hostess knows,
is crucial in shaping the pattern of social interaction. Clubs
arrange their seating differently - some in rows, some in a
circle, some round tables. Leaders have different ideas about
the ideal arrangement though once fixed, physical
arrangements are very hard to change. Changes are
occasionally introduced in the interests of friendship and
intimacy. But attempts to move people from their customary
place come up against strong resistance. Chairs become
identified with people. 'My friend Mrs X' (with a nod at an
empty chair) or 'that lady' (again indicating her chair in her
absence) return after a break knowing that their places, of
perhaps 18 years standing, will have been preserved for them
by their friends. Rather as in a traditional segmentary
society, where dispositions on the ground reflect genealogical
relationships, so in the club seating is an expression of social
distance and cordiality. This is ignored at the leader's peril.
Leaders who wish to promote friendship and integrate
newcomers are faced with a dilemma. The provision of
friendship is the main stated objective of most clubs. The
word 'friend' crops up constantly in prayer, song, formal and
informal utterances. But, curiously, despite an ideology of
friendship, it transpires that clubs are not the place in which
to make friends. Existing friendships normally have their
origins outside the club. Indeed, it is said that you need a
friend to join with, and it is common for friends to drop out
when the partner dies or moves away. Friendship groups
provide the sort of intimacy and companionship which lonely
newcomers lack. But it is not easy to penetrate an existing
friendship group. The talk among friends is of mutual
acquaintances and personal events. A reluctance to ask
personal questions leaves both long established and newcomer
ignorant of any common ground which might provide a basis
for conversation. The majority of members, it seems, go to
the club in order to exchange personal information with
friends whom they meet only in this setting. Going to the
club together is an act of friendship. This is taken to
extremes in some cases where the conversation and laughter
continue unabated through the games playing session. The
friendship requirements of members sometimes conflict with
the goals of the organisation, and there is much hushing until
order is restored. The contradiction between the ideology of
friendship which underpins the organisation of the club and
the reality of friendship among members is potentially one of
the most interesting features of this study. This is
particularly so in the case of Age Concern clubs, though
space does not permit me to elaborate here.
Friends provide obvious kinds of support and
companionship. Through their chat, often inconsequential

354

and trivial, friends engage in what psychologists call verbal grooming, equivalent to physical grooming among primates. A friend's very existence adds to one's sense of personal significance and self-worth. Friends engage in a series of emotional exchanges which may be underpinned by material items. At club meetings, magazines can be seen handed from one member to another. As in some classical trading system, copies of the War Cry, The People's Friend and the Brighton Leader are loaned and borrowed, providing a basis for other, non-material transactions: enquiries about health, promises of help, reassurances of self-worth, support for a viewpoint.

Given the system of multiple membership, information about people and events circulates widely. Members are part of an extensive system of support and control. Personal histories cannot be obliterated by transferring from one club to another and starting again. Within the clubs there are clearly defined norms of behaviour with regard to noise, invasion of privacy, personal restraint and so on. Club members are intolerant of authority and resist it by defiance or mockery. 'Bossy' or 'noisy' are the adjectives most frequently used in relation to unpopular leaders or over-assertive members. Nicknames like 'the Fuhrer', 'the SS', 'the Wardress', 'the Queen', 'Sergeant Major', 'School Marm' and others can be heard sotto voce.

One of the favourite topics of conversation is clubs, per se. There is much talk and critical comparison of different clubs. Pairs of friends sample clubs together, influencing their fate by bestowing or witholding support. Multiple membership, viewed in this light, is not seen as a sign of deprivation and need, as some voluntary agencies are inclined to see it, but as a rational consumer activity in which members are independent and discriminating in their selection of clubs to attend.

Through contact with other members, people are helped to come to terms with adversity: the death of a partner, the failure of a child to visit or provide a home; a disappointment over a rehousing application; the onset of ill health. There is much talk of death, for 'death: that's life', and so bereavement is put into perspective and people are socialised for widowhood. In this society of widows, the woman who cannot cope by herself is 'a poor thing'. The new widow is led ceremonially to her seat and reassured by well-wishers that in three months she will begin to feel better.

There is constant talk of health and ill health, which initially strikes one as morbid, self-centred and complaining. Details of symptoms, treatments and responses to them are endlessly compared, and people derive a standard against which to evaluate their own performance. If X feebly gives up coming to clubs as a result of a particular operation, is Y to be blamed for deciding to cut down her activities after a similar course of events? Are there extenuating circumstances in her case? Z had the same thing and kept going. But didn't she have certain advantages? And so on. In this way, rules of appropriate sickness behaviour are negotiated.

The norms established through interaction at the club offer guidelines for behaviour at a time when there are relatively few role-requirements, and cultural images tend to be negative. Thus social reality is constructed and sustained through conversation at the club. Participants are involved in a world of shared meaning and experience. Through the welcome given to the returning members and the birthday rituals, the achievements of age and triumph over adversity are celebrated. Thus attendance at the club is life-enhancing, indeed, 'a life line', as the people themselves put it.

Conclusion

A detailed analysis of the material promises a rich reward in terms of the issues outlined in the introduction, and others which do not occur in the literature. Several themes can be identified. The first is normative and ideological. The members' models of successful ageing, to be imitated, and examples of unsuccessful ageing, to be avoided, need to be understood in relation to those current in society at large. Attitudes toward health and sickness, fitness and sexuality, to disability and death are a part of the normative system which members have constructed between them. A critical dimension seems to be acceptable levels of dependence and independence, both in relation to families and to each other. A second theme is interactional: the pattern of attachment to kin, friends and other members of the personal network. The findings of the research are relevant to the work on primary groups and the ways its members are called upon in different circumstances. The evidence here of working class friendships would appear to contradict some of the assertions in the friendship literature about class variations. A third, psychological dimension to be further explored concerns the allocation of leadership roles and relative importance of instrumental and expressive activities. The evidence of the study seems to support claims in the literature for the predominance of expressive activities in later life. But at the same time gender differences appear to be marked, with increased instrumentality on the part of older women. The assertiveness of club members in relation to club procedures and decision making needs to be examined in relation to both the life span and cohort experiences of this group of people.

The question of cohort membership introduces another theme, potentially the most interesting. Clubs may be seen, in anthropological terms, as the property of particular age sets passing from one age grade (young old) to another (old

old). The tendency for the club to age with its members rather than recruit from younger age sets is problematic. The literature on cohorts and generations is highly relevant here. The question might be: what makes a cohort into a generation, with all that implies of social distance and cultural autonomy in relation to other age groups? Through the development of these themes some contribution may be made to both theory and ethnography: to our understanding of the mechanisms of age differentiation in this society and to our knowledge of the lives and concerns of a particular generation of elderly people.

Notes

(1) See Danigelis (1985) for a useful summary of this research.
(2) See Harris (1975) and Jerrome (1985) for a more detailed discussion.
(3) For a discussion of such concepts as liminality and age differentiation see Keith (1982).

References

Abrams, M. (1980) Beyond Three Score Years and Ten, I and II, Age Concern, Research Department, London.
Breytspraak, L. et al. (1985) 'Voluntary Organisations as a Support System in the Ageing Process', in Petersen, W. and Quadnago, J. (eds.) Social Bonds in Later Life, Sage, California.
Danigelis, N. (1985) 'Social Support for Elders Through Community Ties, the Role of Voluntary Organisations', in Sauer, W. and Coward, R. Social Support Networks and Care of the Elderly, Springer Publication Company, New York.
Dono, J. et al. (1979) 'Primary Groups in Old Age', Research on Aging, Vol.1, No.4, pp.403-433.
Eisenstadt, S. (1956) From Generation to Generation, Routledge and Kegan Paul, London.
Fry, C. (ed.) (1980) Aging in Culture and Society, Praeger, New York.
Francis, D. (1981) 'Adaptive Strategies in the Elderly in England and Ohio', in Fry, D. (ed.) Dimensions: Aging, Culture and Health, J.F. Bergin, New York.
Harris, C. (1975) The Process of Social Ageing, Unpublished Ph.D. thesis, University of Wales, Swansea.

Me Darby, You Joan!

Harris, C. (1983) 'Associational Participation in Old Age', in Jerrome, D. (ed.) Ageing in Modern Society, Croom Helm, London.
Hazan, H. (1980) The Limbo People, Routledge and Kegan Paul, London.
Hess, B. (1972) 'Friendship', in Riley, M., Johnson, M. and Phoner, A. (eds.) Aging and Society, Vol.III, Russell Sage Foundation, New York.
Hunt, A. (1978) The Elderly at Home, OPCS, London.
Jerrome, D. (1981) 'The Significance of Friendship for Women in Later Life', Ageing and Society, Vol.1, No.2, pp.175-197.
Jerrome, D. (1983) 'Lonely Women in a Friendship Club', British Journal of Guidance and Counselling, Vol.1, No.11, pp.10-20.
Jerrome, D. (1984) 'Good Company: the Sociological Implications of Friendship', Sociological Review, Vol.32, No.4, pp.696-718.
Jerrome, D. (1985) 'Voluntary Association and the Social Construction of Old Age', in Butler, A. Ageing: Recent Advances and Creative Responses, Croom Helm. London.
Karn, V. (1977) Retiring to the Seaside, Routledge and Kegan Paul, London.
Keith, J. (1980) 'Old Age and Community Creation', in Fry, C. (ed.) Aging in Culture and Society, Praeger, New York.
Keith, J. (1982) Old People as People, Little and Brown, Boston.
Linton, R. (1942) 'Age and Sex Categories', American Sociological Review, Vol.7, No.5, pp.589-616.
Myerhoff, B. (1980) Number Our Days, Simon and Schuster, New York.
Rosenmayr, L. (1982) 'Biography and Identity', in Hareven, T. and Adams, P. (eds.) Ageing and Life Course Transitions, Tavistock, London.
Rosow, I. (1967) Social Integration of the Aged, Free Press, New York.
Unruh, D. (1983) Invisible Lives, Sage, Beverly Hills.
Wenger, G.C. (1984) The Supportive Network, Allen and Unwin, London.

Acknowledgement

This research project was completed with the help of ESRC Grant No. G0125005.

Chapter Thirty

NEGOTIATION AND CONTROL -

A PERSPECTIVE ON VALUES IN LATER LIFE

Robert Elmore

Introduction

It is argued that an understanding of those values which are
associated with the final stages of life for any individual
needs to encompass the attitudes and values of all those
people whose presence is deemed crucial. The thesis is
advanced that this terminal stage - and the term is used
loosely - has characteristics which distinguish it from any
other period in the life-cycle and, hence, needs to be
examined in a way which reveals its distinctive nature.

It is suggested that a broad interactionist perspective
can offer profound insights both into the dynamics and the
value context of this terminal phase and that these insights
may have importance for the training and education of those
proffering care and contribute to a fuller understanding of
the feelings, fears and expectations of those who have come
to terms with the prospect of dying.

Although in this paper there will be some discussion of
the period immediately before death, the main concern is with
the later years of life when dependency is increasing, that
period which the Rapoports (1975, p.308) suggested is
concerned with 'life before death', when medical intervention
has become primarily palliative, except perhaps, for the
occasional acute episode, and is concerned with reducing pain
and discomfort for an undetermined period. It is also when
the individual concerned begins to forfeit personal control
over his or her life. The experience derived from hospices,
although extremely important, is discounted in this paper,
primarily because most old people in this 'terminal phase' do
not experience hospice care.

A recent survey of terminal care cases (excluding
hospice care) reported that the quality of life in the final
illness was categorised by the community nurse as 'poor' or
'very poor' in 44 per cent of the cases considered. The
review also concluded that the differing perceptions of the
individuals involved in the caring 'reinforce the need for more

integrated care and a knowledge of, and respect for, the views of those involved, including patients and relatives' (Wilkes, 1984, p.952). Such findings justify an exploration of the issues affecting the terminal phase of life.

Making Sense of the Situation

It is well-recognised that the salience of particular values for the individual is influenced both by the social context in which they are articulated and the stage in the life-cycle reached by the individual expressing them. Thus with a collection of values which may remain constant for the individual throughout life, the ordering of them may vary at different times. Indeed, this variable ordering is seen by some sociologists as being part of the process of acquiring, varying and discarding social roles and statuses, along with their associated values. However, although there is much validity in such an approach, the conceptualisation of the passage through life solely in terms of a series of roles into which the individual is socialised, both for particular contexts and the more general incorporation into the customs and practices of society, is curiously unsatisfactory in offering understanding of the later years of life.

A number of reasons can be offered for this feeling of unease. First, that the latter years of life have a much 'looser' sociological structure when more of the status-creating and influential roles have been abandoned, discarded or removed. Secondly, and perhaps more importantly is the relatively limited value of those views which place great stress on socialisation and age stratification in facilitating understanding of this period of life, primarily because they fail to give due weight to imperfect socialisation and individual variation. That is why for sociologists who maintain this position '.... the transition to old age represents a special problem in adult socialisation because it differs markedly from other status passages' (Rosow, 1974).

A different approach is the interactionist one which is concerned with exploring the social construction of the reality being experienced; how the individual makes sense of the 'situation' and endeavours to gain control over it or negotiates a position which is understandable, even if it is not desirable. Thus in considering the 'life before death' phase in respect of an individual, the 'social realities' of all the parties needs to be determined. It is to this interface between the personal attempt of the individual concerned to make sense of the situation and the professional and personal responses of those others who are closely involved that attention is directed.

If one starts from the basis of role-theory or age-stratification theory with their normative dimensions one is likely to get a different response from one reflecting an interactionist perspective. As one doctor has written, reviewing the work of a seminar on terminal care:

The patient dies as he has lived. If the doctor can make the diagnosis of how (my emphasis) he has lived, then he can help him to a less painful death by co-operating and accepting this life style as the way to this patient's death style.

The fighter fights, and must be helped by the doctor to fight, though both doctor and patient may know that defeat is certain and the fight is in some ways unreal.

The complainer complains and the doctor must accept these complaints and his inability to do much about them, for this is all this patient really expects and may even enjoy having something to complain about at last.

The split personality remains split, and the doctor must accept the degree of unreality this brings to the dying situation and not to try to force the painful truth on an ego too weak to bear it.

The whole person dies whole and with dignity, accepting his mortality as that which has been ordained, treating the doctor as friend, not expecting or demanding anything more than friendship and understanding, but giving and teaching the doctor much in return.

The overall diagnosis of the 'life-situation' of the patient, whether it be good or bad, is important. These ideas seem central to managing the doctor/patient relationship during the terminal illness yet the seminar has not defined them in any way. No clinical signs or symptoms are suggested to assist in the diagnosis ; good and bad are very subjective (Green, 1972, p.238).

This view of the importance of understanding something of the 'life-situation' when dealing with the terminally ill receives support from Hinton when he suggests that their habitual manner of dealing with life, their style in facing difficulties or acquiring social position offers an important indication of the most appropriate response that a doctor, or indeed anyone else, can make (Hinton, 1972, p.137).

Increasingly old age brings with it decreasing options - part of a process which starts with retirement - and although emphasis may be placed on the fresh opportunities that retirement offers, with advancing age comes increasing vulnerability to physical disorders and psychological and emotional distress. Along with these comes the greater possibility of intervention by professionals, welfare agencies, well-meaning relatives and friends proffering a variety of advice. In addition to the physical restraints which may accompany the ageing process there may be others coming from society. Alison Norman, commenting on these writes:

> there are many ways in which society further restricts this narrowing range of choice by imposing on elderly people forms of care and treatment which are the fruits of social perception, social anxiety, convenience and custom rather than inescapable necessity. (Norman, 1980, p.7)

I wish to argue that by taking a broad interactionist perspective some of the issues Alison Norman hints at may be more adequately understood and hence resolved.

Much of the data gathered about this age group has come from the suppliers or providers of services and is based upon their understanding and their perceptions. Even the Rapoports (1975), in their important study Leisure and the Family Life Cycle, did not extend their comprehensive studies to the later phases of life where physical illness and disability tend to be a significant feature. We need to know more of the needs of this age group directly from their own experience.

As part of the context of an interactionist perspective it is important to recognise that the values and attitudes of the professionals and others concerned are not independent of the values existing in wider society. For example, many doctors find it difficult to communicate 'bad news' to patients. Buckman (1984) and Hoy (1985) offered a number of reasons for these difficulties including the fear of being blamed for the failure of the patient to get better and, perhaps more immediately relevant to our discussions, the fear of unleashing emotions from both patients and themselves, and of being involved in a situation for which they are not trained. What applies to doctors also applies to health care and social welfare professionals equally, not to mention the relatives and informal carers who go virtually unmentioned in much of the literature. There is also an hierarchical dimension to all this. If, for example, a consultant declines to impart relevant information, or gives misleading information, the whole interactive chain can be affected.

Access to information is an essential element in making realistic choices and negotiating outcomes and it may be that a refusal to impart information results in a markedly reduced capacity on the part of the older person to control or negotiate issues of importance. Yet this essential information may be withheld, abridged or even distorted in the interests of patient care. Whatever the reason, it constitutes an attack on an individual's autonomy. Thus there may well be a conflict between the professional's perspectives and that of the older patient or client. As Friedson has argued:

... that objective difference in perspective between physician, patient and uncertainties inherent in the routine application of knowledge to human affairs make for incipient conflict between patient and physician. Conflict occurs especially when the patient, on the basis of his own lay perspectives, tries in some way to control what the physician does to him. It is more likely to occur when the patient defines his illnesses as potentially critical than when he sees it as minor and ordinary. (Friedson, 1962)

What an older person believes of a situation is for that person true - regardless of the objective truth of what is believed - as it is for anyone else! What follows from a perception of the reality is an attempt to control or influence relevant outcomes. Whether or not effective control can be achieved depends upon the nature of the situation, the appraisal of options and access to facilities.

Two sociologists, Glaser and Strauss (1965; 1967; 1971), have been particularly involved with the development of ideas concerning status passages, that is the routes people may follow in relation to different periods in the life cycle, and in particular have developed some interesting ideas of the process of dying as a special form of status passage. The curious fact is that although there are extensive references to their work in much of the literature it has not been used by others to develop additional insights. Their theories, which may be subsumed under the broad head of interactionist theory, perceive ageing as a status passage comprising a series of personal negotiations when moving from one age-linked status to another. The whole series constitutes a status passage terminating in death. Status passages may have various dimensions and characteristics and they have been conveniently summarised by Marshall:

Objectively, any status passage can be defined in terms of physical and social time and space. The duration may be long or short, and given meaning as such by others. The passage may be treated as preparatory, initiatory, educative, selective and ritualistic. The passage may involve physical movement, or horizontal movement or lateral movement in social status. It may be viewed by others as desirable or undesirable, inevitable or optional, voluntary or involuntary, reversible or irreversible, repeatable or unique. The passage may occur collectively, aggregatively, or solo. It may be guided by others, or self, or collectively guided or controlled. If undergone with others, the degree to which sub-passagees may communicate with others at the same stage of the passage, or ahead of them, might vary. The passage may vary in moral authority or societal legitimation.

Subjectively, people may be aware, in different degree, that they are actually undergoing a passage. Awareness of any of the aforementioned objective properties of the passages may vary. One may, or may not, decide, for example, to voluntarily accept an inevitable passage (e.g. to accept one's dying). One may attempt to seize, or may surrender, control over the passage. The passage, or sub-passages may be viewed as a crucial or trivial importance. (Marshall, 1980)

The core of the status passage perspective is that the lives of ageing persons will be shaped by their own actions in the context of those of others. It recognises the importance of normative theory but reduces the certainty that socialisation has and emphasises the individual's attempts to control and negotiate his own life passage.

If one uses the status passage dimensions as developed by Glaser and Strauss, then ageing is objectively an inevitable status passage - there is no escape: there is 'no exit' to use Marshall's term, except in death. This single exit makes the ageing status passage unique. All other status passages are concerned with something to come; they have about them an element of futurity. But with ageing comes an acute consciousness of the passage of time, the reduction of options and a consciousness of repeated farewells: subjectively the response may vary widely.

This perspective suggests that the typification of old age essentially as a period of role discontinuity, status loss, increasing personal deficits and so on fails to give due weight to the control and negotiation dimension which is present.

Responding to the Situation

If we conceive of the latter years of life as a sub-passage within the broader status passage of ageing, what are some of its dimensions and characteristics? In a research study, Isaacs et al. (1971) seem to have identified an extremely important status passage with certain characteristics. They write: 'It seems that many of those who survive into old age enter a phase of 'pre-death' in which they outlive the vigour of their bodies and the wisdom of their brains.' They argue that the diseases commonly associated with this phase are incontinence, dementia, arteriosclerotic brain disease and the like, and together they constitute one of the outstanding community health problems of today. This 'pre-death' phase in some instances can be quite long drawn out. Isaacs et al. (1971) reported that the average duration - and the consequent need for hospital care - increased with advancing age.

Although 'pre-death' is not the most felicitous term, it does serve to mark a significant point in the ageing process. Before this state is identified the individual is seen as having some futurity, although limited by prudential considerations. When the 'pre-death' phase has been identified a subtle change seems to occur in all intimate relationships, though the old person may not be aware of it. There will also be a significant change in the treatment regime, in all probability.

Who are the people likely to be involved? Consultants, family practitioners, nurses, spouses, close family, neighbours, social workers, home helps, care-assistants, clergy and casual visitors - the list is not exhaustive and will vary in different cases. Each will be concerned in one way or another with the well-being of the old person.

The main issue now is whether the perceptions of, to use a useful term, the significant others match those of the older person. Unless there is a cognitive collapse where the person concerned is quite unaware of the situation, certain decisions have to be taken and arrangements made, and these may certainly include a consideration of the appropriateness of informing the several parties involved, including the patient.

The pattern of intervention at this stage is likely to be different from other interventions. As Thompson (1979) has indicated in Dilemmas of Dying, when a terminal phase has been identified the ordinary 'contract' or 'understanding' between doctor and patient with its assumption of therapeutic optimism has to be profoundly modified. For example, the re-negotiating of the informal contract may involve the doctor admitting his total helplessness and inability to cure. And although pain relief and palliative care may be available, it does constitute a marked change.

At this stage the doctor - or whoever, though it really is the doctor with the professional knowledge who is crucial - has to decide whether to tell the patient, and if so, how much; and if not, whether to tell the spouse or relatives. Sometimes the doctor is constrained from telling the patient by the relatives. It is here that serious moral issues may be raised which, although sometimes dealt with as if they were solely professional matters, need to be considered as they may dramatically affect the autonomy of the individual.

Glaser and Strauss in their book Awareness of Dying attempt to analyse this kind of a situation through awareness theory. They suggest four models:

closed awareness - where the patient does not recognise impending death, though others do;

suspected awareness - where the patient suspects what the others know and attempts to get confirmation or denial;

mutual pretense awareness - where both parties are aware of the situation but pretend that the others are not; and

open awareness - where all parties are aware and the situation is openly acknowledged.

The impact on each of the parties of their perceptions of the awareness context is profound and undoubtedly influences behaviour. The two kinds of awareness context which seem to be the least stressful for the patient are the 'open context' and the 'mutual pretense awareness' because in either case the individual has a much higher degree of control. These awareness contexts also have their problems but, at least, they are more compatible with the control dimension. One great problem with the 'open awareness' context is that if it persists for too long it can lead to the patient being treated as socially dead by staff, relatives and friends in anticipation of biological death.

Even where an 'open context' or 'mutual pretense context' exists full recognition of the need for the expression of grief has to be considered. The grief that a dying individual experiences is not significantly different from the anticipatory grief experienced by the survivors. Differing grief responses may in some degree account for the seemingly unaccountable changes in the dying person's reactions to social involvement as the movement towards death progresses.

The psychological care of the dying involves the identification, or at least an awareness, of the individual's particular concept of death in order to reduce fear and maintain morale. 'The doctor must therefore be a good psychologist and a genuine philosopher, in the strictest sense of the word' (Popa and Hanganu, 1979). And these authors quote Rilke's 'I want to die my own death and not my doctor's death.'

Conclusion

Briefly, what might all this mean for the understanding and education of professionals, volunteers and family of this latter period of life? First, it could be argued that as a person ages options become more limited. If the opportunities for control and negotiation are important, and I believe they are, then help must be given to ensure that unnecessary institutional or professional rules do not arbitrarily restrict opportunities for exercising them. Thus approaches need to be person-centred and not normatively centred. In other words books or programmes which prescribe 'rules' for dealing with the older person ought to be treated with a marked degree of circumspection. Secondly, training needs to be given to help those working in this area to deal with their own fears, tensions and prejudices. This happens almost invariably in hospices, but rarely elsewhere. Thirdly, skills have to be developed for the sensible and sensitive communication of 'bad news' along with all the ethical implications. Fourthly, special sensitivity needs to be developed for all those in close and intimate contact with this group of older people to the consequences of both formal and informal communication and personal interaction. Just to be kind may not be enough. Fifthly, we need systematically to develop research methods for assessing the moral, emotional, cultural and spiritual quality of life for older people: we know a great deal about the physical dimensions but very little about these others. It is here that the interactionist perspective which is concerned with the 'realities' of the situation for the participants may be invaluable.

All these points may seem obvious and perhaps even trivial but because they are so obvious we think they occur naturally. The fact is, they do not. With the massive concentration of caring, helping and doing things for the elderly, we may be failing to allow them to use their own resources. One general approach which could almost be formulated into a regulative proposition is that all education and training should attempt to facilitate the elderly person's capacity to exercise control and, even within declining options, to negotiate choices.

References

Buckman, R. (1984) 'Breaking Bad News: Why is it Still so Difficult?', British Medical Journal, Vol.288, pp.1597-1599.

Friedson, E. (1962) 'Dilemmas in the Doctor-Patient Relationship', in A.M. Rose (ed.) Human Behaviour and Social Processes, Routledge and Kegan Paul, London.

Glaser, B.G. and Strauss, A.L. (1965) Awareness of Dying, Weidenfeld and Nicolson, London.

Glaser, B.G. and Strauss, A.L. (1968) Time for Dying, Aldine, Chicago.

Glaser, B.G. and Strauss, A.L. (1971) Status Passage, Routledge and Kegan Paul, London.

Green, R.G. (1972) 'The Doctor-Patient Relationship During Terminal Illness', in P. Hopkins (ed.) Patient-Centred Medicine, Regional Doctor Publications Ltd., London.

Hinton, J. (1972) Dying, Penguin Books.

Hoy, A.M. (1985) 'Breaking Bad News to Patients', British

Journal of Hospital Medicine, August, pp.96-99.

Isaacs, B. et al. (1971) 'The Concept of Pre-Death', The Lancet, i, 26 May, p.115.

Marshall, V.H. (1980) 'No Exit: An Interpretative Perspective on Aging', in H.V. Marshall Aging in Canada, Fitzhenry and Whiteside, Ontario.

Norman, J.A. (1980) Rights and Risk, Centre for Policy on Ageing, London.

Popa, G. and Hanganu, E. (1979) 'The Faces of Death', Journal of Medical Ethics, Part 5, pp.71-72.

Rapoport, R. and Rapoport, R.N. (1975) Leisure and the Family Life Cycle, Routledge and Kegan Paul, London.

Rosow, I. (1974) see discussion in V.H. Marshall op.cit., p.52.

Thompson, I. (1979) Dilemmas of Dying - a Study in the Ethics of Terminal Care, ,University Press, Edinburgh.

Wilkes, E. (1984) 'Dying Now', The Lancet, i, 28 April, pp.950-952.

Details of Contributors

S. Arber, Department of Sociology, University of Surrey.

D.A. Atkinson, Health Care Research Unit, University of Newcastle-on-Tyne.

H. Bartlett, Centre for the Analysis of Social Policy, University of Bath.

M. Bernard, Beth Johnson Foundation, Stoke-on-Trent.

A. Blaikie, Department of Social Policy, Royal Holloway and Bedford New College, University of London.

J. Bond, Health Care Research Unit, University of Newcastle-upon-Tyne.

T. Booth, Department of Sociological Studies, University of Sheffield.

B. Bytheway, Institute of Health Care Studies, University College of Swansea.

L. Challis, Centre for the Analysis of Social Policy, University of Bath.

A. Dale, Department of Sociology, University of Surrey.

B. Davies, Personal Social Services Research Unit, University of Kent.

S. Dixon, 5, Larkhall Place, Larkhall, Bath.

R. Elmore, Department of External Studies, University of Oxford.

C.L. Estes, Institute for Health and Aging, University of California, San Francisco.

M. Evandrou, Suntory Toyota International Centre for Economics and Related Disciplines, London School of Economics.

M. Featherstone, Department of Administrative and Social Studies, Teesside Polytechnic.

G. Fennell, School of Economic and Social Studies, University of East Anglia.

G.N. Gilbert, Department of Sociology, University of Surrey.

S. Di Gregorio, 48, Park Avenue North, London N8 7RT.

B.A. Gregson, Health Care Research Unit, University of Newcastle-upon-Tyne.

G.O. Hagestad, College of Human Development, Pennsylvania State University.

J. Harris, Department of Applied Social Studies, Lanchester Polytechnic.

J. Henderson, School of Applied Social Studies, University of Bradford.

M. Hepworth, Department of Sociology, University of Aberdeen.

C. Itzin, 19, Knatchball Road, London, SE5 9QR.

V. Ivers, Beth Johnson Foundation, Stoke-on-Trent.

D. Jerrome, Centre for Continuing Education, University of Sussex.

D. Kelly, Newlands House, Bennett, Keresley, Coventry.

M. Kuhn, Gray Panthers, 6342 Greene St., Philadelphia, Pennsylvania 19144.

F. Laczko, Department of Sociology, University of Surrey.

P. Lyon, School of Social Studies, Robert Gordon's Institute of Technology, Aberdeen.

J. Macnicol, Department of Social Policy, Royal Holloway and Bedford New College, University of London.

370

A. Murdock, Essex Social Services Department, Ongar.

H. Qureshi, Hester Adrian Research Centre, University of Manchester.

A. Sixsmith, Department of Geography, King's College, University of London.

C. Thompson, Age Concern Institute of Gerontology, King's College, University of London.

C. Victor, Department of Community Health, Queen's Medical Centre, Nottingham.

A. Walker, Department of Sociological Studies, University of Sheffield.

A. Weir, Department of Psychology, University of Glasgow.

G.C. Wenger, Department of Social Theory and Institutions, University College of North Wales.

For Product Safety Concerns and Information please contact our EU
representative GPSR@taylorandfrancis.com
Taylor & Francis Verlag GmbH, Kaufingerstraße 24, 80331 München, Germany

www.ingramcontent.com/pod-product-compliance
Lightning Source LLC
Chambersburg PA
CBHW070542270326
41926CB00013B/2174

* 9 7 8 1 0 3 2 7 1 5 9 7 1 *